CHURCH AND REVOLUTION IN RWANDA

Above *Archbishop André Perraudin*. Below *Bishop Aloys Bigirumwami*

IAN LINDEN
with JANE LINDEN

Church and revolution in Rwanda

MANCHESTER UNIVERSITY PRESS

AFRICANA PUBLISHING COMPANY
NEW YORK

©IAN LINDEN 1977

Published by
Manchester University Press
Oxford Road, Manchester M13 9PL

UK ISBN 0 7190 0671 6

North America

Africana Publishing Company
a division of
Holmes & Meier Publishers, Inc.
101 Fifth Avenue
New York, New York 10003

Library of Congress Cataloging in Publication Data

Linden, Ian.
Church and revolution in Rwanda.

Bibliography: p.
Includes index.
1. Christianity — Rwanda. 2. Missions — Rwanda.
3. White Fathers — Missions. 4 Catholic Church in
Rwanda. 5. Social classes — Rwanda. 6. Rwanda —
Politics and government. 7. Rwanda — Social
conditions.
I. Linden, Jane, joint author. II. Title.
BR1443.R95L56 1977   266'.00967'571   76-58329
ISBN 0-8419-0305-0

Printed in Great Britain by
Lowe & Brydone Limited
Thetford, Norfolk

Contents

Acknowledgements

Firstly an explanation of the 'with' in the co-authorship: Jane Linden thoroughly rewrote several of the earlier chapters and completed the major task of pruning a doctoral dissertation down to half a book. She provided a number of ideas and helped with proof-reading. The book could not have come out without her.

I should like to thank my supervisor at the School of Oriental and African Studies, Professor Richard Gray, for his unfailing help, and Professor T. O. Ranger for his encouragement over the years. The School of Oriental and African Studies, University of London, provided me with a small research grant for which I am most grateful. Professor Marcel d'Hertefelt of the Institut National de Recherches Scientifiques, Butare, Rwanda, used his *bons offices* to facilitate my stay in Rwanda and helped me with a number of stimulating suggestions.

A should like this book to be thought of in the tradition of concerned scholarly writing about Africa that has marked the publications of the White Fathers as a religious society. Certainly my research would have been impossible without the kindness and co-operation of both Mission and Rwandan Church, to whom I owe an immense debt of gratitude. But, in particular, Père René Lamey, archivist in Rome, showed me not only great kindness but also great trust, which I hope I have not abused. I should also like to thank the staff of the CMS Rwanda mission in London for their help and assistance at their archives.

After three years in Nigeria at Ahmadu Bello University my colleagues Paul Clough, Bob Shenton, Patrick Redmond and Lorne Larson stand out in my mind as having taught me a lot. At the very least they understand that mixture of melancholy and popery that besets the unemployed academic; at most some of their insights will appear on the following pages.

For assistance with, and permission to reproduce, photographs I am indebted to the White Fathers' Archives, Rome (pp. ii, 32, 55, 58, 105, 140), the Rwanda Mission, CMS, London (p. 185), and Professor Marcel d'Hertefelt, Photo Rudipresse (p. 263). The illustration on p. 51 is from Mecklenburg's *Ins Innerste Afrika* (1911), p. 115.

A note on methodology

I TERMINOLOGY

Feudalism. The loose use of the feudal model applied to African societies has come in for considerable criticism, and its use in this book requires some justification. The first major criticism came from E. M. Chilver in Audrey Richards's *East African Chiefs.*[1] Redmayne, in a major discussion of the topic, suggested that comparisons with other African societies might be more fruitful than the slavish application of European terminology.[2] Goody wanted analysis 'with less worn counters, with more operational concepts' than feudalism.[3] Beattie came to reject the concept of feudality as inadequate as a description of Nyoro society.[4] De Heusch,[5] following Mair,[6] preferred to place feudalism in the broader category of clientship States. The most telling part of Goody's argument was the disparity between the raised value of land in Europe, created by feudal technology, and the low-yield land of Africa, where labour is at a premium; African technology would be too underdeveloped and land too poor to sustain feudalism.[7]

Two major distinctions are made in these critiques: on the one hand feudalism as 'feudo-vassalage' in the socio-legal sense of Maitland and Pollock, described by Ganshof as 'a body of institutions regulating the obligations of obedience and service — mainly military service — on the part of the free man (the vassal), towards another free man (the lord), and the obligations of protection and maintainance on the part of the lord with regard to his vassal'.[8] On the other hand there is the more comprehensive 'feudal society', a political and governmental category characterised by a type of land holding, legal system, decentralisation of authority, and relationship between king and nobility. Feudalism in this second sense is normally presented as a process model drawn from the sequence of historical changes in Western Europe from the ninth to the thirteenth centuries. Thus feudalism arises as the result of the breakdown of an empire and gives rise to powerful kingships, not through the growing power of the king's men but by the monarch establishing himself at the head of a pyramid of feudal lords.

The use of the comprehensive definition, even abstracted to the level of a process model, effectively precludes all debate, as Beattie's discussion of Nyoro kingship demonstrates.[9] It is clear that the European sequence of political processes has not repeated itself in Africa; the feudal model in the African context is used as an explanation of State formation, not as a description of disintegrated States and empires. Kagame is typical in this respect in that he refuses to use the word 'feudal' for Rwanda because the nineteenth century was characterised by the growth of an 'absolute monarchy'.[10] He will, however, like Maquet,[11] use the word in the limited socio-legal sense for the 'contrat de servage', *ubuhake*.[12] Much of this debate has centred round the interlacustrine kingdoms that ended up as British colonies and the focus of anglophone historical study. Kagame alone was in print at any early date on Belgian Rwanda, and his position is obviously coloured by the pejorative overtones of the term 'feudal' in post-war Rwanda. The recent French Marxist school of African historians, of course, has found no difficulty in applying feudal terminology to Rwanda and Burundi.

There is certainly no problem with the limited use of the term 'feudal' as 'feudo-vassalage'. In the second half of the nineteenth century central Rwanda became a complex pyramid of clientship ties headed by the king; the early type of vassalage was military service in the *ngabo*, and a military class grew up, not on the basis of ownership of equipment, horses and weapons, but as the product of lengthy training in the *itorero*. A garagu passed through a formal rite of subordination and exchanged service for protection, while the relationship was recorded by a benefice of movable property over which the garagu had usufruct rights (fief comes originally from *vieh*, cow, even in the European context).

Nor are many of the criticisms levelled at the comprehensive model valid for Rwanda. Chilver's insistence on land holding being strictly and legally tied to political office in a simple cause-and-effect relationship, with the incumbent movable at the king's behest, is both static and Eurocentric in the extreme, and begs the question of whether

A note on methodology

there is an overall *de facto* connection between political office, clientship and land holding. There certainly was in Rwanda.

Ces deux structures politiques et l'institution de clientèle étaient corréla-
tives. Les fonctions politiques aidaient les Tutsi à accroître le nombre de leurs
clients, et la structure de clientèle leur permettait d'obtenir des fonctions
politiques et de les conserver. Les relations entre le seigneur et le client
constituaient un modèle pour les relations entre les gouvernants et leurs
sujets.[13]

As D'Hertefelt points out, powerful landowners and patrons
represented in microcosm the political power of the State as a coercive
organ of the ruling class. Political office allowed a powerful man to
extend his land holding as clients alienated land for protection, and to
gain clients as the weak escaped the threat of expulsion in personal
relationships.[14]

The Goody critique also needs to be looked at carefully in the
context of Rwanda, where there was considerable land shortage in
some provinces by the 1950s. The kingdom was only about 100,000
square miles and had to support a leisured class of some 2,000 chiefs
and about 50,000 Tutsi who never tilled the soil. The high productivity
of the land, well manured by cattle, with bananas and a wide range of
grains and leguminous crops, made land valuable, especially when
large tracts served as pasture for the Tutsi herds. While they could not
match the feudal technology of Europe, Rwanda's direct producers
did provide surplus labour to sustain a small class of leisured lords.
The existence of a class of landless labourers in the nineteenth century
would also have 'stoked the fires of land hunger and given force to the
right of exclusion'.[15]

What both European and Rwandan feudal societies had in common
was an internal tendency towards an equilibrium in which a military
aristocracy ruled through a chain of clientship relations checked on
one side by the monarchy, the king's men, and on the other by
lineages and clans. Both twelfth century England and nineteenth
century Rwanda were marked by the dominance of ideology and
political power over society. But it is also clear — and here the level of
abstraction of the French Marxist school helps to prescind from many
difficulties — that the particular texture of society which these two
States had in common was the product of a mode of production in
which a class of lords controlled land and labour. The dominance of
ideology and political power in Rwanda's colonial history, the central
theme of this book, finds its rationale in Rwanda's feudal mode of
production.

ix

The advantage of the use of a feudal model for Rwanda is simple: changes in society after the 1930s can be understood as part of a process in which the insertion of the capitalist cash economy into a feudal mode of production is intimately connected with colonial tampering with political structures and more indirectly related to changes in the ideology of the Mission Church. This insight can be gained only by allowing the degree of abstraction involved in the use of feudal terminology. The use of feudal terms does not, of course, imply the existence of homologous structures in Europe and Africa any more than the use of terms like 'State' and 'army' assume exactly comparable institutions.

Caste, class or ethnic group. Some of the difficulty encountered in using feudal terminology recurs in giving an adequate account of Rwanda's social stratification. 'Caste' inevitably carries with it religious overtones from India that are incongruous in the Rwandan context. Furthermore D'Hertefelt's work on the multi-class nature of Rwandan clans has demonstrated that much intermarriage occurred in the past,[16] and denies an essential aspect of 'caste'.

'Ethnicity' is a way of perceiving socio-economic differences and can hardly be used as an objective description of the differences between Tutsi, Hutu and Twa. It was common in Europe for the nobility of a supposedly racially homogeneous society to emphasise 'Noble blood' and 'aristocratic features', in short to present class differences as if they had biological bases. I will therefore prescind from the question of the genetic differences between Tutsi, Hutu and Twa, since these are of no operational significance. In the colonial period, when access to political office was limited to the Tutsi, defined by the Belgians as an ethnic group, the disparity between the perceived divisions in society and the real divisions becomes most marked; at this point it will be necessary to discuss 'ethnicity' as a component in Tutsi ideology.

Therefore 'class' is used in the text, defined in a way applicable to pre-capitalist formations as a group of people having the same relationship to the mode of production. The Hutu are therefore a class in as much as they are direct agricultural producers in a feudal mode of production. The Tutsi are a class in as much as they appropriate surplus labour in the same mode of production. But since the feudal economy was limited to central Rwanda, albeit extended by colonial rule, these 'classes' do not apply to all of the country. The isolated Tutsi households of the north were simple cattle-herders in an exchange relationship with Hutu farmers. In such regions production was dominated by kinship.

While it is possible to assert, as does D'Hertefelt, that by the end of the colonial period all Tutsi shared to some degree in the political power and ideological supremacy of the nobles, certainly not all Tutsi were able to appropriate surplus labour. The 'petits Tutsi' provided labour and services for the nobles; rich Hutu employed labour or gained clients in *umukonde* relations. The perceived social stratification, based on premises of ethnicity, into Tutsi and Hutu did not correspond to two real classes. Thus the class struggle, expressed in the form of the Hutu social democrat protest and finally peasant revolt, took place within the framework of the dominant ideology of the colonial period 'ethnicity'. The Tutsi as a group with a monopoly of political power and a shared ideological supremacy are referred to as 'the ruling class', in this context a term with ethnic connotations; the degree to which the Tutsi 'ruled' varied, of course, considerably, from a few noble lineages controlling the chieftancies to a 'petit Tutsi' with one or two clients representing in miniature the coercive power of the State. The 'elite' refers to educated members of the ruling class, the 'counter-elite' to educated Hutu by definition debarred from the ruling class.

2 MISSION AND SOCIETY

The mission in Rwanda is discussed at three levels. Firstly as part of Rwandan society as a whole and therefore reflecting its structure and divisions. Secondly as a unit in its own right, a discrete institution with its own history, structure, channels of authority and ideology, with a degree of 'programmed development' irrespective of context. Thirdly the Church as a collection of individuals with shared beliefs and goals, but nonetheless with differing secular experience, choice of means to achieve goals, and conclusions drawn from the belief system of the institution, itself having certain contradictions.[17]

The central unit of study in the book is therefore the Church, a multi-class, multi-racial institution. It is the operation of this body as a source of ideology and political force that is studied in the Rwandan setting, both as an organised totality and from the viewpoint of its disparate individual members.

The ideology and political power of the Church are considered primarily in terms of three major points of conflict within Rwandan society: the struggle between king and nobles, between the different economies and societies of the northern clanlands and central Rwanda, and between the ruling class and the governed. Since these points of conflict, and, of course, the Church's political power and ideology, were strongly influenced by the policies of colonial rule, that of the Germans and Belgians, these interactions are discussed fully in the context of colonialism. Each chapter attempts to encompass the three points of conflict, their development through time, and their dynamic interaction with the Church. Finally, I have kept to the old orthography used by the White Fathers, i.e. Musinga instead of Musiinga.

NOTES

1 Chilver, E. M., 'Feudalism in the interlacustrine kingdoms', in *East African Chiefs*, London, 1960, 378-93.

2 Redmayne, A., 'The concept of feudalism in African ethnology', B.Litt. thesis, University of Oxford, 1961.

3 Goody, J., 'Feudalism in Africa?' *Journal of African History*, vol. IV, No. 1, 1963, 16.

4 Beattie, J. H. M., 'Bunyoro: an African feudality?' *Journal of African History*, vol. V, No. 1, 1964, 25-36.

5 De Heusch, *Le Rwanda*, 401-12.

6 Mair, L., 'Clientship in East Africa', *Cahiers d'Études Africaines*, vol. VI, 1961, 315-25.

7 Goody, J., *Technology, Tradition and the State in Africa*, Oxford, 1971.

8 Ganshof, F., *Feudalism*, London, 1952, xvi.

9 Beattie, *Bunyoro*, 25-36.

10 Kagame, *Le Code*, 7-11.

11 Maquet, *The Premise*, 133.

12 Kagame, *Le Code*, 11.

13 D'Hertefelt, M., 'Le Rwanda', in *Les Anciens Royaumes de la zone interlacustre méridionale*, ed. D'Hertefelt, M., Trouwborst, A. A., and Scherer, J. H., London, 1962, 69.

14 It is noticeable that in Chilver's brilliant article Rwanda is made an exception; see *East African Chiefs*, 382, though, since the article is dealing with the interlacustrine kingdoms as a whole, the point is not developed.

15 Hindness, B., and Hirst, P. Q., *Pre-capitalist Modes of Production*, London, 1975, 226-228, 245.

16 D'Hertefelt, *Les Clans*, appendices.

17 Most of the emphases advocated by Beildelman, T. O., 'Social theory and the study of Christian missions in Africa', *Africa*, vol. XLIV, No. 3 July 1974, 235-49, are developed here. This article describes in somewhat grandiose style the very simple approach to missions that is taken in this book.

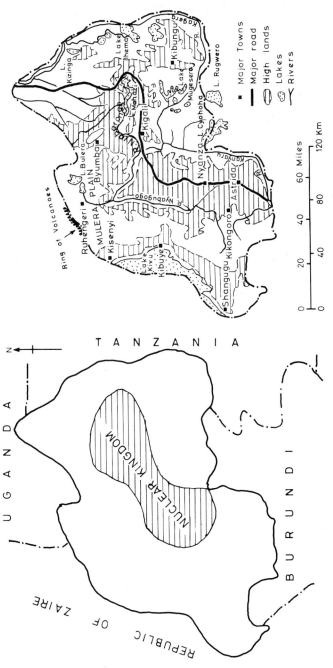

1 (left) *The nuclear kingdom in relation to modern Rwanda*
2 (right) *Rwanda: physical features*

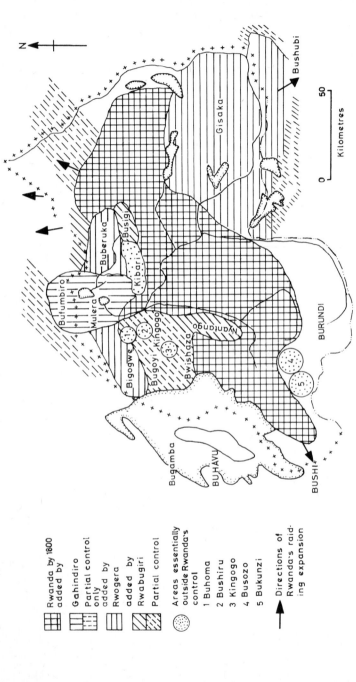

3 *The expansion of Rwanda in the nineteenth century. After Rennie.*

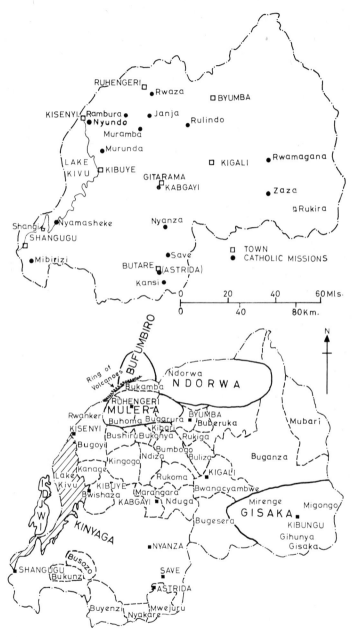

4 (above) *Catholic mission stations before Belgian occupation.*
5 (below) *Provinces of Rwanda.*

xv

Abbreviations

AA   Archives Africaines, Ministère des Affaires Étrangères, Place Royale, Brussels

CMS   Church Missionary Society Archives, London

CO   Correspondence Officielle, correspondence between missionaries and civil authorities, Archbishop's House, Kigali, Rwanda

CR   Correspondence Religieuse, correspondence within the mission, Archbishop's House, Kigali Rwanda

Derscheid papers   J. M. Derscheid collection, microfilm No. 325.6757 D 438c, Yale University, copy at School of Oriental and African Studies, University of London

NAT   National Archives of Tanzania

No. 095 series and dossiers   Correspondence between Rwanda and the White Father Mother House, in White Fathers' archives, Rome.

P series   Microfilm of Bujumbura German archives, now in Archives Africaines

Rwaza correspondence   Loose papers found at Rwaza mission, Ruhengeri, Rwanda

WFAR   White Fathers' archives, Via Aurelia 269, Rome.

Introduction

S'ils ne changent ni n'augmentent les choses pour les rendre plus dignes d'être lues, les historiens en omettent presque toujours les plus basses et les moins illustres, d'où vient que le reste ne paraît pas ce qu'il est.[Descartes' *Discours de la méthode*, quoted by Father Pagès.]

The encounter between Roman Catholicism and Rwandan society apparently provides an ideal topic for a 'culture contact' study. Yet the model of one culture meeting another to generate within it far-reaching changes seems incongruous in the case of Rwanda; there were only a handful of colonial officers and some dispersed missionaries set in a large State and ranged against an ancient monarchy. The subject of study will rather be the Catholic Church and Rwanda's changing political system[1] in the colonial period, and this system included administrators, Fathers, anthropologists and the few business concerns. This is not to say that the few Europeans brought nothing new to change the material conditions and ideology of Rwandan society, simply that the changes they wrought are dealt with here within the framework of dialectical development and homeostasis in a complex and enduring political system.

The ideology of colonial rule came not from the high scientific culture of rectory and university, from Darwin, Lyell and Hooker, but was mediated through a host of minor evolutionary sociologists and physical anthropologists.[2] The subservience of man to eternal, immutable laws, the survival of the fittest, craniology, caucasoid versus negroid divisions were not ideas debated as abstractions in the Boma but were the received wisdom of an age informing policy decisions. It was 'an ideology which sanctioned as natural and necessary a polarisation of the rulers and the ruled, the bearers and receivers of culture', the ideology of imperial adventure.[3]

1

The attraction of the Hamitic hypothesis for colonial administrators was that physical attributes were linked to mental capabilities; Hamites were seen to be 'born rulers' and were granted, at least in theory, a right to a history and future almost as noble as their European 'cousins'.[4] In the tinkering post-military phase of Indirect Rule it was common sense to assess the 'direction' and internal dynamics of pre-colonial 'Hamitic' States, even to worry about sources of conflict and dysfunction within them. So the historian who tries to analyse missionary activity within the framework of the internal evolution of an African State, whether Fulani[5] or Tutsi, is doing nothing essentially new. He is perhaps more aware of the pitfalls: firstly the ever-present danger of a facile reduction of a complex history to a linear, evolutionary sequence; secondly the difficulty of getting behind the historiographical premises in an orally transmitted history.

Rwanda's oral traditions are a prime example of the subservience of history to political ends.[6] René Lemarchand poses the problem succinctly: 'All cultures are myth sustained in that they derive their legitimacy from a body of values and beliefs which tend to embellish or falsify historical truth. But some more so than others.'[7] If this introduction is obliged to dwell on Rwanda's historiography, it is not just that the country's oral and written history provides a pre-eminent example of the effects of ideological restraints in a feudal society, but also that a particular account of the past, shaped in the Tutsi court and promulgated by the Catholic clergy, influenced the political consciousness of Rwandans and Europeans alike.

The Europeans who came to Rwanda brought with them the preconceptions of late nineteenth century Europe; they saw rulers and ruled, slaves and masters, and directed their sympathies according to their personality or social class.[8] The White Fathers were the most important group in the sense that not only did they outlive two colonial regimes, but their presence had a far more immediate impact on the lives of individual Rwandans than the few colonial administrators; Rwandan autobiographies testify eloquently to this fact.[9] Furthermore the Catholic Church in Rwanda grew into a type of 'First Estate' which both nobles and Belgians had to accommodate.

From the outset the stratification of Rwandan society accentuated the inherent contradictions in Catholicism, between the egalitarian ideology of Christian brotherhood and the centrality to salvation of a hierarchically organised institution through which Grace flowed from the top downwards. The problem facing the Fathers was that not a single member of the ruling class[10] was willing to convert before the

2

mid-1920s, while a flourishing and largely theocratic peasant Church grew up around the isolated mission stations. Cardinal Lavigerie had insisted that the White Fathers should evangelise through the chiefs, so the vicariate was put under considerable strain as mission practice increasingly conflicted with official policy — both that of the Mission Society and that of the Germans, who had, inevitably, decided to rule through the 'Hamites', the Tutsi nobles.

German rule, never in reality more than a handful of soldiers and administrators, did not change the nature of the Rwandan State; it remained the coercive instrument of Tutsi rule. Although freelance raiding was stopped, Tutsi regiments fought in a number of campaigns, including the First World War, and German *askari* worked largely in the interests of the ruling class, extending the court's control to the formerly uncolonised northern clanlands. Martial virtues still had a *raison d'être*, and ruling class behaviour and ideology, particularly the religious aspects of the Rwandan kingship, made the Tutsi refractory to the intrusive religious system, with its new ritual and ethical norms. The king and nobles had resolved the problem posed by the religious demands of the missionaries by limiting their evangelisation to the peasantry, but the rise of the Hutu Church with an educated clergy and a separate clientship network brought this strategy into question.

After some initial vacillation the Belgians attempted to impose a uniform policy on Rwanda, to rule through a reformed nobility, and to educate a bureaucracy. As educational attainment became the key to political office under Belgian patronage the Tutsi strategy of keeping the missionaries at arm's length was abandoned: the missionaries ran the schools. The deposition of the king, Musinga, in 1931 came as the climax to a process of assimilating Catholicism which he opposed in the face of Tutsi 'progressives' to the end. The message of his reign was not lost on the court, and the new mwami, Rudahigwa, became a Christian king; the ruling class turned to Catholicism to legitimate their role as inheritors of Rwanda's wealth, custodians of its culture, and occupants of the country's political offices.

But although the ruling class wrested from the European presence every last advantage, they were fighting a rearguard action. Rapid and major political changes and slower economic developments began to alter the texture of society. While the old feudal system[11] apparently survived intact through the 1930s, within it new types of relationships grew up with employment opportunities afforded by the Church and Belgian administration. Educated Hutu took to teaching, cash cropping, truck driving and a host of part-time jobs as carpenters, masons, seasonal plantation labour, or they emigrated for periods to Uganda.

Most dramatic for the nobles in the 1930s was the virtual scrapping of the complex interlocking system of chieftaincies and feudal ties, which had grown up in the nineteenth century, for a pyramid-shaped hierarchy organised increasingly as a chiefly bureaucracy for the Belgians. Ascriptive began to give way to achievement criteria; minor Tutsi families were able to scramble up the educational ladder to Belgian patronage and political power. On the other hand, after a few failed experiments at introducing Hutu chiefs, which foundered on the entrenched opposition of the Tutsi, the Belgians insisted on drawing their bureaucracy from the ruling class, the 'Hamites'.

The successful conversion of the Tutsi in the 1930s meant that myths of Christian brotherhood temporarily gave way before the triumphalism of a Tutsi-dominated Church. The Mission fitted in with the administration's wishes, schools were streamed, with segregated classes of Hutu, and the missionaries were required to put up with the chiefs' failures to comply with ethical norms for the sake of the Christian kingdom. This segregation was explained largely in Thomist terms as a necessary and natural difference of function in an organic society. In reality what had once been a fluid ethnic boundary between two socio-economic groups hardened under Belgian rule into an unchangeable barrier between Hutu and Tutsi defining access to the political class.[12]

Yet, while the ethnic qualification for political office reinforced the ruling class's sense of superiority and tribal exclusiveness, the other changes of the colonial period sapped Tutsi "ethnicity";[13] the martial virtues and much ruling class behaviour were inappropriate in the context of a Belgian bureaucracy, but, what was more important, the Tutsi no longer owned the means of coercion.[14] With military force the prerogative of the Belgians, they had to rely on manipulation of the political and judicial system, with the increasing risk that educated Hutu might appeal higher. It is perhaps in this context that the cultural renaissance of the 1940s and the historiography of colonial Rwanda should be seen: not so much the discovery of a national heritage as the quest of a weakened ruling class for new sources of solidarity and unity. It was the Roman Catholic Church, Rwanda's First Estate, which wiped away the nobles' tears and eased them into their new role as Rwanda's guardians.

Father Pagès' *Un Royaume hamite au centre de l'Afrique*,[15] first published in 1933, the earliest of the Catholic 'Hamitic' histories, was certainly not consciously the propaganda of a court historian. Just as the colonial administrator found among 'the sullen peoples' an aristocratic collaborator, so the Fathers found a lapsed Catholic, or at least a lapsed Monophysite; Pagès thought the Tutsi had come from Christian stock on the borders of Ethiopia, and he wanted to begin again where Coptic Christianity had left off.[16] He drew heavily on Tutsi informants and court traditions, *ibitekerezo*, to provide an account of the expansion of the Rwandan State in the form of a dynastic history.

The second mainstay of Catholic orthodoxy in the colonial period was an equally fascinating book by Chanoine de Lacger, *Le Ruanda*.[17] He elaborated on Pagès' work to present Rwanda's pre-colonial history as the type of an African Old Testament. Stimulated by the massive influx of Tutsi into the Church, he was disinclined to subject colonial society to deep criticism, and his assessment of the past was coloured by a romantic projection of feudalism into early Rwandan society. The historical superiority of the Tutsi and their divine right to rule was, however, balanced by panegyrics to the Hutu peasant, whose function in society was no less glorious.

C'est le cultivateur qui s'empare de la terre, la transforme, lui imprime un cachet d'humanité, crée le paysage historique . . . Au Ruanda ce conquerant, ce transformateur ce fût le paysan bantu, le muhutu. C'est lui qui a fait reculer la forêt, a tracé le premier réseau de sentes durables, a parsemé la campagne d'enclos verts et de foyers; lui, qui, se multipliant comme les étoiles du ciel et le sable des mers, a rempli de sa présence les soixante mille kilomètres carrés où se parle sa langue.[18]

The Rwandan court found its first talented propagandist when Abbé Alexis Kagame began publishing in 1938.[19] Coming from a family of *abiru*, court historians, he had unique access to the royal esoteric codes. In his work the cultural riches of the court are presented from the viewpoint of a Tutsi nationalist historian. If Pagès is obeying the directives of his Society and dipping into local culture, and de Lacger writing the edifying story of the first Christian State after Ethiopia, Kagame is skilfully setting out the cultural and historical justification for the future independence of Church and State under Tutsi control.

To quote Vansina's harsh verdict, these three clerics produced 'un déformation systematique' of Rwanda's history.[20] On the authority of Kagame the Tutsi Nyiginya dynasty was given a spurious longevity and continuity. By using an Île-de-France model of the nuclear Rwandan State (see map 1), projecting the clientship relationship of cattle vassalage into the past, and ignoring the important question of the ancient clan system, Kagame presented Rwanda's history as a progressive domination of other Tutsi States and minor Hutu kingdoms through conquest and the institution of cattle vassalage. The direction of this process was expansion, consolidation by clientship and centralisation of power in the person of the Nyiginya mwami. Like Africans in old colonial histories, the Hutu's role in this saga was that of passive recipients of more or less good Tutsi government. Obviously a gross oversimplification, this was essentially the story gleaned by missionaries and Residents from the Catholic–court orthodoxy.

Vansina's seminal essay *L'Évolution du royaume rwanda des origines à 1900*,[21] researched before 1961 in a period of mounting political consciousness among educated Hutu, went a long way towards a demythologisation of 'Hamitic' history. He demonstrated convincingly the devices used in traditions to disguise defeats and foreign conquests which overthrew dynasties. By laying bare the stereotypes and disposing of many early *abami* as mythical he reduced Kagame's chronology by some four hundred years and lent weight to the hypothesis that the supposedly Nyiginya hero king, Ruganzu Ndori, was a usurper from Karagwe.

D'Hertefelt took the process further, accusing Vansina of 'pan-tuutsisme'[22] for his uncritical acceptance of Tutsi clans whose class distribution, d'Hertefelt demonstrated, indicated a Hutu origin. D'Hertefelt was the first author to address himself to the issue of the multi-class character of Rwandan clans, the problem that Hutu, Tutsi and Twa belonged to the same clan. Using numerical data from election returns, he put the social structure of the pre-colonial State in a new perspective. His analysis of class distribution demonstrated that marriage between Hutu and Tutsi was not the rarity that had formerly been supposed; in the past Hutu became ennobled while Tutsi slipped into the agriculturalist stratum of society through poverty or misfortune. In contrast to Maquet's picture of a closed caste system in which impoverished Tutsi were supported by their peers,[23] d'Hertefelt, like de Lacger,[24] emphasised the importance of social mobility and rejected Maquet's idea of 'récupération fonctionelle'.[25] The development of a distinctly ethnic rather than social boundary[26] between Tutsi and Hutu seems to have been the product of the nineteenth century and increasing stratification of society.

This was by no means simply an academic debate. The arrival of social democrat priests from Europe after the second world war, the pressure put on the Belgians by the United Nations to instigate reforms, and visits by Hutu leaders to syndicalist circles in Belgium increased demands for fundamental changes in Rwandan society. The Hutu, educated in Catholic institutions where they came face to face with Tutsi in situations of expected equality, especially in the seminaries, where there was no 'overt' discrimination, developed a new consciousness of themselves as Hutu. When they left the seminaries they met an ethnic 'ceiling' on their ambitions, the only positions left for them were in schoolteaching or small businesses. When they read about their country they were confronted by the crushing weight of 'Hamitic' culture and history. The debate about development within the Church that had been conducted in the supra-ethnic idiom of *évolué* began to break down as the Hutu spokesmen increasingly identified themselves as a competitive ethnic 'counter-elite'.

Confronted by the dichotomous analysis of Rwandan society[27] that appeared in the Catholic Press, and particularly in the Bahutu manifesto of 1957, the Tutsi elite were torn. The Church-sponsored cultural renaissance with its Hamitic overtones gave weight to their rejection of the European presence and fuelled the elite's anti-colonialist rhetoric; however, an outdated traditionalist stance and feudal idiom were becoming a liability in the face of the Hutu's divisive yet democratic propaganda. Thus it became essential for the ruling class to stress themes of unity, exaggerate past social mobility and deny ethnic distinctions. The mwami, as transcendental source of unity for the kingdom, and the new ideology of nationalism, provided myths of unity for both the 'traditional' and 'modern' sectors of society.

The Church could now no longer provide an integrative religious ideology to buttress the State. Each member of the clergy had to organise his experience of the political crisis in the late 1950s to make it comprehensible; the models chosen were essentially secular and drawn from European history. The unity of the fatherhood of God and the communion of saints was objectively negated even in the pews, where the Tutsi had privileged positions. The Christian king was clearly the partisan of the Tutsi minority. The formation of political parties in 1959 split the Church even further. The polarisation of society on either side of an ethnic boundary, largely created by the Belgians, divided Tutsi from Hutu Abbés and their White Father advisers. The Tutsi laity, finding they 'could not live on Catholicism', the social Catholicism of the new missionaries, turned on the Mission Church.[28] After the explosion of racial feeling in the *Jacquerie* of

November 1959 the Church as a 'first estate' had effectively dis-integrated.

In the period before the PARMEHUTU take-over of January 1961, the Hutu leaders shook themselves free from the restricting framework of Catholic social teaching to follow their ethnic critique to its logical conclusion. Seizing on the Hamitic histories, the Hutu spokesmen upbraided the Tutsi as invaders;[29] the language of anti-colonialism, used to such effect by the Tutsi in Rwanda and at the United Nations, was turned against them. The Hutu were now able to equate nation-hood with the solidarity of the Bantu Hutu people; the Tutsi were foreigners in their own land. For many of the Tutsi the Catholic Church had become the agent of Belgian imperialism and the advocate of Hutu tribalism; for the Tutsi Abbés the religious problem remained. How were they to justify their rejection of their religious Superiors? The answer was to see the White Fathers as an aberrant offshoot of the Universal Church, and to see Rome as uncontaminated by the social heresy.

In Rwanda the two great currents in Catholicism, the unifying force of Christian equality and the hierarchical principle of order, were never in equilibrium. The stratification of Rwanda's society produced the extraordinary phenomenon of first a Hutu and then a Tutsi Church driving a wedge into the Mission Society of White Fathers, until finally, in the crisis of 1959, the Church as a unified institution existed only on paper. It is this story of the growth of Catholicism in a stratified society that the following chapters set out to describe.

NOTES

1 See 'A note on methodology'.

2 For a fascinating discussion of the wider social context of natural science in the nineteenth century see Young R., 'The historiographical and ideological contexts of the nineteenth century debate on man's place in Nature', in *Changing Perspectives in the History of Science*, ed. Teich, M. and Young, R., London, 1973, 344-438.

3 Macgaffey, W., 'Concepts of race in the historiography of north-east Africa', *Journal of African History*, vol. VII, No. 1, 1966, 1.

4 For a very helpful account of the development of the Hamitic hypothesis see Sanders, E. R., 'The Hamitic hypothesis: its origin and functions in time perspective', *Journal of African History*, vol. X, No. 4, 1969, 524-6.

5 It was, of course, because of the concern of historically minded admini-strators like Temple, Meek and Palmer for the 'Hamitic' emirates, and the unifying factor of Islam, that Christian missionaries were kept out of the major Muslim towns in northern Nigeria. See Church Missionary Society archives, G3/A9/01-04, Hausaland 1899-1914 series, CMS, London.

6 Vansina, J., *Oral Tradition*, London, 1965, 164-71.

7 Lemarchand, R., *Rwanda and Burundi*, London, 1970, 31.

8 See, for example, Kandt, R., *Caput Nili*, Berlin, 1921, 239.

9 Codere, H., *The Biography of an African Society: Rwanda, 1900-60*, Annales Serie in 8⁰, Musée Royal de l'Afrique Centrale, Tervuren, No. 79, 1973.

10 See 'A note on methodology'.

11 See *ibid.*

12 See Barth, F., *Ethnic Groups and Boundaries*, London, Bergen and Oslo, 1970, 27-8.

13 See 'A note on methodology'.

14 I have taken this useful term from Goody, J., *Technology, Tradition and the State in Africa*, Oxford, 1971.

15 Pagès, Rev. Père A., *Un Royaume hamite au centre de l'Afrique*, Institut Royal Colonial Belge, Mémoires in 8⁰, Brussels, 1933. (Henceforth publications in this series will be referred to as IRCB, Brussels).

16 *Ibid.*, 8.

17 De Lacger, L., *Le Ruanda*, Kabgayi, 1939. The copy I have seen contained an appendix written by the Rev. Père Dominic Nothomb which took the history up to 1959 on an extended pagination from the 1939 edition.

18 *Ibid.*, 32.

19 'Répertoire bibliographique de Monsieur l'Abbé Alexis Kagame, 1938-66', MS, cyclostyled, University of Butare, Butare, Rwanda.

20 Vansina, J., *'L'Évolution du royaume rwanda des origines à 1900*, Académie Royal des Sciences d'Outre-mer, Mémoires in 8⁰, vol. 26, Brussels, 1962, 9. (Henceforth abbreviated to ARSOM.)

21 *Ibid.*

22 D'Hertefelt, M., *Les Clans du Rwanda ancien: éléments d'ethno-sociologie et d'ethnohistoire*, Annales Serie in 8⁰, Musée Royal de l'Afrique Centrale, Tervuren, vol. 70, 1971, 45. (Henceforth abbreviated to MRAC.)

23 Maquet, J. J., *Le Système des relations sociales dans le Rwanda ancien*, MRAC, vol. 1, 1954, 162-4.

24 De Lacger, *Le Ruanda*, 60-1.

25 D'Hertefelt, *Les Clans*, 62. A similar stress on social mobility is found in Holy, L., 'Social stratification in Rwanda', in *Social Stratification in Tribal Africa*, ed. Czechoslovak Academy of Sciences, Prague, 1968, 89.

26 Barth, *Ethnic Groups*, 27.

27 Kuper, L., 'Race structure in the social consciousness', *Civilisations*, vol. 20, 1970, 88-103.

28 'On the contrary, it is the economic conditions of the time that explain why here politics and there Catholicism played the chief part.' (Marx, K., *Capital*, I, 81 n.)

29 The fact that 'Hamites' were invaders was also used as a legitimation for the British conquest of Fulani-ruled northern Nigeria; see Lugard to Secretary of State for the Colonies, 15, 23 January 1903, C.O. 446/30.

ONE

Religion, king, clan and clientship in pre-colonial Rwanda

The first observers in Rwanda noted a division in society between the cattle-owning Tutsi, the farming Hutu, and the Twa, who either lived in the forests or worked as potters around homesteads. The three groups had distinctive physical characteristics,[1] occupations, behaviour and culture, and it was often assumed that they represented three different stages in the colonisation of the country. But the Hutu certainly owned cattle before the arrival of the Tutsi,[2] so the hunter-gatherer, agriculturalist and pastoralist modes of life offer no evolutionary sequence.[3] Nonetheless, since much of Rwanda was once forested, its earliest inhabitants must have relied heavily on hunting and gathering, supplemented perhaps by a few crops planted in clearings and along the edge of swamps. Rwanda's agriculturalists are known to have made iron hoes and 'roulette' decorated pottery, planted sorghum and made inroads on the primeval forest.[4] This process of clearing land, *kwica ishyamba*,[5] continued until the nineteenth century, a period when many Hutu date their ownership of a particular plot to the toil of an ancestor who cut into the woodland.

The smallest Hutu social unit is today the minor patrilineage, *inzu*, of up to six generations in depth, but in the north the major patrilineage, *umuryango*, is functionally more important. Hutu lineages together make up a clan, *ubgoko*, which may be subdivided into sub-clans. Land is held communally by an *inzu* head and his descendants, though uncultivated land may be allotted to strangers by the lineage head. It seems likely that this form of kinship-based economy and lineage leadership is ancient and perhaps typical of the pre-Tutsi period.

As long as there remained forest to be cleared, population increase could be accommodated and new arrivals settled. In the northern province of Bugoyi land could be given out for usufruct for a year in exchange for a hoe and part of the pea harvest. True patron client relationships grew up in the system of *ubukonde* in which land was alienated and marked out. The client was allowed two years in which to cultivate, sending the occasional calabash to the patron, then had to provide the landowner with two days labour in the sowing season, October to November, and during the May sorghum harvest. Often the *umukonde* formed a blood pact with the client or a marriage alliance with his *inzu*.[6] This development of the kinship-based economy was typical of the rich volcanic plain to the north-west (see map 3) and extended into Uganda.[7]

Social structure was defined by ownership and exchange of the means of production. Relationships within the patrilineage involved the provision of land and labour and were characterised by mutual help and protection. Relationships across lineage lines were created by the exchange of land, women, animals or hoes, and implied some degree of subordination. Vendettas could be ended by the provision of a woman to give birth to a substitute for the dead member of the *inzu*, and the payment of eight cows or goats.[8]

Lineage religion was centred on the veneration and appeasement of ancestors, whose invisible presence was felt to be important for the well-being of the *inzu*. Deceased lineage members were offered symbolic sacrifices of small pieces or food, and sometimes 'married' to young girls who attended their spirithouses. The ancestral spirits, *abazimu*, were generally thought to be malevolent in their activity, and personal misfortunes were attributed to them after divination by an *umupfumu*.[9] The lineage head was in charge of the spiritual well-being of the *inzu*, with the same communal responsibility as he exercised over the (conceptually related) land.

The link between the local *umuryango* and the scattered, widespread clan was of a purely ritual kind, a common totem and annual sacrifice at the Erythrina or sycamore tree. Several of the northern Hutu clans appear to have kept such ritual objects as blocks of hyaline quartz and ivory horns as clan fetishes. An essential element in such supra-lineage religion was the provision of powerful spiritual protection for clan members.[10]

It seems likely that lineages from the Singa, Sindi, Zigaba, Gesera, Banda, Cyaba and Ungura clans, through a combination of land ownership and ritual expertise, managed to impose themselves on settlers from diverse clans to form small priest-led kingdoms.[11] The kingdoms that survived into the twentieth century revolved around the religious powers of the Hutu priest-king, called *umwami* in the south-west and *umuhinza* elsewhere. Such kingdoms seem to have been privileged remnants, isolated by forests and unsuitable for cattle-grazing, of a more extensive type of political organisation found throughout Rwanda.[12]

The *umuhinza* of Busozo in south-west Rwanda (see map 5) lived in complete seclusion until a male heir reached seven years of age. He wore only barkcloth and always conferred with his elders from behind a partition. All food given him had to be carefully washed, covered by banana leaves, and tasted only by pre-pubertal children. No person with sores or deformities was allowed to approach the royal enclosure, and the king himself was not permitted to cross a near-by river. He ruled in conjunction with a Queen Mother, herself constantly attended by two applauding women; all visitors were required to leave her presence bent double, with hands touching the ground. A future *umuhinza* was believed to be born clasping a calabash of milk in one hand and seeds in the other; after the age of seven he had to be secluded in the royal enclosure.[13]

People in the Hutu kingdoms who alienated land, in exchange for two or three hoes or a goat per hectare, paid one hoe to the *umuhinza*. Delimitation of cleared land also required the presence of the local Twa chief, who received a goat for the right to 'open up the forest'; families moving on to this land paid a further sickle to the *umuhinza*. The first fruits of the harvest were sent by all landowners to the Hutu king.[14] Land was thus not reified property; rather, different groups claimed spiritual jurisdiction over different aspects of its productive potential. The *umuhinza's* spiritual authority rested on the belief that he controlled the key to agricultural production, rainfall; he was *mwami w'imvura*. Ndagano, the priest-king of Bukunzi, for example, was said to live sometimes in the clouds.[15]

The divinised persons of the Hutu kings had a similar role to that of the eponymous ancestors; they were symbols of inter-lineage unity and watched over that part of life which fell outside the narrow confines of the *inzu* and the lineage spirits. This structural position as guarantor of the reproduction of the entire socio-economic system had the necessary corollary that the spirit of the *umuhinza* would pass through a number of transformations before becoming *umuzimu*. The body of a deceased king was smoked and dried, the spirit being thought to pass first into a worm and then into a leopard.[16]

The dating of the Tutsi's arrival is largely conjecture; the thirteenth century, from south-west Ethiopia as a dispersal point, has been suggested, and their language may have been Cushitic.[17] More solid is De Heusch's brilliant analysis of myths associated with the Cwezi cult, which suggests an immigration route through Karagwe and Uzinza via Gisaka.[18] The cattle-herding Tutsi would have settled along the valleys of south-east Rwanda, where they perhaps traded milk, skins and meat for local grains.

Probably for reasons of defence, a number of Tutsi lineages around Lake Mohasi in Buganza had developed a major chieftancy by the beginning of the fifteenth century. Ndahiro Ruyange, the first mwami, was doubtless little more than *primus inter pares* of a number of cattle-rich and nomadic chiefs.[19] The cohesion of the nascent Rwandan

State was doubtless no greater than that of the Hutu kingdoms, with their ritually powerful *abahinza*, a congeries of war lords gathered together for raids and protection of their herds.

The rise of Rwandan kingship and the expansion of the State cannot be dated accurately, though some of the important processes involved may be tentatively reconstructed. The assimilation of neighbouring kingdoms would have involved a number of related events: colonisation by pastoralists, formation of secondary vassal kingdoms, and the incorporation of religious specialists into the entourage of the Rwandan mwami. Cattle, used to recruit followers and reward military service, were clearly basic to the king's power; his weakness lay in only tenuous claims to rights over land and hence ritual authority. Hutu specialists incorporated as ritual experts around the mwami would have partially answered both these needs. Vansina suggests that Tsobe lineages were incorporated as *abiru* at court as a result of Mwami Mukobanya's conquests in the sixteenth century.[20] The ideology of pre-existing Hutu kingship assimilated by the Rwandan king would have strengthened the mwamiship.[21]

Nonetheless the invasion of warlike clans from the Nyoro region of Uganda pushed the Banyarwanda into retreat and inflicted a serious defeat on them. When the Rwandans fell back into the neighbouring Hutu kingdom of Nduga its *umuhinza*, Mashira, was put to death.[22] Vansina has suggested that these defeats were a spur to the development of what was to be the key to Rwandan expansion and the development of the State, a well organised army.[23] Each regiment, *ngabo*, was placed under an army chief, *umutware*, who gathered around him an elite corps of troops known as *ntore*. The *ntore* were given long periods of training as young men in the *itorero*, where they were taught the martial virtues and turned into competent soldiers and athletes. Whole Hutu lineages were recruited *en bloc* for major raids to perform behind the vanguard of *ntore*.

The willingness of lineage heads to join an *ngabo* may have been dictated by the need for protection and support in interfamilial and inter-clan disputes; there was no effective way of enforcing verdicts given by an *umuhinza*, and disruptive vendettas were common in the north. The social significance of the army was that it provided scattered lineages with a new corporate identity and source of strength, the *ngabo*. Each regiment had its title and recruited from a wide area; its exploits were built into a body of traditions familiar to its members. By raiding, an *umutware* could add to his stock of cattle; distribution of booty, plus judgement of disputes between lineages and kinsmen, allowed him to become a territorial chief in his own right. On coming to power a new mwami could reduce the power of rival regiments by summoning their elite troops into a new regiment formed on his accession.[24]

The proliferation of the *ngabo* system and the successful raiding of the sixteenth and seventeenth centuries may have provided conditions conducive to the growth of cults above the level of lineage and clan religion. In this sense the spread of the cult of Lyangombe and the success of Mithraism in the lower ranks of the Roman army were perhaps comparable developments.[25] The *mandwa* spirits of the Lyangombe cult were thought to be of a higher order than lineage spirits, against whose malevolent designs they were said to provide protection. They related the initiate to a spiritual world more extensive than that of the *inzu* and hill settlement, just as the *ngabo* united the peasant to lineages scattered throughout the Rwandan State. A sacrificial warrior hero, Lyangombe, headed the spirit order.

It is possible that under the influence of *ngabo* service the type of protective ceremonies formerly associated with clan heads became more popular, incorporated warrior heroes, and came to encompass members of different clans. From traditions that link Lyangombe to a conflict with the usurper mwami, Ruganzu Ndori, at the beginning of the seventeenth century, the cult hero may be identified as an *umuhinza* from the marches of either Ndorwa or Burundi, whose defeat and death in a Rwandan conquest is disguised in cult mythology. The Nduga *umuhinza*, Mashira, for example, also turns up as a *mandwa* spirit in the cult.[26] The model of a progressive assimilation of foreign religious sources of power is consistent with the idea that a cult of deceased heroes would be tolerated in the Rwandan State.[27]

Cult membership was controlled by diviners who diagnosed the need for *mandwa* protection. In his first initiation the neophyte underwent the usual humiliations of transition rites; he was dragged along naked, accused of being a rebel, *umugome*, and covered in cow dung. The neophyte then had the right to attend cult sacrifices without being chased away; he had entered a new 'family' in which a second grade might be taken elevating him to the rank of one of the thirty or so spirit mediums who represented the *mandwa* spirits.[28]

Initiation guaranteed not only protection from dangerous lineage spirits but eternal bliss with the *mandwa* in an after-life on Muhavura volcano. The lobelia growing round the crater of this volcano, in the north-west of modern Rwanda, were said to be tobacco plantations guarded by Lyangombe's sacred sheep and cow. The future paradise was a mundane utopia with a liberal supply of beer, meat and tobacco. The uninitiated were condemned to perdition inside the crater of a second, active, volcano called Nyiragongo, where they would be imprisoned by Lyangombe's warriors. The salvific theme recurred in traditions which presented Lyangombe as a sacrificial saviour, a stereotype also to be found associated with some Nyiginya *abami*, the *abatabazi*, kings who died to save their people.[29] Since these volcanoes remained outside the Rwandan State until the nineteenth century, the *mandwa* may only have been moulded into a *culte de salut* during the traumatic upheavals of Rwabugiri's reign, just before the Europeans' arrival.

According to Kagame, initiation was first prescribed for everyone by the court diviners during an epidemic in the mid-seventeenth century.[30] This may have been retained in tradition to explain the first movement of noble lineages into the cult. Vansina dates the first arrival of *mandwa* mediums at court a century later;[31] from this time onwards there was a permanent group of court mediums, the *mpara*, headed by a delegate of the king, the *mwami w'imandwa*. Cult organisation was not centralised, however: the *mpara* exerted no more control over mediums on the hills than was exercised by the royal diviners over local *abapfumu*. The king himself was ineligible for initiation, and convoked the *mpara* for two to three months' court service, when they guarded his residence in groups of six to ten.[32] They were a spiritual shield for the mwami in the same way as a peasant would seek *mandwa* protection from troublesome lineage spirits. Similarly, they were in charge of the ritual purity of the realm.[33]

As the Lyangombe cult reached the court, Rwandan kingship was reinforced by the accretion of religious mystique; royal votive huts to deceased members of the mwami's lineage were set up,[34] and the mwami may at this time have been associated with Imana, the creative power of the spirit world.[35]. A royal ideology developed which emphasised the eternal and cyclical nature of the mwamiship; *abami* followed each other in a cycle of four rulers: Kigeri following a Mutara or Cylima, Mibambwe after Kigeri and Yuhi after Mibamwe, the reign of each exemplifying a particular value like conquest or peace. To reduce the power of individual Tsobe lineages who controlled the succession the number of *abiru* was increased, and to limit inter-clan jealousies and fratricidal strife the Queen Mother, at least in theory, was chosen successively from four different lineages and clans.[36] As more lineages came to have access to power at court so the mwami became progressively 'divinised' and 'detached'[37] as a transcendent source of unity.

A major expansion of the Rwandan State began at the end of the eighteenth century (see map 3). Mwami Cyilima Rujigira (*c.* 1740-65) pushed out frontier posts into Bugoyi and the north; Ndorwa was subdued and a royal residence built there. As the large independent States of Gisaka and Bugesera were defeated many men and rich tracts of land were brought under at least nominal Rwandan jurisdiction; but in most regions this expansion was not followed up by effective colonisation. Collection of tribute, *ikoro*, was erratic in the north, and when Yuhi Gahindiro put an ennobled Twa over the province of Buhoma its *umuhinza* led a major revolt. Bushiru was never effectively colonised until Belgian times.[38]

Raids from Burundi, Ndorwa and Gisaka were sufficiently intense at the beginning of the nineteenth century for a number of frontier posts to be set up, controlled by resident *abatware*.[39] These army chiefs became landowners in their own right, and before 1830 Yuhi Gahindiro had instituted a new type of chieftancy, the *abanyamukenke*, with rights in pasture land, to break their power. He and the next mwami, Rwogera, also increased their own land holdings by granting *ibikingi*, one to several hills, as pastoral fiefs to their personal agents and retainers.[40] By such land grants dotted throughout the kingdom and by the extensive use of Twa spies the Rwandan kings were able to keep the pretensions of powerful landowners under control. The mwami surrounded himself with a host of ritual officials and increased the number of *abiru* again; many of them were Hutu.

The increased size of the Rwandan court did not alter its essentially nomadic character. The *abami* circulated round the royal residences, placing a wife and retainers in each; the land was controlled by permanent province chiefs, *abanyabutaka*, often kinsmen who provisioned the residences from the peasants' fields. By usurping the position of local lineage heads by sheer force, or by interfering in land disputes and litigation, the chiefs came to control more and more land, exacting crop dues and labour from the unprotected serfs. Although cattle wealth symbolised the richness of the nobility, in reality it was control of land that was linked to political power. Bananas, possibly introduced in the wake of the invasions from Bunyoro,[41] increased the value of fiefs and, despite the lack of agricultural technology, a rich soil manured by the Tutsi herds was the basis of the Rwandan feudal order.[42]

The expansion of the Rwandan State, the coercive instrument of Tutsi hegemony, in the nineteenth century increased the division in society between an oppressed peasantry and a cattle-owning ruling class. Individuals began to seek the protection of powerful nobles in whose patronage they might avoid the onerous *ubuletwa* imposed by the province chiefs. Such commendation, though, was rarely the result of a considered alliance between peasant and pastoralist, rather the product of a power struggle between a nuclear feudal cluster gathered round a Tutsi homestead, and a local Hutu lineage, in which the latter was worsted.[43] The client was obliged to pay court, often for a considerable time, before the patron accepted him in *ubuhake*. Commendation took the form of the Hutu presenting his *shebuja* with a symbolic sheaf of grass; in exchange he was given usufruct rights over a cow. The bonded man, *umugaragu*, was obliged to render his lord dues and customary service, the most important duty being the repair of his enclosure; if a garagu failed to perform this duty annually, all *ubuhake* cattle were forfeit and the relationship terminated.

The institution of *ubuhake* seems to have begun as a relationship between army chiefs and their warriors as a type of noble vassalage negotiated by the spoils of war, cattle. Its spread amongst the Hutu weakened them, since individuals increasingly sought protection with rich patrons rather than in the solidarity of their lineage as of old.[44] Despite the defiant taunt that to be without a lineage was to be 'like a dog'[45] the *imiryango* began to break down as some of their members communally fulfilled obligations to *abatware* and *abanyabutaka* while others sought individual immunity in the patronage of a powerful noble.[46] With their social supports undermined, the Hutu were ruthlessly exploited;[47] by the end of the nineteenth century the imposition of Tutsi rule had reduced many peasants to the level of destitute journeymen, wandering in search of food, work and protection.[48]

The breakdown of the Hutu lineages within the Rwandan State was correlated with the transformation of the Tutsi nobility into a well defined social class whose eating habits, deportment, culture and ideology were designed to instill, in Maquet's celebrated phrase, 'a premise of inequality', which was a charter for their monopoly of the surplus wealth created by Hutu labour.[49] Ruling class behaviour was learnt in the *iterero*, the training school for *ntore*, the elite troops; there they were schooled in the three principal virtues: *ubutware*, military prowess, *ubugabo*, manliness and fidelity, and *itondo*, self-mastery.[50] Articulateness and self-control were the virtues of the Tutsi home.[51] Hutu were invariably segregated for military training.[51] Ownership of cattle defined broad class lines which were reinforced by a training that gave even minor families a sense that they had a right to rule.

Court traditions and oral history extolled the glories of the Nyiginya dynasty and the valour of the Rwandan regiments. The stratification of society was explained and justified by a Tutsi Genesis myth: Kigwa descended from heaven and had three sons, Gatwa, Gahutu and Gatutsi. A calabash of milk was entrusted to each for one night. In the morning it was discovered that Gatwa had drunk the milk. Gahutu had spilt it, while only Gatutsi had carried out his commission. Therefore only Gatutsi was qualified to command. Gatwa personified the stereotype of the Twa glutton, and Gahutu that of the clumsy peasant.

Perhaps more important in the mystique of the ruling class was their elevation of the pastoral way of life from a particular socio-economic niche to a source of values, almost aesthetics. The cow hung like a great ikon over Rwandan society, for it no praise was too great and for it a man would alienate both self and family. The king owned uniquely beautiful herds, *nyambo*, and court poetry abounded with pastoral imagery.[52] For the poor Tutsi the cow was a seal on an ennobling relationship with a rich lord, and at times an object-in-itself, to be paraded on the arrival of a chief at his provincial seat — though for the Hutu, dazzled as they were by prospects of cattle ownership, the cow was still seen in a more utilitarian light as a source of income and indirectly protection.[53] This pastoral ideology dominated Rwandan feudalism, justifying Tutsi rule, in which pasture ate into arable land and 'cows ate men'.

Possession of cows was the first step on the social ladder that led into the cattle-owning, and therefore land-owning, class. A garagu's humiliating duties, the night watch, bringing beer, accompanying his lord on journeys to court, and clearing his night soil, were compensated by ownership of cattle and freedom from *ubuletwa*. A socially acceptable outlet for feelings was a joking relationship with the *shebuja* in which mutual insults were exchanged, though this was extremely formalised and could have provided little relief.[54] Around the Tutsi household the peasant was able to learn the sophisticated language and manners of the ruling class, and keep in touch with intrigues. And some of it rubbed off; a garagu was not quite as other 'free' Hutu. But the ladder was in reality narrow, and a *shebuja* was more likely to take one of his clients' wives than accept his garagu's sons as husbands for the Tutsikazi of the house. Enough did pass up it for a garagu to cherish the illusion that his humiliations were the first painful steps to ennoblement and riches. Confronted with the elaborate paraphernalia of court life, with its nuanced poetry and measured disdain, the peasant outside Tutsi patronage readily came to believe that, apart from being physically smaller and materially poorer, he was intellectually and morally inferior. Marx's statement that 'the ideas of the ruling class are in each epoch the ruling ideas . . . the class which is ruling material power in society is, at the same time, its ruling spiritual power'[55] sums up the situation.

Although ruling class ideology and behaviour accentuated the ethnic boundary between Hutu and Tutsi,[56] the objective structure of society was more complex. There were perhaps about 50,000 adult male Tutsi in Rwanda by the end of the nineteenth century for a total of about 2,500 chieftancies and political offices in the State. Rwandan society was thus ruled by a minority of about 5 per cent of the Tutsi, men with herds counted in the tens of thousands and corresponding ownership of vast tracts of land. Far below them in wealth were rich Tutsi with from thirty to several hundred cows, then the majority of pastoralists with from ten to one animal. Many poor Tutsi had fewer cattle than rich Hutu who, themselves, were a minority above the level of the main body of the peasantry. At the bottom of the scale were an indeterminate number of journeymen, despised by all and little better than the Twa outcasts. Rich Hutu employed journeyman labour by providing a hoe in exchange for two days' work out of five. The words of commendation — 'Make me rich!' — were meaningful for the Hutu garagu, for a cow or two put him high in the Hutu social order. The problem for all the Hutu was, of course, that the rise of the Rwandan State turned independent farmers into the serfs of Tutsi chiefs.[57] Under such cicumstances religion might justly be called the opium of the Hutu; while Hutu hero spirits in the *mandwa* pantheon ruled in concert with a classless divine king the genitals of defeated *abahinza* adorned the Nyiginya dynastic drum, Kalinga, and the king's men took the peasants' land and labour.

In the north-east, though, where Tutsi colonisation had not been consolidated, religion was more an expression of local dissidence. The Nyabingi spirit dominated the religious life of the region. Nyabingi was probably a late eighteenth century 'quèen' of Ndorwa; when the kingdom was destroyed by repeated invasions a cult to her spirit grew up, controlled by mediums who broadcast her alleged wishes.[58] Cattle traders from Gisaka made contact with the mediums and heard about their spirit, known as Mugole, the Lady; on their return from Uzinza they too claimed to be possessed by the powerful *mandwa* spirit. This innovation gained them the opposition of the local Lyangombe cult officials, since the new mediums rallied opposition against Tutsi rule and had a considerable following among the peasantry.[59] When they began collecting tribute to the detriment of the mwami's *ikoro* an expedition was mounted against them.[60]

By manipulating the traditional symbols of kingship and claiming supernatural powers the Nyabingi priestesses remained a potential focus of opposition to the Rwandan mwami throughout the nineteenth century. Later observers described them as 'une autorité révolution-naire, un État dans l'État; elle abuse de la haine née du "muhutu" pour tout pouvoir établi et fait tourner cette haine à son profit'.[61] Their main centre remained Mpororo and the northern marches of the Rwandan State, where Tutsi control was sporadic. Rutajira Kijuna, for example, *c*. 1870, was accorded the royal greeting '*kasinje*' and given the praise names 'Rutatangira omu Muhanda', She who is Unstoppable, and 'Akiz'abantu', Saviour of the People. Social organisation aped that of the Rwandan State; mediums maintained a number of 'temples' — residences — and had clients, *bagirwa*, who shared the leading priestess's spiritual power. Like *abahinza* they gave audiences from behind a partition and, it was said, could perform miraculous cures. Unlike the *mandwa* mediums of the Lyangombe cult, who served the established order at court, Nyabingi shamans moved freely over the hills, offering a genuine contestation of the Rwandan system, cutting across ethnic and lineage lines.[62]

It was during the long and militarily spectacular reign of Mwami Rwabugiri that the contours of the Rwanda seen by the first Europeans were formed.[63] In a series of over sixteen major campaigns, far from all successful and lasting from 1860 to 1895, Rwabugiri raided as far north as Nkole, into south Kivu and onto the island of Idjwi in Lake Kivu, and into northern Burundi, while keeping hold of Gisaka and the east. This incessant military activity produced a supply of cattle and pastures new to keep royal favourites well rewarded and threatening nobles fully occupied. After the Ega had provided four successive Queen Mothers in a row, Rwabugiri inherited a backlog of inter- and intra-lineage tensions; these he kept in check by terror and selective assassination in the leading families of the realm. By taking over the hereditary principalities of murdered chiefs, and multiplying the number of royal residences, Rwabugiri's reign took on the character of an absolute monarchy.[64]

The need to provision his *ngabo* and newly formed residences, the demand for new troops and allies in his struggle with the nobles, dictated a policy of co-operation with Hutu authorities. A Tutsi ambassador to the kingdom of Busozo, able to demand the annual tribute of honey, never set foot in the region. Bukunzi sent a boy and a girl known as the mwami's pillows, *imisego y'umwami*; the boy was killed and his blood used for ritual purposes while the girl was made a concubine.[65] The first fruits from the little kingdom of Bumbogo were sent to Rwabugiri, who sent back a hoe.[66] Beyond these ritual exchanges such little kingdoms were left in peace. Agents, *ibisonga*, were dispatched to the northern clanlands to reside and collect tribute but rarely dared to make more than occasional sorties into the countryside.[67]

It would be broadly true to say that the mwami's effective rule decreased with distance from the old nuclear kingdom of the sixteenth century, but a better description of the political map would be a temporal and spatial patchwork (see maps 1 and 3). While Rwabugiri and his troops were in a region, the successful collection of *ikoro* and the levying of carriers and supplies would have been assured; when he left his agents were liable to be chased out. Even at Save in the Rwandan heartland the mwami was not safe from attack.[68]

Rwabugiri's policy of breaking the great Tutsi families and relying on ennobled Hutu favourites and Twa spies earned him the image 'bon pour le peuple, terrible pour les Batutsi';[69] the average life expectancy of Tutsi in political commands was about ten years.[70] Like a northern Shaka, Rwabugiri forged the State of modern Rwanda through a mixture of military tenacity, shrewd politics and utter ruthlessness, though his control of long-distance trade may have contributed to his success.

European trade goods had first appeared in the country at the beginning of the nineteenth century. Rwabugiri did not underestimate their significance; ivory and skins were taken east through Gisaka to his agent, the chief of Mirenge province, Ruyange, who exchanged them for cloth and trade goods coming from Bukoba. An attempt by Chief Kabaka of Gihunya province to divert the trade led to his assassination. The mwami's foreign goods included a gun and an umbrella; the bulk of incoming cloth was handed on to the nobles, who paid for it in cattle added to the royal herds.[71]

Despite a meeting with the Arab slaver Rumaliza on the Ruzizi river, Rwabugiri spurned the possibilities of the slave trade. Although a slave market grew up at Kivumu for caravans from eastern Kivu, visiting Arabs risked being attacked or poisoned on the king's orders. The Tutsi seem to have frowned on the slave trade; the selling of women and children flourished only in times of dire famine, and buying commercially was limited to ambitious Hutu. At its peak in famine years the trade probably did not amount to more than 1,000-2,000 Rwandans taken into Tanganyika territory.[72]

The Hutu had a number of important markets for agricultural goods, produce and luxuries. At Kamembe, in the south-west, goats and cattle from Rwanda were exchanged for iron hoes manufactured by the Bunyabungo. Rwerere, at the foot of the volcanoes, was a major centre for tobacco and fibre bracelets, *ubutega*, while salt from distant Katwe came down to markets in Buberuka.[73] These local markets were not under the mwami's direct control, though specialist produce of a region, the important items of exchange, were demanded by the court in the annual *ikoro*;[74] Rwerere and Nyundo markets, for example, were taxed by clan heads.[75] Mwami Musinga set up a market at Gitwe *c.* 1896 but largely to control the importation of cloth from Bujumbura.[76]

With the exception of royal residences, where large numbers of Hutu had to be in attendance, markets provided one of the few centres where Hutu from different hills could meet and exchange news. They were at the periphery of the Rwandan State; for the northern Hutu the other principal centres were the courts of the Nyabingi prophetesses. A 'Queen of Ndorwa' became sufficiently powerful for Rwabugiri to engineer her death at the hands of the chief of Mfumbiro, and later to find it politic to deny responsibility for the deed.[77] Tradition has it that her severed head upbraided the mwami, a nice allegory for cult figures who arose, hydra-like, at intervals in the north until the 1920s.[78] Stanley spoke of a priestess, 'Wanyavingi', in 1876 and called her 'Empress of Rwanda'.[79] Emin Pasha gave another interesting account of a medium in 1891:

The Queen of Mpororo . . . said to be a woman named Njavingi . . . has never been seen by anyone, not even her own subjects. All that they ever get to know of her is a voice heard from behind a curtain of bark-cloth. Such theatrical practices have gained her, throughout Karagwe, Nkole, etc, the reputation of a great sorceress.[80]

The threat of these Nyabingi mediums was to be fully realised only in the colonial period.

Rwabugiri's more immediate problems lay closer to home in the corporate power of the *abiru*, who controlled the succession. Some were sent to distant fiefs and others murdered until their power was broken. Finally their ritual prohibitions were simply ignored in the selection of the mwami's successor, Rutalindwa. As Gravel wrote of politics in Gisaka, 'sheer power . . . determined the rules'[81] in Rwabugiri's cavalier treatment of tradition. His wife's brother, Kabare, was a similar 'secular' spirit, a military man with a pragmatic grasp of political expediency and naked force.

The mwami's first encounter with Europeans is said to have taken place on Lake Edward during the Nkole campaign of 1892-93. He was impressed by their use of written messages, which, allegedly, was interpreted as a power to read people's minds, and invited them to come to Rwanda to manufacture cloth.[82] A skirmish with Von Götzen's troops must have changed this first favourable impression. News of the devastating effect of the Europeans' cannon, *umuzinga*, reached the king, who sent anxiously to Karagwe to enquire of the Haya chiefs what policy to adopt towards the whites. News came back from this informed source that Europeans were invincible and should be greeted in a friendly fashion. Nonetheless the court was divided and cows sacrificed to decide whether the kingdom needed the death of a saviour king, *umutabazi* or an offensive war. Traditions maintain that a decision was reached that the whites should be greeted peaceably but the mwami shielded from their supernatural powers.[83]

When Rutalindwa was nominated heir in 1889 his mother was already dead, and a substitute Queen Mother, Kanjogera, was appointed from amongst the Ega. This was not only contrary to precedent but unwise; Kanjogera had a son of her own and enjoyed the support of the powerful Ega statesmen, Kabare and Ruhinankiko. Within a year of Rwabugiri's death in 1894 Rutalindwa was dethroned in an Ega *coup* and Musinga, Kanjogera's son, appointed mwami. By flouting tradition Rwabugiri had finally delivered his kingdom into Ega hands. The young Rutalindwa had suffered a crushing defeat at the hands of the Belgians, and, humiliated, his *abiru* support depleted by assassination, the young king was easy prey for the well prepared Ega.[84]

When the Germans marched into Rwanda in 1897 Musinga had barely been on the throne a few months. The court was offered protection from the Belgians, support for the king and a demonstration of German fire power.[85] The offer of support was timely; followers of Rutalindwa had risen in revolt, and the Teke sub-clan in the north took the opportunity to drive out the Tutsi, sparking off waves of Hutu attacks on isolated Tutsi settlers. A leader for the movement arose called Bilegeya, claiming to be a son of Rwabugiri, but the northern revolt, fragmented and unco-ordinated, was quickly quelled by Musinga's regiments.[86]

The Ega consolidated their position by killing Nyiginya nobles; the situation, nonetheless, was intrinsically unstable, with a Nyiginya mwami in an Ega court, a usurper brought to power after the suicide of the legitimate heir. Rwabugiri's brilliant career as a warrior hero lay behind, and the mwami's effective area of jurisdiction had already shrunk since his father's glorious campaigns. Poised on Rwanda's borders were Europeans whose military might was uncontested and whose supernatural powers might be a grave threat to the realm.

On the eve of missionary penetration Rwanda had thus undergone a serious political crisis and several decades of military campaigns. The centrifugal tendencies of the nobility had been checked and the rigid stratification of society cemented by the spread of *ubuhake* in central Rwanda. The mwamiship itself was a source of both stability and social mobility. 'Le mwami contribue pour une bonne part à cette fusion des races at aux changements brusques de condition,' wrote de Lacger. 'La cour, dit-on, foisonne de parvenus.'[87] The situation in the north was, of course, different; the process of infeudation had not yet reached there, and even in central Rwanda many Hutu owned cattle in their own right. The term *umuhinza* came to mean 'an opponent of the mwami';[88] many lineages retained their autonomy, history and veneration of their ancestral spirits, so the Hutu were far from being the 'slave race' depicted by the first Europeans. On the other hand the process of infeudation seems to have been gaining momentum in the last decade of the nineteenth century, and the 'ethnicity' of Tutsi rule was not entirely in the eye of the beholder. Perhaps the last word on social structure should be left with Marc Bloch, whose comprehensive definition of European feudal society[89] summarises conditions in central Rwanda at the beginning of Musinga's reign.

A subject peasantry; widespread use of the service tenement (i.e. the fief) instead of salary, which was out of the question; the supremacy of a class of specialised warriors; ties of obedience which bind man to man . . . fragmentation of authority — leading inevitably to disorder; and in the midst of all this, the survival of other forms of association, family and State. [90]

But while the texture of society was feudal, Rwanda was also clearly part of a uniquely African historical tradition, the interlacustrine kingdoms; the parallels with Nkole, Bunyoro and Buganda, and, of course, the differences in particular institutions, are equally worthy of note. What particularly characterised the Rwandan State was not the existence of autonomous clan lands (*cf* the *butaka* in Buganda), nor a kingship standing over and against a powerful nobility (*cf* the Nyoro *Mukama*), nor the court's ability to assimilate foreign religious elements and manipulate history (*cf* the Nkole kingship and ruling class),[91] but that institutions found in other interlacustrine kingdoms had, as it were, following their own internal dynamic and developing under the impress of conflicts within the entire territory controlled by Rwanda, achieved a greater degree of elaboration to the point of luxuriance. The Tutsi class had become almost a closed caste. The mwami, more than a Kabaka or Mukama, had surrounded the kingship with a complex ritual aseity. The rich and mystifying ideology of divine kingship and the hierarchy of clientship ties had grown apace to produce a society of great internal complexity. The mwami, source of justice, promoter of the lowly, was the negation of the stratified society over which he ruled. While the kingship never achieved a monopoly of religious symbolism, the mwami became an occult presence in the realm, the projected father image of the Hutu. Reared in an authoritarian patrilocal society, Rwandans thought of the king not as a Nyiginya Tutsi struggling to stay in power but as a transcendental source of creativity, authority and unity. No one would have faulted Father Brard when he wrote in his first letter home in 1900; 'C'est une grave insulte de dire que le roi et sa mère sont des batousi; ils sont rois (abamis).'[92]

NOTES

1 Hiernaux, J., *Analyse de la variation des caractères physiques humains en une région de l'Afrique centrale: Ruanda-Urundi et Kivu*, Annales, Musée Royal Congo Belge, Tervuren, No. 3, 1956, 34-60; the following table is taken from Codere, *The Biography*, 13:

	Tutsi	Hutu	Twa
Stature (cm)	176·5	167·5	155·3
Weight (kg)	54·4	59·5	48·7
Nose height (mm)	55·8	52·4	50·7
Nose width (mm)	38·7	43·6	45·5
Nasal index	69·4	82·5	89·8
Face height (mm)	124·6	120·5	114·7
Facial index	92·8	86·5	85·3

2 Rennie, J. K., 'The pre-colonial kingdom of Rwanda: a reinterpretation', *Transafrican Journal of History*, vol. 2, No. 2, 1972, 15.

3 Hiernaux, J., 'Note sur une ancienne population du Ruanda-Urundi; les Renge', *Zaire*, April 1956, 351-60, suggests that the hunter-gatherer Twa displaced Renge agriculturalists.

4 D'Hertefelt, *Les Clans*, 76-7.

5 Literally 'to kill the forest'.

6 Pagès, A., 'Notes sur le régime des biens dans la Province du Bugoyi', *Congo* (Revue générale de la Colonie Belge), 1938, 8-9.

7 Classe to Mortehan, 3 May 1928. Correspondence Officielle, White Fathers' Archives, Kigali (henceforth abbreviated to CO); Edel, M. M., *The Chiga of Western Uganda*, Oxford, 1957, 93-104.

8 De Lacger, *Le Ruanda*, 76.

9 Pauwels, Rev. Père M., *Imana et le culte des Mânes au Rwanda*, ARSOM, vol. 17, 1958, for details.

10 De Lacger, *Le Ruanda*, 79-80.

11 Such a model of 'State' formation is suggested in Horton, R., 'Stateless societies in the history of West Africa', in *History of West Africa*, vol. I, ed. Ajayi, J. F. A., and Crowder, M., London, 1971, 114-15.

12 Rennie, 'The pre-colonial kingdom', 18-25.

13 The most detailed description of Hutu kingship is contained in a rambling article by Pauwels, M., 'Le Bushiru et son Muhinza ou roitelet Hutu', *Annali Lateranensi*, vol. 31, 1967, 205-322. The primary sources are the Mibirisi mission diaries, White Fathers' Archives, Rome.

14 Pauwels, *Le Bushiru*, 310-12.

15 Mibirisi mission diary, 14 April 1904.

16 The Tutsi mwami was believed to undergo similar transformations; for similar beliefs among the neighbouring Havu see Verdonck, Rev. Père, 'Décès du Mwami Rushombo; intronisation du Mwami Bahole', *Congo*, I, 1928, 294-308.

17 This appears to be the opinion of Professor A. Coupez of the Institut National de Recherches Scientifiques at Butare; see Des Forges, A., 'Defeat is the only bad news: Rwanda under Musiinga, 1896-31', doctoral dissertation, Yale University, 1972, 1.

18 De Heusch, L., *Le Rwanda et la civilisation interlacustre*, Institut de Sociologie de l'Université Libre de Bruxelles, 1966, 342-8.

19 Vansina, *L'Évolution*, 48; Rennie, 'The pre-colonial kingdom', 25.

20 Vansina, *L'Évolution*, 47, 63. Dr Michael Twaddle would, however, date this at the end of the fifteenth century.

21 The Gesera, Zigaba and Singa clans, *abasangwabutaka*, 'those found on the land', were still required in the colonial period to legitimate Tutsi settlement and the installation of huts on new land. When royal residences were being built, officials of the Zigaba clan acted as intermediaries with Hutu spirits and interceded for the mwami. The Zigaba are therefore known as *abase* of the leading Tutsi clans of the Nyiginya and Ega; the Singa have the same relationship with the Sita. The presence of the wagtail, *inyamanza*, the Gesera totem, is also said to have been necessary before any Tutsi would contemplate settling on a hill. See Bourgeois, R., *Banyarwanda et Barundi*, vol. I, Brussels, 1957, 43-4.

22 Delmas, Rev. Père L., *Généalogies de la noblesse du Ruanda*, Kabgayi, 1950, 183; Pagès, *Un Royaume*, 543-6. The dating is contested.

23 Vansina, *L'Évolution*, 66-7.

24 Codere, *A Biography*, 21-3; Kagame, Abbé A., *Le Code des institutions politiques du Rwanda précolonial*, IRCB, Vol. 26, 1952, 17-73, and *L'Histoire des armées-bovines dans l'ancien Rwanda*, ARSOM, vol. 25, 1961.

25 Pastor Ernst Johanssen made this comparison in a little known paper, 'Mysterien eines Bantu-Völkes. Der Mandwa-Kult der Nyaruanda verglichen mit dem antiken Mithras-Kult'; a copy is in the possession of Professor Marcel d'Hertefelt, INRS, Butare, Rwanda.

26 Géraud, Rev. Père, F., 'The settlement of the Bakiga', in *A History of Kigezi in South-west Uganda*, ed. Denoon, D., 1972, 31, suggests that Lyangombe was king of 'Gitara, Muzingo and Muriro' on the Ndorwa border.

On the other hand Pagès, *Un Royaume*, 361, gives a tradition in which Lyangombe came from Kibingo in Nyakale Province, and many of his exploits are associated with the Save region (pp. 626-33).

27 The theme of religious assimilation by the Rwandan court forms the topic of an important unpublished paper by Catherine Robins, 'Rwanda: a case study in religious assimilation', Dar es Salaam/UCLA conference on the History of African Religions, Dar es Salaam, June 1970.

28 Arnoux, Rev. Père A., 'Le culte de la société secrète des Imandwa au Ruanda', *Anthropos*, vol. VII, 1912, 287-90, 541-3, 840-75.

29 De Heusch, *Le Rwanda*, 163; de Lacger, *Le Ruanda*, 266-70. De Lacger gives a remarkable account of an *umutabazi* who was nailed to a tree and brought back to life by Imana, suggesting some Christian contamination of traditions; *ibid.*, 541-3.

30 Kagame, A., *Les Milices du Rwanda précolonial*, ARSOM, vol. 28, 1963, 62.

31 Vansina, *L'Évolution*, 70.

32 Arnoux, *Le Culte*, 292.

33 Delmas, *Généalogies*, 96.

34 It may be that both the votive huts and the *mandwa* were connected with royal fears about Nyiginya ancestor spirits, a dual tactic of appeasement and protection being followed.

35 Nothomb, D. Rev. Père, *Un Humanisme africain*, Brussels, 1969, 91-111, gives a stimulating, though surely Christianised, account of the Rwandan concept of Imana.

36 Vansina, *L'Évolution*, 68.

37 See Beattie, J., *The Nyoro State*, Oxford, 1971, 98, for the term.

38 'Enquête générale', Province du Bushiru, 1925, Derscheid papers.

39 Vansina, *L'Évolution*, 69.

40 Rwabukumba, J., and Mudandagizi, V., 'Les formes historiques de la dépendance personelle dans l'État rwandais', *Cahiers d'Études Africaines*, vol. XIV, No. 53, 1974, 13.

41 Vansina, *L'Évolution*, 66.

42 The connection between the introduction of bananas and the growth of the Rwandan army may have been that the new crop freed men for military service; see Wrigley, C. C., *Buganda: an Outline Economic History*, *Economic History Review* Series, 2, 1957, 71, and Kottak, C. P., 'Ecological variables in the origin and evolution of African States: the Buganda example', *Comparative Studies in Society and History*, vol. 14, No. 3, June 1972, 355-7.

43 Gravel, P. B., *Remera: a Community in Eastern Rwanda*, The Hague, 1968, 163, 179.

44 For the spread of *ubuhake* into Kinyaga see Newbury, C., 'Deux lignages au Kinyaga', *Cahiers d'Études Africaines*, vol. XIV, No. 53, 1974, 26-39.

45 Vidal, C., 'Enquête sur la Rwanda traditionnel: conscience historique et traditions orales', *Cahiers d'Études Africaines*, vol. XI, No. 44, 1971, 532.

46 Newbury, 'Deux lignages', 36.

47 Pagès, A., 'Au Rwanda. Droits et pouvoirs des chefs sous la suzeraineté du roi hamite: quelques abus du système', *Zaire*, April 1949, 372; Bourgeois, 'Rapport de sortie de charge', Shangugu, 1934, Derscheid papers.

48 Vidal, C., 'Économie de la société féodale rwandaise', *Cahiers d'Études Africaines*, vol. XIV, No. 53, 1974, 62-7.

49 Maquet, J. J., *The Premise of Inequality in Ruanda*, Oxford, 1961, 160.

50 A good summary of ruling class behaviour is contained in Lemarchand, *Rwanda and Burundi*, 41-4.

51 Codere, *The Biography*, 22.

52 Coupez, A., and Kamanzi, T., *Littérature de cour au Rwanda*, Oxford, 1970, for examples.

53 Vidal, 'Économie de la société féodale', 70-4.

54 Gravel, P. B., 'Life on the manor in Gisaka (Rwanda)', *Journal of African History*, vol. VI, No. 3, 1965, 328.

55 Marx, K., and Engels, F., *Die deutsche Ideologie*, Berlin, 1953, 44.

56 D'Hertefelt, M., 'Mythes et idéologies dans le Rwanda ancien et contemporain', in *The Historian in Tropical Africa*, ed. Vansina, J., Mauny, R., and Thomas, L. V., London, 1964, 219-38.

57 Vidal, 'Économie de la société féodale', 56-67; Codere, *The Biography*, 20.

58 Freedman, J., 'Ritual and history: the case of Nyabingi', *Cahiers d'Études Africaines*, vol. XIV, No. 53, 1974, 170-81.

59 The much debated question of whether the Lyangombe cult was integrative or a contestation of the established order is only meaningful given two major premises; that the cult underwent no historical development and the Hutu-Tutsi division has always been manifest and important. Neither seems likely. Certainly no Rwandan *abami* feature in the cult, and as de Lacger says, 'La geste des Imandwa se déroule en marge des annales glorieuses de la patrie' (*Le Ruanda*, 288). Cult groups in the colonial period were usually either entirely Tutsi or entirely Hutu, hardly integrative (personal communication from Professor Marcel d'Hertefelt). Vidal has even suggested that the groups reinforced commitment to the established order; see 'Anthropologie et histoire: le cas du Ruanda', *Cahiers Internationaux de Sociologie*, vol. 43, 1967, 143-57. Here the contrast with the Nyabingi cult is very marked.

60 Nicolet, P., Rev. Père, 'Notes sur quelques traditions religieuses au Lukyiga (Kabale) et Mpololo et sur le cas "Nyabingi" en Lukyiga-Ruanda', MS, handwritten, 1928, WFAR; Philips, J. E. T., 'The Nabingi: an anti-European secret society in Africa', in 'British Ruanda, Ndorwa and the Congo (Kivu)', *Congo*, I, 1928, 313-14.

61 Nicolet.

62 Bessel, M. J., 'Nyabingi', *Uganda Journal*, 1938, vol. VI, No. 2, 73-6; Nicolet.

63 Newbury, D., 'Les campagnes de Rwabugiri: chronologie et bibliographie', *Cahiers d'Études Africaines*, vol. XIV, No. 53, 1974, 181-92.

64 Bourgeois, *Banyarwanda*, vol. I, 145-65; Vansina, *L'Évolution*, 71-3.

65 Bourgeois, 'Rapport de sortie de charge', Shangugu, 1934, Derscheid papers.

66 Martin, Rev. Père, 'Notes sur la province du Bumbogo', 23, November 1924, Derscheid papers.

67 Wouters, 'Territoire de Mulera. Rapport établi en réponse au questionnaire adressé en 1929 par M. le Gouverneur du Ruanda-Urundi à l'administrateur du territoire de Mulera', Derscheid papers. (Hereafter called Mulera report, 1929.)

68 People around Save related with relish how ambushers attacked the mwami by hiding in trees and raining down arrows.

69 Kabgayi mission diary, 7 February 1906.

70 An example of six *abatware* appointed and executed in a province in thirty years is given in Vidal, C., 'Le Rwanda des anthropologues, ou le fétichisme de la vache', *Cahiers d'Etudes Africaines*, vol. IX, No. 35, 1969, 398. The Derscheid papers give, on average, four or five chiefs in the period 1860-95.

71 Testimonies collected by Kagame, A., in *Grands Lacs*, 15, September 1950, 9-10. This was a half-centenary issue of the magazine full of interesting oral history but unfortunately with no sources attributed by the writers.

72 De Lacger, *Le Ruanda*, 344-6; the estimate is Father Brard's, made in 1899; see Brard Alphonse, 'Au Ruanda', MS, handwritten, 1900, WFAR.

73 Leurquin, P., *Le Niveau de vie des populations rurales du Ruanda-Urundi*, Louvain, 1960, 42-7. An example of the salt trade in Bugoyi is contained in the Nyundo diary, 24 December 1911.

74 For a typical list of items see Servranckx, 'Rapport de sortie de charge', Shangugu, 10 May 1930, Derscheid papers.

75 The Gwabiro clan head taxed Nyundo market, and the Sekwa head that of Rwerere, see Pagès, *Notes sur le régime*, 36.

76 Classe to Resident, 4 January 1928, CO.

77 Bessel, *Nyabingi*, 76.

78 An exhaustive coverage of these movements from archival sources is contained in Hopkins, E., 'The Nyabingi cult of south-western Uganda', in *Protest and Power in Black Africa*, ed. Rotberg, R. I., and Mazrui, A. I., Oxford, 1970, 258-337.

79 Stanley, H. M., *Through the Dark Continent*, vol. I, London, 1878, 454.

80 Schweitzer, G., *Emin Pasha: his Life and Work*, vol. II, London, 1898, 173, 177.

81 Gravel, *Remera*, 179.

82 Kagame, *Grands Lacs*, 10.

83 *Ibid.*, 14.

84 Testimony of Kayambele, who claimed to be a son of Rutalindwa, given to J. M. Derscheid, 1 January 1931, Derscheid papers. For Ega machinations during this period see Des Forges, *Rwanda under Musiinga*, 18-22.

85 Pagès, *Un Royaume*, 359; Kagame, *Grands Lacs*, 16.

86 Des Forges, *Rwanda under Musiinga*, 25-7.

87 De Lacger, *Le Ruanda*, 60.

88 Interview with Dominique Baziraka, Rukubankanda hill, Rwaza mission, June 1973.

89 See 'A note on methodology'.

90 Bloch, M., *Feudal Society*, vol II, London, 1971, 446.

91 Karugire, S. R., *A History of the Kingdom of Nkore in Western Uganda to 1896*, Oxford, 1971.

92 Brard, 'Au Ruanda': 'It is a serious insult to say that the king and his mother are Tutsis; they are kings, *abami*'.

TWO

The days of the askari-catechist

The first great period of the Society of the Missionaries of Our Lady of Africa came to an end on 25 November 1892 with the death of Cardinal Charles Lavigerie. He had given the White Fathers a spiritual formation and missiological technique better adapted to Africa than that of any other Catholic missionary body. Founded in the disease- and famine-ridden city of Algiers in 1868, the Society numbered 172 members in its first ten years; by the turn of the century forty-eight of them were dead.[1] Its rules emphasised self-discipline, personal sanctification and communal life; its evangelisation was based on an intensive four-year period of preparation for baptism.

Since the Central African missions had arisen as an expansion of the Fathers' work in Islamic North Africa, many features, like the patient in-depth coverage of one small area, and even dress, may be traced back to missionary practice in Tunis and Algiers. The strength of Islamic culture had impressed on the Society the need for adaptation.

The spirit that must prevail in everything is that we must draw as near as is prudently possible to the African way of life; that is to say in everything compatible with Christian and priestly life.[2]

However, the compatability of indigenous culture was a subjective judgement left largely to the missionary in the field. The cultural gulf between North and Equatorial Africa, and the premise of degradation that increasingly motivated the evangelical fervour of Christians,[3] influenced mission thinking and practice.

In the early days the Society had employed Jesuit novice masters, who were trained to produce, in Lord Grey's words, 'willing parts of an admirable machine set in motion . . . for the service of humanity and God'.[4] They set the style of seminary education and, as Retreat masters, reinforced its impact on priestly life. The authoritarianism of the training gave a strong scaffolding against the shocks of alien cultures, while Ignatian spirituality tempered the steel with the flames of hellfire. But the structure had disadvantages. Accurate information about conditions at the local level diminished with distance up the Society's hierarchy; rules and regulations, detailed and numerous, were imposed uniformly from on high with redress only at infrequent meetings of the General Chapter.

The renewed study of patristics and early Church history in the nineteenth century suggested a number of parallels for those meditating on the christianisation of Africa. At a time when Liberal, anti-clerical Europe was pushing the Church relentlessly back into the cloister Constantine and Charlemagne had a nostalgic appeal. Was it not possible that the ground lost in Europe might be made good in Africa? It was hardly surprising that when Cardinal Lavigerie turned his thoughts to Central Africa he insisted on the patient courting of chiefs.

Concentrating on the African court and tolerating negligible commitment by chiefs to Catholic ethical codes was the norm before colonial rule. But then the missionaries had little choice. The setbacks in Uganda failed to destroy the White Fathers' predilection for centralised African kingdoms and the conversion of sub-imperialist groups like the Ganda. Cardinal Lavigerie had taught them not to expect instant success. These events did, however, suggest to some that, if necessary, African potentates were as well eliminated as wooed.

The interlacustrine kingdoms remained the White Fathers' chosen targets, and, armed with the revived Thomism of the nineteenth century, they worked for the creation of Christian States in the centre of Africa, but their attempts were jeopardised by the persistent expansion of the Protestant missions. For the mission clergies there was little difference, as far as the eternal salvation of souls was concerned, between Protestantism and Islam.[5] The Catholics felt obliged to pour in personnel at the turn of the century not so much to evangelise one region in depth as to open up new areas, to stake their claim. After the humiliation of the loss of the Papal States a Catholic laity who had become *émigrés de l'intérieur*[6] in Europe were offered the exciting prospect of sponsoring the aggressive advance of the Church in Africa, and were consoled by the firm belief that outside this Church there was no salvation. Although individual missionaries might concede that many Protestants were in 'good faith', they saw the expansion of Protestantism in Africa as the spread of the malignant disease of heresy. Much of the human aggression submerged or sublimated in an intense spiritual training was given vent in combat with opposing denominations.

The Catholic assault on the kingdoms of Rwanda and Burundi was slow and painful; after the massacre of a group of White Fathers by a minor chief in 1881 it was only with the placing of a German military post at Bujumbura in 1896 that two priests dared open a Burundi station. They were forced to flee within two months. A second attempt was made that year, and at a station near Bujumbura the missionaries met their first Rwandans, slaves taken by Congolese rebels from the Dhanis column. Two permanent Burundi missions were begun early in 1898, taking the White Fathers up to the Rwandan border. With a large mission at Bukumbi in Tanganyika as a main supply base, it was now feasible to launch missionaries into Rwanda from the south-west.[7]

Already the British CMS had reach south-west Uganda and German Protestants were threatening in western Tanganyika,[8] so fear of being beaten to the Rwandan kingdom by their rivals was a strong spur to Catholic advance. In November 1897 Katoke mission was founded some fifty miles from the south-east tip of Rwanda.[9] The missionaries used Jinja traders, middlemen in the Rwanda slave trade,[10] to get up-to-date information about the country, and bought a number of Rwandan boys from them at twenty copper bracelets each.[11] Both Belgians and Germans had set up military camps on Lade Kivu during 1897-98,[12] and the Catholics had every fear that the Germans might send in Protestant nationals to support their territorial claims. 'Il faudrait occuper sans retard le Rwanda,' wrote Monsignor Hirth to his old friend Leon Livinhac, the Superior General of the White Fathers. 'Tout le monde en dit merveille.'[13]

Monsignor Jean-Joseph Hirth spoke excellent German with a pronounced Alsatian accent. Born in Alsace in 1854 but trained in French seminaries, he had been ordained a priest in 1878 and accompanid the first White Fathers' expedition to Central Africa. A pioneer of the African missions who had lived through the martyrdom of the Uganda Christians, he was consecrated Vicar Apostolic of a vast region called 'Nyanza Méridional' in 1890, a territory stretching from Kilimanjaro to Rwanda and including the Kaiser's imperial realm in East Africa. Although he had earned Lugard's contempt in Uganda, he seemed an ideal choice for liaison officer between the German administrators and the White Fathers.

Experience dictated that the missionaries move slowly; presents were first sent to the Rwandan king and Queen Mother. Only a year later did a delegation of twenty come to Katoke to investigate the Fathers and inform them that any approach from the east would be frowned on; court traditions allegedly held that those from the east were invaders.[14] A return visit from Ganda catechists therefore passed through Burundi but were stopped at Muyaga mission, where an uncomprehending Father Superior sent them packing.[15].

Experience had moulded missionaries and their catechists alike; after the 'Religious Wars' in Uganda and the flight to Lake Victoria,

Monsignor Hirth in 1895.

Catholics moved in heavily armed groups. A caravan of Ganda catechists was not immediately identifiable as a team of peace-loving evangelists.[16] Father Alphonse Brard had left a trail of hurt feelings and deposed chiefs from Uganda to the Burundi border; his Ganda retainers had fought off attacks on Marienberg mission, on an island in Lake Victoria, and approached the task of evangelisation like crusaders. So when Monsignor Hirth set off to found the first Christian mission in Rwanda on 11 December 1899 it was like a small army on the move, a caravan of 150 porters protected by Sukuma guards and twelve Ganda auxiliaries, carrying the Fathers' extraordinary mixture of seeds, liturgical paraphernalia, agricultural implements and books.[17]

But experience had limits; only one of the Ganda knew any Kinyarwanda, and the missionaries were at a disadvantage when they arrived in the Rwandan capital of Nyanza in February 1900 acting through a court interpreter fluent only in Swahili. Not that the nobles were any more certain of the new arrivals; forewarned by runners of the large caravan in the south-west — they had, of course, followed the southerly route — the nobles had debated tactics. Religious opinion wanted the newcomers isolated with other foreigners at Kivumu slave market. The major policy-maker, the Queen Mother's brother, Kabare, suggested two provinces where the court's authority was particularly weak. All agreed that the missionaries should be limited to the Hutu.[18] Dr Kandt, the able German administrator who was doing research at the time, wanted them, equally for political reasons, on Lake Kivu, and pressed a cheque for a hundred roupies on the Vicar Apostolic.[19] Hirth was adamant; nothing short of a site in the heavily populated south near the Burundi supply stations.

Each side scored in the encounter. The missionaries were presented with the insulting gift of a hundred goats — only cows were a worthy gift — and they were duped by a Tutsi pretending to be the mwami.[20] Monsignor Hirth got his southern station on Mara hill, though orders were sent that no food or water should be given to the Catholic party; the hill was a fief of a court rainmaker, so it was perhaps hoped that even rain might be withheld.

The caravan was given two escorts, a *mwiru* whom the Queen Mother wished to kill, and the province chief, Cyitatire, a brother of Musinga, who was also on the Ega assassination list. Ega tactics were to compromise prominent nobles at court by association with the mission, then eliminate them by disgrace or death. Within weeks the *mwiru* was executed.[21] But Cyitatire was not so easily ensnared; he allowed the Catholics to move on to Save hill, a gentle rolling upland with a population of over five thousand people and some sixty thousand within a five-kilometre radius, and set his Hutu to work building four huts to house the missionaries.[22] It was the first intimation of the Fathers' later role as powerful allies in court politics.

The first Catholic station of Save was within range of the German posts at Shangi on Lake Kivu and Bujumbura, the centre of an administrative *Bezirk*, and only twenty kilometres from Nyanza, so Hirth had got his way.[23] The mission was dedicated to the Sacred Heart and known as Markirck; the former name was a respectful reference to Pope Leo XIII's dedication of the universe to the Sacred Heart of Jesus in 1898, while the latter, more parochial, was the name of a celebrated Marian shrine in Alsace.[24] It had more in common with a *Militärpost* than a shrine: the Ganda, each with a rifle, occupied a perimeter of huts where they kept night guard, changing like sentries at fixed hours and firing into the air to frighten off intruders.[25] 'They were perfectly organised and on the slightest alarm each knew his place in the defence of the mission.'[26]

When the general of this Catholic expeditionary force surveyed his conquest it was through the distorting prism of nineteenth century stereotypes.

Le pays est asservi par les Batusi ou Baima; le reste de la population, les Bahutu, est absolument esclave; ceux-ci au moins viendront à nous, si les premiers manquent . . . Jamais, en dehors de l'Ouganda, je n'avais vu les missionaires si bien reçus par la population; on dirait que ces pauvres soupiraient après notre venue.[27]

The welcome came not from a slave class but from the impoverished and patronless, who sought in the Fathers the protection of powerful feudal lords. Hirth's view of the mission as 'saviours' was not inappropriate provided it was translated into the Rwandan context. After one visitor to their camp had been cured of sores the missionaries were considered by the Save people as diviners, *abapfumu*;[28] their camp was inundated by sick peasants seeking medicine.[29] The mwami himself was later to request them to make rain, possibly in consequence of a freak thunderstorm that had broken while they were at Nyanza.[30]

Early evangelisation was the work of Ganda catechists, some dedicated, others simply combat-hardened. Father Brard jogged along the narrow hill paths on his ass, accompanied by Tobi Kibati, a catechist who had worked with him for ten years, losing in the process all his family. He had refused to marry after his wife's death and his celibacy was noted at Save; to remain a virgin became known as *kutobia*. Brard would talk of God in a mixture of Swahili and Jinja while Tobi explained the catechism in Kinyarwanda picked up from bought slaves. A complex and rich language, which took the missionaries two years to learn for simple conversation and preaching, but ten to fifteen years to speak elegantly in the style of the court, Kinyarwanda as spoken by Tobi was described deprecatingly as *umunyu*, salty.[31]

Brard's methods were simple but effective, a few handfuls of beads thrown on the ground to entice children into the inner enclosure of the mission, and soon the station was thronged. Father Jovite Matabaro was lured in by the beads as a child and stayed on to work for the promise of some cloth. Fear of contracting some impurity from the foreigners drove him home. The Ganda pursued him, and in a tearful scene chased him out of a corner of his father's hut to the mission, where he entered the *internat* for catechists. By April 1900 fifty had been taken in for training. Many were called but few could be said to have chosen.[32]

The mission buildings soon shot up. Labour was cheap — two spoonsful of salt for workers requisitioned by Cyitatire and for children bringing wood. With some hundred or so patients visiting daily, and scores of children flushed out of their banana groves by the Ganda, Save mission must have given the court an impression of unwonted success. Cyitatire kept away from Nyanza for fear of execution; rumours were rife that he was going to lead a revolt against the Ega. On the missionaries' request two *abatware* came from court to certify that no sedition was afoot;[33] they were treated with undisguised hostility by the local people.[34]

The Fathers' success in handling the devious manoeuvres of the court quickly convinced the Hutu that they were merely agents of the mwami after all. The welcome changed to hostility. Rumours spread that children taken in for instruction were destined ultimately for the mwami, who would hand them over to Nyina'rupfu, Mother Death. Tradition had it that Nyina'rupfu had trapped Mwami Rwabugiri in a cave during the Nkole campaign and released him only on the promise of many Rwandans' lives as ransom. The children dreaded that those in the *internat* were the first contingent; seeing themselves as saviour heroes who would die for the realm, they waited patiently and fearfully for the day Terebura — Father Brard — would dispatch them to Nyanza. As the children of the journeymen and landless were handed over by the chiefs to the catechists the braying of Terebura's ass became the signal for parents to hide their families.[35] In reality the young catechumens lived in comparative luxury, with a good supply of meat and benefiting from the temporary protection of the mission.[36]

To keep up the level of recruitment the Ganda were unleashed to beat the hills on their own. Their technique was to 'select' children who were given the lofty, but dubious, title *intore*, the chosen ones.[37] Protest was useless. The Ganda requisitions soon enraged the Tutsi, who saw their *ubuletwa* being cornered by interlopers; it delighted the missionaries, for whom it was 'a big movement of conversions'.[38] Not all the Ganda, though, were bullies; Abdon Sabakati, who had been through the thick of the Uganda fighting, was a gentle and friendly catechist who attracted crowds. Tobi Kibati went to court and sufficiently gained the mwami's confidence for him to enquire about the Christian religion.[39] He was killed on the way to found Nyundo mission by a Hutu who may have seen the Ganda as the vanguard of a Tutsi invasion.[40]

Tobi's death was indirectly a product of Ega strategy towards the missions. Musinga may have seen the White Fathers as potential allies against his mother's lineage; he followed Kabare's suggestion and allowed the White Fathers two new sites in areas contested by the court. The first was Zaza mission[41] in Gisaka, where the local dynasty had remained the focus of resistance since Rwabugiri's reconquest of the region.[42] On 4 April 1901 Nyundo mission was founded in the equally troubled and unsettled clanlands of Bugoyi. The obstructive behaviour of the guides and Tobi's murder suggested that neither of these stations had been granted with the wholehearted assent of the Ega.

Trouble for the Zaza missionaries was not long in coming; a rising broke out in March 1901 led by a certain Lukara who claimed descent from the Gisaka royal line.[43] His entourage included a group of eighty Ganda bandits-cum-traders who had drifted into eastern Rwanda in the wake of the missionaries. The Ganda who led this band had 'acquired' 100 rifles in Bukoba, and was helping Lukara open up Gisaka for Christianity and commerce.[44] He even produced an old letter from a German officer to prove the authenticity of his claim. But the Fathers, seriously compromised by the riff-raff posing as German or mission agents, were not impressed. With an *ngabo* on the way from Nyanza, they sent him packing; a year in Rwanda had taught a little wisdom.[45]*

The peasants nonetheless rallied to the cause of a restored Gisaka monarchy. Three years of poor rains and famine had decimated the region; the Tutsi, scattered thinly three or four to a hill, presided over abandoned banana plantations and starving Hutu.[46] Court agents were deeply resented. Nyanza retained Gisaka at this point thanks to German punitive raids, with their rich bounty of stolen or confiscated cattle.[47] The mission had also played its part, and Musinga thanked the Fathers for their refusal to treat with Lukara.[48] The White Fathers' initiation into the complexities of Rwanda's regional politics had begun.

Their tactics a year later were less assured. Mhumbika, chief of the Zaza area, descendant of the Gisaka kings and a mission protégé, acquiesced in the replacement of a sub-chief who had killed a catechumen.[49] Musinga, outraged, deposed Mhumbika and complained to the Save missionaries of their colleague's interference.[50] Brard, as pioneer theocrat, reacted by forcing Mhumbika's reinstatement,[51] just at the moment the Zaza Superior was dutifully clearing Mhumbika's cattle off the mission hill.[52] Another error. The cattle, it transpired, were the mwami's, given in *ubuhake* to Mhumbika, and had to be hastily returned to their pasture.[53] Musinga now turned to manipulation of the Germans,[54] and induced them to force Mhumbika to court, where twenty of his followers were slaughtered.[55] The effect on Zaza was immediate.[56] 'These poor people think that all whites form a solid block and the order given by the military commander was, if not inspired by us, at least approved,' wrote the Zaza Superior.[57] The Germans[58] followed up with a punitive raid on Gisaka, leaving thirty dead around the mission.[59] The missionaries had either to follow the German line and support the court or suffer the consequences.

Exactly the same rationale behind the court's assent and characteristic problems beset the fourth and fifth stations, Mibirisi in the south-west and Rwaza in the northern province of Mulera, founded in November 1903.[60] Although the fifty Sukuma armed guards that had been sent to Rwaza robbed the local Hutu of cattle and crops, they were under better control than the Ganda.[61] Banyagisaka catechists were employed at Mibirisi, and the German commander at Shangi assisted with labour for building.[62] But even without the exactions of the Ganda the missionaries confronted the basic difficulties of operating in regions distant from the court.

The northern province in which Rwaza was sited was nominally divided between three chiefs. Kayondo, an Ega notable, was *umutware w'umuheto*, chief of the bow, and in charge of levying *ngabo*. Local

Hutu had fought for Musinga's father, Rwabugiri; they remembered the battles and booty, and Kayondo was the best liked of the chiefs.[63] Neither of the two landowners, *abanyabutaka*, both Nyiginya,[64] dared reside to the north of the river that flowed by the mission hill; these dealt with clan heads almost in the manner of Indirect Rule.[65] Each lineage was supposed to send an annual tribute of one calabash of honey, one hoe and a platter of beans to the mwami;[66] in reality the king's man appeared once every three to four years and counted himself lucky to return safely to Nyanza.[67] Tutsi commoners steered clear of the hills and lived as isolated pockets of settlers in the plain, dealing on equal terms with their Hutu neighbours. In near-by provinces there were still *abahinza*, Hutu priest-kings. Though the missionaries perhaps exaggerated the degree of anarchy to impress their readers in Europe, much of the north was controlled by bandits.[68] To escape the turmoil and hardship many of the Sigi clan, for example, migrated north to Kigezi; since the 1840s forests had been growing back over once cultivated land.[69]

Within weeks of pitching their tents half way up Rwaza hill the missionaries could see the difficulties ahead: 'it will hardly be the Tutsi who will come to our assistance. They have no authority and nobody listens to them.'[70] Their instructions from Monsignor Hirth on the Tutsi were 'to speak highly of their authority and of the power of the king',[71] but, as the Father Superior remarked with some anxiety, 'all you need is the chiefs to say one thing for the people to do the exact opposite'.[72] The only escape from the conflict between common sense and episcopal directives was to turn the Tutsi into what they were supposed to be, powerful chiefs. The king's man was chased away from a watering spot by the river in March 1904;[73] to show the flag a Father led the mission Sukuma into a major battle from which Kakwandi, the king's man, emerged victorious.[74] Within a week all the station's workers had drifted away in disgust.[75]

We were the friends of the Tutsi and wanted to bring them back into the country. Where had those dreams of the early days gone? All the chiefs chased out by the Europeans, only the Bahoutou masters and lords of the mountains and cattle . . . Disappointment! [76]

Within the borders of Rwanda as defined by the Germans there was not a homogeneous State nor was there an 'established order' that the missionaries could easily support. Some missionaries might speak of 'taxes' levied on the Rwaza people or 'faults on both sides'[77] as if there was a history of central government, but the conditions of anarchy[78] went back to the nineteenth century, and diffuse clan authority existed before that. Others at Zaza were more blunt about 'government'. 'The king is represented in Gisaka by chiefs to whom he has given full power to pressurise and pillage the local Batuale.

Consequently there are compaints every day from the latter against their oppressors.'[79] Here regional identities brought Hutu and Tutsi together in opposition to the foreign invader. To support Nyanza meant losing local clients; there was no way round it.

The Fathers' first description of Rwanda had been 'a perfect hierarchy in which one chief is subordinated to another under the all-powerful and supreme authority of the king'. Father Brard first admired the Tutsi for their 'intelligent air, alert, curious yet discreet and well-mannered in their deportment',[80] and had despised the Hutu. But after a few months of frequent and frustrating dealings with the Tutsi the mystique wore off. In Brard it became almost a loathing of the chiefs and their Tutsi garagu; some were humiliated by being forced to carry bricks, and one was put under house arrest until he agreed to supply Save with logs for building purposes. 'Ce n'était pas une petite joie pour les Bahutu de voir leurs chefs, toujours si fiers ennemis de la peine et de la contrainte porter des briques du matin au soir . . . Et puis cette protection que nous exerçons lorsqu'ils sont manifestement tourmentés est bien de nature à leur inspirer la confiance à notre égard.'[81] For the other Uganda veteran, Father Paul Barthélémy, the Tutsi were 'real Jews; they are rapacious flatterers and above all hypocrites'.[82] It was a far cry from Cardinal Lavigerie: 'You will not neglect to make them realise that Christian doctrine is completely favourable to their authority, since it teaches that they are the true representatives of God in the temporal realm.'[83]

The spiritual dynamism that drove men out of the cosy parochial backwaters of rural France into the African bush easily became deformed by isolation and frustration into physical violence. Zeal for souls was quickly transformed into theocratic tyranny not readily checked by colonial officers or religious superiors. After long years veterans like Brard and Barthélemy had grown impatient. Instead of God's representatives they saw brutal and ignorant despots barring the door of Heaven to their subject populations. Unaccustomed to being treated like an inferior race of wild animals, they found it impossible to remain calm when the Tutsi treated them with the arrogance and contempt that informed ruling class behaviour, what one priest called 'un dédain superbe, un mépris conscient'.[84]

The distinction between temporal and spiritual realms, much trumpeted in theory and much ignored in practice, was forgotten in Rwanda. After long years in Africa the missionaries accepted a definition of religious leadership that was profoundly African. Their behaviour and position, not unlike the Nyabingi prophetesses with their court and clients, became a threat to the Tutsi in central Rwanda and negated their political importance in the provinces. The chiefs around Save began preventing peasants from frequenting the mission as early as August 1901; 'they fear our authority is increasing at the expense of theirs', a Father explained.[85]

Whatever the missiological implications of the Fathers' conduct, it seriously jeopardised the White Fathers' position with the German administration. 'Nos missionaires au Ruanda sont regardés comme voulant accaparer pour eux l'autorité dont le gouvernement est si jaloux,' Hirth wrote back to Algiers.[86] In one very grave incident Dr Kandt discovered that the Ganda had beaten a thief so severely that he had later died.[87] Father Brard always worked, Hirth continued ruefully, with 'a good number of Baganda; they are really more *askari* than catechist'.[88] Father Barthélémy was, as the Germans pointed out, 'of the Father Brard school'; Von Grawert wanted his deportation from Rwanda for personally avenging Tobi's murder.[89] The Vicar Apostolic might loyally defend his missionaries' inexcusable behaviour to Bujumbura, but he was resolved to get rid of Brard and keep the new generation of missionaries out of his school.

_ After two years the mission stations at least appeared less like garrisons. Save's day began at dawn with prayers for the Ganda and each man being allotted his task. Catechists were now changed from hill to hill to prevent their building up a personal following. But there was still the martial air; the punishment for fighting was a whole day's work cultivating the mission gardens; penitents could be seen hoeing by firelight. Catechumen/catechists were under the same strict regime. One Hutu who disappeared for a long time was roundly denounced from the pulpit on his return; the priests had assumed he was murdered by Musinga's agents before he came back trailing goats, sheep and cattle. Religious expeditions were still profitable.[90]

Attendances at Save school in October 1901 ranged from eighty to a hundred.[91] Terebura drummed in the catechism, another priest taught reading and writing. If any pupil was unable to recite the set catechism passage off by heart the whole class was sent out hoeing. *Timor Tereburae* drove them to study in the evenings. The catechism itself was a strange hotch potch of Rundi, Swahili and bastard Kinyarwanda. 'The Book which explains the teachings of Religion' (*Igitabu cyo gusobanura amagambo y'idini*) had as its title, for example, *Ekitabu kyo kufutula bigambo bye dini.*[92] In as much as the students could understand it they were presented with an account of the developing dialogue between God and man. 'This format intrigued us,' wrote Father Jovite Matabaro, 'and we followed with curiosity the procession of prophets, these men who had spoken with God.'[93] The idea, so similar to the claims of the Nyabingi prophetesses, must have been consolingly familiar; by the middle of the catechism, though, they were to discover that this prophetic strand disappeared from Catholic Christianity. Only in the 1930s, with the arrival of the Church Missionary Society, would the promise of the early pages be realised.[94]

The Fathers were fortunate to be teaching a doctrine of salvation in a society with a rich religious culture. Ideas of Heaven and Hell, or at least the divergent destinies of different classes of spirits, had developed in the Lyangombe cult, only 'salvation' was linked to initiation without consideration of moral conduct. The White Fathers' long preparation for baptism and ban on catechumens attending mass certainly emphasised the ritual and numinous quality of the Christian transition rite, but the Ten Commandments and Christian behaviour were stressed as equally essential.

The period of postulancy for the first recruits was shortened, and they became catechumens as soon as they could read.[95] New catechumens were given a medal of the blessed Virgin to signify their changed status and a piece of cloth as a prize. Terebura's insistence on the correct repetition of the doctrine of the Trinity made progress slow, but, when others took over, the pupils rapidly absorbed the principal Christian dogmas. However little their conversion corresponded to the Jesuit ideal of an intellectual assent to the truths of the Faith, not all cases could be dismissed as results of pressure and fear, or as epiphenomena of patronage. One of the first neophytes was Wencelas Nyirambinda, a devout Christian whose son became Abbé Laurent Sikubwabo and whose daughter, Mama Mechtilda, rose to be head of Byimana Girls' School. The first converts later came to have considerable status in the Church and were known as 'those who have eaten off the baskets' after the makeshift tables in the Ganda camp; they had unusually close contact with the Fathers, who were making special efforts to get a first Christian generation trained. Abbé Jovite Matabaro was in this early group; in some cases lives were undeniably changed by contact with the mission.[96] But many of these first Christians slipped away to the more powerful patronage of the German *askari*, where immediate rewards were greater.[97]

At Save the numbers of those given the medal rose from 782 in 1900 to 1,836 in 1901 and 4,656 by the end of 1902. Missionary effort was rapidly transformed from intensive training of a select few to the diffuse administration of a huge catechumenate. On Holy Saturday, 12 April 1903, seventeen Hutu and nine Tutsi, mainly orphans and all but four boys, were solemnly baptised at the mission. They had survived three years in the *internat*. At Zaza there were eight hundred on the catechists' books, with a nucleus of fifty in the *internat*; thirty of these were due for baptism at Christmas. Nyundo, with its requisition system, was beginning to fill its catechism classes. A Catholic catechist was allowed to teach the mwami and six other Tutsi at Nyanza. On the surface it seemed a hopeful young mission. The reality was far less encouraging, as Monsignor Hirth found when he made his first visit to the stations in 1903.[98]

His stay at Save allowed him to observe at first hand what had become of the mission he had founded three years earlier. A weekend with Terebura was a daunting experience for the Vicar Apostolic. On Saturday the Ganda called in their groups of catechumens to the mission, each with its own *kapitao*. On Sunday while the Christians were all in church the catechumens were assembled in a large open shed surrounded by their Ganda directors.

There was always a tumultous scene, especially when the women came. They never learned the difference between the Christian religion and the cult of the ancestral spirits. When they were told to kneel they did so as you would for the Lyangombe ceremonies.[99]

Clouting the women to keep them quiet, the Ganda taught the crowd their letters and the sign of the Cross. After the lesson, as the Christians were coming out of mass, Terebura would sweep in bearing the Good News. In the afternoon there was Benediction of the Blessed Sacrament, games and dancing.

The Vicar Apostolic saw enough to be profoundly shocked. Father Brard, like an old wine, had lost what little sweetness he once had. He was forbidding local chiefs to take presents to court, and the Germans now refused even to call at the mission; violent incidents were common. The situation at other mission stations was little better. In an unusual show of wrath Hirth complained bitterly to the Superior General in Algiers:

When we came to this country in 1900 it was agreed with the king that none of these villages should be taken over by the missionaries, but despite everything they have got their hands on 3,000 hectares of land on which about 8,000 people live; they exercise the authority of a king over this property, not only judging many cases but conscripting labour, ordering fatigues for construction materials, chasing out polygamists, removing amulets, demolishing the little huts for sacrifices, replacing even a chief whom they have expelled, and imposing on the chiefs catechists . . . from the *armée roulante*.[100]

The *armée roulante* was the Ganda again. In June 1902 a veritable avalanche had descended on Zaza.[101]

His immediate response was to send the missionaries a list of instructions for reform of the system. All the Ganda catechists were to be withdrawn from the hills and no Sunday mass meetings were permitted. Henceforth the Banyarwanda were to proselytise amongst their neighbours, each catechumen bringing with him two postulants. At Zaza alone permission was given for the Ganda to continue working, provided they operated in regions distant from the mission; close by the station the Banyarwanda had to teach the Faith on their own. For Brard it amounted to 'the least possible noise so as not to arouse the sensibilities of the King or the Tutsi'.[102] But the days of the Ganda *askari* catechist were over.

The concessions at Zaza were attributable to the presence of the 'dove-like' Superior, Father Pouget, who had redeemed earlier mistakes by a strict policy of non-interference in politics. He was perhaps typical of missionaries in Rwanda, outwardly complying with Monsignor Hirth's instructions but inwardly still firmly with the Hutu.

Ah, if only we were able to tell them that their conquerors [the Tutsi] were to be shown the door, or at least stopped from harming them, they would be more zealous [for Christianity]. Several come because of a secret desire for our protection and listen to us with interest. Alas, it takes a long time for them to understand that *regnum meum non est ex hoc mundo*.[103]

But it was not the average missionary who was most noted by either the Germans or Rwandans. In the light of the flourishing theocracies around the five mission stations the Hutus' incomprehension was scarcely culpable ignorance.

In these early years the hill communities did have great difficulty in understanding what the missionaries were about. Many believed that the catechumens' medal was a type of Swahili amulet, *burozi*, with magical powers to harm. Parents beat their children when they found them wearing it, and when priests baptised dying babies they were liable to be accused of sorcery. The picture of the Sacret Heart of Jesus at Save soon gave rise to the idea that the Fathers ate the hearts of their catechumens, who were marked out for destruction by the medal.[104] The disturbed political circumstances were conducive to the spread of fantastic stories involving the missionaries. They were said to have heralded *Bwirakabiri*, a solar eclipse; anyone who left home in the darkness would change into a ravenous beast and eat the occupants of his hut. Some imagined that the Save Fathers had a tunnel under their compound through which the catechumens would be taken to Europe.[105]

It is difficult to gauge accurately from European records how widespread such beliefs were or, indeed, whether the Fathers were not misinterpreting their informants' remarks. Misunderstandings were common, owing to language difficulties; the view of the African peasant as a superstitious child was unquestioned and liable to lead to hasty conclusions. But it does seem certain that the world which grew up around each station provided a focus for myth-making and story-telling. Father Brard's ass was credited with the ability of braying to disclose the presence of poisoners and sorcerers; others imagined that the Fathers used the animal to sniff out a suitable site for a mission. A missionary's bicycle produced a similar crop of stories when he cycled to court.

Although a Nyabingi prophet had predicted the imminent arrival of whites in the 1890s, and the Germans had been travelling through the country for over six years, most people still seem to have found the

White Fathers prodigious and alarming. This was largely due to the limited amount of information available to people on the hills; outside the network of court agents and spies, who served the nobility, communications were limited by the rugged, mountainous terrain. Apart from a visit to a major market, an annual trip to Nyanza with the royal *ikoro* or a trek to find food in time of famine, a peasant had little access to information beyond his own group of hills. When privileged Tutsi like the Ega Ruhinankiko thought that Jesus was the leader of the White Fathers and the mass an appeasement of the major White spirit, it may be imagined what Hutu made of their local mission station.[106]

The rumours and strange beliefs that grew up had common themes and expressed both Rwandan fears about the whites and the tensions and anxieties of their own society. The missionaries mistakenly imagined that the stories emanated from the court, but they seem rather to have grown spontaneously out of the confrontation between mission stations and hill communities. Rwanda's stratified society at this time was one of ceaseless internal conflict as lineages jockeyed for position around the rich Tutsi and their retainers. Hunger was never far from the door and was followed annually by the king's *ikoro* collectors. The ravenous wild animals, transformations, sorcerers and poisoners to which the Fathers were related as saviours, prophets or *abapfumu* and witches, were in part the psychic detritus of a highly competitive society in which the reward for success was great wealth and for failure sudden death.

Through this kind of communal rumination on the nature of the missionaries Rwandans came slowly to assimilate their alien presence. They were given praise names like valiant warriors in the *ngabo*; the Vicar Apostolic became Imputabigwi, he whose exploits follow each other rapidly; Father Zuembiehl, the first missionary in the south-west, entered the language inadvertently as *umuzumbiri*, meaning merely a European Father. It was above all the political dimension of their presence that the Hutu acknowledged and which the court found such a disturbing aspect of the five mission stations.

The religious pretensions of the Fathers were easier to accommodate and, in the Rwandan context, relatively modest. Despite the daily round of high liturgy at Nyanza the court's religious experts had no assured position in the State. A succession of rainmakers were executed during the drought period of 1903-04, and troublesome *abiru* were liable to be murdered. Some time before the White Fathers' arrival the *mwami w'imandwa* was deposed as a supporter of Rutalindwa.[107] Kabare was famous for his remark that even if the new Ega leaders did not have Kalinga, the dynastic drum, they had the mwami and a drum could be made.[108] His attitude to religion was instrumental, almost secular, and highly political, far from any slavish adherence to archaic court ritual. It was Musinga and the Queen Mother who cared about, and needed, the full religious scaffolding of their office to offset the memory of regicide. So there was no essentially religious opposition to the Fathers from an established priesthood, nor from the mwami, provided his ritual authority was not threatened.

The one advantage of the catechism's use of *Mungu*, the Swahili version of the name of the Christian High God, was that it left the mwami secure as a transcendental source of authority for Rwanda;[109] Mungu belonged to the foreigners, the mwami belonged to Rwanda. When the court tested the religious expertise of the missionaries the experiment proved something of a flop. Court messengers asking the missionaries to make rain explained cautiously that the mwami would 'ask Imana and we [the Fathers] should ask Mungu'; Father Brard replied with a little lesson on Lulemo, 'Master of all he has created and therefore of the rain', and declined.[110]

There was a clash with the Lyangombe cult, but, lacking any central direction from Nyanza, the mediums were unable to put up any co-ordinated opposition. Furthermore, by the time the missionaries began recruiting from amongst the cult's adepts it had tended to merge with the household veneration of lineage spirits. An *inzu* would have its own favourite *mandwa* who was called upon in times of grave distress; a man might ask an initiated son to represent the spirit in order to save his cattle.[111] The Tutsi also consecrated young girls to Lyangombe in order to gain the *mandwa's* favour in cases of serious illness; the girls were then unable to marry and wandered from kraal to kraal, living as concubines.[112] This trivialisation of the cult to the level of intercessory lineage religion made it difficult for the missionaries to eradicate, lacking as they did any suitable substitute for household religion, but posed no threat to Christianity as a High God monotheism. In September 1902 something akin to a national festival of sacrifices took place among the Hutu in thanks for the sorghum harvest; the Fathers were amazed to see their catechumens trooping off to join in the offerings to the *mandwa* mediums.[113] This was the only occasion when the cult appeared to be a force to be contended with; the context of the cult and its social functions seem to have been seriously affected by the decline of the *ngabo* in the colonial period.

Coming from Uganda, and having spent a decade in Karagwe, the White Fathers were accustomed to the Bacwezi cults from which the religion of Lyangombe and Kiranga had developed. But this made them far from tolerant;[114] transposing their own dualism on to the religious system they found, they immediately assumed that Imana was a High God, and therefore 'good', so Lyangombe and Kiranga, it followed, were 'bad'.[115] The Burundi Fathers described the local ceremonies as a 'Devil's Sabbath',[116] while the Rwanda Fathers called the *mandwa* spirits 'a whole host of demons that have kept them [the

Banyarwanda] enslaved for centuries'.[117] If household lineage religion was idolatrous superstition the Lyangombe cult was worse, demonic possession. Catechists who attended cult ceremonies risked a beating at the hands of Father Brard, and uninitiated Christians who strayed too close to the sacrifices were chased away and sometimes assaulted.[118] The Fathers' attitude might have the authority of the Christian centuries but it missed the point; their fulminations about *Shitani* and 'suppôts du Satan' fell on deaf ears and the neophytes sought *mandwa* protection with good heart, sure in the knowledge that Lyangombe was the benign saviour of Rwanda.[119]

The White Fathers were therefore fortunate in finding in Rwanda a court with an instrumental, sometimes cavalier, attitude to religion, and a Hutu population which could find a place for Mungu, and a Saviour, in its religious culture. Their initial success in starting five stations had been the result of divisions at court, lack of control over certain provinces and sheer Ganda muscle; they were a political force operating in fortuitous political circumstances. These circumstances were not to last. The Ganda and strong-arm missionaries were unacceptable to religious and colonial authorities alike. The missionaries registered a change of mood at court early in 1904 which stemmed from the death of Musinga's last two natural allies, important Nyiginya nobles killed in a clash with Kabare's troops.[120] All power now lay in the hands of the anti-Christian Ega, the Queen Mother and her brother. Mission protégés feared for their lives, and rumours abounded that Kabare was planning an attack on the mission stations; his rival Ruhinankiko was said to be on the execution list.[121]

The missionaries' only support came from their congregations, drawn from the lowest class in society. They had found initial Hutu response fickle, dependent on immediate advantage; in the north they were to find it more fickle still. The White Fathers were entering a period of crisis when they would again be thankful for the presence of the Germans and their *Schutztruppen*.

NOTES

1 Duchêne, Rev. Père, *Les Pères Blancs, 1868-92*, vol II, Maison Carrée, Algiers, 1902, appendix.

2 The White Fathers' Rule, quoted in Burridge, W., *Destiny Africa*, London, 1966, 104.

3 The change that took place in Christian attitudes during the nineteenth century is well illustrated in Ajayi, A. J. F., *Christian Missions in Nigeria, 1841-91*, London, 1965.

4 Quoted in Ranger, T. O., *Revolt in Southern Rhodesia, 1896-97*, 1967, 313.

5 A good example of this equation of Islam and Protestantism as co-equal threats is found in correspondence over Mozambique; see Bishop Auneau to Gebhard, 29 September 1922, Montfort archives, Rome.

6 This was the name given French Catholics in the nineteenth century owing to their defensive reaction to secular society. For an excellent evocation of French Catholic attitudes see Gorres, I., *The Hidden Face*, New York, 1959.

7 *Chroniques Trimestrielles des missionaires de Notre-Dame d'Afrique*, No. 73, January 1897, 129 (hereafter abbreviated to *Chroniques Trimestrielles*); Monsignor Gorju, *En Zigzags à travers l'Urundi*, Namur, 1926, 13-20.

8 See Hellberg, C. J., *Missions on a Colonial Frontier West of Lake Victoria*, Studia Missionalia Upsaliensia, VI, 1965.

9 Austen, R. A., *Northwest Tanzania under German and British Rule*, New Haven, Conn., 1968, 45.

10 Van de Meire, Rev. Père, 'La Grâce au Ruanda', MS, typewritten, undated, notes on mission settlement by a White Father, Derscheid papers; de Lacger, *Le Ruanda*, 381.

11 Nothomb, D., a printed but unpublished Church history of Rwanda, p. 9. This history formed the basis of Father Nothomb's appendix to de Lacger's *Le Ruanda*, and I am most grateful to him for lending me his original annotated copy (hereafter called Nothomb, *Church History*).

12 Louis, Roger W. M., *Ruanda-Urundi, 1884-1919*, Oxford, 1963, 43.

13 Hirth to Livinhac, 30 November 1897, No. 095033, Dossier 95, WFAR.

14 Vanneste, Rev. Père, 'Le Vicariat Apostolique du Ruanda', MS, typewritten, undated notes by a White Father, Derscheid papers.

15 Testimonies collected by Abbé Joseph Sibomana in *Grands Lacs*, 1950, 27.

16 The settlement was attacked by Chief Rukonge; see Austen, *Northwest Tanzania*, 42-4.

17 Save mission diary, prologue, WFAR; *Bulletin des Missions d'Afrique*, 1900, 289-92.

18 Testimonies collected by Abbé Alexis Kagame in *Grands Lacs*, 1950, 20-1.

19 Hirth, J. J., 'Diaire du Ruanda', an undated letter to his brother, *c.* 1900, No. 095307, Dossier 95, WFAR.

20 The false mwami was discovered soon after by the mission interpreter, Karondã. Dr Kandt also worked out that the mwami should have been in his teens and realised that a trick had been played. After this initial trickery the Ega councillors allowed the mwami to deal directly with the Europeans in their presence.

21 Hurel, Rev. Père, 'Histoire du Sacré-Coeur d'Issavi', MS, handwritten, 1909, Dossier 112, WFAR.

22 Save diary, 8 February 1900.

23 Rwands had originally fallen within *Bezirk* No. 20 of German East Africa, which had its headquarters at Ujiji. Ruanda-Urundi became a separate military administrative unit in 1899 with its centre at Bujumbura.

24 Nothomb, *Church History*, 11.

25 Lecoindre to his family, 7 October 1903, Dossier 112, WFAR.

26 Testimonies collected by Abbé Joseph Sibomana in *Grands Lacs*, 1950, 29.

27 Hirth to Livinhac, 20 February 1900, No. 095048, Dossier 95, printed in *Bulletin*, 1900, 291.

28 Testimonies collected by Abbé Alexandre Ruterandongozi in *Grands*

Lacs, 1950, 31.

29 Hurel, 'Histoire du Sacré-Coeur d'Issavi'.

30 Save diary, 23, 27 October 1902; Hirth to his brother, undated, No. 095307, Dossier 95, WFAR.

31 Testimonies collected by Abbé Joseph Sibomana in *Grands Lacs*, 1950, 28. Tobi's family had been wiped out in 1895, when the Catholic settlement on Tanganyika was attacked.

32 Testimonies collected by Abbé Jovite Matabaro, *Grands Lacs*, 1950, 43-4.

33 Save diary, May 1900. The chiefs sent were Kaizuka and Kaningwa.

34 Hurel, 'Histoire du Sacré-Coeur d'Issavi'.

35 Save diary, November 1900.

36 Testimonies collected by Abbé Joseph Sibomana in *Grands Lacs*, 28-30, 48-50.

37 From *gutora*, to choose.

38 Save diary, December 1900.

39 *Ibid.*, January 1901.

40 Abbé Joseph Sibomana's version in *Grands Lacs*, 1950, 25, is that the king's guides deliberately led the Catholic party into a trap. *Rapports annuels*, 1910-11, 393, also suggests that Tobi's death may not have been accidental. Ngoma Yombi was found at Nyanza in 1911 by Father Pagès and subsequently executed by the Germans.

41 Save diary, June 1900.

42 D'Arianoff, *Histoire des Bagesera*, IRCB, 1952, 88-112.

43 Des Forges, *Rwanda under Musiinga*, 49-51.

44 Hirth to Livinhac, 31 December 1901, No. 09065, Dossier 95, WFAR; Save diary, March 1901.

45 Save diary, March 1901.

46 *Chroniques Trimestrielles*, No. 90, March 1901, 86-7.

47 Save diary, June 1901.

48 *Ibid.*, March 1901.

49 *Ibid.*, July-August 1901.

50 Kaizuka, who had being killing Tutsi thought to be disloyal to the court, was again the mwami's agent. Despite complaints from Rugambarara, the Rwandan *umutware*, the court had been reluctant to move against Mhumbika earlier because of his mission support; see Zaza diary, 9 May 1902.

51 Zaza diary, 12 June 1902.

52 'Interminable complaints from the Banygisaka, who want not a single one of the Rwandan *abatware*'; see Zaza diary, 9 May, 2 June 1902.

53 Save diary, 25 June 1902.

54 Louis, *Ruanda-Urundi*, 117.

55 Save diary, 9 October 1902.

56 Zaza diary, August 1902.

57 *Chroniques Trimestrielles*, No. 97, April 1903, 71.

58 Save diary, 16 October 1902: 'a great army moving east'.

59 Hirth to Livinhac, 31 December, No. 09077, Dossier 95, WFAR.

60 Save diary, 15, 30 September 1903, 8 January 1904; Zaza diary, January 1904.

61 Interview with Joseph Rugirankana, Rukubankanda hill, and Leon

Rukeratabaro, Rubona hill, Rwaza Mission, June 1973.

62 Mibirisi diary, 22 December 1903.

63 Rugirankana and Rukeratabaro.

64 These were Rwangeyo and the very influential Nshozamihigo.

65 The head of the Sigi clan, Munyusangabo, was, for example, called the garagu of Rwangeyo; see Rwaza diary, 26 August 1905.

66 Rukeratabaro.

67 Mulera report, 1929.

68 Classe, in *Dix-huit mois*, 369-70, relates how the Fathers were directed by the Tutsi on to a hill used by the Chakohogo lineage as a base for their attacks on travellers along the Changabe river. Some of the bandits, like the *ibirongozi*, ex-porters of the Germans, offered protection in exchange for crops and tribute, like Livingstone's Kololo in Malawi. (Interview with Ignace Renzayo, Gashunga hill, Rwaza, June 1973.)

69 Mulera report, 1929; Denoon, *A History of Kigezi*, 15.

70 Rwaza diary, 26 November 1903.

71 *Ibid.*, 22 February 1904.

72 *Ibid.*, 6 February 1904.

73 By the powerful Hutu leader, Ntibakunze; see Rwaza diary, 27 March 1904.

74 Dufays, Rev. Père, *Pages d'épopée africaine: jours troublés*, Librairie Coloniale, Ixelles, 1928, 21.

75 Rwaza diary, 4 April 1904.

76 Classe, *Dix-huit mois*, 372.

77 *Ibid.*, 368.

78 Denoon, *A History of Kigezi*, 213, uses the apt phrase 'extravagantly decentralised'.

79 *Chroniques Trimestrielles*, No. 105, April 1904, 188.

80 Brard, A., Rev. Père, letter of 15 February 1900 in *Bulletin*, 1900, 294-5.

81 Save diary, July-August 1901.

82 *Chroniques Trimestrielles*, No. 90, March 1901, 87.

83 Un Père Blanc, 'Les idées principales du Cardinal Lavigerie sur l'évangelisation de l'Afrique', *Revue d'Histoire des Missions*, vol. II, No. 3, September 1925, 386.

84 Arnoux, A., Rev. Pere, *Les Pères Blancs aux sources du Nil*, Namur, 1953, 19.

85 Save diary, July-August 1901.

86 Hirth to Livinhac, 31 December 1901, No. 09065, Dossier 95, WFAR.

87 *Ibid.*

88 *Ibid.*

89 *Ibid.*

90 Testimonies collected by Abbé Joseph Sibomana, *Grands Lacs*, 1950, 29-31; Des Forges, *Rwanda under Musiinga*, 43-6.

91 Save diary, October 1901; *Grands lacs*, 1950, 30.

92 Published in 1902 by Benziger & Co., Einsiedeln, Switzerland. A copy may be found in the library of the archdiocese of Kigali.

93 Testimony of Abbé Jovite Matabaro in *Grands Lacs*, 1950, 44-5.

94 See the end of chapter eight.

95 The period before baptism was divided into the postulancy, which

usually lasted sixteen months, and the catechumenate proper, lasting thirty-two months.

96 Testimony of Abbé Jovite Matabaro in *Grands Lacs*, 1950, 44. Abbé Matabaro was ordained with Abbé Isodore Semigabo in 1919.

97 Hirth to Livinhac, 20 July 1903, No. 095082, Dossier 95, WFAR.

98 For example, see the angry tone of the diary entries for Save, 12 April, 5 August 1903.

99 *Grands Lacs*, 1950, 29.

100 Hirth to Livinhac, 20 July 1903.

101 Zaza diary, 9 June 1902.

102 Save diary, 7 July 1903.

103 *Chroniques Trimestrielles*, No. 101, June 1903, 186.

104 Save diary, March, 5 September 1902.

105 *Ibid.*, 8 June 1902, 15 May 1903.

106 Testimonies collected by Abbés Joseph Sibomana and Alexandre Ruterandongozi in *Grands Lacs*, 1950, 28, 31, 32.

107 Arnoux, *Le Culte*, 291; Pagès, *Un Royaume*, 359.

108 'Hagum' umwami, ingom' irabazwa . . . Tout Kabare est dans cette parole'; Pagès, *Un Royaume*, 207-8.

109 The catechism contained other bizarre translations, e.g. the opening words of the Magnificat, 'Mwoyo wange utinye Mungu', failed to use the Rwandan term 'Roho' for spirit and 'Imana' for God.

110 Save diary, 23 October 1902.

111 De Lacger, *Le Ruanda*, 308.

112 Save diary, 6 January 1903.

113 *Ibid.*, 19 September 1902.

114 For general attitudes to African culture see Kieran, J. A., 'Some Roman Catholic missionary attitudes to Africans in the nineteenth century', *Race*, vol. X, No. 3, 1969, 341-59.

115 *Chroniques Trimestrielles*, No. 76, October 1897, 496: 'All around, a mass of women and girls perform their religious dances, accompanied by songs of supplication. This is because the woman has henceforth become Kiranga, that is to say, the favourite priestess of Yangombe, the evil spirit, the Ahriman of the Rundi, compared with the Ordmudz, the principle of Good.'

116 *Chroniques Trimestrielles*, No. 73, January 1897, 130.

117 *Ibid.*, No. 97, April 1903, 224. The Save diary, 30 December 1903, describes the dancers as 'suppôts de Satan' — 'hell-hounds'.

118 For instances of violence occasioned by the dancing see Mibirisi diary, 12 May 1904; Save diary, 30 December.

119 Arnoux, *Le Culte*, 287-9.

120 These were Kyaka and Sebuharara; see Save diary, 7 April 1904.

121 Save diary, June 1904.

THREE

Clientship in the south, revolt in the north

The military might of the Kaiser in Rwanda amounted to two German officers and twenty-five *askari* in 1902.[1] The telegraph from Dar es Salaam stretched only as far as Tabora, ten days' march to Bujumbura.[2] This token force denied Rwanda to the Belgians; the string of camps along Lake Kivu pointed as much westwards into King Leopold's Congo as eastwards into the Tutsi-ruled highlands of Burundi and Rwanda.

Governor Von Götzen's formulation of policy towards the chiefs — 'sustain their authority . . . in such a fashion that they become convinced that their salvation depends on their attachment to the German cause'[3] — might be vague but its spirit was clearly ignored by Captain Von Beringe's attack on the Rundi mwami in 1903.[4] The removal of Von Beringe, whose exploits around Zaza had damaged the mission's popularity,[5] did not in itself improve Catholic prospects, for now there could be no doubt that the first duty of a German officer was to uphold the authority of the two kings at all costs. On the other hand the mwami, at this time the least determined of the mission's opponents, had the support of German troops to counterbalance the ambitious and anti-Christian Ega. German hopes for Ruanda-Urundi were summed up in the imperialist cliché 'expansion of trade and civilisation': expansion of a trade the court did not want because it could not control it, and of a civilisation which brought with it meddlesome clerics. Musinga and the Fathers now had to struggle to extend their influence in Rwanda under the growing shadow of German rule.

Kabare was in a commanding position at court and determined as ever to bring the missionaries to heel. Aware that the Germans would protect the European personnel of the stations, his tactics were to avoid a direct confrontation while gnawing away at the Fathers' supports; first by disrupting the missionaries' communications and attacking the Ganda, whom he saw as their mercenaries, and secondly

A Tutsi high-jump of 2·5 metres (8 ft 2½ in).

by involving them with the Belgians, thus discrediting them in German eyes.[6] It was the type of subtle, indirect strategy that had brought the Queen Mother's brother to power at court. By 1904 there was enough general resistance to the missionaries to put it into practice with good effect.

Mission expansion had merely magnified the impact of the Catholics on Rwanda. There were 1,500 registered postulants waiting to enter the catechumenate at Save and 226 baptised Christians working as

instructors, teaching prayers and catechism to the catechumens.[7]
The Ganda were now 'confined to barracks', but as the numbers
within the Catholic net increased so did disputes between mission
protégés and pagans. Each Father Superior was drawn increasingly to
intervene, either directly or indirectly, in complex litigation. Mission
recruits were virtually all poor Hutu, with a handful of impoverished
Tutsi, so in central Rwanda the basic friction was between a Hutu
Church and a Tutsi-dominated society.

Worse still, there were five times as many White Fathers as
Germans in the country. To find Rwandans going to the mission
rather than the few isolated German camps to settle cases annoyed the
administration. Even with the best intentions the missionaries gave
offence.

On some occasions Natives neither belonging to the mission, nor working
there, have first addressed themselves to the missionaries, who have quite
properly sent them on to the fort at Ischangi. Now among these it has
happened that some were given a written statement setting down their Shauri
[court case.]As a result the opinion has grown up among a section of the
population that judging Shauris is within the competence of the mission, the
station at Ischangi being merely the executive arm of its judgements.[8]

Privately Von Grawert made the point to the Governor more openly;
he felt that were Monsignor Hirth given a free hand 'the Government
would go to hell and he would establish an African Church State'.[9]

With the Germans thoroughly irritated by the mission's theocratic
tendencies, Kabare was ready to put his plans into action; orders were
sent out from Nyanza that all foreign traders in Rwanda were to be
killed. Von Grawert himself, oblivious of the fate in store for the
Ganda and Indians, had two skin traders chained and deported as a
gesture to the court.[10] Scores of traders died. Von Grawert's apparent
acquiescence in the repression was widely read as a triumph for
Kabare. The Save Fathers learned from their spies at Nyanza that
people openly proclaimed him 'master of the land'. The court diviners
set about sacrificing cows to find out whether, at last, times were
propitious for an attack on the mission stations. The spirits, it was
said, indicated that they wanted the White Fathers driven out of the
country. The spirits, as all the missionaries knew, spoke the mind of
the court.

Such was the opposition to the missions that other spontaneous
risings took place at the same time as the more orchestrated resistance
in central Rwanda. The dry season of 1904 proved a cruel judgement
on the missionaries' accumulated errors. *Nyamparas* sent out on 13
July from Rwaza to collect wood were attacked. From every quarter
the Fathers got wind of impending revolt. Within the week a Father
was attacked and one of his catechists killed; the mission replied with

a raid by their Sukuma militia. The Hutu allowed the Catholic forces to expend their cartridges in loose firing, then sent them fleeing with a hail of arrows.[11]

Popular feeling about events was diffracted and spread by countless rumours, some emanating from Nyanza, many arising from the peasants' own beliefs, which were also influenced by court traditions. The stories articulated a widespread sense of the fragility of the European order, and contained the same message: the real, and therefore spiritual, power of the Europeans could be reduced to nothing, their technology and powerful leaders could be neutralised. It was said that 'the whites' guns will fire only water or goats' droppings'.[12] A saviour from the south-west was supposed to have slain Von Grawert.[13] In another version the conquering mwami Ruganzu Ndori had returned and smitten him: to save his life the European had agreed to become a garagu of Musinga.[14] The rumours spread fast and could soon be heard from Save to Rwaza. Disconnected events at opposite ends of the country, distorted in the telling, added to a common store of stories which shaped the direction of further events. Rumour both expressed an ideology of resistance and was its first practical realisation.

Rwanza was under siege from 24 to 30 July. Opposing clans united against the common enemy after spearmen had taken up a threatening position around the mission. The night calm was interrupted by sporadic gunfire and alerts until reinforcements arrived from Nyundo.[15] Pots of honey taken to be a peace offering from the Hutu attackers turned out to be poisoned. On 5 August the Hutu clans united in a full-scale assault on the station, which was defended by sustained fire from over twenty guards, with the priests using their hunting rifles. The final raid seems to have been triggered by the arrival of Tutsi who had come up from the plain to help the missionaries. On seeing the huge force of Hutu they quickly changed sides.[16]

The deterioration in the situation at Nyanza was first marked by the permanent withdrawal at the mwami's request, of the Catholic catechist.[17] At Save the arm of a new-born child was thrown on to the mission steps as an evil charm, but the expected attack never materialised.[18] At Zaza catechists were unable to get catechumens to come in and mails were repeatedly pillaged.[19] In both stations careful watch was kept at night.

Kabare had succeeded by September in cutting all the main tracks across Rwanda and in intercepting mission mails from Karagwe. The Save Fathers heard reports that in a single day over sixty traders were killed in Nduga.[20] An agent was sent from the capital to Rwaza to encourage the Hutu to press their attacks home, telling them how few Europeans there were in the country.[21] The Ega were on the point of moving from indirect opposition to straightforward military action.

They were restrained by the arrival of Von Grawert and his troops. Tutsi nobles knew how to handle rifles and boasted that they were no longer frightened of the Europeans, but *Tikitiki's muvuba*, Von Grawert's Maxim guns, were recognised as irresistible.[22] The traders were less lucky than the missionaries. Some wounded Ganda managed to stagger into mission stations but most were slaughtered.[23] Rwanda had struck a devastating blow against foreign invaders.

The other aspect of Kabare's policy was no less successful; suspicion had been thoroughly sown amongst the Europeans. Von Grawert commented peevishly on Father Zuembiehl: 'For him the main principle is to have two irons in the fire and never to forget that the Belgians may become masters of the presently disputed territory and therefore to pay them frequent visits.[24] Indeed, the suspicious Father Brard saw the Belgian issue behind Von Grawert's reluctance to take reprisals for the traders' death. 'That would be simply to add more disorder,' he wrote, 'and let the Belgians in the Congo see that there have been disturbances in the country; that is what he most fears.'[25]

Von Grawert could not, however, let the pillaging of mail caravans go unanswered. The inevitable punitive raid was as indiscriminate as it was brutal. The repression at Rwaza was so severe that the Fathers, albeit combat-hardened, ended by pleading for their assailants' lives.[26] Punishment and policy statement went together. 'What was done to the Europeans was as good as done to the mwami, and vice versa,' the assembled farmers were told, a point they had not overlooked. The Tutsi were their legitimate chiefs, Von Grawert informed them, 'a point which they could hardly understand', as Father Classe remarked.[27]

The country-wide resistance to the White Fathers and their agents that erupted in 1904 was largely spontaneous and far from an integrated rising. All sections of Rwandan society, the autonomous provinces as much as the court, were reacting against the power exercised by the missions. The journeymen and landless could see possibilities of emancipation in mission patronage, the northern Hutu might also hope to use the local mission stations as a bulwark against Nyanza, but official White Father policy dictated that such aims were unacceptable. The Mission Society did not want to be a political instrument wielded against central authority, nor was it happy with the usual first converts of African States, the slaves, serfs or destitute. In what it had done, and what it had failed to do, the mission had earned the armed resistance of the majority of Rwandans.

After the crisis Kabare was still in control and wanted the Germans to execute his Ega rival and co-conspirator Ruhinankiko.[28] Father Brard now talked of shutting down the northern stations and failed to send on mails. Musinga as ever vacillated on mission questions in the face of the Ega nobility. The Save missionaries sent their leading

Father Brard (in foreground) at Musinga's court in Nyanza, 1905.

catechist from Bukumbi to press for a new station in the Tutsi stronghold of Marangera,[29] but their presents were returned. Musinga replied that Europeans came to pay court only in order to eat up the land. Yet a month later the mwami was asking his catechist to return to Nyanza to continue his Swahili lessons.[30] The threat of nationwide armed resistance was past; the northern missionaries had learnt a political lesson they were to find difficult to forget.

After Christmas Monsigner Hirth went to court to gauge feeling and again request the concession of a new mission in Nduga. A dutiful Brother cranked up and played a gramophone while the mwami's leading ministers looked sternly down on the proceedings. Musinga was flanked by Kabare and the rising lights Rwidegembya and Ntulo. The Vicar Apostolic spoke directly with the king in Swahili. The charged atmosphere was well evoked by the diarist.

Yet our good sovereign, who is not, after all, master in his own house, dared not take upon himself the responsibility for giving an affirmative answer. He turned towards his uncle, Rwidegembya, to ask him what he ought to reply; the latter retorted at once with some animation, 'We have given you Issavi, Nsasa, Nyundo, Rwasa, Mibirisi, yet you still ask for Nduga.'[31]

The Ega also cannily pointed out that to alienate land required German permission.[32] Not to be outwitted, Monsignor Hirth set about getting it.

The Nduga mission proved something of a test case. The court was adamantly opposed to a station within an hour's march of the royal tombs and out of Nyanza's direct control. Rwidegembya's reply to the Vicar Apostolic, 'Nidukomeza kuguh'ciy'ushatse cyose, tuzasi-garan'iki?' ('If we add what you ask what will be left?'),[33] is still remembered, indicating the emotional as well as political significance of allowing whites into the Tutsi heartland.

If Von Grawert forced Kabgayi mission on the court it was because he felt the nobles could be, and should be, made to submit, whilst the Fathers were marginally less trouble than they were worth. The power of Nyanza and the fragility of European control of Rwanda had been amply demonstrated in 1904; the co-operation of the missionaries was clearly essential if a handful of officers were to 'govern' the country. Not the least consideration was that the mission stations provided excellent intelligence centres; the tight little German camps were isolated islands, while the Catholic catechists ranged far and wide. Only Dr Kandt, after over a year in the bush, spoke a little Kinyarwanda, all official correspondence being in German or Swahili. Most of the missionaries could preach an intelligible sermon and were now able to cross-check the information they received. It was brought home to the king that any refractory behaviour and refusal to co-operate over Kabgayi would result in two detained white cattle rustlers being unleashed on the north.[34] But it was to be the last concession to the Fathers for some time.[35]

After the 1904 crisis there was an unwritten *entente* between the court, the White Fathers and the Germans. Each party recognised that any lasting alliance between the other two could render it impotent. Each was restrained by prudence, fear or formulated policy from too overt a verbal or military attack on the other; the court understood well that the battle against the Christian colonisation of Rwanda had henceforth to be a rearguard action.

Catholic teaching on the separate spheres of Church and State should have reduced conflict between missionaries, Germans and Tutsi to a minimum. Yet, by leaving nineteenth century Europe, where the distinction existed in practice, imposed on a reluctant Church by secular States, the Fathers were able to see the past century of European history as an aberration; the astringent memories of *Kulturkampf* and Garibaldi must have easily faded before the enticing spectacle of Rwanda's feudal monarchy. The spiritual gold rush in which they staked the first claims had as its dreams the Golden Age of Church history, and as its pioneers rough-hewn men like Brard. In the dream Musinga appeared in the role of Charlemagne,[36] and Dante's comforting Thomism depicted the Church's earthly fulfilment.

Let Caesar therefore observe that reverence to Peter which a firstborn son ought to observe to a father, so that, illuminated by the light of paternal grace, he may with greater power irradiate the world over which he is set by Him who is the ruler of all things.[37]

But Popes no longer vied with kings. Reality was a gangling young Tutsi with protruding teeth and the portly, buttoned-down, moustached figure of Von Grawert, both equally immune to the 'paternal Grace' of the mission.

If the peasants accused the priests of being 'kings'[38] and the Germans suspected them of wanting to create a Church State, the Fathers would have been quick to deny the charges. They did not consciously and deliberately plan to become rulers wielding secular power, but, defined by their Rwandan context, they were as truly 'kings' as the Nyabingi prophetesses were 'queens of Mpororo'. There was no clear-cut 'temporal sphere' or 'purely religious' office in the society in which they worked. The philosophy of Church State relations which, *faute de mieux*, emphasised these distinctions was inapplicable, so they abandoned it in practice whilst proclaiming it insistently in theory.

Rwandans judged the Fathers by what they did; for the first two years they could barely understand what they said. The priests laid down the law with chiefs unless Rwandan resistance, or the Germans, forced on them honeyed words and compromise. And even when

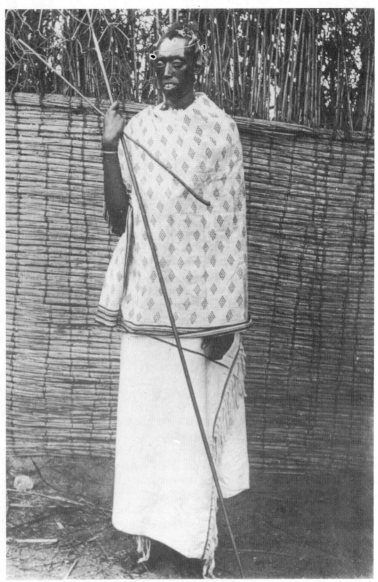

Mwami Musinga in 1905.

conflict arose and the Fathers tried to explain their peculiar view of the world, it was no less subversive:

Mungu commands all the other Bamis, so much so that if they order wicked things, you are not obliged to obey them but to obey Mungu alone; he commands them all, even Musinga.[39]

It went without saying that the officials of Mungu were also able to command *abami* on his behalf; a garagu spoke with the authority of his lord. The Hutu understood the missionaries even if they rarely understood themselves.

The question was not whether the Fathers would become politically involved but how they would become involved. Most of their early work drew them inexorably into the network of feudal relationships which dominated Rwandan life. At all stations the first five years were ones of intensive building activity. When the residential side of the mission was completed the Fathers turned to erecting huge churches. They needed labourers, bricklayers, porters and a permanent staff for cooking, gardening and cattle-herding. Huge teams of men were required to cut and transport logs, sometimes from distant forests; forty to fifty carriers were needed for a nine-metre tree, ten thousand men fetched the beams and supports for Zaza church.[40] Musinga and the court were stunned by such an unprecedented mobilisation of manpower.[41].

The exhilaration of commanding a peasant army working for the glory of God seems to have blinded the missionaries to the impact they were making on the king; chiefs too took offence at requisitions which depleted their own work force; for the peasants this heavy labour was simply another form of *ubuletwa* commanded by the new white chiefs. Although the workers were usually given some form of payment the Brothers who supervised them were not always endowed with the most delicate sensibilities and demanded the maximum effort; Von Grawert described even Father Barthélemy as 'peasant-like and cloddish'.[42] In regions like Rwaza where *ubuletwa* was unknown, forced labour was a source of grievance and helped precipitate the 1904 rising, whilst the thoughtless plundering of sacred groves growing on old residences of the *abami* infuriated the court.[43] The levying of labour, a right claimed by Tutsi nobles, identified the priests in the peasants' eyes as powerful men belonging to the ruling class, and by the same token it made local chiefs their convinced opponents.

The impression that the Fathers came as a new white nobility was enhanced by their extensive land holdings. Save mission grounds spread over 220 hectares, Zaza over 164 hectares, Mibirisi 130 and Kabgayi 125 hectares.[44] The Fathers believed that all the land in Rwanda was owned by the mwami, and the initial arrangement seems to have been akin to that between the king and a Tutsi lord; they held the land 'on his pleasure' and paid him tribute.[45] With greater security they began pressing for a Western style of title and showed little concern for their earlier agreements. For Zaza 250 roupies had been decided, but they paid only 200.[46] Apart from the ineffectual blandishments of Monsignor Hirth the missionaries had a free reign till 1904, when the Germans demanded precise boundary surveys and properly agreed contracts. These documents did little to ease the situation at stations surrounded by a large population with several sub-chiefs and overlapping jurisdictions, where a perpetual tug-of-war went on for the Hutu's allegience.

After purchase, the occupants of mission land were considered to be tenants of the White Fathers while remaining subjects of Musinga. Father Zuembiehl told the people of Mibirisi that 'from now on they would have to submit to the authority of the Superior of the mission; it would be for him to *Kukazera* and *Kutaka*'.[47] The local hill chiefs lost not only their land but their jurisdiction over people.

The hill chief reproached us with having stolen it [the land] from him. It had to be explained to him what had happened — that if we left the people free to take him wood, *pombe*, etc, it was from the kindness of our hearts. The people could not be held for *corvées* [by him]. He then wanted to know if we hated him. Far from that, we are ready to accord you the greatest good.[48]

It was debatable in what sense the king 'owned' the land even in central Rwanda. In Rwaza, where the priests merely grabbed a large tract of land, his lack of real power made payments purely ritual.[49] There the missionaries became the effective rulers and each *umuryango* brought them beer and bananas just as they would have done for *ibirongozi*.[50]

The Tutsi's interest in cattle was also shared by the Fathers. At Nyundo the sale and purchase of cows dominated the annual budget.[51] Punitive German raids with their booty of livestock supplied the stations with cheap cattle and, with intelligent buying from the Tutsi the Fathers not only had a liberal supply of meat but were able to finance their building by trading. The mission herds were sometimes tended by Christians but more often put out to graze with rich Tutsi who owned pasture land. These cattle were sometimes handed on to garagu and formed, like any other cows, the currency of a multitude of exchange relationships. Certain Fathers even had personal herds which moved with them when they changed station.[52] The defective concept of 'mission property' was unable to deal with multivalent bonds created by a cow in Rwanda and caused endless difficulties.

The habit of granting cattle to neophytes and catechumens compounded the difficulties. The Tutsi frequently withdrew cattle from garagu who went to the mission for instruction, considering that relationship with the Fathers precluded *ubuhake* with a Tutsi patron;

they would have agreed wholeheartedly that the Hutu could not serve two masters as the more ultramontane of the priests declared. To recompense their Christians the Fathers gave dispossessed catechumens a cow or two from their herds for usufruct. These cattle could then be withdrawn for backsliding and moral lapses of a serious kind. Soon peasants were flocking to the missions in the sole hope of being granted a cow. Zaza mission, which looked after more than two hundred cows confiscated from a rustler,[53] became embroiled in such a tangle of half-understood feudal relations that the missionaries breathed a sigh of relief when Von Grawert recalled the cattle.[54]

So it was that their need for land, labour and cattle drew the White Fathers into clientship relationships. Without a disembodied radical brand of Christianity — an impossibility for a Church which saw itself as Christ's continued incarnation in the world — no missionary could have stayed outside the feudal nexus yet lived and preached in Rwanda. Free association of individuals was rare; journeys for commerce, *gutunda*, or to buy food, *guhaka*, were the few occasions on which individuals banded together in a type of voluntary co-operative.[55] A chain of clientship marked the social structure of central Rwanda.

The greatest obstacle to evangelisation is the way the country is administered. The king has all the important chiefs as his clients; they in their turn have all the minor Tutsi, and these, the influential Hutu; it all forms a compact mass that is difficult to attack. They all agree that to frequent the whites is to become their clients and to set up as a rebel against the king; you cannot serve two masters, they think, God and the king.[56]

Such a view of society was not totally alien to the White Fathers. Despite the Christian assertion of the fundamental equality of all men in the eyes of God, Catholics believed that the Church mediated this radical possibility: the Church for them was a visible hierarchical institution united in the Pope. Ultimately it was the visibility of an internally differentiated community and not the faith of individuals that counted.[57] Sacramentality, the way God was in the world with men, could not be divorced from the essential hierarchy of the Church, the subordination of its different orders. The conscious goal of the missionaries, therefore, remained the planting of a precise social institution through which Grace could trickle and then pour down on their African converts. They were, of course, profoundly influenced by Protestant individualism and pietism, but not to the point of forgetting the cardinal Catholic insight that the Church was a sacramental hierarchical institution.

There was little in the Catholic ecclesiology, as understood by the Fathers, to give the missions immunity to the clientship around them. Pioneering priests were born patrons. The Fathers were powerful men, and there was only one relationship in the experience of the Hutu which was appropriate to dealings with the powerful, that of clientship. To become a catechumen for the peasants represented, among other things, a formal submission to the white invaders.

The young Church bore the impress of the society around it, and the mission log books show the Fathers with earthly cares if heavenly thoughts. These cares increased with the number of Hutu catechists and the attendant proliferation of patron client relationships. The catechists settled on the hills and soon used their contact with the mission to obtain a banana grove, goats or often cattle. By threats of denunciation to the Fathers for making sacrifices, or by overloading recalcitrant peasants with labour at the mission, with or without the collusion of the hill chief, the catechist could use his position as mission agent to wield power.[58] One group merely *posing* as catechists travelled around collecting hoes from all who worked on Sunday.[59] During the famine of 1905-06, when the cry of slave dealers, 'All those with *baja* bring them',[60] could be heard over the hills, and when soft-hearted priests like Father Pouget[61] were buying scores of women and girls on the way to Kivumu market,[62] Monsignor Hirth inadvertently enhanced the gains to be made by mission adherents; he forbade the opening of an orphanage.[63] The ex-slaves who could not be housed at the missions were then given for adoption to Christian households.[64] To gifts of cattle were added garagu. The catechumenate, defined increasingly by the Hutu as allegiance to the Fathers, became a particularly rewarding form of clientship, bestowing both wealth and protection.

As the Hutu Christians extended the base of the social pyramid developing around each station the Tutsi were left in no doubt that the Fathers, as they had expected, were going to act like powerful *abanyabutaka*. When the Queen Mother wanted to dispossess a Christian living on Mara hill of his banana grove she politely informed the mission, as he was 'their man'.[65] Just as the Tutsi's garagu repaired their enclosures and kept night watch, so the whites' garagu were expected to labour at the mission and learn strange phrases by heart.

By weathering the storms of 1904 the Fathers had demonstrated that they were as strong as the court. And by becoming garagu of the whites the Hutu could share in this power and remove themselves from the more oppressive exactions of the Tutsi. It was in vain that the missionaries began preaching Monsignor Hirth's directives on obedience to lawfully constituted authority. Baptised Christians at Rwaza went out on full-scale razzias and elsewhere others drifted away to the patronage of German troops when allegiance to the mission became insufficiently rewarding.[66]

The feudal nuclei that had grown up around Tutsi households in the nineteenth century had seeded the young Church, and no amount of weeding by Vicars Apostolic was going to remove the overgrowth. Its very luxuriance in these early years showed how quickly the Hutu could convert the mission. On reflection the Fathers realised that their entanglements had brought them into a deeper and more serious opposition to the Tutsi than they had ever intended. In relation to the court they were rebellious nobles. The Father Superior at Save stated that far and wide the catechumens were being proclaimed *inyangarwanda*, haters of Rwanda, and *abagome*, rebels. Sub-chiefs were said to have been instructed to send anyone frequenting the mission to court.[67] The Zaza Christians so aroused the usually friendly Banyagisaka chiefs by their repeated insults that complaints were lodged at Nyanza.[68] According to the missionaries, the slogan 'Death to the Christians' could be heard from Save to Nyanza.[69] The mwami and his Ega councillors seem to have realised, though too late, the implications of their policy of throwing the Hutu to the 'wild animals' from Europe.[70] Yet in contrast to the missionaries' national policy towards Tutsi rulers there was no Tutsi national policy towards the missions, rather a series of local *ad hoc* adjustments.

Rwaza might have been in a different country and the northern Fathers saw themselves almost in a separate mission. The Tutsi were absent except on the Mulera plain. Chiefs plied the missionaries with gifts and sent their garagu to pay court.[71] The year 1905 marked the onset of an invasion of Tutsi from central Rwanda who came to build and stay. Chiefs who had not visited since Rwabugiri's days appeared at Rwaza and shamelessly expressed their thanks to the missionaries for enabling them to collect crop dues.[72] The Mulera Tutsi, poor families who had been eking out a living around Ruhengeri, were as outraged as the Hutu and sent groups of *abapfumu* to curse the Fathers.[73] The Banyanduga wanted, in Monsignor Hirth's words, 'to profit from the presence of the missionaries to settle and saddle the people with the most arbitrary of taxes'.[74]

The price of the mission's acquiescence in the imposition of rulers from central Rwanda was a permanent force of twenty armed auxiliaries and a nightwatch of two to three men on the alert for attacks. Despite these precautions a workshop was burnt to the ground during a Hutu raid.[75] Tension was heightened by the arrival of the Anglo-Belgian delimitation commission in the north. A fortnight later a major assault looked likely. The Hutu had been aroused and were waging a regular campaign against the newly arrived Tutsi and their clerical patrons.[76]

The variation in the court's approach to the different stations depended not only on the local political context but also on the changing role of the mwami. While Musinga was overshadowed by Kabare and the Queen Mother, the missions offered him an uncomfortable way of increasing his stature. A catechist returned to Nyanza in December 1904; a few months later the Fathers were reporting that the mwami was speaking tolerable Swahili. By August 1905 there was a second teacher at court, a Hutu called Wilhelmi, giving reading and writing lessons to the king and fifty *ntore*.[77] The king could now manage without interpreters and thus had an advantage over his uncles in dealings with the Europeans.

Musinga's use of mission teachers did not indicate any change of heart; he remained undecided in the face of conflicting pressures. In July 1905 he summonded a neophyte to Nyanza to quiz him. Had two recently disgraced nobles visited the mission in recent months? Did the Fathers believe that Musinga was the legitimate king? Did they intend to leave the country one day? He later confided in Wilhelmi that he had nothing personally against Christians. 'Their salvation does not please,' he merely remarked, perhaps comparing unfavourably the Lamb of God with Lyangombe's sheep, and the plucking of harps with the alcoholic revels on Muhavura.[78] It was his entourage who hated Christians, he alleged, adding, however, that mission men did not clap their hands respectfully before him in the style to which he was accustomed.

The Fathers did their best to please him, sending off to Mombassa for the special beads and rough cloth that he liked.[79] But against a background of squabbles connected with building and woodcutting it was not easy to gain or to keep the mwami's good will. The priests' lack of tact was sometimes prodigious. Since the mission had neither men, materials nor population to warrant building at Kabgayi, an impoverished Tutsi was sent in as a kind of caretaker.[80] On the very spot which Musinga had been so reluctant to concede to the Catholics their agent, with their tacit approval, pillaged a keeper of a royal tomb. Such blunders and obstinacy drove Musinga towards the Ega policy of overt resistance to mission penetration.

Monsignor Hirth did attempt to bring about another wave of reforms during his 1905 visits; after a further two hundred Easter baptisms were performed at Zaza he asked for 'fewer and better' neophytes:[81] 'Le difficile partout, c'est d'obtenir un vrai catéchumenat, et non pas seulement quatre années pour la forme et pour satisfaire à la lettre.'[82] Problems over land were slightly eased by old *internat* student marrying and settling around the stations.[83] The Vicar Apostolic banned the building of a big church at Rwaza, to avoid trouble; he told the Zaza missionaries not to 'disturb the people' and to supervise catechumens personally. He was still unhappy at the amount of force being used, and the failure of his directives in the face of recidivist missionaries.[84]

At the end of September 1906 the Fathers first noted that Musinga was dealing with European affairs alone; Kabare and Rwidegembya were not present at audiences. His *ntore* classmates had been dismissed, and he was having lessons with only three others.[85] Contemporary with this unifying of State authority in the person of the king came the creation of a permanent Residence for Ruanda-Urundi under Von Grawert at Bujumbura. Rwanda was served by his able and experienced plenipotentiary, Dr Richard Kandt, whose expertise in Rwandan affairs made him more than a match for the missionaries.[86] Kandt, both diplomat and administrator, soon began to turn the *entente* between court, Germans and White Fathers into the more orthodox colonial structure of Indirect Rule, mediating as much as possible between Musinga and the missionaries. He made it plain that curtailment of mission excesses was to be a priority: 'it was not the moment,' he said, 'to multiply the grievances of the native "authorites".' More important, there was to be a temporary ban on mission expansion.[87]

The Maji-Maji war had broken out in Tanganyika at the end of July 1905. That Christmas Von Grawert issued instructions to all the missionaries that in the event of attacks defensive laagers should be formed at Shangi and Save.[88] The Germans were fighting for their lives, and the 1904 'bullets to water' stories were very close to the ideology of Kinjikitile which was sustaining the rebellion and helping its spread.[89] At Rwaza, reminding the Fathers of the Zaza levy of ten thousand men, Kandt told them: 'Never would the government at the coast countenance that sort of thing.' And if the Catholics persisted in ignoring the chiefs, he added, the Lutherans[90] would get them all.[91] This was no idle threat; he was already making moves to get the German Protestant mission societies to come to Rwanda.[92] On the other hand he was shrewd enough to recognise the value of Christianity as a bulwark against risings legitimated by primal religions; at least, he gave the priests that impression.

In short, the good doctor seems ready to favour us; he knows well enough that our Christians will be the people on whom he can count in case of attack. He would like to see as many as possible . . . He told us, 'Above all, do not cross the king right from the beginning . . or there will be no end of trouble.' [93]

In February 1906 Von Grawert showed the flag at Rwaza, and two months later the missionaries were able to dispense with their guards.[94] Local politics resumed their normal pattern, with a bloody dispute between clans; the Tutsi agents struggled against each other, and whenever a *nyampara* made a nuisance of himself collecting wood the show of Hutu spears was met with mission guns.[95] The Germans offered the northern Fathers a period of relative peace, but they, in their turn, were expected to further the expansion of the court's influence, the mainstay of German policy in Rwanda.

Late in 1906 Terebura, the greatest single obstacle to easy relations between Kandt, Musinga and the Vicar Apostolic, was removed to Italy, where he entered a Carthusian monastery.[96] At Save his place was taken by Father Léon Classe, a pious *apparatchiki* who within months became in all but name the bishop's official representative.[97] Marked out early for distinction in the White Fathers' Society,[98] Classe served at Nyundo and Rwaza before coming south, where he was 'totally amazed to note that the king had great authority and was not the dog friends of Nyundo and Rwaza mission called him'.[99] He became, therefore, something of a renegade northerner to his old compatriots. The Church's teaching on authority seemed to Save's new Superior the *sine qua non* of both Catholicism and civilised society. 'The absence of respect due to authority,' he wrote in the annual report of 1906, 'can moreover be harmful to us; for this critical attitude to authority will be carried over into their relations with missionaries. God preserve us from Christians of that sort.'[100] For Classe the Tutsi were a caste like the Brahmins in India whose conversion would guarantee the success of the Rwanda mission.[101] That the Germans saw them as the lynchpin of their colonial policy made the argument all the more cogent.

We must force ourselves by all means in our power not to leave the Batussi on one side. Our dear mission . . . can look forward to some dark days if we take no interest in the apostolate to the ruling class, if, by our acts, we give ground for the opinion that the Catholic faith is that of the poor.[102]

Whatever the theological self-image of the Roman Catholic Church at the turn of the century, it did not in reality transcend the profound class divisions of Europe. Cardinal Lavigerie and members of the White Fathers' Conseil Général had moved in the company of aristocrats, officers and government ministers;[103] the next generation lived in an anti-clerical State but lost nothing of their predilection for the ruling class. The missionary in the bush, like Barthélemy and Brard, often came from small towns, went to seminary in the provinces, left for North Africa and disappeared from Europe without having frequented a single salon. The Brothers were hewers of wood and drawers of water, highly valued in theory, shabbily treated in practice. Promotions to positions of leadership went to those like Classe who combined experience with a willing subordination to authority. The latter ability was as much a product of class behaviour as of spiritual formation, and those whose duty it became to deal with bourgeois colonial officials and their aristocratic superiors generally came from their class, or at least shared their view of government.[104]

In the colonies the hierarchy of Vicar Apostolic, Fathers Superior and missionaries was therefore paralleled by that of Governor, Residents and Africans. The world of the Vicar Apostolic and Vicar General in Rwanda was made up of incessant communication with the lower orders in their own Society, but also of frequent 'horizontal' communication with colonial authorities. Hirth and Classe remained missionaries yet became honorary members of the colonial ruling group. Similarly, the missionaries who spent much of their day with Africans, the Pougets and Brards, came to identify with their interests and sometimes to see the world through their eyes; but they were also local representatives of the Vicar Apostolic, concerned with the maintainence of the visible structures of the Church. As a result there was a gap between the theological niceties of Papal directives and encyclicals and mission practice in the bush. The gap was to be located not in the geographical distance from Europe to Africa but in the hiatus between Vicar Apostolic and common missionary, created often by their structural position in relation to colonial, and European, society.

After 1906, and the setting up of a German civilian administration, the waywardness of the individual missionary became increasingly unacceptable as Hirth and Classe assumed positions in relation to the colonial administration. The early years of German rule with the *Schutztruppen* had seen their share of conflict with the bush missionary; the threat of an African 'Church State' had already cost the White Fathers a ban on expansion and the summoning of Protestants. Cardinal Lavigerie's missiology, Classes's facility in dealing with nobility, both Tutsi and German, and his memories of Rwaza under arms, now conspired to make future mission policy a foregone conclusion. Once amongst the Tutsi 'he was . . . the leader, doubly so because a gentleman and "mututsi"'.[105] Although friction was by no means at an end, and Classe had the difficult task of gaining the co-operation of his fellow missionaries, it was now clear that the Mission Church, despite its clientship and largely Hutu membership, was going to play its part in creating a Rwanda fit for its German and Tutsi rulers.

NOTES

1 There were only *Unteroffizier* Erhardt and four men at Kisenyi. Lieutenant Von Parish commanded Shangi, the main camp, linked by Lake Kivu to the small base at Kisenyi. At the main post of Bujumbura were two sections of the IX Company.

2 Bujumbura was referred to as Usumbura at this time.

3 Von Gotzen to Von Beringe, 9 October 1902, quoted in Ryckmans, P., *Une Page d'histoire coloniale*, IRCB, vol. 24, 1953, 6.

4 Louis, *Ruanda-Urundi*, 115-17; Ryckmans, *Une Page*, 8.

5 See chapter two.

6 Kabare's agents tried to draw the missionaries into their disputes with the Belgians at both Rwaza and Mibirisi; see Rwaza diary, 23 May 1904; Mibirisi diary, 19 July 1904.

7 Hirth to Livinhac, 31 December 1906, No. 095127, Dossier 95, WFAR; *Chroniques Trimestrielles*, No. 114, March 1905, 140.

8 Trans. German of letter in Mibirisi diary, Von Nordeck to Father Superior, Nyundo, 23 June 1904.

9 'Angelegenheiten der Gesellschaft der Missionare von Afrika. Weise Vater', vol. G9/19, vol. I, 1902-06. National Archives of Tanzania, Dar es Salaam, contain a brief correspondence on missionary misdemeanours at Mibirisi and Zaza reported back to the Governor; for quote see Louis, *Ruanda-Urundi*, 176.

10 Save diary, July 1904.

11 Rwaza diary, 13, 21, 22 July 1904. This technique had been successful against the German frontier expedition of 1902.

12 Save diary, July 1904.

13 He was called 'Muchuzi'; see Rwaza diary, 22 July 1904.

14 Save diary, July 1904.

15 Fathers Barthélemy and Loupias led a forced march to the rescue; see Rwaza diary, 30 July 1904.

16 Rwaza, 1-5 August 1904; Dufays, *Pages*, 39-41.

17 Prestanci was temporarily withdrawn in February when the first fruits ceremonies were closed to apostates from traditional court religion; see Save diary, 15 February, July 1904.

18 This was placed there as a *bulozi* by Rwakilima, a neighbouring Tutsi; see Save diary, 10 August 1904.

19 Zaza diary, August-September 1904.

20 Save diary, 14 August, 9 September 1904.

21 It is perhaps significant that it was Ruhanga, Nshozamihigo's agent, not Musinga's man, Kakwandi, who was stirring up trouble; see Rwaza diary, 20 September 1904.

22 Rwaza diary, 17 March 1905.

23 Save diary, July 1904.

24 Louis, *Ruanda-Urundi*, 177.

25 Save diary, 1 October 1904.

26 Hirth to Livinhac, 30 September 1904, No. 095095, Dossier 95, WFAR; Zaza diary, September 1904; Dufays, *Pages*, 42.

27 Rwaza diary, 21 October 1904.

28 Save diary, 13 November 1904.

29 Kabgayi diary, November 1904; Zaza diary, November 1904; Save diary, 13 November 1904; de Lacger, *Le Ruanda*, 392. The Missionaries used 'Nduga' vaguely for a large region of central Rwanda whose population were known in the north as Banyanduga. Marangara was a province in the north of this region. The Belgians used 'Nduga' and 'Marangara' as names for two discrete provinces.

30 Save diary, 4 December 1904.

31 Also present beside the king was Ruharamanzi; see Kabgayi diary, 27 December 1904.

32 *Chroniques Trimestrielles*, No. 125, March 1906, 168.

33 Nothomb, *Church History*, 17.

34 These were Pretorius, a Boer, and the half Austrian Schindalaer; see Dufays, *Pages*, 43-5. Pretorius was a bandit who travelled with a large retinue

of armed men and had been pillaging cattle in the north. He was arrested after losing a pitched battle in Ndorwa; see Rwaza diary, 29, 31 January 1905.

35 Musinga gave the missionaries Kabgayi hill in February 1905 with much annoyance. With a sandy soil and low rainfall the population, save in the north of Marangara, was sparse, so it is hard to understand Hirth's insistence; see Kabgayi diary, 6 February 1905. The hill had belonged to Kanyabujinja, a garagu of Nshozamihigo; see Kabgayi diary, 10, 13 February 1905.

36 Schumacher, Rev. Père, 'Échos du Kivu', *Missions d'Afrique*, 1913, 95-6, in Derscheid papers.

37 Quoted in Ullman, W., *A History of Political Thought: the Middle Ages*, Harmondsworth, 1965, 193.

38 The first reference to this label comes in the Kabgayi diary, 22 August 1907, when the Fathers report that Germans in the Duke of Mecklenburg's suite are referring to them in these terms. De Lacger, *Le Ruanda*, 397, also mentions this name, and it is taken up by Des Forges, A., 'Kings without crowns: the White Fathers in Ruanda', in *East African History*, ed. Bennett, N. R., McCall, D. F., and Butler, J., Boston University Papers on Africa, vol. III, New York, 1969, 176-202.

39 Mibirisi diary, 26 May 1904.

40 Rwaza diary, 3 October 1906; Des Forges, *Rwanda under Musiinga*, 79-80.

41 Kabgayi diary, 15 February, 16 March 1906.

42 Louis, *Ruanda-Urundi*, 177.

43 Kabgayi diary, 15 February 1906. This was not always the fault of the Fathers: Rwakasina once tried to cut wood on a royal *ikigabiro* for himself, pretending at court that he was doing it on the Fathers' orders; see Rwaza diary, 7 June 1906.

44 Classe to Kaiserliche Resident, 18 January 1907; Kaiserliche Resident to Classe, 10 November 1907, P.1735, film No. 167, Microfilm of the Bujumbura German Archive, Archives Africaines, Brussels (hereafter called AA).

45 At Save they handed over 450 roupies' worth of cloth which found its way on to the nobles' shoulders; see Hirth to his brother, undated, No. 095307, WFAR; Save diary, 29 June 1904. In the Duke of Mecklenburg's *apologia* for Indirect Rule it is explained that Musinga is sultan 'nicht als Landes, wohl aber Stammesherrn an'; see Herzog zu Mecklenburg, A. F., *Ins Innerste Afrika*, Leipzig, 1910, 85. This German view was meant to pave the way for white settlement, and meant that the White Fathers were essentially in German hands when it came to the question of land concessions after 1904.

46 Classe to Kaiserliche Resident, 18 January 1907, AA; Lecoindre to Kandt, 18 January 1907, CO; Mibirisi diary, 24 January 1906; de Lacger, *Le Ruanda*, 387-8. The contractors were now king, mission, Germans and relevant nobles. Under German pressure in 1906 money was handed over for Zaza, Mibirisi and Kabgayi.

47 To levy traditional land and labour dues; see Mibirisi diary, 28 January 1906.

48 Mibirisi diary, 30 January 1906.

49 Kandt to Father Superior, Kabgayi, 17 July 1908, CO; Rwaza diary, 18 June 1904, gives details of the initial settlement.

50 Rukeratabaro.

51 Account books of Nyundo mission for the period 1903-04 are in the possession of Monsieur Bernard Lugon, Department of History, University of Butare, Rwanda, to whom I am grateful for this information.

52 Classe to confrères, 5 July 1907, Correspondence Religieuse, White Fathers' Archives, Kigali (henceforth abbreviated to CR).

53 See note 34.

54 Hirth to confrères, 7 August 1906, CR; Zaza diary, 13 January, 22 September 1907; *Rapports annuels*, 1906-07, 162.

55 Schumacher, P., 'Das Sachenrecht in Ruanda', *Koloniale Rundschau*, 1932, 292.

56 *Chroniques Trimestrielles*, No. 114, March 1905, 143.

57 Adam, K., *The Spirit of Catholicism*, London, 1929, 31-45.

58 Save diary, 19 September 1905, 16 April 1907; Zaza diary, 13 March 1906.

59 Rwaza diary, 16 August 1905, gives an example of a man who had been collecting tribute merely by brandishing a converted hoe handle made to look like a gun and some fake cartridges. See also Kabgayi diary, 11 February 1906, for a similar case.

60 Rwaza diary, 30 April 1906.

61 There was a major caravan halt at Rukira, not far from Zaza, where trading took place; see Zaza diary, 24 November 1906.

62 Dr John Iliffe has kindly informed me that there were two slave markets in Buha in 1903; see Sergeant Kummer to Bezirksamt Ujiji, 16 January 1903, RKA 290/235, Dar es Salaam Archives of Tanzania. Rwandan slaves were most likely sent to Ujiji at this date rather than to the coast. Only one of about eight major dealers was Tutsi; see Kabgayi diary, 21 May 1906.

63 Hirth to confrères, July 1906, CR.

64 A strong adult was worth about seven or eight goats, while a sexually attractive girl might fetch up to fifteen; see Rwaza diary, 28 September 1905, 27 April 1906.

65 Save diary, 2 June 1905.

66 Rwaza diary, 3 January 1905.

67 Save diary, 17 February 1905.

68 Zaza diary, March 1905.

69 Save diary, 17 February 1905.

70 The name *ibisimba*, 'wild animals', seems to have been given to Europeans after Von Grawert's savage punitive raids in the north; see Rwaza diary, 17 November 1904; Dufays, *Pages*, 78. The same name was given by the Rundi, who called them *vikoko*.

71 In January 1905 Ruhanga arrived with one of Nshozamihigo's concubines and offered her in marriage to the Father Superior; see Rwaza diary, 3 January 1905. It was a familiar tactic to form marriage alliances with powerful and troublesome local leaders, and the practice continued into the 1950s: see chapter nine, the offer of a daughter by Jean-Baptiste Rwabukamba to Bicamumpaka.

72 Rwaza diary, 14 April 1905.

73 *Ibid.*, 12, 20 April 1905.

74 Hirth to Livinhac, 24 March 1905, No. 095098, Dossier 95, WFAR.

75 Rwaza diary, 24 April 1905, and see note 12.

76 Rwaza diary, 17 May, 30 July 1905.

77 Save diary, 4 December 1904, 17 August 1905.

78 *Ibid.*, 5 July 1905, 6 October 1906.

79 Hirth to confrères, July 1906, CR.

80 This was Leon Rutwaza. He told the Fathers that his conversion to Christianity had resulted in his virtual destitution; his uncles, Lwiyamwa and Rubuya, he alleged, had stolen all his cattle, and, bolstered by his position as mission representative, he set about getting them back. The mwami, already sensitive about Kabgayi, was outraged and wanted Leon's head. The Germans requested his removal, though he was still hanging round Kabgayi several months later; see Kabgayi diary, 2, 24 March, 24 July 1906, 5 January 1907.

81 *Chroniques Trimestrielles*, No. 119, September 1905, 430; No. 125, March 1906, 170.

82 Hirth to Livinhac, 24 March 1905.

83 Rwaza diary, 12 October 1906; Zaza diary, 11 November 1906; *Chroniques Trimestrielles*, No. 125, March 1906, 164-6.

84 Hirth to Livinhac, 30 June 1906.

85 Kabgayi diary, 8, 30 September 1906.

86 Louis, *Ruanda-Urundi*, 105-6, 145-6; Austen, *Northwest Tanzania*, 72.

87 Von Grawert to Father Superior, Kabgayi, 11 July 1906, Dossier 112, WFAR; Hirth to Livinhac, 30 September 1906, No. 095124, Dossier 95, WFAR; G9/19, vol. I, 1902-06, NAT; Kabgayi diary, 24 March 1906.

88 Von Grawert plainly intended only to hold the south-west, Kinyaga, where Kandt had established two camps, as well as the post at Shangi. He made a point of warning the Rwaza Fathers that they settled in the north-east at their own risk; see Dufays, *Pages*, 18.

89 Gwassa, C. G. K., 'Kinjikitile and the ideology of Maji-Maji', in *The Historical Study of African Religion*, ed. Ranger, T. O., and Kimambo, I. N., London, 1972, 202-19.

90 See Mirbt, C., *Mission und Kolonialpolitik in den deutschen Schutzgebieten*, Tübingen, 1910, 30-6, for details of Protestant missions in German East Africa.

91 Rwaza diary, 3 October 1906.

92 Kandt had pointed out in the 1905 edition of *Caput Nili*, 226, that Rwanda would go by default to the Catholics if they did not make a move. Dernburg particularly wanted German Protestants on Idjwi Island, contested with the Belgians; see Hellberg, *Missions on a Colonial Frontier*, 96-8.

93 Kabgayi diary, 24 March 1906.

94 Rwaza diary, 14 February, 16 April, 18 August 1905; Save diary, 20 July 1905.

95 Rwaza diary, 4 October 1906, 30 January 1907.

96 Father Brard seems to have been on the verge of a nervous breakdown, and left, overtly to attend the General Chapter of the Society; see Save diary, 26 August 1905; Hirth to Livinhac, 12 September 1905, No. 095103, Dossier 97, WFAR; Nothomb, *Church History*, 20.

97 Save diary, 9 December 1906.

98 Born 28 June 1874, Classe was ordained in Carthage 31 March 1900 and appointed secretary to Monsignor Livinhac; see Van Overschelde, Father A., *Monseigneur Léon Paul Classe*, 28 June 1945, booklet in White Fathers'

Library, Rome. Classe was something of a 'son of the Church'. He left his birthplace, Metz, and went with his parents to Paris at the age of six, where he first studied at St Nicolas du Chardonnet. When he first joined the White Fathers in 1896 he stated his parent or guardian on the forms as 'Abbé Sterney, Curé de St Denys et de l'Estrée (Seine)'. So it may be assumed that both his parents had died before he was twenty-two. (Personal communication, Rev. Pere Réné Lamey, Archivist, WFAR.)

99 Lecoindre, Rev. Père, 'Le Ruanda: raisons qui ont nui beaucoup au développement de la mission au Ruanda', MS, handwritten and undated, *c.* 1918, WFAR.

100 *Rapports annuels*, 1905-06, 184.

101 It seems likely, given the White Fathers' Jesuit novice masters, that Classe had been influenced by Da Nobili's success in India.

102 *Rapports annuels*, 1905-06, 184.

103 The two factors, a missiology based on the history of the Church's missionary activity and 'secular' considerations of social class and the position of the Church as an institution within the State, reinforced each other. Lavigerie's esteem for the methods of St Rémy and Augustine fitted in well with contemporary secular needs for keeping in with the French State; see Beildelman, T. O., 'Social theory and the study of Christian missions in Africa', *Africa*, vol. XLIV, No. 3, July 1974, 235-49; Shorter, A., *African Culture and the Christian Church*, London, 1973, 72. In the famous 'Toast of Algiers' made by Lavigerie to French naval officers on 12 November 1890, at the Pope's behest the Cardinal put his considerable weight behind the republic.

104 This was equally true of other mission societies such as the CMS, where solid 'Varsity' men would be viewed with more favour by administrators than missionaries drawn from the lower middle class and working class; see G3/A3/01-04, CMS archives, London.

105 Van Overschelde, *Classe*, 5.

FOUR

Hutu Church and Tutsi court

'In der Person des Herrn Pater Classe einen geeigneten Leiter . . . haben,' wrote Von Grawert complacently to Monsignor Hirth.[1] His complacency was not shared by the missionaries, who resented Classe's eager support for the court, his apparent defection from the northern camp,[2] and his obvious determination as Vicar General to impose discipline on the Catholic ranks. Classe, showering the Rwanda missions with reams of directives and missiological reflections of great delicacy, did not endear himself to gun-toting priests.[3] His superior manner and excessive piety aggravated them; his thunderous calls for adherence to the rules of the Society were provocative:

Let those of our missionaries who do not believe they can reconcile the apostolate with the practice of our Rules look for a Society which has as its Rule only the caprice of its members . . .[4]

Yet Classe was to more than make up for the divisions he created among his missionary brethren by his adept handling of Musinga and Dr Kandt; the principal result of the 'Brard method',[5] fisticuffs before diplomacy, had been a ban on new stations in 1906 which was to last till 1908.[6] During this period of enforced stagnation the worst Catholic fears were realised: Pastor Ernst Johanssen, a Lutheran from the Bethel bei Bielefeld mission,[7] arrived in Rwanda, was well received by Musinga and was given land at Zinga, five hours' walk from Zaza.[8]

Although the initial contacts between the White Fathers and the Lutherans were superficially friendly, the priests helping the pastors with the language and giving them tips on brick-making,[9] alarms were being sounded behind the scenes. The Vicar Apostolic asked the Fathers to reduce contact to a minimum. Catechists were to be trained immediately and placed 'incognito in threatened spots'.[10] Mission adepts were henceforth to be referred to as *Bakatholika* and, in case there was any confusion, chapels to the Virgin Mary were to be erected at each station.[11]

There was indeed a little confusion, as the Lutherans were called *Bafransa* in Buganza.[12] In a flush of ecumenism, or in the hope of slipping in unobtrusively, the Protestants had not, it seems, emphasised their differences with the Catholics while at court. Musinga told Father Classe accusingly that the Lutherans were proclaiming the same doctrine as the White Fathers and were similar to them. 'Yes,' replied the Vicar General with great panache, 'in the same way as a Mututsi and a Muhutu are similar.'[13] The humour was certainly not lost on the king; the choice of site for the Lutherans indicated that Musinga hoped to contain the Catholics with Protestant competitors.[14]

Although the new Governor of German East Africa, von Rechenberg, was an aristocratic Catholic educated by the Jesuits in Madrid, the White Fathers were at an obvious disadvantage against German Protestant competitors.[15] The Society, strained to the maximum, still provided only five German priests for Rwanda by 1912 as against nineteen French.[16] It was true that five out of the six Brothers were German, but some Hutu mistook them for the Fathers' *garagu*, their role was clear to all,[17] and such distinctions running along national lines could not have pleased the imperial administrators. The Lutherans were even told when they arrived that the country belonged to the *Bafransa*, a word that was synonymous with *Basarcedoti* — priests.[18]

Rechenburg, a Catholic in a strongly Protestant or freethinking administration — Kandt was an adept of Nietzsche — was unlikely to flaunt his religion.[19] He preferred the company of Muslims, whom he saw as the natural heirs to the colony.[20] The success or failure of the Catholic missions hinged, therefore, not on the religious affiliation of officials at the coast, nor in the Reichstag and colonial service, but on the Fathers' willingness to support German policy and behave in Rwanda in a way likely to win the approval of the court.[21] And that depended in some measure on Monsignor Hirth and his Vicar General turning their missionaries into the 'admirable machine' their Jesuit predecessors had striven to create.

Any attempt to check the impetuosity of individual missionaries met with a multitude of instances when intervention in local affairs seemed justified. When a Tutsi chief near Kabgayi fell ill his Hutu were accused of having poisoned him; within a few days twenty-five peasants were given a potion that made them mentally deranged. Taking their induced madness as a sign of guilt, the chief had them executed one after the other. A Father stopped the slaughter.[22] The next day he was proclaimed *mwami wa bahutu*, king of the Hutu. In Bukunzi, when a child was born with teeth and was therefore about to be killed, the Mibirisi Father Superior hastily put a medal round its neck, saying 'This child belongs to us.'[23] Such actions were surely blameless, yet for Rwandans around the stations they were just as much unwarranted interference as less highly motivated behaviour.

If the conduct of individual missionaries was a question of discipline within the Society, and therefore open to correction, the missions' drift into clientship confronted Hirth and Classe with a Sisyphian task. Disputes at Zaza between Christians and their chiefs were endless. Father Pouget conscientiously called in the Tutsi to judge cases, but it was generally recognised that decisions went to the man with the most powerful supporter. The penalty for mission failure to sustain this support was 'backsliding into Pagan ways'.[24] Reflecting gloomily on Zaza, Monsignor Hirth confided to Livinhac that he well understood why the Germans had banned further missions in Rwanda.[25]

The situation at Nyundo was equally fraught with difficulty; since the Germans had made Kisenyi into a large base, the Fathers had been obliged to support the Tutsi.[26] In June 1908 there was a minor Christian uprising; Tutsi chiefs' huts were burnt and their cattle pillaged. The next day the nobles arrived at the mission with an escort and were met by a large but well armed group of Christians. In the presence of the Father Superior the Hutu spokesman demanded that the Tutsi should rule in a more moderate fashion in future, then the cattle were handed back.[27]

The missionaries were not often directly responsible for the insubordination of Christians so frequently bemoaned by Kandt. They felt that there were faults on both sides; the chiefs tried to push their peasants to the limit, the peasants 'try to do the least possible, neglecting no means to that end and even going to take instruction [i.e. catechism] if they think it has some utility'.[28] Yet whilst the missionaries were supposed to cajole the Hutu into obedience, the Germans did little to curb Tutsi exactions. Richard Kandt, a Jewish medical practitioner, latter-day explorer and linguist, and from 1908 Resident of Rwanda, saw no alternative to support for the harsh regime of the Tutsi.[29] Only through them would it be possible to rule the country. If he saw the Kaiser's 'civilising mission' as anything more than respecting the Tutsi order it was as injecting rationality into the ruling class through education. In Tanganyika his colleagues were able to call on literate and moderately trustworthy Muslims from the coast, but he had quickly realised that the Tutsi's aversion to foreigners would vitiate any attempt to employ the Muslim elite in Rwanda; he badly needed educated and able Rwandan auxiliaries.

Kandt saw little to praise in six years of Catholic educational effort and asked querulously why the priests did not run a proper school at Nyanza instead of a mud and straw hovel.[30] In 1900 the German government had decided to subsidise mission schools where German was taught,[31] but the French White Fathers had done little to further the imperial language policy.[32] Monsignor Hirth the Churchman and Dr Kandt the statesman both saw African education as the generator of an elite, but whilst Kandt wanted docile rational nobles for an enlightened feudal order Hirth sought pious exemplary Rwandan priests and laity for the *corpus christianum*. Kandt dealt in the practical realities of ruling a highly stratified African State; Hirth clung to the radical possibilities of his Christian faith. Not for him to call a halt when after ten years' effort in German East Africa only seven of the 160 seminarians who had passed through his hands still persevered.[33] It was popularly said that the Tutsi were 'for the *Badatchi*' (Germans) but the Hutu 'for the *Bafransa*'; in reality Monsignor Hirth was indifferent to the class or ethnic origins of his seminarians.[34]

For the Vicar Apostolic the creation of an African clergy was the immediate and primary aim of missionary endeavour. Only with the formation of an indigenous priesthood did the Universal Church become fully incarnate in African societies as a visible and Grace-giving institution. Rwandan Fathers were not an additional colourful touch but the essential constituent of the Rwandan Church. This was an article of faith for Catholic missionaries; in Monsignor Hirth it was a blinding vision that dominated the last years of his episcopacy to the exclusion of more mundane considerations.

Any German reading Hirth's circulars on education would soon have realised that Catholic schools were going to be of only incidental help to imperial administration. His goals were purely religious; the teaching of writing was a reluctant concession, 'only what would be adequate to give a certain amount of preparation to a small elite to become assistants to government functionaries'.[35] However, all catechumens were expected to be able to read; already the proofs of the first Kinyarwanda books of piety, like Father Ecker's *Book of Prayers*, were being circulated, so it was important for the Fathers to press on with reading lessons.[36]

Save mission at this time had a theoretical catechumenate of two thousand, but only 750 received regular instruction of a formal kind from the three trained catechists and their fourteen helpers, yet the main thrust of missionary work was directed at the young catechumens;[37] neophytes got little attention after baptism. As the missionaries tried to remain aloof from Hutu-Tutsi conflicts there were increasing signs of 'backsliding' amongst the Christians.[38] The Vicar Apostolic was convinced that under these conditions pious reading was vital to keep Christians from slipping into the diffuse outer orbit of the mission and finally being lost.[39] Whilst the priests struggled to win back Hutu who felt deserted by their erstwhile patrons, even providing pupils with paid work to induce them to come to school, Monsignor Hirth circulated his lofty thoughts on the role of teachers[40] and dreamed of neophytes doing spiritual reading in the *rugo* (enclosure). Small wonder that this insistence on education, albeit integrated with and almost indistinguishable from catechesis, was not shared by all; 'certain missionaries are over-doubtful about their role as educators. Has it not been said even to myself [Hirth] . . . "What is the use of a school for these blacks?".'[41]

The station school was usually a large open shed lacking even books and slates. Instruction in both reading and religion was based on passages from the *Histoire Sainte*. When the younger pupils were dismissed at eleven the older ones continued with forty minutes of writing practice. The priests were not supposed to use corporal punishment, and the pupils were expected to show a mimimal level of decorum; in the stifling atmosphere of the classroom there were lapses on all sides.[42] Perhaps the most important teaching and learning took place in the afternoons, when the Brothers gave their schoolboy workers simple training in brickmaking, carpentry and construction, and demonstrated the cultivation of new crops such as coffee[43] — much of a mission's modest income was derived from its gardens[44] — but the Germans were not satisfied with this informal technical instruction.[45]

Right from the first baptisms the Vicar Apostolic stressed the need to select bright pupils for his seminary. Every two years groups of boys aged between thirteen and fifteen, chosen for their 'solid piety, open respectful and amenable personalities and good health',[46] left for Tanganyika. In October 1904 ten boys from Save marched for six days to meet six from Zaza, then the group headed east across Gisaka to Kianja; among them was the future first priest of Rwanda, Donat Leberaho. Once at Rubyia, three hours' march from lake Nyanza, they began learning Latin before many of them knew enough Swahili to converse with their fellow students.[47] In October 1906 a second contingent, which included Jovite Matabaro and Isidore Semigabo, left Rwanda;[48] they and Leberaho where the only three of the seventy-five Rwandans sent to Rubyia who reached ordination. Not surprisingly, many missionaries were sceptical; they had little reason to believe that the motives of boys who agreed to make the journey to Rubyia were entirely spiritual. Their Hutu catechists assumed, and declared openly, that seminary life was easier than working under a Tutsi lord in the fields. 'And do you really think,' one catechist asked a missionary, 'that those going to Rubyia are drawn by any other motive?'[49] With the prospect of guaranteed mission protection and no fear of persecution Hutu seminarians left Tutsi jurisdiction and reprisals for good.

Yet, in the Rwandan context, material and spiritual motives for joining the Fathers were not contradictory. The idea of a holy alliance between poverty and piety was as alien to Rwandan society as to the Semites of the Old Testament. The political power of the Fathers did nothing in the peasants' eyes to detract from their religious claims; far from it. In the face of pessimism amongst his priests that at times degenerated into racism, Monsignor Hirth admonished them, 'Knowing that the vocation comes from God, we are too inclined to forget that it only flowers and bears fruit through the work of Man.'[50] Nonetheless, whenever the missionaries detected material motives in their catechumens they felt apprehensively that the Hutu were misunderstanding them and ignoring their religious office. To aim at the material comforts of seminary life — a relative comfort indeed — instead of the perfection of an ascetic sarcedotal ministry was deplorable to men who had given up their own comforts in search of spiritual excellence. The misunderstanding was mutual and never fully resolved.

The premature return of all but a tiny fraction of those who went to Rubyia is perhaps explicable solely in terms of its inhuman lifestyle and the strain of separation from family and country. Donat Leberaho spent nine years away from Rwanda, living as a celibate among strangers, speaking a foreign language, and studying philosophy and theology in Latin.[51] Yet since these boys had got to Tanganyika it must be assumed that they were to some extent attracted by a vision of the priesthood, a vision which did not correspond to the reality of Rubyia.[52] It seems likely that the major seminary beckoned its students like a great Catholic court; few of them could have imagined that the rewards of this court, the power and the glory of priestly office, were granted only after ten years of patient spiritual and educational effort; the Hutu seminarians, observing the rise of Tutsi courtiers, had learnt on the contrary that dissimulation, cunning, violence and flattery led to office and success. Behind them lay the deadening inertia of peasant life under the Tutsi yoke and before them the demands of priests reared in a long tradition of spiritual striving reinforced by bourgeois notions of meritorious industry; faced by such a conflict the majority decided to go home.

Peasant culture, however, did contain elements which a glib Freudianism might have labelled highly favourable to the Christian message and especially to the Catholic concept of priesthood. The Hutu family was marked by an extreme dependence on the father, continuing even after marriage. The authoritarian father of the patriarchal *umuryango* was projected into the political kingdom in the person of the mwami. The great Patriarch was magnificently distant from the harsh, humdrum life of the peasant. He reigned with the Queen Mother as the source of all authority, having the right of life and death over his brothers and sisters. In this heroic figure were epitomised all the noble deeds held up in court culture for the admiration of the masses. In their stead he realised both the psychological and political yearnings of the peasantry.[53]

The place of the White Fathers in this pattern of values was assured. They were seen without contradiction as *abami* and *abayeyi*, parents; titles like 'Saviour of the poor' and 'The feet have come' were bestowed on them.[54] They were endowed with powers to detect robbers merely by using a piece of paper with writing on it, to control rain, cure the sick and bewitch the recalcitrant.[55] To go against their will could be dangerous. A Christian from Save left home to sell skins in Gisaka against the Fathers' orders and advice. While away he had a vision of Christ, who told him of the coming conversion of Rwanda and chided him for leaving home.[56] The image of the dominating father, diffracted through the patrilineage to the court itself, was focused on the Catholic Fathers, and by extension on their God, through their ready use of paternalist and authoritarian methods. These methods, it seems, attracted rather than repelled the Hutu of central Rwanda, even though few became priests.

With the exception of a few impoverished Tutsi, Church education was the prerogative of the Hutu throughout the German period. In 1903 Musinga threatened Von Beringe that he would move his capital if the Tutsi at Nyanza were forced to go to school,[57] a priest visited Nyanza occasionally from Save, and Catholic catechists sent as teachers gained the mwami's confidence, but attendance at the small straw-roofed school house at court remained erratic. In August 1905 Musinga, who was now trying to use education against his Ega councillors, asked the Fathers to put up a permanent brick building. Relations between Terebura and Monsignor Hirth were at their most acrimonious, and the Vicar Apostolic seems to have declined the opportunity on the grounds that anything that took Father Brard to court would be damaging.[58]

Once Hirth could provide a teacher acceptable to the Germans, the court and himself, he wrote to Bujumbura for permission to begin.[59] Von Grawert replied giving his assent, provided there was no proselytising or religious instruction. He felt that such education would make the Tutsi more amenable to European influence, and a good teacher might, by example, lead them to Christianity without arousing immediate hostility. He could hardly refuse a school in which Classe promised to teach the Tutsi German and Swahili, and about which the mwami was unusually encouraging.[60]

Musinga's renewed interest in literacy seems to have been linked with his increased participation in trading. A 1906 ordinance banning African traders with firearms from entering Rwanda had been liberally interpreted by Von Grawert to mean that traders could return provided they were unarmed.[61] Ganda and Haya caravans began to creep back cautiously, going straight to court, where they traded cattle for cloth and roupies. Musinga soon got rid of the money to his favourites, and the Tutsi flocked to Kabgayi mission to buy cloth.[62]

The mwami, who had been dealing alone with European affairs since October 1906, was beginning to flex his muscles. The place of

Ruhinankiko in the highest councils of State had been taken over by the rich Ega landowner Rwidegembya, and his estates in Gisaka had gone to an old Nyiginya chief, Kanuma.[63] Less actively engaged in the persecution of the Nyiginya nobility than his fellow Ega, the young Rwidegembya was favoured by Musinga, who pitted him against the combined might of Kabare and the Queen Mother.

At the beginning of January 1907 the court suffered a liturgical calamity: the sacred fire that was lit at the beginning of each mwami's reign, only to be extinguished on his death, was allowed to go out. The extinction of the royal fire was a trigger which released all Nyanza's latent tensions. Musinga ordered the execution of all the *Bayamuliro*, the fire keepers, and Kabare was accused of having bewitched the fire.[64] Supported by the canny Rwidegembya, the mwami was able to force his uncle on to the defensive and his final disgrace was averted only by turning the king's fears towards foreign invaders. It was a familiar tactic: the foreign campaign to keep rebellious *ngabo* out of mischief, and the foreign threat to close ranks at court. A rebel group who had taken refuge in Burundi were accused of having the fire put out and were said to be plotting to return and kill the king. Musinga was not yet able to dispense with Kabare's services and was ready to believe the story.[65]

The drama of the royal fire delayed the opening of the school,[66] but by May 1907 the catechist Wilhelmi[67] was able to begin writing lessons. It was soon clear that the king was more interested in the prestige of writing than in acquiring the skill itself. He would casually wet his pencil in the mouth of a Twa servant and trace out the letters of the alphabet. He learnt how to sign his name and little more; for the rest an amanuensis was employed. At this time his reading knowledge of Swahili was minimal, and when letters arrived Wilhelmi was summoned to translate them.[68]

Despite a natural anxiety about which missionary would head the school, Musinga finally gave his permission for a brick building in June. A priest called every fortnight, although the Kabgayi Fathers were sometimes summoned daily to Nyanza when the mood took him. Attending the school, or at least spending some of the day leaping through its windows, were eighteen *ntore* selected from unimportant Tutsi families.[69] The boys, accustomed to purely physical training in dancing, jumping, spear-throwing, archery, swimming and court etiquette, were thoroughly bored by the long classroom lessons, and few attended regularly. Their exercise books were sent off weekly to Kabgayi for correction. Once several people at court were competent Swahili speakers the mwami pressed to make some improvement in his German. The *ntore* had little incentive to persevere, since an unspoken rule of the school was that the mwami stayed one step ahead of the rest.

The king's fears, sharpened by the bad augury of the extinguished fire, never left him. When Save church was officially blessed he sent a representative; Wilhelmi told the Fathers that fear of possible sorcery had kept the king away.[70] But when the king had his terrors under control he performed a skilful juggling trick with the Germans, the Ega and the White Fathers, balancing the power of one group against the other. The missionaries had grown into a counter balance to his Ega councillors, and he made concessions to them as he would have done to any other powerful faction in the country. When the European side of the balance became too heavy, as during the influx of whites for the Duke of Mecklenburg's visit in 1907, he would frantically try to reduce it.[71]

Pressure was put on the White Fathers the moment the king learned of the size of the duke's caravan. The Save Fathers were surprised to hear from Von Grawert that the Catholics were refused permission to start any further missions because the king was worried about the amount of land they controlled.[72] No request had been made. A week later the priests received another letter complaining that they stopped Christians going to court and favoured them in local disputes. The Save missionaries had food sent to Nyanza during their visits; the king now found their behaviour insulting to his hospitality. Christians were denounced for burning huts, when, at court with the priests, they were miles away from the incident.[73] While the Duke of Mecklenburg loomed on the horizon the Catholics could do no right.

Musinga correctly judged that the Germans would help him curb the missionaries. When German and missionary interests coincided, as over the smooth functioning of Nyanza school, he called in the Ega. The Save Fathers learned in September that Kabare and Rwidegembya had been summoned to court, where they were required to reside permanently next to the school. They joined Cyitatire to form a baleful education committee.[74]

On the whole Musinga's diplomacy worked. The royal *ikoro* poured in to fill the Nyanza granaries, and the power of the leading nobles was undermined as men and land were taken from them. To keep up their interest in the well-being of the throne the mwami married their sisters.[75] Nyiginya, like Ntulo, who had risen too rapidly, he disgraced. Reflecting on the changed situation at court, Father Classe wrote in June 1907, 'Musinga is no longer a minor; he has become a *mugabo ukomeye* [a powerful man].'[76] As a result of shrewd manipulation of the Ega and the White Fathers, and after a three-year struggle, the young mwami now dominated the court. Perhaps seeing the import-ance of the Catholics in the equation, Kabare began sending his *ntore* to pay court to the Kabgayi Fathers.[77]

While Musinga had rapidly proved himself in the inter-Tutsi politics of the court, his position in relation to rebellious Hutu distant from

Nyanza improved only slowly, despite European assistance. The *umuhinza* of Bukunzi used the proximity of Mibirisi mission as an excuse for refusing to send the tribute of two slaves for sacrifice. The Germans he ignored altogether, and would not appear before the commander at Shangi. A German patrol with Tutsi auxiliaries was sent to capture him in April 1907, but he slipped through their hands, and despite being formally deposed continued to hold power in Bukunzi. Fearing that the royal herds would perish and calamities come on the realm if someone of the *umuhinza's* ritual prowess were banished, Musinga insisted on his reinstatement. The German attacks on the famous rainmaker alienated the population, and few catechumens came to the mission while he was in hiding.[78]

The Nyabingi prophetesses of Mpororo did not make the mistake of ignoring the Europeans. A German patrol even left confiscated cattle in the custody of one, while the famous Muhumusa co-operated with Anglo-Belgian survey parties belonging to the frontier commission.[79] By enlisting support from among Hutu lineage heads and by claiming supernatural powers Muhumusa became an influential medium and built up a large following. Young girls from her entourage were married to chiefs and formed sub-centres through which she could exert her control over Mpororo and south into Rwanda. In 1905 a German patrol found a young girl behind a curtain who claimed to be Nyabingi's servant. The girl told them that Nyabingi had flown up to the sky but had asked her to pay eighteen cows fine and request German assistance in putting down rebellious chiefs in the district.[80] Musinga was wary of Muhumusa's spiritual powers and large following,[81] but her law-and-order messages from the spirit world had convinced the Germans that Nyabingi was harmless.

The submission of the north was one of the few desiderata to which Musinga, Kandt and Classe, the triumvirate who now ruled Rwanda, could all subscribe. The mwami wished to emulate his father's glorious exploits, whilst the rich spoils of Bugoyi and Mulera were a gratifying source of dissension amongst his nobles. Dr Kandt was worried that the activities of Twa and Hutu bandits, such as the notorious Lukara lwa Bishingwe,[82] under the noses of the British and Belgians in the north would damage German colonial prestige. Whilst negotiations over Mfumbiro continued he could not afford to be seen presiding over a rabble of war lords.[83] Monsignor Classe was perturbed by the arrival of more Lutheran missionaries and wanted to stake claims as soon as possible to unoccupied regions of the north. The three disagreed over the advisability of using Catholic missionaries as a vanguard; the idea appealed to Kandt, it distressed Musinga.

The Duke of Meckenburg's visit coinciding with the arrival of the Lutherans had been an unprecedented show of European strength.[84] Like some exhibit in an ethnographic museum Musinga had been brought out for the visitors' inspection and thoroughly humiliated.[85] He now saw that the ban on new missions had been only temporary, and his former changeable attitude hardened into an abiding hatred of the whites, who were too numerous to attack. 'The Sultan once said in the course of a discussion with our Superior, Father Classe, in Nyanza that he would indeed have been able to contemplate war at an earlier date (i.e. prior to 1909) but that the dwellings of the Europeans had increased to such an extent that expressions of violence could no longer be envisaged.'[86] The mwami was too well schooled in Tutsi etiquette to show his emotions and was usually courteous to the Fathers. Faced by their demands, he prevaricated. When forced to give his permission he strove to nullify its effects but at times the impassive façade would crumble. When one of the Lutherans' porters was executed at court there was great excitement. A Father visiting Musinga was shown the savagely beaten corpse, with the warning that the same could happen to him;[87] yet when Classe visited court in April 1908 the mask of politeness was once more in place.[88]

After the Protestants had opened their second station Monsignor Classe began to prepare the ground for expansion. He chose the occasion of the blessing of Nyundo church to make his first move. Relations between Kisenyi Residency and Nyundo mission were coldly correct; the Fathers had been a little too welcoming to the Belgians, though they had tried to make amends by going to celebrate the Kaiser's birthday. Dr Kandt in return accepted an invitation to attend the inauguration. 'It is worth repeating,' proclaimed Classe in his welcoming speech, 'that missionaries as such are agents of no country and that here they are working towards the same goals as the government; they on their side and the government on its.'[89] Already that year the Vicar General had agreed to undertake the upkeep of roads near missions, and after the speech he made a formal request that the ban on new stations be ended.[90] Kandt's reply was cautious, but he agreed to intercede with the imperial government. The proposed new station at Kanage would strengthen the German position on Lake Kivu, and one in Busigi would extend German influence among the people of Mulera and the northern Hutu.[91] The mwami promptly sent Kandt a cow. 'As a matter of fact Musinga asked, citing the numerous stations which he had already conceded to the mission, that there should be no new foundations.'[92] Kandt's reassurances that the Germans would curb the Fathers' land hunger and prevent their assuming jurisdiction over more Hutu did not satisfy Musinga, who feared that his own *abatware* would lose faith in him if he made more concessions. Despite open protest Kandt's interest in using the missions for political ends meant that he would push through two more stations whatever Musinga's feelings.[93] In December 1908 fifty Christians set out from Rwaza to begin building on Rulindo hill in

Busigi.[94] The reaction at Nyanza was predictable. All effort to keep the pupils at school in order ceased, and Wilhelmi could teach nothing. A new wave of complaints began reaching the missions in central Rwanda about their Christians' conduct. The Vicar General, seeking audience with the king in February 1909, was categorically refused. Classe gently warned that if the king continued in this fashion he would be passed over by Dr Kandt; since the Resident was already overriding the mwami the argument had little substance and was ignored.[95]

The mission's attempt to reverse the court's formula, using the Germans to threaten the king, was a measure of Kandt's growing hold over the country. There was talk of taxation. Nobles took the opportunity to collect goats from their Hutu on the pretext that they would deliver them to the German Residence in Kigali; hundreds of goats were removed as 'tax', and Hutu besieged the mission with complaints. It was not so much that the raids were orchestrated from Nyanza but that the nobles at court were able to convey politically valuable information to their local representatives; their garagu on the hills could then gauge how far they could go with the Christians. Conversely the mwami was the centre of a constant stream of complaints about Christians' activities in the provinces. The wrath of Musinga and the persecution of the Christians around missions were sometimes causally linked, but not by any simple chain of command. Tutsi around provincial stations had their own grievances and needed no authorisation from Nyanza to erupt into violence.

The Europeans continued to console themselves with the anachronistic belief that the intermittent hostility at court from 1908 to 1909 was emanating from a group which they called 'the war faction', Kabare, Rwidegembya and the Queen Mother.[96] A Rwandan proverb says that it is never the mwami who executes but his councillors, and the pliant monarch surrounded by unscrupulous advisers was a common theme of colonial mythology, used to explain why Indirect Rule failed to achieve results. On the contrary, it was Musinga and not his councillors who determined policy now. In August 1908 the king had Rwidegembya's leading garagu, a chief with over four thousand cattle, executed at court.[97] Kabare was forced out of Nyanza under a cloud in January 1909 and meekly turned up at Save mission in March to present the Fathers with a cow.[98] His disgrace was confirmed when Kanuma and the Gisaka chiefs appeared at Zaza mission to warn the Fathers not to give Kabare sanctuary.[99] The only independent Ega left at court was the shadowy figure of the Queen Mother.

The arrival of the first White Sisters and a contingent of new Fathers at the beginning of 1909 was a further blow to the king. He had granted a third Protestant station but was still holding out against Catholic expansion.[100] On the other hand, in March, 150 *askari* and five German officers had engaged in a number of inconclusive skirmishes in the north against the Twa Basebya and demonstrated to the court that the imperial government was willing to subdue the mwami's rebellious subjects.[101] Two months later a patrol brought in a great prize, the priestess Muhumusa.[102]

The king was now delighted at the Europeans and wrote Classe a fulsome letter asking why he no longer came to court.[103] His pleasure was short-lived. Muhumusa was put under a kind of house arrest at Kigali, and since the Germans had only Musinga's word for her nefarious influence she was well treated.[104] It was a serious miscalculation. The presence of such a powerful medium was a magnet for court dissidents; visitors trooped to see her and it was not long before she was summoning important *abatware* from Gisaka.[105] Feeling grew at court that it was a monstrous trick and that this 'Queen of Ndorwa' had been brought south of the Nyabarongo river to overthrow the mwami.[106]

The missionaries were the first to suffer for the Germans' inept handling of the Muhumusa affair. The mwami allowed gangs of Tutsi youths to wreck Nyanza school and informed Kandt's deputy, Indrumm, that he wanted no priests permanently at court.[107] Indrumm, preoccupied by rumours of an anti-European rising,[108] bundled Muhumusa off to Bukoba[109] and prepared to launch a major expedition on the north.[110] The mwami was informed that the *askari* were being sent to police the frontier against Belgian and British intrusion,[111] but the spectre of rebellion in South West Africa and Tanganyika was certainly in the forefront of the German Colonial Office's thinking. The missions, with their several dozen Mausers and hundreds of cartridges, could afford to be complacent. 'I am convinced that the Watussi will take the first opportunity to settle affairs with the Europeans,' wrote a Father, 'but we are so accustomed to such rumours we do not assume the situation to deteriorate unless we have strong reason.'[112] Slowly the rumours died down, leaving Musinga stronger in relation to the Ega — the small army in the north had demonstrated the folly of their talk of destroying the Germans[113] — but still weaker in relation to the colonial government. Teaching was resumed at Nyanza,[114] and the mwami's representative signed a contract for land on which Murunda mission in Kanage was founded.[115]

By 1910 the mission was in an anomalous position; there were seven stations and some 4,500 Christians, mainly Hutu. Already young Hutu seminarians were working their way towards ordination. Yet as an institution the Catholic Church relied entirely on the Tutsi, who resisted all thought of conversion, and on the *bons offices* of the Germans, whom they succeeded in irritating through their clientship network and theocratic tendencies. The court, on which in theory they should have concentrated for the conversion of the nobility, was a hotbed of intrigue and resentment at European high-handedness. Yet the very same Europeans were putting down risings and extending Rwanda's frontiers back to their limits in Rwabugiri's glorious days. The situation was fraught with contradictions, the most serious of which for the missionaries was the growth of a Hutu Church in a Tutsi State.

Classe, who might have been expected to put things right, was now performing most of Hirth's duties; the Vicar Apostolic, on grounds of failing eyesight,[116] had retired into the confessional at Nyundo, where he sat for hours forgiving the sins all his refinements of the cate-chumenate had failed to prevent.[117] Outside, a disciple of the Brard school drove in the penitents.[118] Described by Governor Schnee as 'a tall fine figure of a man, honoured and esteemed by everyone',[119] Hirth still could not contain the violence of his priests, catechists and converts. Classe, as Vicar General, fully committed to supporting Tutsi rule, made every effort to suppress pro-Hutu tendencies among the clergy, but he lacked the authority of a Vicar Apostolic, for though Hirth was inactive he did not renounce his office.[120]

This split jurisdiction that existed *de facto*, if not *de jure*, in the Rwandan vicariate greatly reduced the missionary Church's ability to respond to the growth of dissension and disunity within its ranks, especially that disunity which sprang from the cultural and political differences, and, therefore, the needs of the north and south. This division, which was of the utmost importance for the Germans and Tutsi, could hardly fail to be equally important for the missionaries. But there was no escaping from a uniform mission policy; there was one vicariate, one Vicar Apostolic and one policy; it could not be otherwise given the Germans' intentions and the will of the court. But Fathers Superior closely involved with local problems could ignore Classe's clear national directives with the excuse that they did not come from the top. Few of the northern missionaries shared the Vicar General's experience of Nyanza; they opposed the imposition of a policy designed to serve the interests of a court they regarded as powerless. Some cherished notions that Christianity *was* the religion of the poor,[121] others felt they could knock a respect for authority into their Hutu Christians without help from the Tutsi. The 'northern' faction could simply see no need for the wily 'atheist' Tutsi in their territory; some saw no need for the Germans either. This was how one Father ruled his theocracy: 'A scare was given these people by putting them through the darkroom treatment, a room with closed shutters and a revolver on the table. The sub-chief, paralysed with fear, sat next to the Father Superior while . . . chains were rattled in side room to add a lugubrious note to this macabre scene.'[122]

Yet once the Catholics saw that the Germans were going to force

Banyanduga on the north they were obliged to take the Tutsi into account. When the translation of the Gospels of St John and St Mark was begun Monsignor Hirth insisted on the language of the court rather than Kiga.[123] The arrival of the Protestants put a new urgency into the debate about coercion of the peasantry and the apostolate to the ruling class. Kandt's prediction of a Lutheran monopoly of the Tutsi was taken seriously.[124] The German Protestants, however, made the same mistakes as the Catholics in their first two years, involving themselves with Hutu-Tutsi disputes and seeing in the 'sturdy Hutu peasant' the future of Rwanda.[125]

During the Kivu-Mfumbiro conference[126] Muhumusa, the Nyabingi prophetess, escaped from Bukoba and remained at large. The eyes of both the Germans and the court were anxiously fixed on the north, where Lukara lwa Bishingwe, at the height of his power, with a herd of 1,600 cattle,[127] camped at the foot of Lyangombe's sacred mountain, Muhavura volcano. In May 1910 the Kaiser signed protocols which handed over portions of Kivu and north-west Rwanda to Britain and Belgium. Although Musinga had only nominal jurisdiction over some of the lost territory, since Rwabugiri's campaigns it had been considered part of greater Rwanda.[128] The loss was a severe blow. The bitter pill of expanding Catholicism had been sweetened by the hope that the Fathers were providing a new foothold in the mountainous north. The loss of his half-brother's land in Mfumbiro, the chieftaincy of Nyindo, more than offset any gains to be made through the missionaries.

Lukara's great prestige as the leader of a mobile military force which had outwitted all Musinga's attempts at capture[129] was increased by his canny manipulation of religious and political symbolism; his camp was named Nyanza, and even White Fathers approaching the sacred mountain where it lay were warned that they risked their lives.[130] The segmentary character of all Hutu groupings, was, however, a built-in restraint on such bands of kin and clients. Early in 1910 two of Lukara's kinsmen[131] led a break-away movement, taking with them over 600 cattle and many followers. Both factions plied Rwaza mission with copious gifts instead of the rotten eggs they used to send. Father Loupias, dutifully carrying out his instructions not to intervene in local conflicts, referred both parties to the mwami[132] Lukara retaliated by denying the mission timber from 'his' forests. Loupias, a giant of a man, set out to find the band and almost came to blows with their leader.[133]

Musinga now made a positive move: he sent a representative to Rwaza mission, presumably in the hope of reasserting his control over the Rashi lineages.[134] Father Loupias could hardly refuse his direct request to be guided to Lukara's encampment. At a large meeting, to which all parties were summoned, Lukara reluctantly agreed to recognise the autonomy of the splinter group. Buoyed up by the presence of the Catholic missionary and his Christian entourage, the Banyanduga tried to press home their advantage. Nshozamihigo's agent stepped forward and called on the king's man to prosecute the rebels for cattle theft. Lukara jumped to this feet. Loupias stood up to restrain him. As Lukara ducked, perhaps on some hidden signal, a hail of arrows struck the White Father, wounding him in the forehead and liver. The mission *nyampara* bore him back to Rwaza, where he died on the evening of 1 April 1910, the first casualty of the policy of co-operation with the Tutsi.[135] Lavigerie's missiology had been followed, central authority had been upheld — more, it had been imposed — but at a high price. The dilemma of the Hutu north, symbolised by Loupias's death, was to remain with the mission throughout the colonial period.

The first years of German civilian rule had inaugurated a pattern of relationships between court and missions which was to last until Belgian rule. Classe, despite an incessant struggle to cut back on clientship relations in the Church, was able to normalise relations with the administration and make gains for the White Fathers. Although the Tutsi remained refractory to the attempts at their conversion, they were willing to countenance missionary activity provided it resulted in strengthening Nyanza's hand with the Germans and in the provinces; the school in the capital was a tangible concession. Meanwhile the first steps at developing a self-supporting Hutu Church with its own priesthood were under way. It was the growth of this Hutu Church that was soon to force the king from a position of resistance to quiet accommodation.

NOTES

1 Von Grawert to Hirth, 31 December 1906, P.1728, film No. 166, AA.

2 See chapter three.

3 1913-14 was a vintage year, capped by a thirteen-page work dated 5 November 1914 on the sacrament of penance.

4 Classe to confrères, 5 July 1907, CR. This denunciation was provoked by no serious moral lapse but by the habit of some Fathers of travelling alone. The rule demanded that they go in pairs.

5 Lecoindre's term, from 'Raisons qui ont nui'.

6 Kandt to Classe, 11 March 1909, No. 101/09, CO; de Lacger, *Le Ruanda*, 397. It was the retiring Von Götzen who had agreed to an embargo after complaints from Von Grawert in 1906.

7 For details of this mission see Johanssen, E., *Ruanda. Kleine Anfänge. Grosse Aufgaben der evangelischen Mission in Zwischenseengebiet Deutsche-Ostafrikas*, Bethel bei Bielefeld, 1915. The Evangelische Missionsgesellschaft für Deutsch-Ostafrika, begun in 1886, was moved to Bethel bei Bielefeld in 1906. It numbered twenty-two missionaries in German East Africa in 1909; see Mirbt *Mission und Kolonialpolitik*, 30-1. The arrival of German Protestants was encouraged by Kandt; see chapter three.

8 Zaza diary, 8 August 1907. This was a stepping stone into Rwanda; a second station at Kirinda was built later in the year.

9 Kandt to Buisson, 17 July 1908, CO; de Lacger, *Le Ruanda*, 406.

10 Classe to Father Superior, Kabgayi, 4 August 1907, CR.

11 Hirth to confrères, 11 April 1908; Hirth to Father Superior, Kabgayi, 13 May 1908, CR.

12 Kabgayi diary, 22 October 1907.

13 Save diary, 31 August 1907.

14 Kandt to Ruccius, 20 September 1907, P.1735, film No. 167, AA; Des Forges, *Rwanda under Musiinga*, 120.

15 Iliffe, *Tanganyika*, 52.

16 Kandt, R., annual report for 1912, P.1728, film No. 166, AA.

17 Kabgayi diary, 18 April 1907.

18 'Intschi hi ni ya mufransa'; see Johanssen, *Kleine Anfänge*, 32, 41.

19 De Lacger, *Le Ruanda*, 420.

20 Iliffe, *Tanganyika*, 199-200.

21 For example, the Catholics were invited to the reception of the Duke of Mecklenburg, probably because of their assistance to Dr I. Czekanowski's caravan. Dufays and Classe attended, while there was no Protestant representation; see Mecklenburg, *Ins Innerste Afrikas*, 125-6; de Lacger, *Le Ruanda*, 419.

22 This was Lwibishenga; see Kabgayi diary, 12 January 1907.

23 Mibirisi diary, 14 March 1906.

24 Zaza diary, 30 January 1907; *Rapports annuels*, 1907-08, 155.

25 Hirth to Livinhac, 30 September 1906, No. 095124, Dossier 95, WFAR. Zaza mission, despite its position on east-west trade routes, was comparatively isolated from the White Fathers' headquarters in Save. Mails between Save and Zaza had to pass through the forest of Bugesera, where they were vulnerable to attack. The king's excuse was that too many traders posed as mission agents for him to be able to protect mission mails. As a result mission caravans took to carrying distinctive indentification marks; see Zaza diary, 5 March 1907; Save diary, 16 April 1907; Kabgayi diary, 25 April 1907; *Chroniques Trimestrielles*, No. 143, November 1907, 647.

26 Hirth to Livinhac, 31 October 1907, No. 095143, Dossier 95, WFAR.

27 Nyundo diary, 21-2 June 1908. The Tutsi were Banyanduga recently arrived in the north and led by a certain Lwakadigi; see chapter six, p. 128.

28 Nyundo diary, February 1909.

29 For Mecklenburg too many whites would be needed to rule Rwanda, so the mwami had, 'unmerklich', to be made into the Resident's right hand. The advantage was the 'absoluter Autorität' of the mwami; see Mecklenburg, *Ins Innerste Afrika*, 77, 82, 85-7. Kandt was equally pragmatic; see Louis, *Ruanda-Urundi*, 146, n. 4.

30 Rwaza diary, 3 October 1906.

31 The White Fathers made an initial agreement with the Germans in 1896 in which it was tacitly asssumed that German missionaries would be sent to Rwanda, Burundi and East Africa. They were included in the 1900 agreements which had been the result of pressure from the Reichstag and in which it was agreed that schools teaching German should be State-aided; see Austen, *Northwest Tanzania*, 70.

32 Swahili was supposed to be the *lingua franca*, while German was taught to the elite. Few of the Fathers bothered to learn German, and most of the German-speakers were, unfortunately, from Alsace. Nonetheless Swahili was taught at Rwaza station school, and Catholic pupils did receive government prizes for good German-speaking at Mibirisi station school; see *Rapports annuels*, 1905-06, 190. Stations with French Superiors do not seem to have persevered in German classes.

33 *Grands Lacs*, No. 10, 1952, 7.

34 *Chroniques Trimestrielles*, No. 125, March 1906, 169; de Lacger, *Le Ruanda*, 434.

35 Hirth, J. J., 'Des Élèves destinés au séminaire', MS, typed, Marienberg, 1907, CR. This alone was in the spirit of the 1900 agreements.

36 *Gitabu tshy'abakristu* and *Gatikisimu mu Kinyarwanda* were printed at Maison Carrée in 1907; see Kabgayi diary, 17 May 1907. This emphasis on reading was perhaps a lesson learnt from long contact with Protestants in Uganda. Though not unknown, it is unusually stressed for a Catholic mission at this period.

37 *Rapports annuels* and baptismal records indicate that the majority of converts were aged between twelve and thirty years.

38 *Rapports annuels*, 1907-08, 155, 157.

39 Classe to Father Superior, Kabgayi, 4 August 1907, CR; *Rapports annuels*, 1907-08, 155. In response to *Acerbo Nimis*, a Papal encyclical of 15 April 1905, which demanded a weekly catechism lesson for youths, Hirth designed a course of twenty-five lessons to be given, when they could be spared from the fields, to children preparing for their first confession. Pope Pius X required a compulsory one-hour Sunday catechism lesson for youths and special classes in preparation for the sacraments of confirmation and penance.

40 Teachers should 'mettre en oeuvre toutes les richesses de leur nature en les élevant et les vivifiant par les ressources divines de la grâce'; see 'Élèves'.

41 Hirth to confrères, 11 April 1908, CR.

42 The Vicar Apostolic complained about the level of violence when he visited the schools; see Hirth to Livinhac, 30 June 1906. On the other hand, Father Léonard, who visited the Rwanda mission from Maison Carrée, took the view that the pupils could not be expected to sit that length of time in the classrooms and such trouble was inevitable; see Leonard to Livinhac, 1 February 1909, No. 09195, Dossier 95, WFAR.

43 *Chroniques Trimestrielles*, No. 143, November 1907, 647. The first successful Rwandan coffee crop was harvested on mission grounds.

44 Kabgayi diary, 12 January 1908 — some stations also had a shop.

45 Austen, *Northwest Tanzania*, 70.

46 Hirth, 'Élèves'.

47 *Grands Lacs*, No. 10, 1952, 8-10.

48 Nothomb, *Church History*, 20.

49 Kabgayi diary, 9 June 1909.

50 Hirth, 'Elèves'.

51 The top class was starting philosophy in Latin and learning German by 1909; see Hirth to confrères, 20 November 1908, CR. Only in 1910 was a 20,000-word Swahili-Latin dictionary available. Despite the extraordinary

difficulties, seminarians became competent in Latin and several pupils corresponded with seminarians in Trier in excellent German; see Schäppi, F. S., *Die katholische Missionsschule im ehemaligen Deutsch-Ostafrika*, Vienna and Zürich, 1937, 162-3, 174.

52 Even Father Classe wrote privately to Livinhac to tell him that the seminarians were disgusted with life at Rubyia and wanted to leave; see Classe to Livinhac, 14 August 1909, No. 095212, Dossier 95, WFAR.

53 De Heusch, L., *Essais sur le symbolisme de l'inceste royal en Afrique*, Université de Bruxelles, 1958, 50-63.

54 Dufays was called 'Rukizaboro' and Lecoindre 'Ibirengebyaje'. Informants at Rwaza spontaneously used the term *abayeyi* when asked how the priests were seen by the first Christians. The same affectionate relationship is recorded in Codere, *A Biography*: see especially pp. 77, 96, 363.

55 Save diary, 13-14 September 1905; Kabgayi diary, 19 January, 9 May, 26 August 1906; *Rapports annuels*, 1906-97, 162. The Fathers' own behaviour could be a mixture of the pragmatic and the magical. For example, they gave a woman in difficult labour a half-glass of holy water followed by black coffee; see *Chroniques Trimestrielles*, No. 146, February 1908, 152.

56 Save diary, 5 December 1906.

57 Indrumm to Classe, 24 August 1909, J. N. 780, CO.

58 Save diary, 17 and 26 August 1905.

59 Hirth to Von Grawert, 8 November 1906, P.1728, film No. 166, AA.

60 Hirth to Von Grawert, 8 November 1906.

61 Rwaza diary, 29 August 1906; Louis, *Ruanda-Urundi*, 168.

62 Kabgayi diary, 7 April 1907.

63 For details of Ruhinankiko's fall see Zaza diary, January 1905; Save diary, 2 January 1905; *Rapports annuels*, 1905-06, 180; Pagès, *Un Royaume*, 624.

64 Kabgayi diary, 6 January 1907; *Chroniques Trimestrielles*, No. 140, August 1907, 454.

65 The crime was said to have been instigated by Sebuharara, a close relative of Ruhinankiko, who fled after the latter's disgrace. Thus Kabare was blaming his Ega rival's lineage; see Pagès, *Un Royaume*, 205; Kabgayi diary, 11 January 1907.

66 *Chroniques Trimestrielles*, No. 143, November 1907, 651.

67 See chapter six.

68 Save diary, 15 May 1907; 22 September 1907; *Rapports annuels*, 1908-09, 169.

69 Save diary, 11, 17 June 1907; *Rapports annuels*, 1908-09, 168-70.

70 Save diary, 9 February, 22 June 1907.

71 The Mecklenburg visit itself provoked an intense reaction. The kingdom was to be taken from the Tutsi. It was Bilegeya returning or a new Ega king. When Von Grawert requested the mwami to appear before the duke in traditional animal skins the rumour quickly circulated that 'the new European king will forbid the negroes to wear cloth . . . Tikitiki (Von Grawert) was only his boy; he had white garagu. What a man!' See Kabgayi diary, 17 July 1907; Save diary, 22 June 1907; Mecklenburg, *Ins Innerste Afrika*, 110.

72 Save diary, 1 August 1907. Mecklenburg reached Lake Mohasi on 28 July 1907 from Tanganyika. The letter was puzzling and must have been

connected with the arrival of the Protestants. Von Grawert was making it plain that nothing had changed and the ban held as far as the Catholics were concerned.

73 The Fathers had merely advised their Christians that they were not obliged to provision the caravan of Dr Czekanowski; see Save diary, 14, 22 August 1907.

74 Lwangampuye was another watchdog; see Save diary, 26 September 1907.

75 Kabgayi diary, 11 March, 13, 22, 24 June 1907.

76 *Ibid.*, 13 June 1907.

77 *Ibid.*, 4 January 1908; *Chroniques Trimestrielles*, No. 146, February 1908, 159.

78 Mibirisi diary, 28 April, 1, 15 November 1907; *Chroniques Trimestrielles*, No. 146, February 1908, 152-3.

79 Hopkins, *The Nyabingi Cult*, 267.

80 *Deutsches Kolonialblatt*, 1905, 279, Derscheid papers.

81 Des Forges, *Rwanda under Musiinga*, 176-8.

82 Lukara was contesting control of the Mulera plain throughout the first half of 1907, with Ruhanga and his Tutsi relentlessly pushing him back. His own Rashi lineage was supplemented by recruited retainers. In August 1907 he narrowly escaped execution at court; Dr Czekanowksi called him away to assist his investigations on the forest Twa in the north-east; see Rwaza diary, 22 August 1905, 16 February 1907, 8 November 1907; Father Superior, Rwaza to Resident, 19 April 1908, Dossier 112 *bis*, WFAR; Dufays, *Pages*, 66-9. In April 1908 his fortunes changed when he mistakenly attacked a Tutsi enemy who had joined a German expedition. The Germans now began to think of their usual punitive raid; see Rwaza diary, 3 April 1908; Zaza diary, 17 April 1908.

83 The negotiations resulted in the local Derche-Kandt agreement of 19 February 1909 in which the Belgians agreed to withdraw from Lake Bulera, occupied by them since November 1908. This was not recognised in Brussels. At the Anglo-German Mfumbiro conference in Berlin on 19 May 1909 it was secretly agreed that Britain should secretly occupy Mfumbiro to present Belgium with a *fait accompli*. Part of Mpororo was to be British; see Louis, *Ruanda-Urundi*, 64, 68-75.

84 The Queen Mother left court, and with 6,000-8,000 people camped around Nyanza the mwami was guarded night and day by 5,000 spearmen; see Kabgayi diary, 17 July 1907; Save diary, 9 August 1907; Mecklenburg, *Ins Innerste Afrika*, 102-6, 111.

85 The king and his entourage watched fascinated as the duke's party blasted away with their rifles at earthen pots far out of his archers' range; see Mecklenburg, *Ins Innerste Afrika*, 109, 118-23.

86 Schumacher to Indrumm, 8 September 1909, P.1734, film No. 165, AA.

87 Save diary, 22 October 1907.

88 Hirth to Livinhac, 30 June 1908, No. 095154, Dossier 95, WFAR. Classe and Schumacher were now visiting irregularly about once every two months. Good relations prevailed during their visit of 27 April 1908; see *Chroniques Trimestrielles*, No. 155, November 1908, 877.

89 *Chroniques Trimestrielles*, No. 139, July 1907, 401; No. 156, December

1908, 140; No. 161, May 1909, 408.

90 Classe to Kandt, 18 August 1908, P.1735, film No. 167, AA; Classe to Kandt, 23 October 1908, CO.

91 Kandt to Classe, 24 October 1908, No. 856/08; Kandt to Classe, 3 November 1908, No. 867/08, CO.

92 The Germans had already turned down proposed extensions of Save and Zaza, and seem to have shared the court's concern about Catholic landlordism. Kandt let the Vicar General know that no future land grants were to exceed twenty hectares and reiterated demands that peasants should be cleared from mission grounds and properly compensated; see Von Grawert to Hirth, 12 February 1907, P.1828, film No. 166, AA; Kandt to Classe, 3 November 1908, CO.

93 He had little difficulty in getting permission from the coast, and blamed the whole ban on Von Grawert; see Kandt to Classe, 11 March 1909, No. 101/09, CO.

94 *Rapports annuels*, 1908-09, 273; Barthélemy, J. B., 'Fondation d'une station au Rouanda', *Missions d'Afrique*, 1910, 271-83.

95 Kabgayi diary, 19 February, 16 March 1909.

96 Indrumm to Classe, 6 September, JN844, P.1734, film No. 165, AA.

97 Mibirisi diary, 27 August 1908; *Rapports annuels*, 1908-09, 266.

98 Rwaza diary, 10 February 1909; Zaza diary, 1 March 1909.

99 Zaza diary, 1 March 1909.

100 Kandt to Classe, 11 March 1909, CO.

101 Langenn to Kandt, 15 April 1909, P.1734, film No. 165, AA; *Rapports annuels*, 1908-09, 277.

102 Gudovius to Kandt, 17 June 1909, P.1734, film No. 165, AA.

103 Musinga to Classe, 1 July 1909, in Kabgayi diary.

104 Des Forges, *Rwanda under Musinga*, 177-8.

105 Rugambarara went, for example; see Zaza diary, 24 June, 25 August 1909.

106 Zaza diary, 7-8 September 1909; Des Forges, *Rwanda under Musiinga*, 176-8.

107 Lecoindre to Indrumm, 19 August 1909; Indrumm to Classe, 14 August 1909, J.N. 711, CO.

108 The rumours were picked up by a German trader, Büchfink, whom Indrumm used as a spy.

109 Indrumm to Classe, 6 September 1909, CO; Louis, *Ruanda-Urundi*, 153.

110 The II Company was ordered to cross into Rwanda from Bujumbura, and a contingent of seventy troops with five officers and two machine guns were already on their way from Bukoba under the leadership of the Resident, Von Stuemer, a veteran of the north who could have confronted Belgians or British.

111 Since November 1908, when Belgium had occupied Lake Bulera, all eyes had been on the north-west; see *Chroniques Trimestrielles*, No. 158, February 1909, 139. Von Stegmann unashamedly asked the Nyundo Fathers to spy on Belgium patrols; see Von Stegmann to Father Superior, Rwaza, 21 September 1909, WFAR. Lindequist, the Colonial Secretary in Berlin, was predicting calamity, a Rwanda torn between the three powers, on the basis of

highly inflated troop estimates; see Louis, *Ruanda-Urundi*, 75 n. 3.

112 Schumacher to Indrumm, 8 September 1909, P.1734, film No. 165, AA.

113 Nyindo, Musinga's half-brother, was Chief of Mfumbiro and in a position to monitor troop movements. His garagu, Muvunandinda, had already appeared at the door of Rwaza in May 1904, and Nyindo came in person in July 1905. Aged eighteen, he strongly resembled Musinga; see Rwaza diary, 19 July 1905. Thus Musinga could gauge the accuracy of the information given him by the Germans.

114 On the other hand, without special permission the school was out of bounds to the missionaries themselves; see Indrumm to Classe, 17 September 1909, JN874; Musinga to Classe, 24 September 1909, CO. Only the Vicar General or his delegate could come, and Wilhelmi had to inform the king on each occasion of their intention.

115 Indrumm to Von Stegmann, 11 December 1909; Classe to Indrumm, 11 December 1909; Véckerlé to Oberleutnant, Kisenyi, 26 December 1909, P.1735, film No. 167, AA.

116 He handed over temporarily while travelling; see Hirth to confrères, 22 April 1907, CR. By 1908 he was sending Classe's reports direct to Maison Carrée; see Hirth to Livinhac, 30 June 1908, No. 095154, Dossier 95, WFAR. Hirth to confrères, 6 December 1908, CR, complains that he cannot go on.

117 Hirth to confrères, circular No. 12, 1907; Hirth to confrères, 31 March 1908, CR; *Chroniques Trimestrielles*, No. 114, March 1905, 146; No. 119, September 1905, 430; No. 125, March 1906, 166-7; No. 149, May 1908, 404; *Rapports annuels*, 1905-06, 186; 1907-08, 154, 160.

118 Lecoindre, 'Raisons qui ont nui'.

119 *Deutsches Kolonialblatt*, 1 September 1913, quoted in de Lacger, *Le Ruanda*, 436.

120 Too much of a Churchman to drop the most significant and symbolic of his functions, to act as a bridge between Rome and the bush stations, he continued to convey to his clergy both the sublime and the ridiculous in the Vatican's thinking. 'For the past two years,' he told his harassed priests, 'we have tried to resolve in the most practicable fashion the question of adopting a new edition of the Gregorian chant.' See Hirth to confrères, 15 January 1910, CR. In 1911 he required them to replace the scapular of the Brotherhood of Our Lady of Mount Carmel, a pious confraternity, with a medal showing on one side the blessed Virgin and on the other the Sacred Heart of Jesus. He faithfully recommended the baubles of Romanesque Catholicism, yet staunchly advocated the speedy development of an indigenous clergy against all criticism and opposition. The worst excesses of what might be called cultural imperialism, and the best support for the Rwandan Church, albeit Romanised, came from the same source, the Vatican, and relied for its impact on the same value, obedience. If there was a cool aloofness about Hirth it was doubtless because he realised how few of his confreres showed his most obvious insights; if the Church had no frontiers it could have no frontier dispensations.

121 For Classe's clear opinion see chapter three.

122 Lecoindre, 'Raisons qui ont nui'.

123 Hirth to confrères, 11 April 1908, CR.

124 Rwaza diary, 3 October 1906.

125 Kandt, R., annual report for 1912, AA; Johanssen, E., article in *Koloniale Rundschau*, December 1912, 752-4, Derscheid papers; Johanssen, *Kleine Anfänge*, 241.

126 The conference was held in February 1910 at the Belgian Foreign Ministry; see Louis, *Ruanda-Urundi*, 79-95, 189.

127 Von Stegmann to Father Superior, Rwaza, 27 July 1909, WFAR; Rwaza diary, 1 April 1910.

128 Des Forges, *Rwanda under Musiinga*, 179.

129 Since Lukara's lucky escape from Nyanza he had never returned to court but kept to caves and temporary hiding places from which he raided the plains below.

130 'Lors d'un voyage des P.P. Classe et Dufays au Muhavura, Kinigamazi, frère de Lukarra lwa Bishingwe, ne leur avait pas apporté de nourriture au pied du volcan, parce-que, disait-on les Blancs ne descendraient pas de la montagne; Lyangombe les y ferait périr.' Rwaza diary, 21 June 1906; *Chroniques Trimestrielles*, No. 136, March 1907, 118.

131 Sebuyangi and Kumana.

132 Lukara sent a representative to court, but could have had no hope of getting satisfaction.

133 Rwaza diary, 4 April 1910. Loupias, about two metres tall, actually struck Lukara on 20 January 1910 when the former staged a fake battle on the plains in order to get Loupias to side with him. A mission *nyampara* told Loupias that the smoke curling up from the villages in the plain, said to be the work of Sebuyangi, was a trap. There are many oral traditions of this death, but a full account is given shortly after Loupias' death in the Rwaza diary.

134 The northern Hutu's use of foreign mediators probably allowed the Tutsi to infiltrate clan lands in the past. Lwakadigi at Nyundo, for example, was called in to mediate a dispute between Lukara and another kinsman, Lugira; see Nyundo diary, 1 February 1908; *Chroniques Trimestrielles*, No. 154, October 1908, 811.

135 *Rapports annuels*, 1909-1110, 318. The impact of Loupias' death on Rwaza may be judged from the fact that several informants could give vivid accounts of the position of his spear wounds while remembering little else of this period.

FIVE

French Catholicism
or
German colonialism

The position of Rwanda's Vicar General in 1910 was more equivocal than he cared to admit. The sacrifice of Loupias' life had touched neither Tutsi nor Germans. The ungrateful mwami put out the eyes of an old friend of Save mission,[1] and sounded out a possible alliance with Lukara.[2] The Germans, charged with finding the murderers, blamed Loupias for his rashness and wept crocodile tears over their painful duty of punishing Mulera.[3] The Hutu closed ranks; even Christian guides did not lead the searchers to Lukara.[4] Those who remained with the mission behaved with more than their usual insolence, burning the huts of a king's garagu[5] and refusing to supply German patrols with food.[6]

Not only Captain Wintgens, with his simple formula 'Give to Musinga what is Musinga's',[7] but Kandt too reproached the growing power of the Catholic Church and its theocratic tendencies. For some time the Church-State clash to which Classe shut his eyes had been inevitable. Sharing his views, on the one hand, were the Germans, the Tutsi and Monsignor Hirth; on the other, their unruly subjects, the missionaries, and northern Hutu thrown together in an unholy mixture of violent and contradictory aims. The fissure lines dividing rulers from ruled had cut into the Church, but in none of his directives did Classe ever avert to this conflict; and Kandt, whilst delivering homilies on missionary conduct, carefully sustained the illusion that the French priests and German colonial officers shared a common purpose. Predictably it was a cattle dispute which in December 1910 brought the latent conflict between bush missionaries and rulers into the open. A Kabgayi Hutu catechumen persuaded Father Schumacher that he had been punished by his Tutsi lord for joining the mission.[8] In a 'frank'[9] letter to the Resident Schumacher denounced Tutsi 'justice' and claimed that he, as Father Superior, was in the best position to judge such disputes.[10] This voicing of Kandt's suspicions and many missionaries' private opinion made the banal case something of a *cause célèbre.* 'Where will all this end?' demanded the mwami. 'Are all the chiefs to be chased out whenever a servant who has had cattle confiscated as a punishment complains to the mission?'[11] From Classe and Kandt poured a fresh stream of injunctions to respect Tutsi authority.

'The policy of the imperial government has to be in all cases to strengthen and make consequent the authority of the chiefs and Sultan, even if this sometimes results in injustice to the Wahutu,'[12] wrote Kandt, stifling protest. 'The Batussi are the chiefs . . . the government cannot change in one fell swoop the deep-seated structures of the country,' reasoned Classe. 'There would be a revolution — something all governments want to avoid at all costs.'[13] 'The Hutu are of savage character, inclined to disobedience and insurrection,'[14] warned Kandt: 'Certain missionaries seem to want to see the Bahutu reigning one day, and especially Christian Bahutu . . . would things be any better?' echoed the Vicar General.[15] 'As long as I have the honour to be Resident here I am not proposing any other policy or principles than those of the imperial government . . . the Mission must adapt itself to this policy if it does not want to endanger its vital interests,'[16] Kandt thundered. 'We are not kings,' Classe reminded his subordinates; '. . . it cannot be a material influence which we hope to wield. We seek to have a moral influence on them, influence as in the Gospel, the only true one.'[17] Such injunctions might be reasonable in the circumstances, might conform with Lavigerie's views,[18] but coming from a German Resident via a 'career' missionary they had much the same effect on militant priests as Tutsi disdain.

Kandt and Classe made the support of feudal monarchy sound a simple affair. Hard-line priests might concede that Christian peasants did have duties towards their chiefs; henceforth they would even instruct them to fulfill these duties, but the simple policy hid a complex reality. What duties were peasants supposed to perform, and to which chiefs? In an attempt to resolve this problem the Fathers began a serious investigation of feudal rights and obligations.[19]

Musinga had continued Rwabugiri's policy[20] of breaking down large Tutsi land holdings even after he began using Europeans to expand his kingdom around 1905. The system of overlapping jurisdictions, deliberately created by the mwami and his father, not only prevented the nobles consolidating their estates and followers in the north and south-west[21] but, since several chiefs would have rights over the same Hutu, ensured that ambitious notables like the Ega would check and contain each other. Around Zaza, for instance, four leading Tutsi chiefs could claim rights of peasant service, and this complicated the already difficult legal position of Hutu on mission grounds. The old Hutu on the Zaza estate told the Fathers that the rights of the 'chief of the bow', the *abatware w'umuheto*, were limited to summoning the *ngabo* and demanding provisions for it. According to the army chief himself the Hutu ought to hoe for him regularly, provide him with beer and produce, in short behave as his *ubuletwa* labourers. The priests were inclined to accept their own people's version. Though the peasants must have been minimising their duties, they were probably presenting an older tradition, whilst the chief was trying to translate his rights connected with the almost defunct *ngabo* into terms relevant to contemporary Rwanda.[22] Feudalism was not static and did not have a fixed code such as the Fathers, with their training in canon law, sought. Taxes, tributes, gifts, laborious duties, all were determined by the ability of the Tutsi to extract them; given the backing of the Germans they were almost bound to increase.

When the Fathers took over their estates the *abanyabatuka* and *abatware* lost their fiefs; the mwami received roupies and cloth in exchange, and he decided whether new fiefs should be given in compensation. Even after 1906, when the chiefs began signing contracts alienating their holdings, they still hoped to be able to maintain the feudal bond between themselves and Hutu now living on mission property, especially in cases where a peasant had fields both inside and outside the mission's boundaries. If the peasant refused to send the tribute demanded, maybe a part of his harvest or a hand of bananas, the Tutsi would try to place another man on his plot.[23] Conversely the Hutu, also thinking in terms of patron-client relationships, treated the Fathers as their new and preferred *abanyabutaka*, playing them off in traditional fashion against the local *abatware*.

Acculturation inevitably took place: the Fathers treated their Hutu as *garagu* rather than tenants, whilst the Tutsi made valiant efforts to come to terms with their idiosyncratic view of property. Ruhinankiko's successor, Rwamuhama, proposed, 'in order that we may have peace together . . . you give me all [the land] that those on the mission ground have outside and I will concede you what my men have within the mission'.[24] This seemingly straightforward solution was rejected after a quick calculation that there would be a net loss to the Catholics; however, the priests promised to make sure that those with external plots sent their *ikoro*. When the advice of Kanuma, the other land chief, was asked he replied only vaguely, apparently at a loss for a suggestion;[25] three weeks later Rwamuhama was demanding that the mission Hutu build him a hut: the missionaries, having agreed to endorse one feudal demand, might after all lend their weight to another.[26]

To disengage from clientship was impossibe. No sooner did the missionaries weed out one set of patron-client relationships than another sprang up. Their profusion strangled every effort of Fathers Superior and defeated the Vicar General's moralising. Behaving correctly, the Zaza Fathers asked the Germans, in collaboration with the chiefs who 'owned' the forest, to assign them trees, and sent out forest guards to protect them till the sawyers could come. The guards soon settled down to become 'masters of the forest';[27] chiefs were refused access to their own timber without a payment. After handing over hoes, goats and cattle to the mission *nyampara* the chiefs were in no mood for a new exaction. They refused to allow Hutu to carry away logs, and the missionaries, for the first time, became aware of their agents' abuses.[28]

The same story was repeated with Zaza's herds. As land grants were now limited by the Germans, the priests had to ask the chiefs for grazing rights. Parts of summer pasture spread over five or six fiefs were assigned them and a mission cowherd was put in charge; cowherds began pushing other cattle off the pasture, selling the grazing rights, which belonged to the land chiefs, for hoes, and building up a private herd.[29] Any relationship with the priests could be turned to profit; catechists, cowherds, timber guards, all took their opportunity. Whether as Tutsi whose resistance divided priests from their bishop — 'What is the use of worrying about these people who openly despise us and take us for their boys?'[30] — or as Hutu who manipulated every aspect of the Church's life, Rwandans were defining the character and internal dynamics of the *corpus christianum* that was being built up on their soil.

Although in 1911 there were still no important Tutsi Christians, none even under instruction, the war of attrition which the court had been waging for a decade had ended. The Tutsi were imperceptibly retreating; their tactics had changed to accommodation, hence the attempts at negotiation at Zaza. It is difficult to attach a definite date to the origins of this movement, but, looking back, the missionaries singled out as its starting point the day, late in 1909, when Kabare shared a calabash of beer with a Christian.[31] For all well born Tutsi such an act had been unthinkable, comparable to eating with a Twa. This gesture by the eclipsed Kabare epitomised a process which had begun in 1908 and was well advanced by 1912. Reliance on Christians for help in collecting *ikoro* and even in dealing with legal cases became a more permanent arrangement.[32] Tutsi began taking Christians into the honourable *ubuhake* relationship, with its mutual duties and rights. Several influential chiefs at court made approaches to Christians, others accepted the advances of ambitious converts, taking them as garagu who could be useful in delicate dealings with Europeans. Although both sides felt that such intermediaries were dangerously contaminated by an alien ideology, they served as valuable channels of information. 'We are pushing our Christians to join the "families" of chiefs. In such a way prejudices will disappear,' wrote Classe, favouring a movement which gave him limited but important access to the ruling groups.[33] Kabare himself took Frederiko

Rwagihange as a garagu and made him his permanent delegate to the Save Fathers. Fearing that Frederiko was now more Kabare's man than theirs, the missionaries sent a trusted employee to pay court to Kabare and become his garagu;[34] it was these two Christians with whom Kabare drank, creating a Catholic myth which might exaggerate the importance of this single act but which did point towards the area in which the Tutsi were coming to terms with the Church.[35]

Musinga himself endorsed this change, using his catechist Wilhelmi as a general factotum and appointing a man who had created a scandal in 1906 by pillaging a royal gravekeeper as his ambassador to the Kabgayi mission.[36] Several old Ega, however, still tried to isolate the Christians by pouring scorn on them. The Queen Mother chased out any Catholic she found working on her enclosure, and Rwidegembya forbade any Hutu wearing the medal to enter Nyanza. This seriously reduced the usefulness of Christian garagu. Their lords often spent sixteen months on end at the capital;[37] failure to perform the two months' labour service at Nyanza when required led to grave punishments. By the middle of 1911 there were more than seven thousand Christians and six thousand catechumens in Rwanda. Selected from among the poor, the patronless and the journeymen they may have been, but their numbers made Musinga unwilling, or unable, to ban them from Nyanza. Probably the humbled but ever pragmatic Kabare influenced him in this decision; in February 1910 Kabare visited Save for the first time, and until his death in 1911 acted as intermediary between the Fathers and the king.[38]

The movement for accommodation gained ground at Nyanza. Musinga failed to follow up the defeat of Schumacher with the usual round of persecution; instead he informed his ambassador at Kabgayi that in future he himself would deal with disputes between Christians and their lords, so that Kigali might not be called in to adjudicate.[39] He almost seemed to suggest a mission-Tutsi *entente* to circumvent the Germans, and declared in public that were it not for the first and sixth commandments he himself would consider becoming a catechumen. 'Musinga is well disposed towards us . . . He asks questions about religion frequently, often sending for catechists from distant stations to enquire what they have been taught,' reported Classe to Algiers, perhaps concealing even from himself the suspicion that Musinga was making a careful assessment of Christianity's political effect.[40]

Throughout 1911 fifteen *ntore* were receiving instruction at Nyanza; Musinga knew of it but turned a blind eye. Attendance at school was still irregular and depended on the king's whims. Some days he would supervise the *ntore*, obliging them to pay attention to their lessons, on others he seemed happy to find the classrooms empty. In the provinces there were still instances of resistance to the mission, but when a catechist in Marangara had his hut burnt down Musinga sent a stiff letter ordering it to be rebuilt.[41] Perhaps Classe had succeeded in the task he had set himself, and the mwami was convinced that Hutu converts would make loyal subjects.

After Kabare's death the king seemed at last to enjoy himself; the departure of king makers is the delight of kings. The Lutherans were summoned to Nyanza to take part in a little ecclesiastical theatre, a dialogue with the White Fathers.[42] With only seventeen baptisms to their credit after four years work, their pastor was still able to summon a fiery eloquence, relating how he had heard the voice of Imana calling him to Africa. How was it, the mwami enquired blandly, that he taught differently from the Catholics? Perhaps recalling the need for white solidarity, the pastor denied it. Why then did the Protestants have wives? Because the White Fathers have a rule of celibacy, was the answer.[43] Behind their impassive expressions the Tutsi courtiers must have relished the entertainment. Musinga himself was probably weighing the political implications of differences between the two Christian denominations. In his summing-up he simply said that he was not yet ready for Christianity, but that he preferred the White Fathers.[44]

The problem of actually converting the Tutsi remained intractable; they still saw missionaries as barbarian, even though they had been forced to recognise their power. At court it was difficult to speak to a noble, let alone convert him to Catholicism. Only those who, like Cyitatire, feared for their lives and fiefs, stayed away from Nyanza for long. Musinga wanted his chiefs near him so that his spies would be free to undermine them in the provinces;[45] he kept them in his company, drinking with them till the early hours of the morning. Each chief had a retinue of thirty to fifty servants camped around the capital; relays of workers from their provincial seats brought in supplies. Those bringing provisions mingled with Hutu carrying *ikoro*, sleeping rough on the edge of the town, often diseased and near starvation. Among the elegant enclosures and huts Twa spies circulated, reporting news to the king; similarly every lord had his garagu listening for him.[46] In this seething cauldron of political intrigue the White Fathers were closely watched. Compared to the supercilious banter of the courtiers and the cruel excitements of the struggle for power and position the Good News of the Gospel must have seemed insipid and naive.

The pretensions of Christian priests were out of keeping in a court where, though an important diviner might have ten *rugos* each with a wife and several thousand cattle,[47] he could, for political failure, or for a minor infringement of ritual, be summarily executed or disgraced. Gisaka was the cemetery of ambitious nobles, and the priests could offer them no protection. An important anti-Christian chief was called to the capital in 1909 and murdered with his two sons by the Twa.[48] The chief who had inherited Zaza lost everything in October 1913. Even a chief like Rwidegembya would make several sacrifices before deciding whether it was safe to return to court.[49]

Life for Hutu and Tutsi alike was constantly threatened by disease. In 1909 Rwaza was struck by cholera and diptheria; an epidemic of sleeping sickness reached the court itself.[50] In the same year six thousand people died of amoebic dysentery within a twenty-kilometre radius of Nyundo.[51] Against such scourges the Fathers offered no spiritual portection; instead they provided dispensaries staffed by White Sisters. At their Zaza clinic, the Sisters reduced infant mortality to six our of ninety-two live births,[52] but they gave no explanation for the six deaths; 'the will of God' was more a pious invocation or religious exclamation mark than a causal explanation,[53] so effective physical treatments by missionaries did not mean the eclipse of diviners and mediums, who could not only cure some conditions but could suggest a spiritual cause for all of them. Missionaries, who had accepted material and scientific explanations for disease, and for the vagaries of the weather, could not and would not respond to demands on their self-proclaimed religious expertise from Rwandans who expected demonstrations of supernatural power, and explanations of the spiritual forces traditionally held to cause suffering and death.[54] As Kandt pointed out, the 'Catholic mixture of orthodoxy and rationalism' meant that the Fathers did not expect their presence to bring about miracles.[55] Medical work remained simply a practical demonstration of Christ's love and a tactic to draw people to the missions; this might satisfy the Resident, but it did not satisfy his Rwandan subjects.

Despite punishments, including sometimes expulsion from mission property,[56] the Fathers were unable to loosen the hold of the Lyangombe cult over their flocks. Some catechumens even attended sacrifices to avert any evil consequences of baptism. 'You know your Christian subjects follow the Wanyaruanda and Lyangombe,' Kandt had written to the king, reassuring him of the Catholics' loyalty.[57] To chiefs like Cyitatire, who lived for some time on the edge of the mission orbit, Christianity seemed unable to protect Rwandans: they were as well off with their own *mandwa* spirits,[58] their indigenous 'good angels'. They had Imana instead of Mungu;[59] they appreciated the stories of demons, since they suffered from *bazimu*,[60] and they saw little differene between the godparents and confirmation ceremonies of Catholicism, and their structural equivalent in the Lyangombe cult. *Byose ni kimwe* — 'It is the same thing' — so why convert to the whites' religion?[61] There was, however, relatively little open conflict; the Christians preferred to attend the ceremonies in secret and, since the cult flourished at the level of the hill communities, outside the control of the mwami, it could never offer a national resistance to Christian influence.[62]

Ten years of mission activity had not made traditional religion irrelevant to most, but it had transformed the lives of a few, and brought almost imperceptible changes to the lives of many. In this the Fathers represented only a facet of the European occupation that was slowly altering the economic life of the nation. Dr Kandt, a staunch free trader, had invited Indian traders to his new town of Kigali,[63] and these, with itinerant Ganda and Swahili, widely introduced the luxuries of cheap cloth and beads. The central Rwandan economy which funnelled surplus wealth created by peasant labour into the hands of the leisured Tutsi class, and thence to Nyanza, was soon affected. Cows, goats and sheep, which had once negotiated relationships of a feudal kind, came to assume a cash value as skins and meat, especially around mission stations. The demand for skins on the Bujumbura market pushed up the price of goats twentyfold between 1897 and 1907. Inflation and fluctuation in prices followed the presence or absence of traders.[64] Rwanda, with less commerce than Burundi, had lower prices, but by 1909 a cow could fetch twenty-three roupies, compared with a previous top price of eighteen;[65] the Fathers received complaints from chiefs that Hutu Christians were selling off *ubuhake* cows.[66]

Bride price seems to have followed the rising value of cattle. From August to October 1909 the Fathers noticed a doubling and even trebling of bride price in the marriages at which they officiated; they were obliged to peg it at seven hoes for their Christians.[67] Cattle had been, and were still, the fundamental index of wealth and value, so as cattle acquired a market price other objects which could not so easily be sold to traders were relatively devalued; more hoes were needed to effect the transfer of genetricial rights from one lineage to another; fertility itself, and therefore brides, were being sucked into the market economy.[68]

The missionaries might solve the problem of bride price among their Hutu Christians, but they were powerless in the face of that other effect of commerce, emigration. Three roupies were needed to clothe a man;[69] clothes had been the perquisite of all the early Christians, and the later ones were not willing to forgo it as the mission entered a period of economic crisis.[70] Whilst their people left them to look for work the Fathers censoriously predicted the outcome, forgetting that it was themselves who had introduced the Hutu to paid labour; 'With the Christians more numerous the need to clothe themselves will push people . . . to chase after the Europeans and traders of all colours. It is the scourge of the missions. These bad examples will quickly corrupt the simplicity of the poor negro.'[71] Many died on the way to Bukoba as porters, perhaps one in ten came back with a profit, but the movement begun in 1910 was not to be halted by moral strictures. In three weeks a porter might earn four roupies and satisfy some of the new needs and ambitions born in the Catholic classroom.[72]

The new sources of wealth brought into Rwanda by the Europeans, and the protection they afforded, started a process that was ultimately to undermine the Tutsi order.[73] As employees of the Germans, and even more as those of the White Fathers, Hutu were able to substitute cash payments for the performance of feudal obligations.[74] Kandt believed that all Hutu joining the misson hoped for an improvement in their social standing, and protection against the lawful and unlawful demands of their chiefs. 'They consider themselves to be the garagu of the mission and as such even gain the respect of other Rwandans.'[75] The German presence was more and more felt; as an alternative source of power and patronage it threatened the missionaries as well as the court. The White Fathers, under German pressure, were losing their position as an important white nobility, and along with the Hutu and the Tutsi were being beaten and harangued into an unnatural passivity. At every point groups worked against one another — nobles, garagu, clan heads, Germans and White Fathers all competing for the one commodity Rwanda could supply in abundance, the labour of her peasantry.

If at Nyundo the Fathers spoke of being asked to *kukiza*,[76] save the Hutu from the predatory Tutsi, farther north they had to recognise a 'spirit of independence'[77] among the peasants; even the Germans admired the way the Kiga worked the rich soil, and it was the Kiga who rallied to Muhumusa when she escaped German custody and returned to Kigezi.[78] Kigezi had been divided by the Brussels frontier agreement of 1910; the establishment of a British post at Kumba, employing Ganda agents, turned the previously quiescent Nyabingi mediums against the Europeans.[79] The new frontier divided only colonial officers; in 1911 it did not even prevent Musinga collecting *ikoro* from the British side;[80] Muhumusa was able to use it to her advantage; on one occasion she seems to have escaped attack because the British assumed she was a German protégé.[81] After three months she formed a small army that swept through southern Ndorwa attacking the delimitation agents and moving the focus of the Nyabingi cult into German territory.[82]

The Nyabingi movement was less an organised religious system than a congeries of mediums with a common claim to supernatural power through spirit possession. Itinerant *ababyakurutsa* used to enter Rwanda from Mfumbiro and were held to be the intermediaries of Biheko, a spirit identified with Nyabingi, who was concerned with the fertility of women and land.[83] Childless women brought Biheko gifts and were asperged with water; those whose crops were poor were given

Basebya and Father Dufays in 1908.

peas that would yield a 'magnificent harvest'.[84] The priestesses also exploited pastoral interests; Muhumusa claimed that if she could find a royal Hinda drum she would raise cows from the ground. This particular assertion was also a distant appeal for the restoration of the Ndorwa monarchy, a recurrent theme in Nyabingi outbreaks.[85]

With British Ndorwa closed to Muhumusa, she began making contacts in Northern Rwanda. By November 1911 the whole region was in a state bordering on uprising. Lukara and the Twa Basebya had formed an alliance in June; Basebya became Muhumusa's main military commander.[86] Meanwhile the Yoka clan revolted against their Tutsi overlords.[87] Christians around Nyundo dared not leave their hills for fear of attack by the followers of *Nyina Ku Humusa*.[88] The priestess was captured in September 1911, having turned the leaders of the Sigi clans against her and antagonised at least one important Lyangombe medium.[89] Her removal to prison in Kampala did nothing to calm the area; it was soon claimed that one of her sons, Ndungutse, had escaped and that he would continue the fight to oust the Europeans.[90]

The mythology of resistance, the stories of rightful heirs and of Nyabingi's shamanistic powers were always at hand; leaders rose up, moulded the mythology to cement alliances between the Twa and Hutu clans, and were themselves moulded by the demands of their followers. Ndungutse was one of many; his power at the end of 1911 sprang from his exceptional ability to respond to the demands of the disparate northern groups, including those of the local Tutsi. But his movement was to pose the most serious threat to the central authority of the court before Belgian rule.

The Rwaza Fathers made a point of telling their people that Muhumusa had been captured, but the Hutu immediately switched their hopes and allegiance to Ndungutse.[91] For some he was the new king of Rwanda, a child of the murdered mwami Rutalindwa, and a descendant of Rwabugiri; for others he was the *kisongo*, the minister who heralded the imminent arrival of a young girl without breasts, the Queen of Ndorwa, Nyabingi.[92] It was a cry against both the Banyanduga invasions and the new demands of the Europeans.[93]

To listen to the pagans on this the king is a sort of messiah . . . First of all he is invulnerable, no one will be able to kill him. The Europeans' bullets will have no effect on him; . . . he will catch them in flight and change them to water in his hands . . . Furthermore this marvellous king has the power to *kuloga* to cast a spell at a distance and so bewitch his enemies. The main reason for his coming is to chase the Europeans out of the country.[94]

But if Ndungutse did evoke the myth of a saviour king, the powerful sorcerer who could defeat even Western technology,[95] his grasp of political realities was firm. He does not seem to have responded at first to peasant hopes of routing the Europeans; he tried hard to gain the White Fathers' support — after all, there were 1,500 baptised Christians at Rwaza and 2,300 at Nyundo, mostly young men between the ages of twelve and thirty.[96] In February he began circulating the story that the White Fathers were his maternal uncles: the claim did not disturb his royal patrilineal descent, but advanced the missionaries, as well as his alleged mother, Muhumusa, as the source of his religious authority.[97] Talk of Rwaza mission being attacked faded away; people openly speculated that the Fathers' flagging opposition to the Banyanduga might be revived.[98]

Ndungutse's claims to the Rwandan throne seem to have gained force as he moved south. His first major attacks on the Tusti took place around Rulindo mission, in the province of Busigi. Proclaiming that the Hutu would henceforth be free of Tutsi exactions, he systematically destroyed the huts of the Tsobe-clan Tutsi, who, as *abiru*, had agreed to Rutalindwa's deposition. The people's response was overwhelming: "the Father was able to verify with his own eyes the ruins left amongst the Batsove [Tsobe] . . . There was nothing left, neither Tutsi nor cows, nor huts save those of the Hutu which had been spared on Ndungutse's instructions.'[99] Now the stories were embellished by imagination; he had only to extend his spear to set huts ablaze; when a Father at Rulindo accepted his gift of a cow it was said that the royal calabashes had been placed in the mission's custody.[100]

Musinga consulted his deviners and was told that the vengeful spirits of Mwami Rutalindwa's murdered brothers were stirring up trouble. Massive ceremonies of appeasement were conducted. A cow was sacrificed, and Musinga stood on the mutilated carcass whilst a diviner drenched him in blood; after he had washed he descended into a deep pit and emerged followed by a young bullock. In a subsidiary ritual the mwami and his Queen Mother stood in a blazing hut before escaping through the back. The cycle appears to have been an extraordinarily cathartic representation of the bloody *coup* which had brought Musinga and the Ega to power. Ritually the victors became victims, and the regeneration of Rwandan kingship was symbolically achieved.[101]

The Germans, thinking they had but another instance of Hutu insubordination to contend with, and perhaps hoping that Ndungutse would return to British territory, were dilatory.[102] Kandt was away, and his deputy, Gudovius, was loath to take responsibility for another major expedition. A mere police officer and fifteen *askari* were sent to halt Ndungutse's triumphal march towards Kigali. The Tutsi read the warning signs correctly. Nyindo arrived at Rwaza mission on 15 February 1912 on the way to summon his *ngabo*.[103] Within days two thousand men were heading for Rulindo and the Mulera plain, only to be turned back by Gudovius' cautious policeman.[104]

Whilst the Germans hesitated Ndungutse used his time well, exploiting the north's different grievances. In Bushiru, Buhoma and Kibali provinces the *abahinza* and Tutsi of long standing were roused by promises that the Banyanduga would be driven out.[105] The Fathers heard on 26 February that a royal drum maker had sent Ndungutse a drum; he was now carried on a litter and had a bodyguard of thirty men. In Bumbogo and Buliza he seems to have emphasised his royal claims and swung most of the northern provinces behind him.[106] On 27 February a party of two *askari*, two house servants and three Christian oarsmen were killed on Lake Bulera. The Hutu responsible was not among Ndungutse's followers, but it was enough to convince Gudovius that he must act.[107]

By the beginning of April Gudovius was faced with a full-scale civil war, and the White Fathers were far from certain of the outcome. Ndungutse had a hard core of Twa mercenaries and could count on Lukara's men; he had support from the Yoka as well as from the conservative Tutsi diviners of Bushiru and Buhoma.[108] The *umuhinza* of Kibali was already staging his own independent rising.[109] The movement was more a temporary alliance of dissident groups than a supra-clan army, but it represented the most serious challenge to Musinga since the first years of his reign. The Fathers in the north talked of a Hutu 'revolution', but Ndungutse, of course, was far less the leader of a revolution than of a legitimist rebellion which had become intertwined with a wide range of peasant grievances.[110]

On 8 April a state of war was declared, and the missionaries were pointedly informed that their Christians would be safe provided they gave no succour to the rebels.[111] By this time Ndungutse had followers within five miles' march of the Nyabarongo river, the sacred boundary beyond which no mwami ever went.[112]

The rebel leader misjudged the missionaries; he sent them presents and offered a pledge not to attack them or their supporters. At their request he even handed over Lukara to the German garrison at Ruhengeri.[113] But when brought face to face with the full implications of their pro-Hutu sympathies the White Fathers drew back; they represented an institution whose historical experience had made it suspicious of revolution, and this was a rebellion legitimated by 'paganism'. When their own Christians headed a revolutionary movement in the 1950s they were to react differently.[114] The day after Loupias' assassin was brought in Gudovius set out from Kigali with sixty *askari*, thirty police and almost three thousand Tutsi.[115] The Fathers ordered their flocks not to co-operate with rebels and gave the Germans valuable information about the disposition of the Twa.[116] At Nyundo they confiscated large numbers of spears, since the Germans had made it plain that they would attack any Christians suspected of complicity.[117]

On 13 April the Germans broke the rebellion, leaving Ndungutse presumed dead in a morass of slaughter and pillage.[118] The German troops were only the vanguard of the Banyanduga who swept through Bumbogo, Kibali and Buhoma, burning and looting.[119] Behind the Mausers the mwami carried out a traditional raid, and to imperial punitive measures was added sub-imperial repression. The scores of women captured and sent back as concubines to nobles of the court became the subject of futile protest by the White Fathers.[120] The wave of Banyanduga receded in the dry season of 1912, leaving behind an assortment of Tutsi like prickly fish in tidal pools. Important nobles returned to Nyanza, leaving garagu to fight for control of their new fiefs.[121] Many Hutu who had previously been free of nobles' exactions, or who had lived under compliant chiefs, now fell within the orbit of unscrupulous *parvenus* who tried to take over as many hills as possible.[122] Lukara's grisly public execution was attended by a large contingent from Rwaza and Nyundo.[123] Basebya followed him to the grave in May 1912, shot on sight by the Germans.[124]

Tutsi central authority had again been upheld against regionalism; the missionaries emerged from the bloodbath smelling like roses. 'Not one of our Christians suffered,' crowed a Father. 'This has been noted everywhere, and our influence has grown correspondingly.'[125] It had taken eight years to bring the northern stations into line with government policy, and the rewards were immediate. For the first time since the White Fathers' arrival in Rwanda the Tutsi nobility attended a church service in strength; there were twelve chiefs present at the benediction of Rwaza church, including a nephew of the king, Nshozamihigo's, son, Nyirimbilima. The church had risen on the ashes of northern Hutu hopes; the last bricks were drying in the mission kilns as the final raids died away. Gudovius returned his gun to its holster on 16 May, dismissed his Tutsi cohorts, and joined Monsignor Hirth in the solemn blessing of the fine new building. The blessing fell as much on the policy and perseverance of Leon Classe.

Yet Classe, that most ardent of Tutsiphiles, had been shaken by the repression and the strength of northern resistance, and was warning his superiors: 'It seems inevitable that the Tutsi with their . . . rank obstinacy and disdain for Europeans, their jealous concern to avoid all education, will in fact be displaced by educated Hutu.'[126] The annual report for 1911-12 emerged clearly Hutu in sympathy. 'The Banyarwanda are tired of the tyrannical yoke which the Tutsi have imposed on them for centuries . . . Not a sod of earth, not one tree, not a handful of grass can they call their own . . . The Europeans are here; some powerful but pitiless, others compassionate but too weak for their liking.'[127] All the contradictions in Catholic thought and action remained, perhaps intensified rather than diminished, after the suppression of Ndungutse.

The White Fathers dutifully spread the news of Ndungutse's death.[128] Dr Kandt, on his return, warmed to them and acted as their spokesman at court. 'I know that there was not a single Christian in Mulera found at Ndungutse's camp,' he told the mwami. 'Not a single Christian bore him gifts.'[129] Once more the northern Fathers were powerful patrons. Nyundo and Rwaza thrived.[130] The Zaza missionaries, on their best behaviour and avoiding conflict, suffered heavy losses as Hutu Christians left for Bukoba, but the *rapprochement* with the Tutsi continued at Save and Kabgayi, and numbers increased.[131] Only at Rulindo, where the Hutu were feeling the presence of newly arrived Tutsi, was a certain distrust remarked. 'The Hutu are turning away, and why? Quite simply because their hopes have been disappointed. And this dates from the attempt at revolution which almost dethroned Musinga and kicked out the Tutsi, but failed following the intervention of the European authorities against the pretender.'[132] Mission success now depended on pleasing the Germans, the Tutsi and the Hutu, in that order.

Yet the north was not completely subdued. Kibali and Bushiru under their *abahinza* remained disturbed. At Rubengera there was already a new Protestant station, and at Murunda, south of Nyundo, a new White Fathers' post.[133] Kandt, who more than ever valued the missions as agents of pacification, was pressing the king for a third Catholic station in Bushiru. Musinga's throne had been saved by German might, Kandt's language did nothing to conceal the brutal fact. "They have received permission from the Emperor Wilhelm to build anywhere in the land . . . Now I hear that you the Sultan refuse to allow this building. You want people to think that you have the honour of being Emperor Wilhelm. But you have not.'[134] A week later Kandt upbraided Monsignor Hirth for having built a school in Bukonja without permission;[135] both the king and the White Fathers were to bow before the reality of imperial power.

Yet Kandt was ready for progressive reforms,[136] furthering what the White Fathers liked to call 'une évolution d'esprit', perhaps even realising their cherished dream of a new Charlemagne.[137] A special training school for chiefs was no new project for Kandt, but now the Fathers gave it serious consideration, spurred on by Governor Schnee's threat of an invasion of Swahili-speaking teachers, graduates of Tanga training school,[138] which, according to Christian sources, was a hotbed of Islam.[139]

Government service and towns proved to be the milieux most favourable to Islam.[140] In Rwanda Kandt had opened the floodgates to large numbers of Muslim traders and was pressing on with the construction of townships at Kigali and Kisenyi, where there were to be Government schools. Christian fears that they were witnessing a deliberate attempt to propagate Islam through trade, schools and the ranks of the police and *akidas* were illfounded;[141] Governor Schnee was almost as anxious as they about Muslim teaching among his government's agents and the spread of Muslim brotherhoods.[142] Catholic and Protestant anxieties were shared by the court; the king's sporadic forays into the alphabet had been greatly stimulated by the prospect of spending half a year in Muslim Kigali under Kandt's supervision. It seems likely that the court knew of the impact of Mohammedan agents in Buganda, Burundi and western Tanganyika, for the Arab slaver Rumaliza had been carefully excluded in the nineteenth century. 'We are not like Muslims,' soothed Kandt, 'who insult the chiefs, calling them *mshenzi*.'[143] And indeed Hirth was soon to ban Christians from using this word to describe a pagan.[144] Kandt's new school at Kigali had the surprising effect of doubling Nyanza school's pupils.[145] Musinga even requested a Catholic school for his nephew Nyimbirilima at Ruhengeri, perilously close to the German camp; similarly Mibirisi mission received an appeal for Catholic teachers when the new government school was opened close by.[146]

Now that good Tutsi pupils were plainly destined for government service the mwami tried to control them by *ubuhake* arrangements; he gave cows to the clever ones and part of a hill to Wilhelmi Mbonyan-gabo, now his secretary accredited to him by the Residence,[147] the court's first political appointment of a Christian.[148] After Kandt introduced an experimental class of Government chiefs in 1911, each with his field for the production of the royal *ikoro*, the king appointed two more Christians to large hills and gave them several hundred Hutu. Kandt's reform of the *ikoro* system[149] provided Musinga with a new style of *ibikingi* or fief to grant, but for the Resident the new chiefs were the forerunners of a more streamlined system of tax collection.

Both Tutsi and Christian missionaries were struggling to come to terms with increased commerce. As new markets were opened and the old grew in importance the Tutsi first opposed them and then tried to tax them. Slowly they were drawn into the Muslim-dominated trading network; Rwabusisi, Rwidegembya's brother, began paying for cloth and goods by loaning traders his *ubuletwa* labourers to carry skins to Bukoba.[150] The Lutherans opened their own shops where goods were exchanged for skins and furs.[151] The mwami himself finally asked the White Fathers to build him a shop in Nyanza.[152] At Zaza, troublesome as ever, the station most affected by rumours and by the trade through Gisaka, the Fathers gave money to selected Christians to start up in competition with Indians and Muslims.[153] Trade and porterage kept attendance at catechism low;[154] the mwami made a handsome profit from the increase in commerce, but the missionaries could only deplore developments that limited their success.

Although the northern stations, restored to their role of patrons, prospered and were almost envied by their southern colleagues, the rift that had grown up among the Rwanda missionaries was not healed. In March 1913 Hirth informed the priests that he was to be replaced by Classe, and went into Retreat.[155] In an attempt to ensure uniform implementation of his policies Monsignor Classe transferred Father Schumacher to Nyundo, where he was shocked to find ' . . . Our brigands of catechists in the out-stations have formed brigand catechumens of whom not a single one could be baptised.'[156] Whilst Father Schumacher inspected the bruises his predecessor, Huntzinger, had given, Monsignor Hirth sat in the confessional;[157] Father Huntzinger himself, now at Save, gaily shot the goats of catechumens who missed their lessons,[158] and Classe released a broadside that had been in preparation for the last two years. He urged his priests to bow to the government's wishes, for, sensing some pro-Hutu feeling among the clergy,

. . . the government turns to the Protestants, who set themselves up as German masters and wish above all else, as they never cease writing, to reach the Tutsi . . . The government therefore reproaches us with, at least, working to form an anti-government party; if it were true we would be working against ourselves, against God by whom we have been sent, and so forming an anti-Catholic party; . . . it is our duty to convert the chiefs. [159]

The impulse for change came from without rather than within. 'Error will soon establish its schools everywhere,'[160] forecast Classe.

'Error' had indeed six stations by 1914.[161] Its schools were few but well equipped, and taught to a higher standard. Rubengera was soon to be staffed by Tanga graduates and become a Normal school.[162] Yet though the Catholics referred enviously to Lutheranism as the 'religion of the government', and worried whenever a Tutsi chief strayed their way, in reality the Protestants were having little success. Their better schooling was making them no short-term gains; they were, it seems, too closely identified with the Germans, the much feared *ibisimba*.[163] Hanging in Lutheran classrooms were portraits of Dr Kandt and the Kaiser; pupils learned the geography of Europe and were given talks on German greatness, victories and virtues.[164] If it is true that Rwandans preferred what de Lacger called 'catholicisme français' to 'christianisme allemand,'[165] it was largely because they saw the German missionaries as the agents of imperial government at a time when imperial over-rule was making itself felt.

In Malawi and Zambia, where Protestant competition was intense, rambling networks of chapel schools and prayer-houses, out-stations and catechists were flung around the missions; in Rwanda there were rarely Christians beyond a three-hour radius of a station.[166] After 1912, when the Catholics began to take Protestant expansion seriously, the pattern changed, but only slowly: the Germans insisted that out-stations have a European in residence, and few chiefs accepted a catechist on their hill without a struggle.[167] The only sure way of placing a catechist was as a chief's garagu, a position which obviously limited his freedom of action. As the Catholic counter-attack began, and out-stations and catechists were placed on distant hills, a new wave of opposition to the mission was encountered.[168] For the first time territorial conflicts typical of other countries arose between Lutherans and White Fathers.[169]

The Catholics' ability to respond to the double challenge of Protestantism and Islam was greatly limited in the short term by Monsignor Hirth's preoccupation with seminary education. A couple of straw-thatched sheds with wooden benches grandly styled Nyaruhengeri Minor Seminary were opened in 1912;[170] the seventeen pupils learned Swahili, Latin and German, with prizes for the best German-speakers awarded by the Resident.[171] A year later they moved to Kabgayi, and were joined by Rwandan students recalled from Rubyia, to form the nucleus of a major seminary.[172] The Rubyia students could speak good Latin, and sometimes had difficulty containing themselves when old European priests used expressions which had 'nothing in common with the language of Cicero'.[173] Even in the heart of Rwanda there was little liberty, and visits from parents and relatives were strictly supervised.[174]

With so much energy expended on the seminarians there was little left for the laity except Hirth's old stand-by, pious reading. Before the beginning of the First World War there were almost 13,000 baptised Hutu, but a lower percentage than in former years were attending mass,[175] and few seemed interested in reading. Classe carefully mixed political and missiological arguments to make his prescription of more education palatable. 'Education is a necessary and indispensable weapon . . . If on the pretext that it is difficult we neglect to assure our catechumens and Christians of its benefits we are putting ourselves in a position of inferiority in relation to the Protestants and the government . . .'[176] This renewed emphasis on education was in fact the corollary to his moment of insight after the Ndungutse rising; should the Tutsi fail to form an elite acceptable to the Germans he intended to have an alternative Christian elite at hand, perhaps Hutu, ready to become government chiefs.[177]

In the second week of August 1914 news began to spread that the *badatchi* were fighting the other colonial powers. German 'civilisation' scarcely reached as far as Rwanda; it petered out, like the famous railway line to Kagera, somewhere near Tabora. Roupies were still not common currency, though the Fathers had begun to give workers their wages in coin, so that they could pay their one-roupie head tax,[178] collected for the first time in June 1914.[179] A few ambitious Christians had turned to crops, such as tobacco and cotton, destined for the external market, but the rich agricultural north was hardly touched by the colonial economy.[180] Imperial rule meant Kandt and his assistants, balancing their weakening of Musinga's authority by the strengthening of their own *askari*. Although the tax chiefs were Kandt's own innovation, he did not hesitate to by-pass the court, and by 1914 was asking the Fathers to send all 'Christian' cases direct to him at Kigali;[181] perhaps even the Germans were secretly doubting their ability to change the proud Tutsi into malleable associates of German rule. Although the Europeans had supported the Rwandan State, extended it in the face of northern resistance and maintained the king's ascendancy over the nobles, they had eroded the mwami's power by substituting Kigali for Nyanza as the administrative capital, and German *askari* for Tutsi *ngabo* as the prime agents of State control; Indirect Rule, it seems, by 1914 was on the point of giving way to Direct Rule. The war's effect on the bicephalous Rwandan State was to raise the value of stability and hence of the ruling class; Musinga's co-operation was essential to the German war effort and the court regained its old importance.

By the beginning of the First World War the White Fathers had still not resolved the dilemma of a Hutu Church in a Tutsi State. As they were training Hutu priests the Germans were shoring up Musinga's shaky authority in the provinces and crushing the Muhumusa-Ndungutse rebellion. The backwoods of Rwanda were just beginning to experience the impact of the colonial capitalist economy;

although the nobles remained unconverted, the court had begun to come to terms with the new, educated Hutu Christians. As the first few assumed positions of authority in the State and the court's weakness in the north was startlingly demonstrated, even Father Classe's faith in the Tutsi began to waver.

German authority was now undisputed; the missionaries were obliged to tow the line; yet the imperial regime was soon to give way before the Belgians. The assimilation of the Hutu Christians heralded a more profound change, the later movement of the Tutsi into the Church, an event which would confirm Classe's faith in the nobility and spell the end of the flourishing Hutu Church. The war was to put the clock back and set king, colonial authority and mission on a path of conflict already once trodden by the Kaiser's agents.

NOTES

1 Save diary, 2 April 1910. Loupias' death was the beginning of a demytholo-gisation of the Fathers. People no longer asked questions like, 'Were missionaries born with beards?' or, when new Fathers arrived, 'Did a return to Europe rejuvenate a man?' In 1912 Rwakabibi attacked a priest with a spear in an attempt to kill him; see Zaza diary, 10 January 1912.

2 Rwaza diary, 2 November 1910; de Lacger, *Ruanda*, 44. Ruhanga arrived at the mission asking whether he should obey the king's instructions and present Lukara with five cows.

3 Rwaza diary, 27 December 1910; Wintgens to Delmas, 19 December 1910, 27 December 1910, WFAR. Wintgens' tears dried quickly: two weeks later his troops killed sixty-five people to avenge the death of a single *askari*, who turned out to have been a rapist; Louis, *Ruanda-Urundi*, 179 n. 1.

4 'Mir stehen gegen Lukarra keine zuvälessigen Leute zur Verfugung.' Falkenstien to Delmas, 8 October 1910, WFAR; Louis, *Ruanda-Urundi*, 178.

5 Wintgens to Delmas, 29, 31 December 1910, WFAR; the Christians had formed a warrior band in defence of the mission.

6 The Fathers, unaware of the reasons why the food was being collected, supported their men. Rwaza diary, 27 December 1910.

7 Wintgens was very annoyed: 'One has heard it announced on more than one occasion that these are the Mission's men, *Missionsleute*, and need obey no one else.' Wintgens to Delmas, 19 December and 27 December 1910, WFAR.

8 During the Basebya campaign a Tutsi chief, R̃uhigirakurinda, had con-fiscated four cows from a Hutu, Rubandahe, who refused to join his *ngabo*. Schumacher's conclusion that the man was being persecuted seems wrong. 'According to the evidence of the witnesses and the man himself, Rubandahe is getting instruction for the very first month. One might suppose that the man went to the mission when the dispute arose so as to take advantage of the mission's help.' Kandt to Classe, 3 January 1911, No. 1356/(German ref.), CO. Extracts of this letter appear to have been sent to Governor Rechenberg in Kandt to government, 3 January 1911, RU III, I/D/33, quoted by Louis, *Ruanda-Urundi*, 180 n. 5.

9 The letter was shown to Governor Schnee on his official visit to Rwanda in March 1911. Schumacher, a headstrong and intelligent priest, later commissioned by Pius XI to study the forest Twa, marched off to confront Schnee himself and was rebuked with the words 'How dare you write to the Resident in such a fashion?' Kabgayi diary, 22 March 1911.

10 Schumacher claimed that Ruhigirakurinda had bribed Kandt's interpreters with two cows, and so the Resident had heard a highly doctored Swahili version of the case. The mission's dispute with Ruhigirakurinda was of long standing; in Kabgayi diary, 13 January 1907, he was reported as moving away from the mission, after accusing a Hutu of bewitching his wife.

11 Kandt to Classe, 3 January 1911; Kabgayi diary, 4 January 1911.

12 Kandt to Classe, 3 January 1911. This statement makes Indirect Rule sound like simple pragmatism, but Professor Hans Meyer, a traveller through Rwanda, noted that officials practised almost a cult of the Tutsi; the richness of the court culture, the splendid *ntore*, the height and dignity of the nobles, all conspired to confirm the Hamitic hypothesis; the Tutsi were seen as a *naturally* superior race among blacks. Classe to Livinhac, 25 November 1912, No. 095319, WFAR; *cf* Baumann, O., *Durch Massailand zur Nilquelle*, Berlin, 1894, 224, for another traveller's equally sceptical view of Tutsi rule.

13 Classe, L., 'Relations avec les Batussi dans la mission du Ruanda', MS, handwritten, undated (*c*. 1912), part of which appears in Classe to confrères, 17 March 1913. This is one of the most interesting pieces of evidence for Classe's social thinking, as these are his private thoughts and notes.

14 Kandt to Classe, 3 January 1911.

15 Classe, 'Relations', 37.

16 Kandt to Classe, 3 January 1911.

17 Classe, 'Relations', 24.

18 Page 176 of Cardinal Lavigerie's *Recueil des instructions* gives the formula for dealing with 'A violent society subdivided into a multitude of tribes living in a patriarchal State'.

19 A renewed concern for Tutsi rights was certainly shown by the Fathers in the second half of 1911. For example, Father Delmas conveyed to the Ruhengeri Resident Tutsi complaints about a ban on cattle movement in an area affected by cattle pest. Ignored, he got Brother Eigenbenster, a German, to write. See Delmas to Resident, 23 August 1911, P.1736, film No. 1846, AA.

20 See chapter one, p. 16.

21 Des Forges, *Rwanda under Musiinga*, 147-52.

22 The Fathers concentrated on the rights of army chiefs because Dr Kandt conceded that *abanyabutaka* had no further rights over land purchased by missionaries. See Zaza diary, 4 April 1911.

23 Zaza diary, 28 November 1908.

24 Zaza diary, 23 April 1911.

25 The reply is stuck in the Zaza diary, 22-6 April 1911.

26 Zaza diary, 15 May 1911.

27 Kabgayi diary, 24 March 1906. Delays over cutting trees were the occasion for the first acrimonious dispute with the Lutherans. See Roehl to Father Superior, Kabgayi, 7 March 1911, CO.

28 Classe, 'Relations', 67-8.

29 Zaza diary, 25 September 1912.

30 A remark quoted in Classe, 'Relations', 12.

31 *Rapports annuels*, 1910-11, 411; de Lacger, *Ruanda*, 403.

32 Delmas to Indrumm, 10 January 1912, CO.

33 *Rapports annuels*, 1910-11. 410.

34 Nothomb, *Church History*, 23.

35 *Grands Lacs*, 1950, 34, 41.

36 Kabgayi diary, 6 June 1909, 4 January 1911; 'En somme, ces maîtres servent plus les intérêts du roi que les nôtres'. See Classe, 'Relations', 31.

37 Kabgayi diary, 10 May 1909.

38 *Rapports annuels*, 1910-11, 411-12; Classe, L., 'Nos relations avec les Batutsi', *Missions d'Afrique*, 1912, 88-9; Save diary, 29 March 1911.

39 Kabgayi diary, 4 January 1911.

40 *Rapports annuels*, 1910-11, 409. With thirty-five priests as well as thousands of adherents, the Church had to be placated. Presents were offered by chiefs, such as Kahuma at Zaza, as payment for leaving certain families alone; Zaza diary, 22 April 1911. Classe, in 'Relations', 52, notes that mission employees demanded bribes from chiefs before taking them into the presence of the Father Superior. Rich Hutu paid catechists not to teach their favourite children. Save diary, 17 October 1907; Classe, 'Relations'. 47. The root of such resistance was the fear that no children would honour a head of *umuryango* when he died if they were all Christian; see Arnoux, *Les Pères Blancs*, 120-1.

41 Kabgayi diary, 10, 18, 20, 21 July 1911. Oppostion to the demands of catechists now came as much from the Hutu as from ruling class.

42 Kandt, annual report for 1910, AA.

43 Kabgayi diary, 21 July 1911. Relations between Catholics and Protestants in Rwanda remained more friendly than between Benedictines and the Berlin Missionary Society in Tanganyika; see Grundler to Manley, 5, 12 December 1912, for a major conflict; G3.A8/02, CMS, London. Some accusations were made — see Kabgayi diary, 28 June 1911; Roehl to Classe, 31 May 1911, CO — but the Fathers were soon helping the Lutherans out by providing them with school Bibles. See Johanssen to Classe, 23 October 1911, CO.

44 Kabgayi diary, 21 July 1911.

45 Cyitatire, Nshozamihigo, and Sharangabo were all Nyiginya and wanted to protect their fiefs against the Ega. From 1906 to 1908 Cyitatire was forced to reside at court to keep him away from the sensitive Save region. See *Chroniques Trimestrielles*, No. 155, November 1908, 872.

46 Classe, 'Relations', 26-30; Mulera report, 1929; Bourgeois, 'Rapport de sortie de charge', Shangugu, 1934, Derscheid papers; Mecklenburg, *Ins Innerste Afrika*, 102-6.

47 Kabgayi diary, 1 February 1909. The fiefs were distributed in Mfumbiro, Mulera, Buganza and Marangara.

48 Zaza diary, 15 November 1909.

49 Kabgayi diary, 16 October 1911. "Il n'y a pas de grande famille qui n'ait plusieurs se ses membres tués par le roi. Cela n'empêche pas les autres de lui faire la cour quand même." See *Chroniques Trimestrielles*, No. 152, August 1908, 657.

50 Musinga to Father Superior, Kabgayi, 1 July 1909, WFAR; *Rapports annuels*, 1908-9; Dufays, *Pagès*, 45.

51 *Rapports annuels*, 1909-10, 317.

52 Classe, 'Nos relations avec les Batutsi', 86; *Rapports annuels*, 1910-11, 388.

53 For example: 'Un de nos voisins Bitangampunzi et son fils chrétien, Antoni, faisaient autrefois à nos néophytes de Sangaza une opposition plus ou moins sourde. Mais la Providence voulut qu-un revers de fortune ou de politique amenât Bitangampunzi et ses deux fils à la capitale, où le roi les fit exécuter'. See *Rapports annuels*, 1909-10, 314. The more educated the missionary generally the less such remnants of 'folk religion' were manifest.

54 The Fathers were aware, for instance, that many flocked to receive baptism hoping for protection from dysentery. Arnoux, *Les Pères Blancs*, 125.

55 Kandt, annual report for 1910, AA.

56 See Kabgayi diary, 22 January 1908.

57 Kandt to Musinga, 23 October 1912, CO, 'Na tena unajua kama wakristu watu wako namna wanyaruanda wanafuata(jo) Lyangombe' — Kandt's brand of Swahili.

58 Arnoux, *Les Pères Blancs*, 143-4.

59 Zaza diary, 14 October 1909.

60 Some even saw Palm Sunday as a Christian form of *Kubandwa* (the sacrifices of the Mandwa cult). See Kabgayi diary, 18 May 1909.

61 Arnoux, *Les Pères Blancs*, 143-4.

62 It could be compared in this to the Emandwa cult of Nkore. See Karugire, S. R., *A History of the Kingdom of Nkore in Western Uganda to 1896*, London, 1971, 84.

63 Louis, *Ruanda-Urundi*, 169-71.

64 Classe to Livinhac, 26 December 1910, No. 095223, WFAR.

65 Von Stuemer to Father Superior, Rwaza, 21 September 1909, WFAR, describes how well the new Kigali market is doing; for prices see Rwaza diary, 9 September 1908; Kabgayi diary, 18 July 1909; *Chroniques Trimestrielles*, No. 14, 7 March 1908, 186; Louis, *Ruanda-Urundi*, 169.

66 Tutsi were not often willing to release cows for sale but the temptation for those Hutu with alternative sources of protection could be overwhelming. Kabgayi diary, 28 November 1909.

67 *Ibid.*, 23 October 1909. This was drastic 'price control'; at Rwaza in September 1908 bride price ran from six to ten goats or a bull plus one to four goats, or a cow in calf. See Rwaza diary, 9 September 1908.

68 It seems unlikely that the higher prices were the result of shortage of Christian brides, even though there were three boys for every girl in school; the children of a mixed marriage belonged to the father's lineage and would therefore presumably be Christian. Vidal, 'Économie de la société féodale', 55, 68, gives examples of relatively stable tax rates and values in pre-colonial Rwanda, e.g. 300 kilos of beans bought a bull; 'taxes' of beans and sorghum were measured in baskets and varied between 4-8 per cent of a lineage's harvest.

69 Brickmakers were paid about one roupie per hundred bricks, teachers about a roupie for four days' teaching, pupils approximately three metres of cloth for a term's garden work.

70 Rev. Père Roussez, 'Carte de visite', 9-17 February 1913, CR.

71 *Rapports annuels*, 1907-08, 161.

72 *Ibid.*, 1911-12, 400; Kabgayi diary, 5 March 1910.
73 Every one was aware of the impact of trade. Musinga began by banning his subjects from visiting Bujumbura market; see Save diary, 9 December 1903. He then tried to control trade and reward his chiefs with imported goods; see Kabgayi diary, 20 March 1907. 'Le petit commerce pour les marchands arabes, indiens et autres . . . semblent pour beaucoup le salut'; Classe to Livinhac, 28 April 1911, No. 095226, WFAR. The Hutu had seen the possibilities.
74 Zaza diary, 13 April 1909, 30 June 1910, 10 December 1913.
75 Kandt to Governor, 1 June 1912, annual report for 1911, AA.
76 Nyundo diary, 1 April 1911.
77 *Chroniques Trimestrielles*, No. 147, March 1908, 234. 'Esprit frondeur' was a common expression, as independence was not a Catholic virtue.
78 Martin Chanock's 'The political economy of independent agriculture in Colonial Malawi: the Great War to the Great Depression', *Malawi Journal of Social Sciences*, vol. I, 1972, 113-29, discusses political thinking among a comparable group of skilled farmers working a rich soil.
79 Ssebalijja, Y., 'Memories of Rukiga and other places', in *A History of Kigezi*, 181-3.
80 Nyundo diary, 29 September 1911.
81 Ssebalijja, *Memories of Rukiga*, 182-3.
82 Hopkins, *The Nyabingi Cult*, 268-73.
83 Nyundo diary, 2 April 1911; Mibirisi diary, 2 July 1916.
84 *Ibid.*; Freedman, 'Ritual and history', 171-4.
85 Denoon, *A History of Kigezi*, 213-16.
86 Rwaza diary, 11 June 1911; Louis, *Ruanda-Urundi*, 153-5.
87 The clan head, Minane, was chased by the Tutsi Lwangeyo for a time; see Rwaza diary, 7 September 1911.
88 Nyundo diary, 12 November 1911.
89 Denoon, *A History of Kigezi*, 214.
90 Rwaza diary, November 1911.
91 Kandt to Father Superior, Rwaza, 7 November 1911, WFAR.
92 *Rapports annuels*, 1911-12, 411; Louis, *Ruanda-Urundi*, 154.
93 The Fathers were to some degree sympathetic to the northerners. Fathers Dufays and Barthélemy knew the Twa well and consulted them; see Dufays, *Pages*, 58-62; Mecklenberg, *Ins Innerste Afrika*, 221; Nyundo diary, 29 August 1911.
94 Nyundo diary, 2 February 1912.
95 Water was almost universally perceived as the 'ground substance' of spiritual force, and technology was usually seen as spiritual power over matter, so the bullets-to-water theme essentially asserted that a sourcerer could reduce a spiritual power to its 'ground state', i.e. reverse the processes that 'empowered' Europeans. Kingship was the pre-colonial expression of maximal power, technology that of the colonial period; Ndungutse was felt to control both.
96 Baptismal records, Rwaza mission; *Rapports annuels*, 1911-12.
97 Rwaza diary, January, 6 February 1912. It is interesting to compare this relationship with that given the Europeans by the Mwari cult medium in the Matopo hills of Rhodesia — 'sister's sons', an inferior but friendly joking

relationship; see Daneel, J. M., *The God of the Matopo Hills*, The Hague, 1970, 84.

98 Rwaza diary, 6 February 1912.

99 *Ibid.*, 20 February 1912.

100 Rwaza diary, 8, 10-11 February 1912.

101 De Lacger, *Ruanda*, 224-6. Before the sacrifice the mwami and his Queen Mother had lain for a day and a night tied to a bed under which were images of themselves. Next morning the images were' placed in a basket tied to the neck of the sacrificial animal. In the second half of June there were even more elaborate rituals, *igihatsi*, for deceased relatives of the mwami and annual ceremonies for the veneration of Nyiginya lineage spirits.

102 The movement was much more of a regional revolt than a simple clash between Hutu and Tutsi. See Chrétien, J. P., 'La révolte de Ndungutse (1912): forces traditionelles et pression coloniale au Rwanda allemand', *Revue française d'histoire d'outre-mer*, LIX, 1972, 645-80.

103 Rwaza diary, 15 February 1912; Louis, *Ruanda-Urundi*, 155-6.

104 Rwaza diary, 21 February 1912; Des Forges, *Rwanda under Musiinga*, 185-91, provides an excellent account of the antecedents to the Germans' later raid.

105 Louis, *Ruanda-Urundi*, 155, 155 n. 7.

106 Rwaza diary, 26 February 1912.

107 This was Banzi, who unlike Shoja, *umuhinza* of Bugarura, seems to have been in revolt without any connection with Ndungutse; see *Rapports annuels*, 1911-12, 410-12; Dufays, F., and de Moor, V., *Au Kinyaga. Les enchainées*, Paris, 1938, 39.

108 Gudovius to Fathers Superior of mission stations, 8 April 1912, Dossier 112 *bis*, WFAR; Rwaza diary, 22 February 1912; *Rapports annuels*, 1911-12, 413.

109 This was Mwijuka; see Dufays and de Moor, *Au Kinyaga*, 39.

110 See Dufays, *Pages*, 75, a passage which reflects the excitement and sympathy of some missionaries. 'Their rights over their property, their fields and their cattle have been done away with for the benefit of a prince thrust aside at birth by his father and reared by a Muhutu on the Burundi border.'

111 Gudovius to Fathers Superior, 8 April, 1912.

112 For the mwami's identification with the land see chapter one. The region of Rulindo mission, Bumbogo and Buliza, was solidly pro-Ndungutse; see Classe to Livinhac, 25 November 1912, No. 095319, WFAR; Louis, *Ruanda-Urundi*, 155.

113 *Rapports annuels*, 1911-12, 412.

114 See chapter ten p. 249. In the Mexican revolt of 1927 the rebels known as 'Christeros' were blessed by their bishops.

115 Louis, *Ruanda-Urundi*, 156.

116 Dufays to Gudovius, April 1912, Dossier 203A, IRU 6692, AA; Rwaza diary, 24 February 1912.

117 Lecoindre, 'Raisons qui ont nui'; Indrumm to Delmas, 9 December 1911, CO, makes it plain that the Germans would certainly have attacked Christians suspected of complicity.

118 Louis, *Ruanda-Urundi*, 156-7.

119 Rwaza diary, 17 April, 3 May 1912; *Rapports annuels*, 1911-12, 413.

120 The Fathers were shocked at the indiscriminate killing of women and children. See *Rapports annuels*, 1911-12, 412; Louis, *Ruanda-Urundi*, 157. Government agents collaborated to the full in raids, accepting women as *abaja* and sharing the booty. Ndungutse's wife, Nyiraguguze, was in the clutches of an interpreter for the Germans when the Fathers offered to buy her back. Gudovius informed them that the woman was a prisoner of war and could not be returned. Gudovius to Father Superior, Rwaza, 26 June 1912, WFAR.

121 Classe to Livinhac, 26 November 1912. 'Après avoir construits leurs residences, ces chefs, voyant les soldats se retirer, ont cru prudent de ne pas pousser plus loin l'occupation de leurs nouveaux fiefs.'

122 Buisson to Indrumm, 30 August 1912. 'Musinga has promised the hill to Sekaganga. Rwabugiri does not want to believe this, and roundly refuses to inform himself at court. He states further that he will drive a spear through any Muhutu who dares to submit to Sekaganga. The consequence of this is great confusion amongst the Bahutu.' Indrumm to Father Superior, Rulindo, 2 September 1912, No. 856/I, P.1736, film No. 168, AA.

123 Lukara slipped his chains and stabbed a guard at the last moment; he was shot down and his dead body hanged in public. *Rapports annuels*, 1911-12, 412.

124 *Ibid.*, 413; Rwabusisi disguised himself as a trader in order to approach the Twa camp and tricked Basebya into surrender.

125 *Ibid.*, 414.

126 Classe to Livinhac, 25 November 1912.

127 *Rapports annuels*, 1911-12, 428. The writer was right at the heart of the Christian dilemma of the Cross or the Sword.

128 Schumacher to Kandt, 20 November 1912, CO.

129 Kandt to Musinga, 23 October 1912, trans, Swahili, CO.

130 Classe to Livinhac, 25 November 1912.

131 Zaza diary, 10 January 1912; *Rapports annuels*, 1911-12, 400, 418.

132 *Rapports annuels*, 1912-13, 445.

133 Roehl to Resident, 30 January 1912, 198A, IRU 6692, AA; *Rapports annuels*, 1912-13, 453.

134 Kandt to Musinga, 23 October 1912.

135 Kandt to Hirth, 30 October 1912, CO.

136 He returned from a Germany, where the Social Democrats were victorious in the Reichstag.

137 Schumacher, P., 'Échos du Kivu', *Missions d'Afrique*, 1913, 95.

138 During Schnee's 1911 visit it was proposed that teachers be placed with all leading chiefs. Classe to Livinhac, 28 April 1911, No. 095226, WFAR.

139 There were three post-primary institutions in German East Africa, at Dar es Salaam, Bagamoyo and Tanga; between 1912 and 1913 they turned out 192 Africans ready for government service. According to Bishop Spreiter, Christians attending these schools were beaten and ridiculed until they converted to Islam. Spreiter to government, 31 July 1912, P.1736, Film No. 168, AA.

140 The missions were very conscious of the increasing vitality of Islam.

The insistence of the Zentrum (Catholic) Party in 1900 on the formation of a Muslim-free elite through Christian schools was the beginning of the issue in East Africa. It remained in the mission and colonial Press; a 'Mohammedan Seminar' was founded in Potsdam in 1909, three years after the Congress of 'Islamic Missions' in Cairo. In 1912 a systematic survey of the spread of Islam in German East Africa was carried out, and the 'threat' was fully heeded by the government. Personal communication from Lorne Larson on the documentation on the survey in the Potsdam archives; Becker, C. H., 'Ist der Islam eine Gefahr fur unserre Kolonien?', *Koloniale Rundschau*, 1909, 266-93; Mirbt, *Mission und Kolonialpolitik*, 203-19; Austen, *Northwest Tanzania*, 69-70.

141 Roehl to Classe, 27 May 1912, CO; an appeal for a common front against the Muslim menace.

142 Confidential circular No. 1024, 28 September 1912, P.1736, AA. See also Classe to Hirth, 1 November 1913, after Schnee's second visit; 'Le gouvernement a décidément ordre de favoriser un peu les Missions pour arrêter du même coup les progrès de l'Islam', Dossier 111, WFAR. Iliffe, *Tanganyika under German Rule*, 199, refers to the German Colonial Society's warning that the spread of Islam was 'a political and a cultural threat'.

143 Kandt to Musinga, 23 October 1912.

144 The term *utazi ibya mungu*, 'not knowing the things of God', was used instead; see Classe to confrères, 10 December 1913, Dossier 112, WFAR.

145 There were an average of forty-three *ntore* at the school, mostly the offspring of unions between chiefs and their Hutu *abaja*, and so ineligible for the highest chieftaincies. Kandt to government, 1 June 1912, annual report for 1911, AA; *Rapports annuels*, 1911-12, 423.

146 Rwaza diary, 19 April; *Rapports annuels*, 1912-13, 437. The wave of government school building in 1912-13 also prompted a second Catholic school to begin on Save; see Musinga to Lecoindre, 27 May 1914, CO; Mibirisi diary, 10, 25 March 1914.

147 Kandt to Governor, 1 June 1912, annual report for 1911, AA.

148 *Rapports annuels*, 1912-13, 423.

149 *Ibid.*, 423; Louis, *Ruanda-Urundi*, 152.

150 Classe to Simon, 21 October 1933, CO (a pre-war reference).

151 Mibirisi diary, 20 February 1914; Johansson, *Kleine Anfänge*, 249-52. The shop was funded by the German Society for Missionary Commerce and was meant to combat the spread of Islam through trade.

152 It was completed by a Brother in 1914; Save diary, 7 March 1914.

153 Gifts of twenty to thirty roupies; see Zaza diary, 29 May 1914. A rumour of 1913 was prompted by the sale of coffee seeds to Christians; it was said the Fathers were going to take all the land for coffee plantations. Zaza diary, January 1913.

154 *Rapports annuels*, 1912-13, 412, 424.

155 Hirth to confrères, 17 March 1913, WFAR.

156 Schumacher to Livinhac, 7 December 1913; Schumacher to Roussez, 15 March 1914, Dossier 112, WFAR.

157 From 8 a.m. until 11.45 a.m., and from 1 p.m. until 5 p.m. daily.

158 During his visitation of 1915 Father Roussez banned the taking out of guns from the stations; 'Carte de visite', 10-20 April 1915, Save mission, CR.

Fathers Pouget and Dufays went back to Europe in the reshuffle, and Rambura was not properly staffed.

159 Classe to confrères, 17 April 1913. He was backed up by Father Roussez; see 'Carte de visite', 27 March-7 April 1913, for Kabgayi, CR.

160 Classe, 'Carte de visite', 1912, CR.

161 At Rukira, Kigali, Kirinda and Dzinga. Contracts signed for Rubengera on 15 July and for Remera on 14 September 1912. P.1735, film No. 167, AA.

162 Kandt, annual report for 1912, P.1728, film No. 166, AA; Classe to confrères, 'Diffusion de Petit Catéchisme et de la lecture', 20 May 1914, CR.

163 Meaning 'ferocious beasts'. Brutal raids in Burundi had gained them the same title, *vikoko*. See *Chroniques Trimestrielles*, No. 113, February 1905, 101 The Fathers were shocked enough by Wintgens' 1910 raids to report them publicly; see *Rapports annuels*, 1910-11, 397.

164 Ryckmans to Franck, 2 December 1922, M.639, AA.

165 De Lacger, *Ruanda*, 406.

166 Classe to Livinhac, 30 January 1910, No. 095218, WFAR.

167 Classe to Livinhac, 25 November 1912; *Rapports annuels*, 1912-13, 413-14.

168 Kabgayi diary, 7 March 1914; Nyundo diary, May 1914; *Rapports annuels*, 1911-12, 396-97, 414.

169 Schumacher to Kandt, 17 July 1913, CO.

170 *Rapports annuels*, 1912-13, 415, 453.

171 The German lessons made the school eligible for a small government subsidy.

172 Classe to Livinhac, 31 July 1918, Dossier 111, WFAR; de Lacger, *Ruanda*, 441; Schäppi, *Die katholische missionsschule*, 156, 162.

173 *Grands Lacs*, 1952, 11-13.

174 Classe to Father Superior, Kabgayi, 9 February 1914, CR

175 *Rapports annuels*, 1913-14.

176 Classe to confrères, 20 May 1914, CR.

177 Classe to Livinhac, 25 November 1912.

178 Classe to confrères, 5 April 1914.

179 There had been earlier minor taxes, e.g. on guns the White Fathers paid two roupies for each per annum. From 1910 a hut tax was levied in Kisenyi, Kigali and Shangi; see Louis, *Ruanda-Urundi*, 159 n. 6.

180 Zaza diary, 7 December 1913, 21 May 1914; *Rapports annuels*, 1912-13, 428-429.

181 Classe to confrères, 20 March 1914, CR.

SIX

*The crisis
of the First
World War*

The Germans could not hope to hold back an Allied army of Belgians and British without the support of the Tutsi;[1] that support was readily forthcoming. Musinga sent them two letters at the end of 1914 pledging his loyalty and troops;[2] he had heard that the Belgians confiscated many cattle and was hoping to regain lost territory in Mfumbiro, where his half-brother Nyindo, with German support, was in revolt against the British.[3]

Kiga dissidence too was directed against the British, as Nyabingi priestesses recruited followers and mobilised the Twa.[4] A certain Bichubirenga, 'The clouds pass by' — perhaps a reference to the transitory nature of European rule — appeared at Rwaza in December 1915. His emblem was a white sheep, and he was said to be the precursor of a new king who would appear when the Europeans were driven out. Less threatening to the Banyanduga than the Nyabingi priests, perhaps because his choice of symbols placed him in the Lyangombe tradition, he quickly gained Tutsi support.[5] Unlike Ndungutse he won Nyindo's friendship and tried to persuade the Germans at Ruhengeri to back him. The White Fathers were his main target; Christians at Rwaza were told not to go to the mission and were asked to send him their children to 'vomit up the poison given them by the whites'.[6] His followers believed that he had gone to the Germans' camp to bewitch their guns, but later he was rumoured to be going to bewitch the Belgians. Bichubirenga's tactics succeeded: Captain Wintgens gave him cows and a promise of support.[7] In January 1916, with two thousand followers, he attacked a Belgian post and was only driven off with minor casualties.[8] The whole affair underlined the White Fathers' unpopularity among the independent Hutu clans as a result of Classe's pro-Tutsi policies.[9]

As an international missionary society the White Fathers, in theory, owed allegiance to no single country. Father Classe appealed for charity and put the Fathers on their honour to be loyal to the German administration. No 'exterior sign' of opposition to the Germans was to be expressed, under no circumstances were missionaries to voice their personal opinions in front of Rwandans.[10] The Church was to freeze into an attitude of neutrality. An illusion, of course; only a few months earlier Father Lecoindre, one of Classe's few confidants, had been complaining about the country's 'Germanic' atmosphere; the war had come just as the missionaries were feeling the pressure of imperial rule and were regretting their former independence.[11]

The war's immediate effects on the mission were material. Money ran out at Bukoba and Mombassa,[12] all supplies were cut off from September 1914, and the price of cloth rose steeply.[13] There were five German Brothers eligible for conscription,[14] and in April 1915 French clergy were asked to move back towards Tanganyika; two months later, after 'Italy's betrayal', two Italian White Fathers were arrested and sent to Tabora for internment.[15] Lack of supplies and restrictions on the movements of priests had begun to disrupt the mission's work by the end of 1915; mission employees could not longer be paid.[16] As the Allied counter-offensive gained ground the mission stations took on a strategic importance. While the Lutherans loyally turned their posts into supply depots, the Catholics negotiated for concessions before following the same course.[17] The Italian priests were allowed to return, and all missionaries permitted to continue with normal work.[18]

Missionary activity had virtually ceased by the beginning of 1916. Save mission was ringed with huts, and the local Tutsi had mobilised the peasants for porterage to Rubengera.[19] Belgian patrols intermittently visited Nyundo, and in February 1916 the staff were evacuated to make way for German troops.[20] Mibirisi was turned into an ammunition dump, and the Fathers were sent to buy beans from the Hutu to provision Ruhengeri camp.[21] The Rwaza schoolmaster was dismissed for lack of money, very few catechumens came to the mission,[22] and since the Fathers could no longer pay the pupils the schools emptied. Many catechists continued working on half or no pay, but their numbers fell from 119 to eighty-two.[23]

The Hutu bore the brunt of the missions' poverty; those on the Rwaza property were no longer required to bring *inzoga*, banana beer, to the missionaries but had to provide labour two days a week for twelve weeks of the year.[24] The Tutsi behaved as usual, using their new importance to force an extra day's *ubuletwa* each week on the Nduga and Marangara Hutu, to increase crop dues, and introduce *ubuletwa* for the first time in the northern provinces. Throughout 1915 the Banyanduga tightened their hold over the regions they had colonised in the wake of the Ndungutse punitive raids. The Hutu also suffered from fresh German demands; hundreds were mobilised to provision the troops, and several chiefs began asking an additional tax of one hoe on the harvests as compensation.[25] Despite a second round of German tax collection in the dry season of 1915 the Hutu were still expected to do forced labour at Kisenyi and Kigali.[26] Movements like that of Bichubirenga directed rising Hutu discontent against the Allied forces. The idea that the war was going to bring European rule to an end was widespread and caused panic in some regions.[27]

As the Belgians, strengthened by British carriers and arms, began to prepare for their major offensive in February 1916 German relations with the White Fathers deteriorated.[28] The priests did their best to avoid becoming embroiled in the conflict, even going to the point of hiding from patrols,[29] but with the Germans heavily outnumbered it was inevitable that the Lutherans responded more readily to demands for supplies than the French White Fathers.[30] Christian joy was easily interpreted as a smirk of Allied triumph.

After two major breakthroughs on the western front Wintgens began a retreat to Nyanza.[31] The Fathers were now under considerable pressure to withdraw with the German columns;[32] both French and German missionaries wrote to Classe asking him to insist that they remain at their stations.[33] The last German communication with Monsignor Hirth gave permission, but suggested that the priests should appear in full missionary attire.[34] Thus when Father Lecoindre came out to greet the Belgian troops advancing on Kigali the Catholics were in the happy position of being the only Christian missionaries and the only Europeans in Rwanda.[35]

'Liberation' was a word that came easily to the missionaries' lips after the Belgians' arrival.[36] That June at Save's Corpus Christi procession they watched 'the dais officially escorted by Christian soldiers under arms and followed by European officers'.[37] The Tutsi as the Kaiser's infantry had been defeated and disgraced;[38] Musinga wrote humbly to explain that the Germans had assured him the Kaiser would win and to ask the Belgians not to 'spoil' his country.[39] The retreating Germans left the Catholic stations, some quite literally, in ruins,[40] but the Fathers, who in Gisaka had been forced to stand back whilst the Tutsi pillaged the Hutu,[41] were now in triumphant possession. From being the reluctant agents of Germano-Tutsi imperialism they became again the principal actors in the colonial drama.[42]

When the Belgian commanders came to consider problems beyond the immediate needs of their advancing columns they could turn to no one but the White Fathers for advice. Their experience in the Congo had little relevance to the problems of ruling a kingdom like Rwanda. Armed with only the vague notion of supporting the local chiefs, all but the most militantly atheist of administrators welcomed the priests' services,[43] and the priests, freed from the authority of the intransigent Kandt, who had forced them to take their place within the framework of

Tutsi hegemony, once more became active Hutu sympathisers. Even Classe, when called upon to outline Rwanda's political organisation, stressed regional variations, political complexity and the limitations of Tutsi sub-imperialism.[44]

The Vicar General's notes began, 'Le régime politique du Rwanda peut être assez exactement assimilé au régime féodale du Moyen-age,'[45] but there followed a far from superficial analysis of Rwandan society. He mentioned how the Tutsi had recently tightened their grip on the country, the levying of arbitrary taxes in Nduga and Marangara, and the northward spread of *ubuletwa*. But Classe still believed that without the Tutsi nobility, even though they were refractory to Christianity, and a strong monarchy, there would be anarchy. He solved the problem to his own satisfaction by distinguishing between a 'good' pro-European faction at court consisting of the Nyiginya, and a 'bad' group of reactionary Ega traditionalists. He was, however, realist enough to admit that Nyiginya support amounted only to enlightened self-interest, and pointed out that the syphilitic old Nshozamihigo's main concern was to protect his fiefs from the Ega. Similarly, while he spoke of the Tutsi's contempt for the Europeans he wanted to differentiate between the 'real' Tutsi and the rabble of petty land-owners who exploited Marangara.[46] On Nshozamihigo's death in December 1916 Classe wrote an unsolicited letter explaining the Nyiginya's pro-European role, emphasising again the power of the Ega Queen Mother, Musinga's weakness, and the questionable legitimacy of the court.[47] It was altogether a remarkably poor reference for the Rwandan ruling class from the champion of Tutsi authority.

The mwami was not acting in a way to attract support; in September 1916 after two *askari* were killed near Save, Musinga contemptuously handed over five innocent men to bear the Belgians' punishment and poisoned the only one who tried to protest.[48] As the main body of the Belgian army moved south away from the capital rumours of revolt grew. Captain Stevens, left in Nyanza with no information save that fed him by Musinga, the Father Superior of Save, and Classe's anti-Ega letters, arrested Rwidegembya, the Ega leader, and imprisoned him in Kisenyi.[49] He later realised his mistake.

Musinga had been long dreaming of dividing up his wealth. Rwidegembya was a victim of plots . . . hatched by Musinga and his satellite Kashamura and a little, as well, of the prejudices of certain missionaries, who represented him as the custodian of the cultural practices and the diabolical arts of the Mtuzi race.[50]

Musinga must have been surprised at the gullibility of the new Europeans, and went on to depose the Zaza army chief, who had made compromises with the missionaries, for a son of the Nyiginya Kanuma.[51] The Ega counter-attack was swift. Rwidegembya's son, Rwagataraka, let the Belgians know of contacts between the mwami

and the Germans. Musinga's secretary was suddenly given an important fief — to pay for his silence, it was assumed — but the Belgians
did uncover a cache of forty rifles at court, and believed the stories of
German messengers and secret letters despite lack of proof. By March
1917 the Belgians were listening to any wild rumour put about by
their ambitious interpreters.[52] Insecure, newly arrived, and lacking a
clearly formulated policy, the Belgians repeated German mistakes in
Burundi and reacted precipitously. 'In short, since we have occupied
his territory,' wrote Captain Stevens, 'Musinga has been simply
laughing up his sleeve at us and scorning the orders we give him. He
intends to play the leading part in the politics of his country and to
relegate the European authorities to the background.'[53]

On 25 March 1917 the new Commissaire Royal at Kigoma
authorised Musinga's arrest.[54] In the most astonishing reversal of
fortune Nyanza had ever known Musinga was bundled off to jail at
gun point.[55] The Tutsi nobility were brushed aside. The Belgians
judged cases at Zaza without reference to the chiefs, and the church
filled again with Hutu who had perhaps got wind of the upheavals.[56]
Minor provincial chiefs avoided paying *ikoro* that year.[57] But the
decapitated Rwandan polity proved ungovernable, and Musinga,
utterly humiliated, had to be released.[58] The passage from conquest to
administration had been telescoped to a single year, but the price in
bitterness and chaos was very high.

The political havoc caused by the Belgian commanders was trivial
compared with the 'natural' disasters that struck the peasantry
throughout 1917. The north-eastern shores of Lake Kivu had been a
key defence line, and the Germans had fought some skirmishes in
Bugoyi;[59] their retreating army pursued a scorched earth policy,
cutting down banana groves which afforded cover and food to the
enemy.[60] Troops had lived off the land since October 1914, and in
1916, when they should have been planting, hundreds of peasants fled
the battle zone. Finally the famine, *Rumanura*, came.[61]

When the Fathers returned to a battered Nyundo mission, pillaged
and overgrown by bush, the roadside was littered with corpses. A
region that had once been the garden of Rwanda was now scrub in
which wild animals and scrawny cattle roamed freely.[62] The missionaries had to decide how to distribute their meagre supplies. They
opted to feed only those fortunate peasants who had got seed into the
ground and so could hope for a sorghum harvest in May 1917. Those
who had escaped the European manhunt for porters by staying
hidden, and who therefore had planted nothing in December 1916,
were reluctantly abandoned to famine and death. Two hundred were
fed daily at Nyundo; one priest sold everything he owned down to his
chalice to buy food in Kisenyi.[63]

With Bugoyi, the granary of Rwanda, depleted, other crop failures compounded the misery. Severe infestations of pests destroyed the main potato and bean crop around Kabgayi, and 276 out of 650 Christians moved either south to Save, or to Kansi, in search of food.[64] The aftermath of mulnutrition was epidemics of smallpox, cerebro-spinal meningitis and dysentery. The missionaries vaccinated thousands, but many died before the end of July 1918.[65] Among the Nyundo Christians, families with privileged access to mission supplies, the death toll rose from about three hundred in March 1917 to over two thousand in July 1918, 50 per cent of the parish's neophytes. In the same period Murunda mission lost 20 per cent of its flock.[66] The Fathers put the overall mortality of the Hutu in some parts of Mulera at 75 per cent; the massive mobilisation of the European war had literally decimated the population of Rwanda.[67]

When Major Declerck arrived in Kigali to take up his position as first Belgian Resident in Rwanda in 1917 brigands preyed on travellers along all major tracks in the north, and rich families had begun to buy domestic slaves in exchange for hoarded surplus food. His troops were without supplies or porters.[68] The missionaries had alerted the Belgians to the severity of the famine when they returned to Nyundo, but no action had been taken for two months.[69] It was only Declerck's arrival at the end of May that brought action, a paltry five thousand francs to buy food for the starving.[70]

Military considerations still dominated the administration. Kisenyi was the western sector's headquarters, and Kigali the eastern.[71] This meant that the Kigali administrator found himself sending troops to support Tutsi chiefs as far apart as Mulera and Bugesera,[72] whilst the administrator at Kisenyi considered getting rid of the Tutsi and redistri-buting their land to the Hutu.[73] As the Belgians misunderstood the political geography, changed posts, and moved from one mistake to the next, the different northern factions took the opportunity to regain ground lost to them during German days.

The Rashi, led by one of Lukara's sons,[74] waived a vendetta with the Sigi clan and began attacking mission employees, alleging that the Fathers had been willing accomplices of Belgian and British pillaging of cattle. In November a Rwaza Christian was murdered.[75] Unchecked by strong rule, the conflict with the Banyanduga grew more intense. The Father Superior of Rambura mission became the figurehead of a movement to chase out the Tutsi, a prophet *malgré soi*, while in Bugarura the Rwaza Christians put up so much resistance that the Banyanduga complained that it was impossible to govern.[76] It was not for want of trying. 'I saw in March of this year,' wrote a Father at Rwaza, 'two Batutsi . . . ask for tax from the same Hutu.'[77] Several of Lwakadigi's[78] residences had been pillaged by the Belgians, but he slunk out of hiding, returned to Nyundo and was soon in control again. The starving Bugoyi Hutu were in no position to resist, and his cattle trampled freely through their few banana groves and sweet-potato patches.[79] The Bukamba and Mulera Hutu were better off because the Belgians had accepted the local clan heads as rightful chiefs,[80] and so they could seek support against southern intrusion. But such innovations created more resentment at Nyanza; in the Commissaire's view 'some territorial administrators favour policies which would tend to divide the kingdom and emancipate the subject race; this cannot help re-establish the confidence of the king and the court'.[81]

Major Declerck was highly thought of by the White Fathers, who esteemed mainly those who heeded their advice and council. He was willing to reunite the kingdom if the Tutsi agreed to reform and uniformity. The Belgians had been paying their porters four francs — about one roupie — for the journey to their lines, and the Tutsi were confiscating it as compensation for the time they had spent away. Declerck got the mwami to sign a decree condemning anyone taking legitimately earned money from a Hutu to up to thirty days imprisonment. He announced before the assembled nobles in Kigali that henceforth no peasant was to be prevented from attending a mission. Finally Hutu were to have five days out of seven free for their own work, and were asked to double their cultivated plots against future famine.[82]

The Fathers, if not the originators, were to be the watchdogs of reform. 'Since it is beyond doubt that the Batutsi will not obey the above decisions,' Declerck told Monsignor Hirth, 'and since it is indispensable to better the peasants' present situation, I would be grateful if the Reverend Fathers would inform the authorities of any abuses that are committed.'[83] The courts, however, were controlled by the Tutsi, so the peasants had no real redress. The Fathers could broadcast the directives as instructed but could not enforce them without falling back into the morass of patron client relationships.

By August 1917 Declerck regretted having delivered himself and his assistants into the welcoming arms of the White Fathers, and issued a directive debarring missionaries from litigation. He had been inspired by another protracted legal battle which, like the Schumacher-Ruhigirakurinda affair, involved an aggrieved Hutu, an ambitious Tutsi, a priestly 'champion of the poor' and a frustrated administrator.[84] For the north he prescribed a ban on blood feuds and the poison ordeal. Tutsi taking Hutu crops were to pay double their value in compensation and were not to allow their cattle to graze in peasants' gardens. Rewooding, ten eucalyptus plants per man, distributed through the missions, was to begin.[85] The reforms were quite impossible to implement.[86]

The Vicar General was still very good at colonial officials; he and Declerck exchanged sugary compliments. For five thousand francs of famine relief, after a year in which death by starvation and epidemic disease had not been allowed to deflect the Belgians from pursuing the Germans, Classe praised Belgian humanitarianism, and told Declerck that for the first time in seventeen years the country had a government which took the natives' interests to heart.[87] The Resident, perhaps thinking of the White Sisters working in Kigali and Goma military hospitals,[88] referred in his reply to 'la Grande et belle oeuvre civilizatrice que vous dirigez avec un dévouement et un désintéressement au dessus de tout éloge'.[89]

But whilst Declerck and Classe played at clipping the Tutsi's wings, telling themselves how much more sensible they were than the Germans, their dependence on Musinga and the court, and on the Banyanduga of the north, was rapidly becoming evident. By the end of 1917 the pressures that had influenced the Germans were being felt by the Belgians, and were pushing them towards support for the Tutsi.[90] A missionary reported sadly that the Kisenyi magistrate had sounded like Kandt, who had once said, 'The Batutsi would not trick me. What would be the point of it? I always decide in their favour, and they know it.'[91] Declerck had reached the same conclusion. 'From one moment to the next,' he wrote to Classe, 'I expect to hear Kandt, that great friend of the Batutzi. That magistrate is out of his stable.'[92]

Whilst the Belgians struggled to understand Tutsi politics the Fathers used their new relations with the administration to extend mission property in central Rwanda and open new out-stations; the Mibirisi Fathers obtained their first footholds in Busozo.[93] Musinga, cowed by his imprisonment, sent Kabare's son to Save school, where the insatiable Father Huntzinger presided; fourteen leading chiefs around Save had been given presents as an inducement to send their children to classes, and a girls' school was planned.[94]

At Save and Kabgayi on Christmas Day 1917 the first leading Tutsi nobles were baptised. They had been allowed to take the medal without the usual sixteen months of postulancy.[95] Amongst them were Semutwa, the son of Cyitatire, and so a Nyiginya prince, and the parents of Charles Naho, a noble controlling some six hundred Hutu. Naho's brother, Chachana, had been on the brink of baptism in 1916 when the mwami sent him to Bukoba with forty porters for the Belgians. Only three men returned, but they said that Chachana, who knew the catechism perfectly, had died a Christian and had baptised all his companions.[96]

The shock of Belgian rule and the missionaries' success among the Tutsi stimulated the court to further diplomatic activity. Already the mwami had made moves to increase his support in the provinces by handing the Gesera several hills that had belonged to the Tsobe Tutsi, a group badly weakened by the Ndungutse rising.[97] Now the mwami encouraged certain Tutsi to educate their children, and the classes for chiefs' sons flourished, though there was still a ban on religious instruction at Nyanza school.[98] The Queen Mother began making public appearances, and the king's four children were paraded in European dress for the edification of visitors. Musinga himself even drank with Europeans on important occasions and offered them cigarettes.[99] The Catholics were filled with naive delight; now that the Queen Mother, in their view the *éminence grise* and 'lynchpin of all Native Administration', was out in the open, they believed, 'the most serious obstacle to our joint penetration has disappeared'.[100]

Many Christians came forward to offer their services as secretaries and interpreters to the Belgians; 'Guten Willens' went into Belgian service under the name of Guillaume in June 1917.[101] Barthélemy Semigabo from Save became a secretary, while Simeon Ndazilamiye and Aloys Kangusa were posted to the Akanyaru river to help supply caravans. The task of provisioning the extended Belgian lines was an opportunity for corruption, and even the ordinary mission catechists became more belligerent in competition with the Belgians' agents;[102] Paul Lungiragugu demanded eight cows from Cyitatire to keep his second son out of Save school; one catechist, Simeon Lutare, was renowned for his bold and fearless treatment of the Tutsi.[103] The monarchy was badly shaken in the first year of Belgian rule and the value of clientship ties was enhanced; stations like Save were once more burgeoning theocracies.

Apart from their immense political power, the missionaries also threatened Musinga's ritual authority; with his powers of life and death over his subjects gone and his *ngabo* defeated, he had little else left. Why, he wanted to know, could Father Huntzinger speak ill of his religion when Tutsi laughing at Christians' medals were liable to imprisonment? 'I do not want their Mongu, why do they want mine?'[104] Missionaries like Huntzinger did not trouble to conceal their pleasure. Save Christians did not make the hazardous journey to Tanganyika; that was left to the Tutsi chiefs and their pagan Hutu.[105] Huntzinger allegedly whispered to the mwami, 'Now you see how big you are . . . I am the chief. The German days are over. You are not the big man you used to be.'[106] The German period became for Musinga a golden age when 'everybody respected me' and when the Fathers kept their word 'that they had only come for Mongu . . . and would not meddle in my affairs'. Then even 'the Fathers feared me', and when the people became Christians they still 'listened to me and saw in me their chief'. But 'The day the Belgians came the Fathers changed completely . . . although they say that a man should not lie they tricked the whites of Bulamatari'.[107]

But those Fathers who thought that Belgian rule had given them a mandate to behave like the Jesuits in Peru[108] were mistaken. Already the Belgians were realising that they needed the Tutsi, and the mwami, after verbal attacks on the Fathers, struck at their followers. The first casualty was Guillaume, dismissed by the Belgians and replaced by a favourite of the Queen Mother.[109] Several of the Christians working for the Belgians were imprisoned for refusing to return cattle they had extorted; Simeon Ndazilamiye was attacked by four *askari* when he tried to hold back part of an illicit herd.[110] Nyirimbilima, on the verge of taking Instruction from the Rwaza Fathers, was dispossessed at the Queen Mother's insistence, but the Belgians were unwilling to uphold this decision.[111] Similarly, when one of the mwami's appointees near Save tried to confiscate Christians' plots, the Belgian listened to Huntzinger and put in one of his men as sub-chief.[112] It was at this point that he fatally overreached himself.

Paulo Lungiragugu, one of Huntzinger's favourites, tried to extort cows from a Tutsi in return for exemption from porterage. When the Tutsi complained Huntzinger replied that if Paulo saved him from Bulamatari then Paulo must be paid, and promptly forced the sub-chief to accept a Christian on land containing a water source. The Christian occupant killed some of the Tutsi's goats when they tried to drink, and the man finally made a public protest.[113]

A letter from Major Declerck arrived at Save mission in April 1918, speaking of the intolerable situation created by Huntzinger, 'a State within a State',[114] and summoning him to Nyanza, where Declerck tried to effect a reconciliation with the mwami. Huntzinger protested that Musinga had been set up as judge, prosecutor and jury. The king questioned the Christian witnesses in Kinyarwanda, then addressed himself to the Belgians' interpreter in Swahili, who in turn translated into French for Declerck. The Belgians were outraged by what they heard. Father Huntzinger made a formal apology,[115] but it was too late. Musinga loathed him, Declerck needed to disengage himself from the Catholics, and Classe had been awaiting an opportunity to get rid of him since 1913.[116] A week later the last of the 'Brard school' was in Tanganyika.[117]

The fall of Huntzinger marked the close of two years of Catholic power and royal weakness. By May 1918 the old balance between mwami, colonial administrators and missionaries was more or less restored. On 11 May Musinga received full military honours and a message from King Albert;[118] in return he sent a telegram of greetings to the *Commissaire Royal* which was splashed across the Belgian papers.[119] Important chiefs around Save took their sons away from the mission school and sent them to Belgian classes at Nyanza; in retaliation the Fathers withdrew their teacher from the capital. At Zaza old Kanuma, always sensitive to changes in the political wind, began confiscating Christians' banana groves and denouncing them as rebels.[120]

Classe once more sent circulars warning the Fathers against involvement in local politics and criticising their tendency, 'no less fatal, of posing as chiefs'.[121] His views coincided with those of Lecoindre, who returned to the north, after war service in Europe, to find missionaries judging cases and catechists policing chiefs. 'There are many cate-chumens amongst the Hutu,' he wrote, 'who are of a "Bolshevik" mentality, and there we have it: all the revolutionaries in the country enrolled in the Catholic Church.'[122] The 'Bolshevik mentality' was not confined to the Hutu. Discontent was rife among the priests, who resented their frequent transfers from station to station[123] and were indignant when in February 1917 their 'average budget per missionary was fixed at about 0.5 francs a day'.[124] Whilst they went shirtless and were plunged in darkness after dusk, the shop at Kabgayi held a stock of shirts for the seminarians and the seminary had a supply of paraffin and lamps.[125] Classe complained to Algiers that he was being blamed for Hirth's policies.[126]

Classe was contending with the effects of the Belgians' early vacil-lations, which had nearly handed the north back to the Hutu and had also returned much influence to the northern Fathers Superior. It was useless for Lecoindre to advise against 'appointing superiors over the missionaries who are too democratic . . . Bolshevism and anarchy will be the result' or to advocate concentration of missionary endeavour on the Tutsi 'class';[127] such lessons, plainly drawn from the political and social turmoil in Europe, ignored the realities of northern Rwanda, which more than a Brard or a Huntzinger shaped the consciousness and practice of the northern missionaries. Father Oomen had been in the north only a short while when the new Kisenyi Resident came humbly to ask his advice.[128] Oomen's blushing reply demonstrated how quickly Nyundo turned a new arrival into an advocate of decentralised regionalism.

After having told him that I only permitted myself the liberty since this was his wish I attempted to demonstrate that to apply the system of Nduga to these provinces, so that the Mututsi become the absolute ruler of all the land and cattle, would destroy the country altogether . . . if the Mututsi can pillage at will it means they are dispossessing the real owners, denying the past history of Rwanda which the government seems to recognise in Bushiru.[129]

Oomen and others had become almost as rebellious as their parishioners; he recorded his reply to the Resident in the station diary for the Vicar General or the Father Visitor to see. Until the Belgians imposed a uniform policy with the ferocity of the Germans, Classe could not prevent priests assuming the roles of absent Tutsi and Belgians.[130]

In April 1917 the northern stations began organising Christian groups on the hills for mutual support during the famine. The Rwaza Fathers also introduced a tribunal to deal with court cases involving Christians and to prevent vendettas. Each hill was headed by a

Christian *mukuru* who led the group, *inama*; *bakuru* (pl.) introduced litigants to the tribunal held at the mission on Wednesdays. Although there was a panel of three Christian magistrates elected by the laity, and no outside representation, even pagan defendants came before the court. Anyone attempting to plead without his *mukuru*, or trying to contact a magistrate before the court sat, automatically had his case thrown out. The mission, of necessity, had substituted itself for the courts of the absent Tutsi and the hard-pressed Belgians. And since the manipulation of disputes between clans and families was the principal means, other than force, by which the Tutsi wormed their way into positions of power, this tended to block the expansion of the Banyanduga into the Rwaza area.[131]

The budding Rwaza theocracy met with few external checks.[132] The Tutsi were feuding amongst themselves. Throughout 1918 Bushako's son struggled with Lwakadigi's for the control of Bugoyi; Nyirimbilima, Nshozamihigo's son, under increasing pressure from Musinga and his mother, finally fled to British territory in November, and was replaced by one of the mwami's men.[133] The Hutu, weakened by famine and war, threw up several minor Nyabingi prophets.

In 1919 the Fathers had to be wooed; their stations were havens of law and order in the north, where the Banyanduga could not impose themselves without the help of the Belgians, and where on occasions the Belgians turned to the White Fathers for help.[134] The difficulties with rebellious Hutu were so great the Banyanduga talked of abandoning Mulera's good cattle land.[135] The *Commissaire Royal* had given Monsignor Hirth *carte blanche* to found new stations provided he avoided Rwabugiri's old residences;[136] the Catholics went ahead and opened Rwamagana mission by Lake Mohasi in Buganza, where the *nyambo*, the celebrated royal herd, was grazed.[137] Musinga could not fail to realise that his victory over Huntzinger was hollow; Kabgayi with its two seminaries now rivalled the court, 'The most frequented place in Marangara', the Belgians said. 'It is the place where natives from all parts of the region meet . . . anyone looking for someone goes first to Kabgayi, where they draw their information.'[138] More insidiously the trickle of young Tutsi into the catechumenate continued.[139]

Kabgayi might be a great centre, but it was in a poor state. During the famine the students had eaten mainly dried vegetables, and some were suffering from vitamin deficiency diseases like night blindness. The roof of the newly built minor seminary started to fall in, and the buildings were infested with ants; some felt that the Brothers' hearts had not been in their work.[140] Until the refectory was completed the seminarians ate their frugal meals, with meat only once a month, in the open air.[141] Since there were no French books until after the war was over, and teaching had switched from German to French within a month of the Belgians' arrival, most of the instruction in the minor seminary was oral. The theology students in the major seminary shared copies of Noldin and Tanquerey, their teachers' textbooks from another century.[142] They were supposed to reach the standards of their colleagues in Europe, but, as the two seminary teachers admitted, their approach was stale and antiquated, and there were simply not enough books.[143]

Monsignor Hirth made the seminary succeed. After two years of probation at a mission Donat Leberaho and Balthazar Gafuku were ordained at Kabgayi in October 1919 and began teaching in the minor seminary. Four pupils who had left the minor seminary were training as Brothers, *Bayozefiti*, whilst at Rwaza there were nine postulants for the *Benebikira* being taught by the White Sisters.[144] In June 1919 three more Hutu priests were ordained, Jovite Matabaro, Isidore Semigabo and Joseph Bugondo. The previous year Mama Maria Yohanna had taken her vows as a nun.[145] The ordination of the five priests made a great impact on central Rwanda; it was a tangible and startling emancipation of the Hutu to the ranks of the nobility.[146] Moreover it demonstrated to the Tutsi just how close a bond the missionaries were willing to form with the peasantry, and demanded from them with new urgency a positive response to the intruding religious system.

Musinga was embittered. He needed to counter the emancipated Hutu, and he saw that the new religion threatened his ritual position. The Tutsi must assimilate European learning to maintain their ground, but not from the 'books that made them the men of the Fathers'.[147] He wrote to the *Commissaire*, 'Bulamatari builds schools everywhere. I hope he will build schools here. The Germans did nothing while the Sultans of Buganda and Bukoba got education.' He was adamant that 'I do not want the Fathers' education for my children, they teach people to scorn the law of our fathers.'[148]

When Van den Eede took over as Resident from Declerck on 6 May 1919 Classe lost and Musinga gained a useful ally. Belgium was struggling for her share of the colonial cake at the Paris peace conference and mandates commission of the League of Nations, and Van den Eede would brook no interference from French, Dutch or German missionaries.[149] He was determined to have at least one showpiece in the chiefs' school at Nyanza, and was happy to please Musinga by sending pupils to the Belgian teacher there rather than to the Fathers at Kabgayi. Father Classe told the new Resident archly that he hoped 'it will soon be possible to arrive at the necessary liberty of conscience that formerly existed before the war'.[150] Van den Eede, with becoming Flemish bluntness, directed the Vicar General to send any complaints to the Belgian headquarters at Kigoma.[151] Belgium was beginning to show her anti-clerical face.

The court's opposition to the Fathers put the Nyiginya chiefs in an awkward position; the fate of Nyirimbilima must have been uppermost in their minds. Sharangabo, a brother of the king, who had stayed away from court from 1906 to 1912 to avoid the purges,[152] faced a number of difficult decisions when Rwamagana mission was opened up in the middle of his fiefs. Sharangabo sent three of his sons to the government school in Nyanza, while two others went to the Fathers' school for chiefs' sons at Rwamagana.[153] When Classe angrily pointed out to the Belgians that one was over sixteen and had the right to go to Rwamagana mission, the school of his choice, Sharangabo simply removed another from the mission and sent him to Nyanza, thus maintaining the ratio three for the king two for the Fathers — perhaps not a bad indication of the wavering nobles' views and certainly a way of maintaining an interest in both camps.[154]

When Musinga realised that important nobles were dividing their allegiance he began to concentrate power in his own hands. Classe detected a change after the 1919 ordinations, 'Musinga is becoming more autocratic, and the people's rights get less and less; the country has taken a real step backwards in the last few months.'[155] As Ntulo, Cyitatire, Kayondo and even Rwidegembya and Rwabusisi moved closer to the missionaries, Musinga began to deal directly with their sub-chiefs and garagu; at Kabgayi especially the situation grew very complex, as the Hutu no longer knew to whom they should refer.[156] The sudden release of the adventurer Lwakadigi, who had been held at court since June 1918 on the mwami's pleasure, and the appointment of his son over Bugoyi were signs of the times.[157]

On 30 May 1919 Rwanda was formally handed over to the Belgians. The administration had already been buffeted back on to the course charted by the Germans; Louis Franck, the Minister for the Colonies, decided on Indirect Rule because Rwanda's political organisation was 'strongly constructed and with authority on a firm foundation'.[158] The Belgians were to be the councillors and tutors at the elbow of the chiefs. The emphasis was on continuity, keeping the system intact rather than instituting potentially disruptive reforms.[159] Franck fell back upon the hallowed formulae of the colonial service. Only very gradual moves must be made to adapt Rwanda 'aux besoins de la colonisation et au progrès économique du pays';[160] thus the introduction of European planters was not ruled out, despite a resolution to 'respect indigenous institutions'. [161]

In 1920 Franck visited Rwanda, and 'did not hesitate to let us [the White Fathers] know that in his opinion the negroes need to be introduced to economic development alone',[162] which seems to have meant training in skills to fit the Hutu to perform their lowly duties in life. "*There should be no question of affecting the very foundation of the political institutions on the pretext of equality*; we find the Watuzis established . . . intelligent and capable; we will respect this situation,'[163] wrote Franck, who kept his socialism at home in Europe. Classe was disappointed — 'He seems to us in no way a partisan of elementary education for the people, for the bulk of the population' — though of course Classe had to admit that 'We ourselves want this education to preserve the Faith and piety of our Christians.'[164]

Most Fathers still saw literacy in an other-worldly context and would, like Franck, have seen the Brothers' technical training as preparing Hutu workers to staff the Tutsi State, but the first year of Belgian rule and the Banyanduga's oppression of the north had produced an upsurge of genuine social concern. In 1912 Classe had written, 'Our Christians need peace to develop; to avoid oppression we must make the chiefs favourable to us'.[165] By 1920 he was advocating substantial reform; 'the situation of the people must be improved and they should be given real rights over private property'.[166] Reversing roles in Rwanda, Franck became the conservative, responding favourably to Musinga's pleas to continue the ancestral cult at court,[167] whilst Classe and his confrères offered to spearhead a kind of bourgeois revolution against feudalism, without an indigenous bourgeoisie to back them.

The White Fathers were not offering to undermine feudalism without understanding what they were about, nor were they uniformly hostile to Rwandan social institutions;[168] it was only in the area of marriage that they had shown themselves determined to impose quite new patterns of behaviour.[169] Confronted with a virile if not virulent feudalism, based on a complex system of exchanges and relationships in which the unwary or the ignorant became hopelessly lost, they set about studying it. Fathers Arnoux, Hurel, Pagès and Schumacher prepared anthropological treatises with the speed of career academics, the rest wrote voluminously in station logs or prepared manuscripts for private circulation among the White Fathers. The result was often shrewd policies of adaptation.

For example, tactics towards the vendetta were informed by a full understanding of customary law. When a Christian was killed in fulfillment of vendetta obligations Classe advocated that the normal compensation of eight goats be paid to the offended *umuryango*. If a Christian performed the killing he was required in addition to do two weeks' work at the station for 'the moral damage incurred by the mission'.[170] Provided the man went to confession and fully repented his act, he could then return to full Church life. When two Christian *imiryango* were involved, the Father Superior was advised to handle the compensation himself to avoid making public the identity of the killer. The Fathers would, however, try to marry off the widow themselves in order to prevent her passing to the deceased's brother.[171]

The Liberal and Socialist Deputies in the Belgian Chamber[172] might come baying after the missionary fox in the Rwandan hen roost, but they were no more able than the White Fathers to harmonise the idea of slow transformation with respect for African institutions. However often the mwami was wheeled out in his plumes, surrounded by his *ntore*, to support the Liberal fiction that imperial rule left native political institutions intact, the destruction of Musinga's kingdom and its way of life was guaranteed the moment the idea of reform was born. The powers of self-deception of Belgian Deputies were admirably demonstrated when the whole of Gisaka was handed over to the British after a plebiscite in which over fifty nobles, several from Gisaka, had declared that they wished to be ruled by the Belgians.[173] The mwami protested formally to the British, but secretly believed the White Fathers were responsible; he now attributed all his troubles to their evil machinations.[174]

Although beset by critics, the mission remained disunited. Discontent among the missionaries finally focused on two main issues. Classe's authoritarianism and Hirth's missiology. A council of priests had met at Kabgayi to decide which of the seminarians should be allowed to become sub-deacons; eleven out of twelve Fathers had voted against Abbé Jovite Matabaro on the grounds of his low intellectual achievements. They were simply overruled.[175] Another seminarian, probably Isidore Semigabo, had spent six days paying court to the mwami for cows; the missionaries were scandalised when Monsignor Hirth pushed him through to the sub-diaconate.[176] 'The seminarians are spoilt,' reported the Regional Superior. 'Nothing is refused them.'[177] When several missionaries protested that they did not think it proper to ordain a man barely fourteen or fifteen years after he had been baptised, Monsignor Hirth not only brushed them aside but created the first all-African parish at Murunda, only loosely supervised from Nyundo.[178]

Some missionaries' sense of powerlessness in the face of high-handedness and obstinacy became allied with what amounted to a racial critique of such rapid development of an indigenous clergy; deep down they did not think Rwandans capable of it. Yet in front of them Murunda mission flourished; hundreds used to come to hear Abbé Donat Leberaho's sermons, and his emphasis on penance so stirred his listeners that they flocked to the confessional.[179] His way of speaking in flowing Kinyarwanda, circling round the main point of the sermon, and employing the rich proverbs of the country, naturally held the congregation more than the faltering phrases of new White Fathers. He became famous for his repeated use of the saying 'Imana iruta ingabo', God is greater than the *ngabo*.[180] The European clergy could find nothing to reproach him with except his superior ability to adapt the Westernised Christianity of the seminaries to his parish. While sub-deacons, and therefore subordinate, the Rwandan clergy had been well received in the stations, but as priests they were more threatening and not always welcomed at the mission table.[181] The Belgian administrators treated them to curt, offensive letters.[182]

When the first complaints against Father Classe reached Maison Carrée in 1918 Monsignor Hirth protected his lieutenant by saying that these were in substance earlier criticisms made against himself. Father Gorju, the Vicar General for the southern half of the Kivu vicariate, despite Hirth's persistent neglect of Burundi,[183] loyally defended Classe and represented him as the scapegoat for Hirth's incompetence.[184] But even within the hierarchical world of the White Fathers Classe could not for ever escape the consequences of the division of authority between himself and Hirth and the vicariate's drift into anarchy. 'The cause of peace demands that Father Classe disappears from Kivu,'[185] Livinhac gravely told Hirth, and in May 1920 the Vicar General was recalled to Europe.[186]

There followed a long silence on the part of Hirth which brought a panic-stricken letter from Livinhac reminding the bishop of his past triumphs and delicately enquiring whether he had resigned?[187] He had. In July Monsignor Hirth wrote to the Prefect of the Propaganda, relinquishing his office on the grounds of failing health and eyesight.[188] He lived on for many years and, for a partially blind man, conducted a surprisingly voluminous correspondence with his family.[189]

The Regional Superior's report on Rwanda was devastating, painting a picture of bush missionaries 'completely discouraged, annihilated',[190] whilst Classe and Hirth avoided accepting responsibility by referring and deferring to each other. 'The poor missionaries do not know which saint to invoke,' though some of the less helpless had taken to tampering with correspondence, whilst Classe, before their angry gaze, continued to hobnob with Belgian administrators. Classe's response to criticism was to try to force dissidents out of the country,[191] choosing to ignore the fact that declining morale had driven some priests to give up work: 'about ten . . . who would have been very good had they been given some support, are not doing a thing'.[192] Yet it was unlikely that a priest such as Léon Classe, with his talent for dealing with government officials, and his strong belief in ecclesiastical authority, should fall permanently from grace as the result of a movement from below. It would have been a denial of religious order. By November 1920 the Superior General felt obliged to inform the Rwanda missionaries that Classe's recall did not mean that he was in disgrace.[193]

The Gisaka issue now loomed large in colonial politics, and it was not long before Classe was moving in the salons of Antwerp and Brussels, seeming, like all born rulers, the indispensable man. With a five-page brief on why it was necessary to return Gisaka to Belgian Rwanda his fortunes began to rise,[194] and by April 1921 he was, at least in Livinhac's eyes, exonerated of responsibility for the disintegra-

Monsignor Classe in 1920.

tion of Kivu vicariate. The Superior General wrote the Rwanda Fathers a stiff letter, summoning the full force of three hundred years of Church history to demand their respectful submission to the Sacred Congregation of Propaganda's famous 1659 directives on mission practice.[195]

By September 1921 Classe was dining with the Minister for the Colonies in his capacity as an expert on Tutsi politics. Captain Philipps, the British Resident destined for Gisaka, had been invited to join the 'Dîner entièrement en maigre . . . assez symptomatique chez un libéral doctrinaire', as Classe privately commented,[196] in order to be persuaded to write Winston Churchill pressing for Gisaka's return to the Belgians.[197] Classe's remarks on the Franck menu had been provoked by the Minister's 'frankly hostile'[198] attitude to Catholicism and his unwillingness to recommend as a kind of *quid pro quo* subsidies for Catholic schools in which forty pro-Belgian missionaries were educating eight thousand children.[199]

Classe's removal had brought little change to Rwanda. Monsignor Hirth continued to overrule the rector of the seminary's decisions, and finally took over the job himself.[200] It was plain that a new Vicar Apostolic ought to be appointed as soon as possible and that the vicariate must be divided in order to give the Burundi mission a chance to develop. For Rwanda there was only one serious candidate — Léon Classe.

The Superior Provincial of the White Fathers in Belgium fully supported Classe[201] and wanted pressure put on the Vatican to ensure his success.[202] Ryckmans, the new Resident at Kigoma, also wanted Classe but felt it inadvisable to 'write in such a way as the Holy See might detect government interference in the appointment'.[203] Franck, less than enthusiastic on such issues, could not help but appreciate the value of a person such as Classe in situations of political delicacy; he therefore informed the Foreign Minister that he wished the Belgian ambassador at the Vatican to indicate Belgian preferences when Livinhac presented the *Terna* in Rome.[204] On 28 May 1922, two years after a missionary revolt had forced him out of the country, Classe was consecrated Vicar Apostolic to Rwanda,[205] whilst a year later Burundi became a separate vicariate.[206]

The First World War had brought to the surface the conflicts between the Mission as a religious organisation with a specific ideology and the varied secular orientations of the missionaries. The post-war crisis was not simply the product of differences of opinion about missiology; it exposed the missionaries in all their personal, social and national differences. It was the latter, exacerbated in the Rwandan context, that triggered the unusual confrontation between Vicar Apostolic, Rome and the bush missionaries.

During the early days of Belgian rule the Hutu Church had continued to grow in strength as the Tutsi were disgraced. The power vacuum after the war allowed full play to the centrifugal tendencies within both Church and State; regional autonomy meant more power to the Fathers Superior. Father Classe remained far from certain of his commitment to the Tutsi. But during this time the Tutsi moved from a cautious process of assimilation to an outright courting of the missionaries, now a powerful force in the country. The result was the beginning of a split in the nobility and a heightening of the tension between mwami and nobles. The swing in Belgian policy to full support for the court, and the return of Father Classe, by concentrating missionary efforts again on the conversion of the ruling class, drove in the wedge further between pagan king and wavering nobles.

NOTES

1 De Lacger, *Le Ruanda*, 449. The Germans had conducted a successful raid on Idjwi island in September 1914.

2 Musinga to Wintgens, 24 September, 9 October 1914, P.1734, film No. 165, AA.

3 Bisamunyu, E. N., 'Baganda agency, 1911-24', in *A History of Kigezi*, 207. Nyindo conducted a raid on Chahafi in January 1915.

4 Rwabihigi, D. Z., 'Chief Katuregye: the man and his times', in *A History of Kigezi*, 150-2; Hopkins, *The Nyabingi Cult*, 283-4. The Germans connived at these activities.

5 Both Ruhanda and Luzilampuhe supported him; see Rwaza diary, 3 December 1915, 6 February 1916; Bessel, M. J., 'Nyabingi', *Uganda Journal*, vol. VI, 1938-39, 82; Hopkins, *The Nyabingi Cult*, 287.

6 Rwaza diary, 9, 10 December 1915.

7 *Ibid.*, 12 February 1916.

8 Bessel, *Nyabingi*, 82.

9 The missionaries were, in this sense, back to their position in 1904 when their station was under attack; see chapter three.

10 Classe to confrères, 8, 9 August 1914, CR.

11 Lecoindre to Classe, 15 January 1914, Dossier 112, WFAR.

12 Classe to confrères, 9 August 1914, CR. Cheques were sent to Trier for cashing.

13 Classe to confrères, 2 September 1914, CR.

14 Wintgens to Klein, 24 October 1914; Wintgens to Resident, 27 September 1914, P.1734, film No. 165, AA.

15 Wintgens to Hirth, 8 April 1915, Dossier 112 *bis*, WFAR; Save diary, 29 April 1915; Rwaza diary, 8 June 1915; *Rapports annuels*, 1917-18, 282, 288.

16 Roussez, 'Carte de visite' for Kabgayi, 22 March-5 April 1915, CR; Classe to confrères, 12 August 1914, contains an order to share reserves between stations; Dossier 111, WFAR.

17 Personal communication from Monsieur Bernard Lugon, Department of History, University of Butare, Rwanda.

18 *Rapports annuels*, 1917-18 309.

19 Save diary, December 1915.

20 Nyundo diary, 5 June 1915, 6 January 1916, 20 March 1916; *Rapports annuels*, 1917-18, 295-6.

21 'Compte rendu des séances de Conseil', Rwaza, 17 January 1916, Rwaza mission loose papers in the possession of the Father Superior, Rwaza mission. The remaining northern station of Rambura, opened in Bushiru at Kandt's request, but never properly staffed by the White Fathers, was also an important supply centre and useful to the Germans. In a reshuffle undertaken by Classe in 1913 to improve relations in the vicariate, Father Pouget and Dufays had left Rambura and returned to Europe. As a result the mission was understaffed at the war, hence the hard bargaining over station facilities for concessions concerning personnel.

22 'Compte rendu des séances de Counseil', Rwaza, 14 February 1916.

23 Nothomb, *Church History*, 36.

24 Widows were expected to provide one day's work for the same period; see 'Compte rendu des séances de Conseil', Rwaza, 24 January 1916, Vicar General's instructions.

25 Zaza Diary, 17 June 1915, for the mobilisation of Kanuma's *ngabo* for service in Mulera; Classe, 28 August 1916, Derscheid papers. Buisson wrote most perceptively: 'Le gouvernment allemand, plus que jamais, devait favoriser l'élément noble: il avait besoin du Nyanza, des Batutsi. Devant le spectre d'une révolte possible à l'arrière, moins que jamais il était disposé à cèder aux Bahutus quoi que ce fût de "L'autorité intangible" des chefs.' See *Rapports annuels*, 1917-18, 284.

26 Nyundo diary, 13 August 1914, 1 April 1915; one roupie per head of *umuryango*.

27 *Rapports annuels*, 1917-18, 289, 305.

28 Louis, *Ruanda-Urundi*, 219.

29 Interview with Leon Rukeratabaro, Rwaza, June 1973. Fathers Delmas and Knoll seem to have been 'on the run' for some time, and, from *Rapports annuels*, 1917-18, 300, Father Knoll seems to have been avoiding his fellow countryman, Captain Wintgens.

30 'Devant les réclamations et les menaces nouvelles du gouvernement qui se plaint que des missionaires. . .' Classe to confrères, 24 March 1916, CR.

31 Mibirisi diary, 21, 26 April 1916. Mibirisi was shelled, and a German Brother killed defending it. Father Cunrath was made prisoner of war. Louis, *Ruanda-Urundi*, 220.

32 Deprimoz, Schumacher, Buisson, Delmas and Parmentier to Classe, 4 May 1916, CR.

33 Von Langenn to Hirth, 12 May 1916, CO.

34 Wintgens to Hirth, 7 May 1916, Dossier 112 *bis*, WFAR; Save diary, 21 May 1916; *Rapports annuels*, 1917-18, 257.

35 *Rapports annuels*, 1917-18, 251.

36 Except for the odd pro-German Dutch priest and the German Fathers, of course; see Save diary, 21 May 1916; *Rapports annuels*, 1917-18, 311.

37 Save diary, June 1916.

38 Nyundo was used against the British until his capture in 1916; see Rwaza diary, 23 May, 20 June 1916; Rwabihiga, *A History of Kigezi*, 151.

39 Musinga to Grand Seigneur des Belges, 20 May 1916, AE/11. 3287, No. 18422, AA.

40 Nyundo diary, 10, 11 May 1916. The station had been bombarded.

41 The Tutsi attacks fell on the Hutu Chaba clan in Gisaka; Musinga also kept Rwidegembya and Kayondo successfully in check. See Save diary, 20 February 1915; Rwaza diary, 12 June 1915; Zaza diary, 10 July, 24 December 1915, 4, 6, 7, 8, 15, 26 February 1916.

42 'The Belgian victory was really a Catholic and Latin victory.' De Lacger, *Ruanda*, 463.

43 In the Congo the Belgians had received welcome support from Catholic missionaries during the Congo reform movement. Slade, R., *English-speaking Missions in the Congo Independent State, 1878-1908*, Académie Royal des Sciences Colonials, Mémoire in 8°, vol. XVI, 1959, 255, 298-300; Morel, E. D., *History of the Congo Reform Movement*, ed. Louis, R., and Stengers, J., Oxford, 1968, 183.

44 He gave the example of Mbare hill, near Kabgayi. Nominally, he noted, it belonged to Nshozamihigo, but the chief had only four Hutu there. The mwami had put on to it Nyabugonde, Sebatwa and Sebakunda, three garagu into three separate *ibikingi*, i.e. garagu of one chief were commonly to be found on the hill of another.

45 Classe, 'L'Organisation politique'.

46 Another distinction he wanted to make was between the much disliked *abanyabutaka* and the *abatware*, the army chiefs, whom he described as 'plus aimés parce qu'ils assistent leurs gens dans leurs procès, leur font rentrer en possession de leurs biens'. Exactly the same distinction was to be made later by Abbé Kagame to justify the legitimacy of the old Tutsi Order before the Europeans destroyed the *ngabo* system. See chapter nine. The White Fathers

generally assumed that they knew more about the societies in which they worked than colonial administrators — they generally did — so to be asked was a great pleasure. Collignon had made the request for information on 28 July 1916; Collignon to Classe, 28 July 1916, CO.

47 Classe to Van den Eede, 6 December 1916. 'Peu en sûreté à cause du très grand pouvoir de la famille des "Bega" et de son hostilité, surtout de celle de Nyina Yuhi, la mère de Musinga, les fils de Lwabugiri, de tout temps, s'étaient rapprochés des Européens et leur étaient favorables tandis que les Bega avec leurs chefs Kabale (1912) et Rwidegembya son neveu, puis Rwidegembya avec Lwabusisi, son frère, Kayondo son cousin germain et Nyantabona, le fils de Kabale, leur demeuraient résolument opposés'. The distinction between the harried royal line and the 'wicked' Ega is not only overdrawn here but certainly overemphasises the pro-Europeanness of the Nyiginya. See also *Rapports annuels*, 1917-18, 248-249.

48 'Rapport mensuel: Corps d'occupation, Zone de l'Ouest', February 1917, No. 1828, AE/11 3287, AA.

49 Save diary, January 1917; Kabgayi diary, 19 December 1916; 'Rapport mensuel; Corps d'occupation, Zone de l'Ouest', December 1916, AA.

50 'Rapport mensuel: Corps d'occupation, Zone de l'Ouest', January 1917, No. 1610, AA.

51 Zaza diary, 15 January 1917. The son was called Lukara. 'Rapport mensuel', February 1917.

52 Save diary, February, March 1917; Collignon to Classe, 29 March 1917, CO; 'Rapport mensuel', January, February 1917. A tale that Captain Stevens's milk had been poisoned was believed. On the other hand, Wintgens had made public a list of Tutsi killed by the Belgians, so the Belgians had grounds for believing that there was contact as some level with the enemy.

53 'Rapport mensuel', February 1917.

54 'Note sur le rapport politique de Ruanda,' 3 January 1919, AE/11, No. 1847, 3288, AA.

55 Des Forges, *Rwanda under Musiinga*, 214-16.

56 Lietenant Carlier seems to have been particularly autocratic in Gisaka; see Zaza diary, 31 January, 8 April, 1917.

57 An interesting example of this was the minor chief Ntolero, from near Mibirisi. He had learned to read and write from a Ganda, and requested Catholic teachers, a common enough case history of the type of Tutsi who wanted to emancipate himself from the court. See Mibirisi diary, 10 March 1914; 'Rapport mensuel', February 1917.

58 Des Forges, *Rwanda under Musiinga*, 217.

59 *Rapports annuels*, 1915-16, 295; Louis, *Ruanda-Urundi*, 215.

60 Classe to Stevens, 22 March 1917, CO.

61 Nyundo diary, December 1916; Malfeyt to Renkin, 29 June 1917, AE/11, No. 1842, 3287, AA; *Rapports annuels*, 1915-16, 300-1.

62 *Rapports annuels*, 1917-18, 245.

63 Oomen to Stevens, 31 August 1917, and undated letter AE/11, No. 1842, 3287, AA; *Rapports annuels*, 1915-16, 302.

64 Classe to Livinhac, 3 April 1917, Dossier 111, WFAR; *Rapports annuels*, 1917-18, 259.

65 Father Hurel was prominent in the struggle against cerebro-spinal

meningitis at Ruhengeri. About two thousand died from epidemics around Save; see Stevens to Classe, 12 October 1917; Stevens to Hirth, 8 December 1917; Lejeune to Hirth, 4 December 1918; *Rapports annuels*; 1917-18, 244.

66 The Nyundo Fathers baptised seven hundred people dying of smallpox. Around Rwaza a Rwandan began inoculating with pus from smallpox sores, explaining that it was like a blood pact and would keep the smallpox's hatred at bay. See Rwaza diary, 20 February 1918; Classe to Commandant, 22 March 1917; *Rapports annuels*, 1916-17, 302; 1917-18, 245-73, 301.

67 Thousands of head of cattle, for example, were requisitioned by the Belgians; Stevens to Malfeyt, 21 May 1918, AE/11, No. 1842, 3287, AA; Nyundo diary, 17 December 1917.

68 Declerck to Stevens, 29 May 1917, AE/11 No. 1842, 3287, AA; *Rapports annuels*, 1917-18, 291.

69 Malfeyt to Renkin, 10 June 1918, AA.

70 Stevens to Classe, — June 1917, CO.

71 'Note sur le rapport politique', No. 1847, AA.

72 Rwaza diary, 12 January 1918.

73 In Malfeyt's words, 'les conceptions politiques de certains fonctionnaires territoriaux tendant à provoquer la division du royaume, et l'émancipation de la race dominée n'étaient pas de nature à rétablir la confiance dans l'entourage du roi.' 'Note sur la rapport politique'; Stevens to Malfeyt, 21 May 1918.

74 Nyirinkwaya.

75 Schumacher to Kisenyi Resident, 12 December 1916, 18 May 1917, correspondence found at Rwaza mission. The man had been sent across the Mulera plain to look for food.

76 Rwaza diary, 25 January, 18 February 1918; des Forges, *Rwanda under Musiinga*, 233.

77 Schumacher to Kisenyi Resident, undated (*c.* 1917), Rwaza correspondence. One was from Lwangeyo and the other from Kanuma.

78 See chapter four, p. 89 n. 27, and n. 84 below.

79 *Rapports annuels*, 1917-18, 301.

80 Rwaza diary, 25 January 1918. One of these, Kadiho, rose to be a powerful force in the north and resisted the later change in Belgian policy towards support for the Banyanduga; see Rwaza diary, 24 December 1919.

81 Malfeyt, trans. 'Note sur le rapport politique'. The Belgians were keen on giving the impression of sound administration to bolster claims when the division of the spoils of war came; see Malfeyt to Rwanda Resident, 26 June 1918, AE/II, No. 1847, 3288, AA.

82 Kabgayi diary, 12 June, 7 July 1917; Hirth to Father Superior, Rwaza, 7 June 1917, Dossier 112, WFAR; Declerck to Classe, 3 July 1917, CO.

83 Declerck to Classe, 3 July 1917. It took about a month for the Hutu to become aware of the reforms by contact with the missions, and then the stations were flooded with complaints; see, for example, Nyundo diary, 9 August, 1917.

84 The Tutsi was Lwakadigi. He had come north from Save as Bushako's garagu *c.* 1903. It seems likely that he was chosen for his abilities and experience in dealing with the Fathers. In the German period he manipulated to the full the patronage afforded by Nyundo and Kisenyi, and was now preparing for a confrontation with Bushako. By June 1917 he had introduced

many of his own garagu into famine-weakened Bugoyi. It was one of these, Seki-bakanya, who was now installed illegally in Magini's, the Hutu's, banana grove. See Nyundo diary, 28, 30 September, 31 October 1917; Oomen to Hirth, 4 November 1917; Soubielle to Classe, 6 December 1917; Hirth to Declerck, 29 December 1917, CO; *Rapports annuals,* 1917-18, 301. For the Schumacher-Ruhigirakunda affair see chapter five.

85 Declerck to Classe, 21 August 1917, CO.

86 For example, it was impossible to keep cattle out of gardens without fencing. Even today cattle stray on to valuable land in the marshes reclamation schemes. Similarly the reforms still needed full missionary co-operation for giving out seeds, hoes, plants, etc.; see Nyundo diary, 30 January 1918.

87 Classe to Malfeyt, 28 October 1917, No. 1847, AA; Classe to Declerck, 22 October 1917, CO.

88 Tombeur to Classe, 19 January 1917; Stevens to Classe, 13 February 1917; Bosmand to Classe, 2 January 1918; Classe to Malfeyt, 10 January 1918, CO.

89 Declerck to Classe, 28 December 1917. Monsignor Hirth responded to this in a similar vein; see Hirth to Declerck, 29 December 1917, No. 1847, AA.

90 Made more acute, of course by the exigencies of running a campaign against elusive German forces, and defending themselves against British claims of incompetence.

91 Oomen to Hirth, 4 November 1917.

92 Declerck to Classe, 18 December 1917.

93 Mibirisi diary, May 1916, 28 August 1916; Save diary, April 1917; Kabgayi diary, 19 March 1918 — examples of out-stations going up. Musinga's grants of extensions could not be ratified by the Belgians because of the temporary nature' of their rule at the time; see Declerck to Classe, 17 August 1917, CO; Malfeyt to Franck, 26 September 1917, No. 1918, AA.

94 Save diary, April 1917; Classe to Roussez, 18 May 1918, WFAR.

95 Kabgayi diary, 27 December 1917; *Rapports annuels,* 1917-18, 262-63; Compte rendu des séances de Conseil', Rwaza, 27 January 1918.

96 Nothomb, *Church History,* 41; *Rapports annuels,* 1917-18, 263.

97 Zaza diary, 13, 22 June 1917. Rugambarara was reinstated and Kanuma presented Zaza with a cow.

98 *Rapports annuels,* 1917-18, 248, 255.

99 *Ibid.,* 249.

100 Hirth to Declerck, 29 December 1917, quoted in Classe to Malfeyt, 10 January 1918, CO.

101 Save diary, June 1917.

102 Both German and Belgian troops lived like locusts on the local population, despite good discipline; see Nyundo diary, July 1915; Save diary, 21 May 1916; Ruhengeri Resident to Father Superior, Rwaza, 19 June 1917; *Rapports annuels,* 1917-18, 244. See also Des Forges, *Rwanda under Musiinga,* 209.

103 Save diary, 14 April 1918; 'Rapport politique confidentiel', Defawe to Declerck, 24 March 1918, Dossier 111, WFAR. The very fact that this document found its way to the White Fathers' archives is another example of the close relations between Classe and Declerck.

104 Save diary, May 1917; translation in Defawe to Declerck, 24 March 1918.

105 Save diary, August, October 1916.

106 *Ibid.*

107 *Ibid.*; *Bulamatari*, 'breaker of rocks', was the common name for the Belgians in the Congo, first given to Stanley in the 1870s.

108 The *reducciones* of the Jesuit mission in Peru provides an obvious parallel to the tendencies found at the White Fathers' stations.

109 It is interesting that Captain Dupuis, the military attaché at Nyanza, pressed Musinga to give Guillaume a hill as compensation. The military authorities obviously needed the *abasemyi*, shared the White Fathers' view of the world, and thought less in terms of long-term social planning than the administrators like Defawe. See Save diary, December 1917.

110 Save diary, 14 April 1918.

111 Rwaza diary, 4 March 1918. Rwaza diary, 7 March 1918, claims that Father Classe saved Nyirimbilima's mother's life by spiriting her out of Nyanza.

112 Sebabangali was ousted in favour of Lwassamanzi; see Save diary, February 1918.

113 Declaration of Lussesabagina, in Defawe to Declerck, 24 March 1918.

114 Save diary, 5 April 1918.

115 *Ibid.*, 16 April 1918.

116 Classe to Hirth, 28 September 1913, Dossier 111, WFAR. Rumours were reaching Nyundo as early as September 1917 that priests had been killed in central Rwanda and that the king had chained up Huntzinger; see Nyundo diary, 28 September 1917. Huntzinger's immediate response to the move against him was to assert that Musinga was wreaking vengeance on Save for the Belgians' mistakes. Since Save mission had been behind some of these mistakes, this was in a sense true.

117 Father Écomard took over; see Save diary, 25 April 1918.

118 Malfeyt to Minister for the Colonies, 27 September 1918, No. 1842, AA.

119 Telegram from Malfeyt to Minister for the Colonies, 23 July 1918, No. 1842, AA. The telegram was published to stem rumours that Musinga was dead.

120 Save diary, 26 May 1918; Defawe to Father Superior, Kabgayi, 28 May 1918, CO;Zaza diary,, 10 May, 2-5, 13 July, 1918.

121 Classe to confrères, 2 April 1918, Dossier 111, WFAR.

122 Lecoindre, 'Raisons qui ont nui'. Charles Marie-François Lecoindre came from the Montfaucon family of Moine, Maine-et-Loire, France. He was forty, four years younger than Classe, and, coming from minor aristocracy, naturally fell in with the Vicar General's *Weltanschauung*.

123 Save diary, February 1917, records a protest when Soubielle was moved to Nyundo; Lecoindre considered this was Hirth's response to the mission's problems; 'Raisons qui ont nui'.

124 'Compte rendu des séances de Conseil', Rwaza, 26 February 1917.

125 Bonneau, H., 'Rapport sur le Kivu', *c.* 1920, Dossier 111, WFAR.

126 Classe to Livinhac, 15 November 1917, WFAR.

127 'Raisons qui ont nui'.

128 Oomen replaced Parmentier in February 1917; see Malfeyt to Minister for the Colonies, 10 June 1918.

129 Nyundo diary, 17 February 1918. The identification with the Hutu could also be detected in letters: 'Il nous semble ridicule, pour ne pas dire un autre mot, d'aider d'un côté en dépensant l'argent du gouvernement, et de l'autre côté, laisser les Batutsi tuer le pays.' Oomen to Hirth, 4 November 1917, CO.

130 Des Forges, *Rwanda under Musiinga*, 220-33. For example, from 1917 to 1918 there were neither Tutsi nor Belgians around Rwaza.

131 Rwaza diary, 18 April, 1917.

132 There are, of course, checks, partly internal, ideological and historical. The way a mission like Rwaza formed a little 'State' from the segmentary lineage society around it has interesting parallels in Islam. I am grateful to Charles Stewart for having drawn my attention to the importance of 'outsiders' with religious legitimation who serve legal functions in societies of this type. It is, though, the absence of a Christian 'Shari'a' and the precedent of the caliphate that provided an *internal* check on the theocratic growth of stations like Rwaza.

133 Nyundo diary, 6 November 1918, May 1919; Rwaza diary, 11 May, November 1918; Defawe to Hirth, 10 December 1918, CO.

134 For example, Rwaza Christians were used as intermediaries between Kalinda and Kadiho's son, who refused to pay *ikoro* and attacked the chief's *garagu*; see Rwaza diary, 26, 31 December 1919; 3, 5 January 1920, 26 February, 5 April 1920.

135 Rwaza diary, 18 February 1918.

136 *Rapports annuels*, 1919-20, 379-80. These were held to be sacred.

137 *Ibid.*, 379. This was, of course, equally provocative.

138 Defawe to Hirth, 10 December 1918, CO.

139 *Rapports annuels*, 1919-20, 363.

140 Kabgayi diary, 15 August 1918; Classe to Livinhac, 31 July 1918, Dossier 111, WFAR; *Rapports annuels*, 1917-18, 270.

141 *Rapports annuels*, 1917-18, 266.

142 *Ibid.*, 272.

143 *Ibid.*

144 De Lacger, *Ruanda*, 455-6.

145 *Rapports annuels*, 1919-20, 364-5; Nothomb, *Church History*, 42.

146 Interview with the ex-rector of Nyakibanda Seminary, Monsignor Matthieu, Rwaza mission, June 1973.

147 Defawe to Declerck, 24 March 1918.

148 Malfeyt to Minister for the Colonies, 23 July 1918, No. 1842, AA.

149 Louis, *Ruanda-Urundi*, 232-54.

150 Classe to Van den Eede, 8 August 1919, CO.

151 Van den Eede to Hirth, 9 August 1919, CO.

152 Classe, 'Relations', 27; Arnoux, *Le Culte de la société secrète*, 291. Sharangabo was a past *mwami w'imandwa*.

153 Van den Eede to Hirth, 28 July 1919, CO.

154 Van den Eede to Hirth, 14 October 1919, CO. Most of the leading nobles also had at least one son in Nyanza school, which the mwami was now favouring; see letter dated 10 July 1919 signed by Nyanza schoolchildren greeting Commissaire Royal, No. 1859, AA.

155 Classe to Livinhac, 7 September 1919, Dossier 111, WFAR.

156 Kabgayi diary, 10 April and 13 February 1920.

157 Nyundo diary, May 1919, 15 January, 1920.

158 Franck to Governor General, Boma, 6 January 1920, AA. 'J'ai décidé que dans le Ruanda et l'Urundi, où il existe une organisation indigène, fortement échafaudée avec une autorité puissament assise, les relations de la métropole avec ses territoires seront celles de l'administration indirecte'.

159 Louis Franck, memorandum, 17 June 1920, No. 1849, AA.

160 *Ibid.*

161 *Ibid.*

162 Hirth to his brother, 9 May 1920, Dossier 111, WFAR.

163 Louis Franck, memorandum, 17 June 1920, No. 1849, AA; underlined in original.

164 *Rapports annuels*, 1919-20, 362.

165 Classe to confrères, 17 April 1913, CR.

166 *Rapports annuels*, 1917-18, 249. See chapter seven for Classe's emphasis on private property.

167 Cunrath to Livinhac, 13 June 1920, Dossier 112; Classe to Livinhac, 16 July 1920, Dossier 111, WFAR. The reason for the request may have been the mwami's personal insecurity at the time of Franck's visit. He had just lost two of his sons. See Defawe to Médecin-Chef Lejeune, 12 November 1919; Defawe to Classe, 2, 20 March 1920, CO.

168 The concept of adaptation was beginning to appear in missionary writings. For example, Huonder, A., *Der Europäismus im Missionsbetrieb*, Aix-la-Chapelle, 1921; see Mulders, A., *Missiologisch Besteck*, Hilversum and Anvers, 1962, 301-16.

169 Mibirisi diary, 24 September 1909; *Rapports annuels*, 1911-12, 404. They were against night celebrations and even the practice of newly-weds wearing veils in church. Or from the viewpoint of a canon lawyer: 'La prépondérance des interventions des parents et de la famille a fait place à une simple mais sereine déclaration des deux fiancés au curé de la paroisse'. See Bushayija, S. 'Le mariage coutumier au Rwanda', Gregorian doctoral thesis in canon law, Brussels, 1966, 186.

170 Classe to Father Superior, Rwaza, 20 August 1913, Dossier 112, WFAR.

171 Rwaza diary, 22 October 1915; 'Compte rendu des séances de Conseil, 'Rwaza, 14 October 1917.

172 The Catholics lost their majority to the Socialists in the 1919 Belgian elections leaving the missionaries symbols of Catholic reaction.

173 Van den Eede to Hirth, 9 December 1919, is the first reference to the coming cession in mission sources. The actual declarations of the chiefs were not without their funny side: some said they wished only the opposite of Musinga; see Zaza diary, 29 December 1918. Chief Katche in Gisaka stated; 'We like the Belgians as well because they have left all the old chiefs in the country and have not chased out the chiefs like the English did in their territory.' No. 1846, AA. Musinga's declaration went as follows: 'I leave everyone free to choose their religion, for now I see that the missions respect me and respect my religious customs. I wish and I order all the Watutsis and Wahutus to learn, and, to give the example, I have first of all put my sons to

school.' AA. Father Classe's description of the process is worth recording: 'L'administrateur lui disait, "N'est-ce pas que tu veux écrire ceci au roi Albert?" "Oui." "Puis ceci?" "Oui" . . . Et chaque fois la rédaction se faisait.' see Classe to Livinhac, 25 March 1920, Dossier 111, WFAR.

174 Van den Eede to Hirth, 18 January 1920, CO; Classe to Livinhac, 24 June 1920, Dossier 111, WFAR. A notable who was receiving instruction was beaten to death at Nyanza at this time; see des Forges, *Rwanda under Musiinga*, 246.

175 Bonneau report; see n. 125.

176 *Ibid.*

177 *Ibid.*

178 *Rapports annuels*, 1919-20, 257.

179 Paas, J., *Unter der Aequatorsonne. Padri Donatus Lebereho*, Trier, 1927, White Fathers' Library, WFAR; *Grands Lacs*, 1952, 18. The Christian concept of sin and the African one of evil were not differentiated by many. Abbé Leberaho's emphasis on 'pure souls' seems to have corresponded to the idea of impurity as a cause of disruption and evil. During the meningitis-smallpox epidemic, for example, Christians came to confession by the thousands; see *Rapports annuels*, 1917-18, 326; 1919-20, 391; *Missions d'Afrique*, 1922, 31.

180 *Grands Lacs*, 1952, 19.

181 Colle to Livinhac, 21 October 1920, Dossier 112, WFAR; *Rapports annuels*, 1919-20, 367.

182 Philippin to Abbé Donat, 8 February 1922, CO.

183 De Lacger, *Ruanda*, 436, *Rapports annuels*, 1917-18, 323, Gorju to Livinhac, 2 August 1919, indicate the extent of the neglect.

184 Hirth to Livinhac, 10 June 1918, Dossier 111; Gorju to Livinhac, August 1919.

185 Hirth to Livinhac, 29 July 1920, quoting from Livinhac's letter.

186 Marchal to Classe, 4 May 1920.

187 Livinhac to Hirth, 18 August 1920.

188 Bonneau report.

189 The first letters from Maison-Carrée after August 1914 reached Rwanda in November 1916; see Classe to confrères, 7 November 1916, CR. Livinhac to Hirth, 28 February 1918, complains of having received nothing from the Vicar Apostolic, so Hirth had failed to correspond throughout 1917.

190 Bonneau report.

191 Apart from Huntzinger, he had been trying to get rid of Father De Bekker; see Classe to Livinhac, 24 March 1917, Dossier 111. On the other hand the Father Superior of Kansi was a definite convert to Classe's viewpoint: 'Un peu partout, en effet, dans le Ruanda la gent muhutu a longtemps caressé l'illusion que les missionaires allaient la délivrer de l'étau mututsi. Aujourd'hui il semble qu'ils sont bien "revenus" de cet espoir et qu'ils commencent enfin à nous voir sous notre vrai jour; *oportet evangelizare et baptizare*. En tout cas, nous na manquons aucune occasion de les éclairer prudemment à ce sujet: la religion ne peut qu'y gagner.' See *Rapports annuels*, 1916-17, 277.

192 Bonneau report.

193 Livinhac to Rwanda missionaries, 17 November 1920.

194 Van den Eede to Classe, 15 October 1921, CO; de Lacger, *Ruanda*, 478.

195 Livinhac to Rwanda missionaries, 1 April 1921, quoting instructions to Vicars Apostolic of missions *ad exteros* 1659, 'hoc vobis certissime persuasum sit rem S.C. molestestissimam facturum eum quicumque se rebus hujusmodi, aut etiam immesceri . . .'

196 Classe to Livinhac, 26 September 1921.

197 Van den Eede to Classe, 27 September 1921, CO; Classe to Livinhac, 26 September 1921.

198 Classe to Livinhac, 2 June, 14 December 1921.

199 Ryckmans to Minister for the Colonies, 21 October 1921, M.634, AA, pointed out the anomaly.

200 Donders to Livinhac, 10 October 1921, Dossier 112, WFAR.

201 Father Ulrix's verdict in a Belgian colony would carry a great deal of weight, as in theory the government would hope to see the Rwanda mission staffed by Belgians trained under him. There were, in fact, very few.

202 Ulrix to Minister for the Colonies, 7 December 1921; note for Minister for the Colonies, 8 November M.634, AA.

203 Ryckmans to Minister for the Colonies, 21 November 1921.

204 Franck to Jaspar, 16 December 1921.

205 Nothomb, *Church History*, 46. To be ordained by Cardinal Mercier, a Catholic hero of the First World War, after Classe's *entente cordiale* with the Germans was a nice touch.

206 *Rapports annuels*, 1921-22, 523.

SEVEN

The conversion of the Tutsi

When Léon Classe returned to Rwanda in 1922 the Tutsi had already abandoned direct opposition to Catholicism for cautious accommodation, and within the next decade were to adopt a third course — conversion. The Hutu inside the Church who had, when expedient, exchanged their Tutsi overlords for a missionary were soon to be overwhelmed by a rush of aristocratic converts which the priests called *La Tornade*. Under Belgian rule education became the portal which gave access to political power, but as Cardinal Hinsley remarked, it was also 'the portal of the Church'.[1] As the Belgians created a new group of literate government chiefs, and the mission schools geared themselves to preparing candidates for political office, Musinga alone, the old source of political power and the representative of the old religion, stood outside the new political and religious structure; his deposition in 1931 and the coronation of his catechumen son Rudahigwa marked the closing of an era of Rwandan history and the opening of a new one.

Despite Musinga's passing gratitude to Bishop Classe for his efforts to bring about the restoration of Gisaka,[2] the loss of eastern Rwanda to the British only deepened his mistrust of Europeans.[3] He had lost a vast pasture region dotted with royal *ibikingi* in 1920, and he feared attempts to restore the Gisaka royal house.[4] By 1922 the partition had become effective; travellers to and from Nyanza required a note from the British Resident countersigned by the Belgians across the 'border'. Gifts could still be taken to the mwami, but too prolonged an absence might result in deposition by the British.[5] Not that there was much incentive to return; the British Resident, seeing the Hutu as the 'underdog', was insisting that Tutsi give back cattle confiscated from their subjects.[6] He was equally revolutionary in his appointments, passing over two important Ega chiefs and giving thirty-five hills in Buganza to a minor Nyiginya; the missionaries were amazed; the mwami, they heard, was furious, since Buganza was reserved for the son of a faithful Nyiginya, Kanuma.[7] Worse was the Resident's threat to put a literate appointee over the multitude of *ibikingi* holders.[8]

The Resident and Isaac Kyakawambara, his Ganda assistant, found themselves, in a short while, leaders of a Hutu-inspired movement for reform.[9] The Christians were the first to take advantage of the possibilities opened up by the new regime. Petro Muhanika, an ex-seminarian who had turned his hand to skin trading and extortion in the past, was taken on as the Resident's *karani*.[10] Joseph Lukamba, who belonged to the Gisaka royal line[11] and served as a catechist at Zaza, which was now British, went off to train as an administrative assistant. He was appointed sub-chief, and at least one noble thought him enough of a rising light to ask for a blood pact.[12] Another of the mission's employees, Simon Nyiringondo, came forward as an interpreter.[13]

The contrast with Belgian rule was striking; it was announced that *ubuletwa* and crop dues were abolished unless they sprang from specific land grants to tenant farmers.[14] When freedom of worship was proclaimed, despite public and cordial co-operation between Resident and White Fathers,[15] complaints against the missionaries poured in.[16] Tsobe Tutsi were brought to the Residence and their diviner's potions burnt.[17] Perhaps because of past Nyabingi disturbances in Kigezi, female chiefs were banned, with the result that the wife of an important Ega chief left the region altogether.[18] A new and more powerful patron had come into the land to make lowly both Tutsi and White Fathers. In October 1922, Joseph Lukamba was made provisional chief of Mirenge province, thus realising the Rwandan Tutsi's worst fears. The Gisaka kings had been resurrected.[19]

Although the reversion of Gisaka to Rwandan rule in 1923 gratified Musinga, it can have done little to dispel his feelings of helplessness and resentment; the case for the Rwandan monarchy had been eloquently presented by Classe[20] and by the Société Belge des Missions Protestants,[21] but the League of Nations mandates commission made its decision after Britain had lost interest in the Cape-to-Cairo railway. Dependent on missionary advocates, and impotent as he now was, Musinga looked back to the past in which he had enjoyed real power and romanticised the German period when he was "respected',[22] He was never to adapt himself to Belgian demands, which, after the return of Gisaka, were consciously intensified.[23]

Late in 1919 a Seventh Day Adventist pastor occupied the abandoned stations of Kirinda and Iremera before making Gitwe the Adventist headquarters,[24] but for four years after the Germans' departure Protestants were no more than a tiny cloud on the White Fathers' horizon; the Protestant intervention at the League of Nations was an unwelcome reminder that 'error' must once more be reckoned with. Kirinda itself was reopened by a French member of the Lutheran Evangelische Missions Gesellschaft and though he might be tarred with the German Brush he was joined in July 1922 by the impeccably Belgian Pastors Josué Honoré and Arthur Lestrade with a trained nurse.[25] Five Christians baptised in German times came forward at Rubengera, where the Protestants were able to start a girls' school.[26] The Church Missionary Society, banned from Belgian territory after enquiries some members had made about the treatment of porters in 1917,[27] but hovering ever since on the Ugandan border, finally entered Gisaka during the period of British rule; they remained after Gisaka had returned to Musinga,[28] to overshadow with their Cambridge medical degrees and upper-class backgrounds their less well endowed Belgian colleagues.[29] In September 1922 they, along with the Lutherans, baptised their first Rwandan converts.[30]

The League of Nations mandate to supervise Rwanda strengthened Belgian resolution to rule the Tutsi and to push ahead with reforms. The CMS lost many adherents who plainly had equated them with British administration and the possibility of emancipation,[31] but they nevertheless sent a Toro Christian to ask the mwami's permission for a station on lake Mohasi, later to be Gahini, a great Protestant centre. 'In the eyes of the natives,' a missionary told CMS readers, 'such sanction is almost of more value than the dictates of European rulers.'[32] There was little evidence to support this observation. The Belgians saw the return of Gisaka as an opportunity for exerting even greater pressure on the king; 'I hope it will allow us to change our tactics with Muzinga,' Classe was told. 'It is a unique chance to obtain from him what must be the basis of his country's development, i.e. stabilisation of property rights.'[33] In an ordinance of 28 April 1917 the Belgians had recognised the Rwandan courts, but this left the Hutu at the mercy of the chiefs; they now tried to have an administrator present at all important cases. *Ubuletwa* was reduced from two out of five, to two out of seven days in 1924, and later to one out of seven. The Tutsi custom of marking and claiming Hutu banana trees and the enforced donation of cattle when the lord's beasts died were abolished. Head and cattle taxes were instituted. Politically more important was the obligation imposed on the mwami to consult the Belgians before making appointments.[34] These decrees, designed to improve the lot of the peasantry, remained largely a paper exercise; the Belgians could only curb the mwami and collect the taxes.

Bishop Classe's support for reform was now public. *Le Soir* quoted from a booklet he had written entitled *Le Royaume de Musinga:* 'Above all, while refraining from bringing up the most serious question of private property I would say that progressive reform is needed. More security for goods, possessions and fields, harvests and even herds is required.' In private Classe sounded more radical, complaining that 'since there is a fear of attacking the basis of the social organisation, we are exposed to half-measures'.[36] In 1924 he still hoped for his 'bourgeois revolution', but this was the low water mark of his feelings about the Tutsi; when the tide turned such thoughts disappeared.

The Belgians were dependent on the White Fathers in minor as well as major matters. The missions were, for instance, expected to supply domestic servants for the administrators and to look after their coloured offspring. Initially the implementation of nearly all agricultural policy depended on Catholic co-operation. The period of reforms after 1924 only increased this dependence.[37] But more necessary to the administration than any other aspect of mission work was the Catholics' extensive infrastructure of minor seminaries and schools.

The Belgian philosophy of education in Africa was essentially that of the 1924 Phelps-Stokes commission, with its emphasis on vocational training and vernacular teaching.[38] The missionaries were ideally suited to this type of formation, but Liberal pressures from Belgium dictated some commitment to secular education. Church control of schools was being hotly debated,[39] and some of the political sound and fury reached the hills of Rwanda; the Kigali Resident removed children from the town's Catholic school in a peremptory fashion and even seems to have claimed the fixtures and fittings.[40] Political conflict in Belgium, and lack of money and men in Rwanda, left the educational system almost entirely in missionary hands, with a few showpiece secular institutions.[41]

Despite debates in Brussels about whether the Catholics in Ruanda-Urundi should be subsidised, the White Fathers were from 1921 the fortunate recipients of 56,675 francs annually sent by mistake from money destined for the Congo Mission.[42] They badly needed it; every seminarian cost 500 francs per annum, and it was often difficult to provision them. Bishop Classe did his utmost to 'sell' his seminaries: 'Pupils destined for the ecclesiastical state will never be more than a feeble minority,' he wrote to the Resident. 'Our goal is to form schoolteachers as well as employees of all sorts.'[43] But standards were too low and the syllabus was too 'religious' for the Belgians.[44] The five or six Protestant missionaries in Rwanda were receiving 25,000 francs — intentionally — as nationals, so it was difficult to make a case for denying the more numerous Catholics equal treatment.[45] The first funds deliberately budgeted for the Rwanda Fathers, 25,000 francs, were sent in 1924, and the sum was raised to 55,000 francs in 1925.[46] Thus the result was much the same in Rwanda as in British territories, an identity of interest between Church and colonial regime, and a mission-dominated education system, the only difference being that the Belgians were more ideologically motivated in their drive for secular schools.[47]

Despite the growth of Protestant missions Catholicism was the official religion of the country; the presence of the CMS was treated with 'unwilling toleration';[48] German Protestants were beyond the pale.[49] The experience of the Congo had not endeared 'Anglo-Saxon' missionaries to the Belgians.[50] Monsignor Hirth and Father Lecoindre were honoured in turn with the Order of the Lion;[51] in hard times the administration rallied round to provide the seminary students with grain.[52] At the opposite pole to the anti-clericals were those who saw in Catholicism a necessary support for colonialism. 'As for the White Fathers,' wrote a Chef de Service in the Colonial Ministry, 'had they not been in the country it would have been sound policy to call them in,'[53] whilst a fanatical Catholic confided in Monsignor Classe:

Both as a Catholic and a colonial I cannot see any value in Protestant education . . . it ignores the special character of our primitive races and hands out a spiritual food which revolutionises their way of thinking, creates anarchy . . . and gives rise to extreme individualism, which tends of necessity to destroy the precious gregarious spirit of our blacks that alone can realise and maintain that latent voluntary and collective submission which is indispensable to all civilising work.[54]

Fascism in Europe had its Catholic supporters, and it is perhaps against this background, and against such movements as Action Française,[55] that Classe's pragmatic conservatism in the '30s should be judged, rather than the radicalism of the missionary clergy of the 1950s.[56]

The first graduates of Nyanza government school emerged in 1923; now the Belgians had the men, the raw material, they needed to carry out their social policy.[57] The thirty or so ambitious young Tutsi leaving Nyanza each year permitted the administration to dismiss old chiefs and replace them by their trained sons, to eliminate anti-European Tutsi from public office and amalgamate jurisdictions under selected new men. Lwakadigi, the *parvenu* of Nyundo, gave way for his son in 1925, and new chiefs began appearing around Rwaza.[58] The process of imposing Banyanduga in the north was given a new impetus, and the *abahinza*-ruled kingdoms of Bukunzi and Busozo were occupied militarily and incorporated in Tutsi-ruled provinces.[59]

While the Belgians extended rule to regions untouched in German times, they did nothing comparable to increase Musinga's personal power. As a result the struggle at the heart of Rwanda's court politics, between king and nobility, swung in favour of the aristocrats; since the Belgians provided their appointees with land, clients and cattle, the system amounted to a feudal bureaucracy, in which the king had less and less place. Major Tutsi lineages courted the new focus of power within the State, the Belgian administrators, and handed over to their sons if they politically overreached themselves.[60]

Bishop Classe was perhaps premature in his identification of a 'pro-European faction' at court in 1916. Five years later the Belgians had transformed wishful thinking into reality. The court began to split into a group that looked to the Belgians for patronage, the *Inshongore* — or complainers[61] — and one that still courted the mwami; these traditionalists were called by the Nyiginya leader Ntulo *Abayoboke* — those who knew only a single way.[62] The *Inshongore* wished to take the process of accommodation further than Musinga would contemplate; there were more ways than one of staying in power.

As the old tension between king and nobles was transformed by Belgian patronage the mwami struggled to keep control of the provinces by multiplying the number of his garagu and providing them with *ibikingi*. 'The king is actively working to dispossess all the province chiefs,' wrote Classe in 1923, 'and to increase his personal power, which was once so great.'[63] But Musinga no longer held the top of the clientship chain; his fury mounted as nobles denounced him to the Belgians, and the Marangara chiefs proudly boasted their independence from Nyanza.[64]

With the Ega chief Kayondo and the Nyiginya chief Ntulo ranged against him, the king had no alternative but to look to his enemies, the White Fathers, for support. To ingratiate himself with the missionaries and tighten his hold on the newly returned Gisaka, Musinga took the unusual step of warning the Gisaka nobles against rival missions.

To my chiefs: much greetings.

Through this present letter I announce to you that the Bapadri are my friends as they have always been. So if they wish to build schools to teach the people of Rwanda, give them land and help them. I am happy under the rule of Bulamatari and for that reason I want there to be Europeans of no other nationality in my kingdom. And you will tell your sub-chiefs what I have told you. It is I, the king of Rwanda.

Yuhi Musinga [65]

There were to be no reformist British, nor their CMS missionaries. Protestants were now refused audience at court, and the Fathers reciprocated by intervening with the Belgians on the mwami's behalf.[66] But the drift away from Musinga was irrevocable; when he tried to set an example and attended the government school several pupils left to join the Fathers.[67]

Signs of the mwami's softer attitude seem to have made a great impact on the ordinary Hutu; after Musinga attended the blessing of Kabgayi cathedral, catechists on neighbouring hills were overwhelmed by postulants. The Catholic missions continued to make gains throughout 1924.[68] Rwabusisi, a nephew of the Queen Mother, was

now openly recruiting for Catholic schools among chiefs and sub-
chiefs.[69] 'All the youth of the ruling class want to learn how to read
and write,' the Fathers observed.[70] Several years' education was now
the condition for retaining or augmenting Tutsi power. Nobles came
en masse to enrol, and soon the catechism classes included young
married men among the children.[71] One of Kabare's sons became a
fervent evangelist at court,[72] but for many the important part of their
classwork came after the catechism lesson, when they learned reading,
writing and arithmetic.

By the beginning of 1925 the Catholics had 17,475 pupils crammed
into their classrooms or being taught in the open air by teachers who
barely managed to stay one step ahead of their pupils. With a 12,000
increase since 1922 the Catholic school system was swamped, and was
sustained only by the eagerness of its clients. In contrast there were
about three hundred young Tutsi in the Belgian school at Nyanza,
sixty of them catechumens. They attended a four- to five-year course
and then spent a year at an administrative post learning the European
tax and court procedures. Until the secular school system was phased
out in 1929 approximately 400 secretaries, chiefs' sons and a few
veterinary students passed through Nyanza, where they received two
years of French and a final year of Swahili. After 1925 the Catholics
ran their own Swahili classes at Kabgayi, but teaching in the bush
schools was, of course, in Kinyarwanda and learning was by rote.[73]

The change in the balance of power between mwami and nobles,
coupled with the new educational definition of eligibility for political
office, combined to make mission patronage highly desirable for
ambitious Tutsi. It cost little now to please Fathers, and sophisticated
nobles soon learnt Musinga's trick of using rival protestant missions
to great effect. When Protestants in Kinyaga requested Rwagataraka's
permission to build, the chief wrote an effusive letter to Father
Lecoindre. 'Ni wowe mukuru,' 'You are my superior,' he declared.
'Njewe inshuti yanyu itabafatanya na Abaportesitani nkabandi bose,'
'I am your friend who will not be taken by the Protestants.'[74] As this
shrewdest of the Ega remarked, 'If a man serves two masters he will
hate one and love the other.'[75] Whether feudal or biblical in inspira-
tion, his words summed up the mood of the times; increasingly the
Tutsi were obliged to make choices between old and new channels of
power and patronage.

The movement of Tutsi into the mission orbit transformed the
position of the Catholic Church. It was appropriate that as Monsignor
Classe moved in as leading spiritual authority in the State so Gashamura, the king's leading ritual expert and head of the Tsobe clan,
should pass out the other door. Gashamura, never forgiven for his
part in ousting the Ega when the Belgians arrived, was haunted by
Kayondo. The Ega chief was jockeying his nephew, Rwigemera,

Musinga's second son, into line for succession and denounced Gasha-mura as a fanatical 'sorcerer', a charge bound to succeed with Europeans.[76] It was in vain that Musinga appealed to the Bishop to save his *umwiru*; the *Inshongore* knew only too well how to manipulate the missionaries.[77]

Musinga seemed to be at a loss how to counter the massive onslaught on the traditional prerogatives of king and court. He reeled from one humiliation and defeat to the next; the Belgians forced him to disband the *ntore* so that he watched helplessly while the pride of his entourage fell under European influence. 'Musinga seems to me very clumsy at the moment,' wrote the Kigali Resident. 'Fear, perhaps, has made him lose a little of what I took to be his political sense . . . it seems to me that we have been frightened of a phantom. Can it be that native institutions are destined to disintegrate at our touch?'[78]

Perhaps the Liberal left hand was at last aware of what the right hand was doing; nonetheless, concession after concession was wrung from the mwami; the first fruits ceremonies were abandoned,[79] and in April 1925 Musinga took the unprecedented step of sleeping away from the capital after visiting Kabgayi.[80] A visit from the Governor brought another humiliation; Musinga refused to acknowledge his presence and was summarily ordered to Astrida (Butare), whence he was instructed to return to Nyanza and receive the Governor with fitting protocol.[81]

The mwami's recourse to the missionaries was not exclusive; any solicitous noble had the Bishop's ear. Kayondo, who was turning his attention to the Nyiginya traditionalists at court, helped the Fathers by provisioning the seminaries in times of scarcity. Ntulo felt obliged to follow suit.[82] At the end of 1926, when an important court case was proceeding at Nyanza, Father Lecoindre was petitioned by Rwagataraka, Ntulo and Serukenyinkware, the latter a litigant;[83] they let the priest know that their correspondence was being kept a secret from the king. More threatening to the mwami than these clandestine letters was the way Rwigemera, his second surviving son, was complaining to Kabgayi that he was 'more and more persecuted by his father because of his *rapprochement* with the Europeans, government and missionaries'.[84] The young prince was another masterful exponent of the art of priest-handling, and laid great stress on Musinga's homo-sexual habits, doubtless after hearing stories of the Uganda martyrs. 'Our Musinga,' Classe was to write, 'has nothing to envy a Mtesa or a Mwanga in old Uganda in this sphere.'[85] The Bishop was informed that Rudahigwa, the mwami's eldest son, had all the king's favours since he had promised to continue the traditions of the dynasty 'over which the famous Bandora has been put as custodian'.[86]

The strategy of the *Inshongore* was clear; they saw Musinga as a spent force and tried to isolate him further by picking off, one by one, his closest *abiru* and allies;[87] seeing the threat of an all-Hutu Church in a Belgian territory, they were manoeuvring to maintain the position of the ruling class and major Tutsi lineages. Their appeal was irresistible to the Fathers. Their 'collaboration' might be contrasted with the traditionalists' 'resistance', but the contrast would detract from the more important point that the struggle between king and nobles, the feudal dynamic, had been transformed by the *Pax Belgica* and the demands of Western Christianity.

The Belgians had thought the worst of Musinga since an insurrection scare at the end of 1924. His behaviour during the Governor's visit had not helped matters, so when Rwagataraka put around the story that Rwigemera was about to be poisoned, on account of his close association with the Fathers, it was readily believed;[88] the scheming prince was moved to the safety of Kigali. Evidence is scanty, but it seems that the administration contemplated deposing the mwami at this point.[89] Musinga certainly began doing his utmost to gain the Fathers' favour. When they sent Rwagataraka to court in November 1926 to plead for a site for Nyamasheke mission, it was granted.[90] The White Fathers considered it a great stroke, because the place chosen, on the shores of Lake Kivu, was an *ikigabiro*, sacred ground on which one of Rwabugiri's residences had once stood.[91] In January 1927 Musinga wrote the Bishop a pathetic letter begging him to be friends again and warning him against rumour-mongers. 'These people [the *Inshongore*],' he wrote, 'want the king to be caught like Gashamura.' To oppose the traditionalists, he explained, was like trying to make an enemy of the thunder God, Inkuba; 'you can do nothing against them but they can harm you'.[92] Perhaps Musinga was a prisoner of the court, to be sacrificed for the survival of the Tutsi State, as he was symbolically in the appeasement ceremonies. Bishop Classe was willing to give him the benefit of the doubt; he went to Bujumbura to plead on his behalf with the Governor, but even he was abandoning the illusion that the Queen Mother was the source of all evil and realising that what he called the *marche-en-arrière* had the king in the vanguard.[93]

Probably the Belgians did not depose Musinga in 1927 for want of a suitable successor. The Vicar Apostolic, it seems likely, was unwilling to cause a disturbance at a time when the Tutsi were beginning to flock into the Church; the number of catechumens at Kigali rose from 353 in 1924 to 2,697 in 1928, and at Kabgayi the numbers doubled. The movement was limited to the Catholic Church; according to the White Fathers the Tutsi were unimpressed by the eschatological doctrines of the Seventh Day Adventists.[94]

The Tutsi were now divided into traditionalists who regretted the passing of court ritual and who frequented the Lyangombe cult on the hills, and progressives who were ready to take a little Catholicism with their education. But disruptive prophetic religion had nothing to commend it, whether represented by Nyabingi prophetesses or Adventist preachers. An interesting spread in the popularity of the Nyabingi mediums between 1924 and 1928 appears to have been limited to the Hutu.[95] Sharangabo, the leading Nyiginya noble in Buganza, viewed both the Nyabingi and the CMS with a jaundiced eye; he had threatened to kill the English missionaries when they first arrived.[96] Whilst the Tutsi were ready to assimilate institutional Catholicism they saw a danger to their monopoly of power in aberrant eruptions of the spirit world.

These were heady days for Bishop Classe. Tutsi diviners were reported to be burning their amulets and equipment, two hundred of the pupils at Nyanza school were catechumens, and, though the old guard like Sharangabo died resolutely refusing baptism, their sons were one step from the font. Musinga's wife, the mother of Rwigemera and so banished from court, asked the Zaza Fathers in February 1928 to build her a hut near the station so that she could receive regular instruction.[97] Unspoken but understood, pretenders were moving forward to be groomed for the role of Christian king.

The vision of a Catholic aristocracy, informed by the Faith and leading a subject peasantry along the paths of righteousness and economic development, now seemed something more than a mirage glimpsed by Lavigerie from across the Sahara. It was a peculiarly Catholic habit to refer to common sense when a point was proven, and to dogma when it was not; reason and pragmatism increasingly characterised Classe's correspondence in the 1920s.

If we want to take a practical point of view, and look to the country's real interests, we have in the Tutsi youth an incomparable element for progress that nobody knowing Ruanda can underestimate. Avid to learn, desirous of becoming acquainted with all that comes from Europe, wanting to imitate Europeans, enterprising, realising well enough that traditional customs have lost their raison d'être, but nonetheless preserving the political sense of the old-timers and their race's adroitness in the management of men, this youth is a force for the good and for the economic future of the country.[98]

Poised at the portal of Mother Church, the Tutsi again appeared to the Bishop as 'born chiefs'.[99]

The Belgians had made a half-hearted attempt to introduce a sprinkling of Hutu chiefs and *karani* but it had foundered on the entrenched opposition of the Tutsi. The impossibility of ruling without the nobles' consent was well illustrated in the case of Joseph Lukamba of Zaza. He rose to prominence in Gisaka during the British interlude on the strength of his literacy and mission connection; in September 1924 he was replaced by one of Gashamura's sons on orders from Musinga. Pressure from the Belgians enabled him to retain two hills for a while, but he was soon chased off and left with control of only

Zaza hill, on which the mission stood.[100] The only career left open to him was within the mission orbit; he later became a school inspector, and his son, a sub-deacon in 1928, was to be consecrated Bishop Aloys Bigirumwami.[101] The Catholic Hutu chief of Ndiza, literate after attending Nyanza school, was in charge of seventy-three hills and 3,913 head of cattle; an administrator described him nonetheless as 'held in low esteem, if not despised by the Watusi'.[102] If Classe could not conceive of a Rwanda ruled by the Hutu, it was because no one else could.

Nor had the *reductio ad anarchia* argument dear to the Vicar Apostolic lost any of its force in the 1920s. The Bushiru *umuhinza* had little control over break-away segments of his lineage, and clan feuds abounded;[103] he was notoriously anti-mission and led a rising in June 1925 with a disaffected catechumen against the collection of crop dues.[104] The last of the independent Hutu kingdoms fell in 1928, when the mwami of Bumbogo was deposed;[105] his lineage had held the office of *umuganura*, bearer of the first fruits to the king of Rwanda. There was little in the Hutu polities to appeal to the Fathers; the Mibirisi Superior saw 'the lack of authority of the chiefs over their subordinates' as 'a very serious cause of the mission's slow progress ... The former belong to the Hutu class and around here Hutu chiefs are little respected.'[106] When Europeans thought of Hutu kingdoms they thought of the rebellious Kiga and the Nyabingi mediums who disturbed Belgian rule.[107] 'A Hutu does not want to be commanded by a Hutu,' one administrator roundly declared.[108]

The visit of Monsignor Hinsley to Africa in 1927 and the Vatican's commitment to educating an African elite[109] pushed the White Fathers further into the Tutsi camp; the Superior General reiterated Hinsley's message on the necessity of preparing clerical and lay leaders for Africa. Classe immediately took up the theme.

The question is whether the ruling elite will be for us or against us. Whether the important places in native society will be in Catholic or in non-Catholic hands; whether the Church will have through education and its formation of youth the preponderant influence in Rwanda. [110]

If, as he suggested to the Belgians, 'the historical privilege of birth must be provisionally maintained',[111] it followed that the historical privilege of the Catholic Church could be assured only by educated Catholic Tutsi. Consensus between Church and administration now existed.

Government subsidies helped the Catholic school system respond to the enormous demands placed on it in the late 1920s. The Catholics produced a formidable array of 467 teachers, 297 of them with basic training and diplomas.[112] The government schools were staffed almost entirely by mission-trained teachers, with only a dozen or so 'secular' teachers for 677 pupils.[113] At Kigali and Ruhengeri the Fathers ran separate classes for the nobles whose education was entrusted to them. French courses were provided for Tutsi pupils at four mission schools, so most of the country's clerks and French teachers were trained exclusively within the Catholic system.[114]

Each mission had a central school around which radiated a large number of bush schools where, after catechism reading, writing and arithmetic were taught. At Kabgayi, for example, there were seventy-five chapel schools, twenty-eight served by catechists with training as teachers, instructing a total of 1,194 catechumen-pupils.[115] Although at least four of these schools had mostly Tutsi children, one with seventy-nine Tutsi from poorer families, only a single teacher appears to have been from the nobility. The ten-classroom central school served 143 pupils who took a four-year course; lessons lasted four hours a morning four days a week, with a month's holiday at the end of July. About a quarter of the teachers at the central school seem to have been Tutsi; Chrysostome Mushumba, the son of a notable, with a *certificat d'aptitude pédagogique*, taught one class in the 'first degree' — the first two years — and Augustino Gatabazi, a married ex-seminarian, taught in the 'second degree' — the last two years.[116]

Bishop Classe concluded a 'Contrat Scolaire' by which the Church assumed responsibility for the entire educational system and the government schools were phased out in the early 1930s. Each pupil was worth forty-seven francs in government subsidies, each diplomaed teacher 600 francs per class of twenty-five pupils.[117] Such was the harmony between Church and State, the shared goals, that the secular schools were redundant. 'You must choose the Batusi,' Classe told the missionaries, 'because the government will probably refuse Bahutu teachers . . . In the government the positions in every branch of the administration, even the unimportant ones, will be reserved henceforth for young Batusi.'[118]

As the mission central schools assumed the full burden of instructing the ruling class Catholic education took on a two-tiered appearance; in several stations an almost segregated stream of Tutsi with well qualified teachers was eligible for special additional subsidies. In 1928 the segregation of Save school was rigid, with Hutu and Tutsi sections in each grade. The Tutsi first year had thirty-seven pupils registered, with an average attendance of twenty-seven; the Hutu class, twenty-nine registered, with an average attendance of eighteen. The school inspector noted little progress among the Hutu; only four or five knew how to read. The second-year Tutsi were taught by Petro Mukangale, described as 'a calm man with a great deal of authority over his pupils, and a very good teacher'; his average attendance was twenty-five out of twenty-nine. The Hutu stream, though, was taught by Joseph Ngendahimana, reported to be an 'élément assez médiocre'; 'very little energy, lacks frankness, has had several absences from his class without explanation, and often leaves his pupils'; attendance in his class was eighteen out of twenty-six. The numbers of Hutu in 'second degree' classes still exceeded that of Tutsi, and the final two classes could read and write Swahili. Ignace Nyayabosha, who had been to the old Dar es Salaam Normal school, took a third section of eight Hutu pupils for vocational training as teachers; Tutsi pupils were given special French classes.[119]

The main centres which reflected the recent inrush of Tutsi were at Kigali and Kansi, where only sixty-three out of 326 pupils and fifteen out of 198 pupils were Hutu. At Zaza forty-eight out of seventy pupils were Tutsi, but attendances were low because Kanuma, the Nyiginya chief, and his son were against the school.[120] Broadly speaking, the picture was one of a pronounced movement into Catholic schools amongst the poor and ambitious members of the ruling class, the 'petits Tutsi', especially where the Banyanduga were influenced by the towns. Around Nyanza, though, it was as if some inhibitory influence radiated from the court. 'The mututsi element,' wrote the Catholic school inspector of nearby Kabgayi, 'is rather the exception in the station school.'[121] The Catholic schools reflected Rwanda's Church history. The majority of the teachers were Hutu, just as were the mission catechists, but among the pupils were many 'petits Tutsi' seeking the advantages of education and church membership.

The Belgian policy of providing a crash programme for their Tutsi bureaucracy spelt the end of the Hutu Church. The educational system, 'the portal to the Church', now became the great generator and stabiliser of class structure. Bishop Classe, lured by the prospect of a Christian ruling class, a 'racial aristocracy',[122] contributed to the process. 'We must not for all that neglect the classes of Bahutu young people and children,' he told the Fathers. 'They also need to be schooled and educated, and they will take up places in mine workings and industry.'[123] It mattered little that the 'reading' schools in the bush were hopelessly overcrowded so long as the central schools kept vaguely to the 1925 government syllabus and did not forfeit their subsidies.[124] The streaming system guaranteed that the Tutsi were given a superior education and was the means by which the Belgians were able to impose an ethnic definition of eligibility on the new political class. However sub-standard the general level of education, the nobility was assured of special attention.

As the streaming system allowed the Tutsi to consolidate their position while undergoing the transformation demanded by the colonial situation, so the tensions created amongst them, as poorer families clambered up the educational ladder, were reduced by an increasing racial solidarity. The ruling class could now identify themselves as 'Hamites' and their subjects as inferior 'Bantu'. Father Pagès' *Un Royaume hamite au centre de l'Afrique* fixed court history for the first time in written form;[125] privileged pupils at school in Kisenyi could hear from Pagès himself the glorious exploits of the Nyiginya dynasty.[126] It seemed to the missionaries that Hamitic history had involved the progressive dilution of some religious essence pre-ordained to flower into the fulness of Christianity.[127] As early as 1907 the White Fathers were speaking of Tutsi history, 'which obviously evokes biblical memories, by their customs, often borrowed from Jewish customs'.[128] The link between the 'Hamites' and Semites appeared to be incontestable at that time.

But what in a writer like Pagès was a pleasant speculation, a bringing together of Church history and Rwandan history, became unmitigated racism in some Belgian administrators. The Banyarwanda could in their view be placed on an evolutionary ladder whose rungs were the crudities of physical anthropology.[129] For such heirs to the evolutionary sociology of the nineteenth century Tutsi rule was un-questionable, 'their intellectual superiority has imposed them'.[130] Hutu, on the other hand, needed fond but firm paternal authority. 'Mahuku is not a bad sub-chief,' wrote another Resident, 'but, Muhutu, you have to supervise everything he does.'[131] Several missionaries agreed that the Hutu were incapable of governing, indisciplined and vulgar.[132] The Hutu Church gave the lie to this, but it had faded into insignifi-cance in the shadow of the Tutsi nobility and the Church triumphant.

The 1920s brought no succour to the Hutu; the initial effect of Belgian legislation was to worsen the lot of the peasants. They suffered the additional burden of unpaid *kazi* labour in public works and compulsory planting of food crops like manioc and sweet potatoes.[133] Tax revenue rose from one million francs in 1925 to almost two million in 1928 as· the three francs fifty centimes were collected more efficiently.[134] Attempts at legal reform were hopeless. Only two or three Residents spoke tolerable Kinyarwanda, and courts could be visited only two or three days each week. The Belgian dependence on Swahili meant that the Hutu could gain access to Residents only through interpreters. Spot checks on the court records were made, but the Tutsi found countless loopholes and many occasions for bribing judges, assessors and secretaries.[135] Since the Tutsi lord could still exert his influence through the legal system, arbitrary exactions continued; to counter the reduction in *ubuletwa* some chiefs began demanding it per individual rather than per *inzu*.[136] Even garagu were asked to hoe for their lords.[137] Tax collection for the Belgians provided an additional excuse for pillaging, so was more and more directly supervised.[138] The administration was too small and too sedentary to control the chiefs' exercise of power; one Belgian admitted that the small Rwandan police force were 'brutes',[139] and it was recognised that the new chiefs, lacking great wealth in cattle and land, were more rapacious than their predecessors. From 1924 to 1930 the good intentions of Indirect Rule gave way slowly to direct, though inadequate, supervision by selected Belgian agents and the harassed Residents.[140]

The Ruanda-Urundi Ordinance of 7 November 1924 on compulsory crop cultivation gave the Hutu an additional incentive to leave Rwanda. Owing to the favourable exchange rate, a good worker could earn one franc a day in Uganda on the cotton estates.[141] The price of hoes rose from thirty-five centimes in 1916 to three or four francs in the mid-1920s, and finally to ten to fifteen francs by 1929, so the cash economy was as much pushing as pulling the Hutu out of Rwanda.[142] The White Fathers were to a man opposed to the exodus, as were the Tutsi, who lost their *ubuletwa* labour; the Zaza Fathers let those leaving know that their banana trees on mission grounds would be confiscated.[143] But it was just as bad to remain if others left; *kazi* and *ubuletwa* labour fell on any unprotected individual, and the numbers available grew monthly smaller in areas of high emigration.

The White Fathers' attitude towards economic development remained equivocal. They saw cash cropping as a safeguard against emigration, but also as a danger. 'The small native producer, too tempted by the lure of profit which exportable products would bring him, may forget or neglect indispensable food crops,' one missionary feared.[144] Yet Rwaza mission stimulated tobacco production in the 1920s by opening a factory which made cigars that were sold throughout Rwanda. Mulera farmers, far from being simple 'subsistence farmers', had in the past profited by provisioning drought-stricken regions out of their food surpluses.[145] In this area where the Hutu felt confident of adequate food supplies a small tobacco-growing industry sprang up around Nyundo market.[146]

Perhaps because of the pre-colonial economy of Mulera, Rwaza proved the most successful of the White Fathers' industrial ventures, with its cigar factory, flour mill and furniture workshop,[147] but there was also basketmaking at Kabgayi, mat-making at Nyundo and pottery at Save, while all the major stations had their carpentry shop.[148] With the arrival of mining companies in search of tin, and the parcelling out of the Rwandan economy to the Banque Populaire Belge, PROTANAG (Syndicat Belge des Produits Tannants et Agricoles), and the Empain and Ryckman de Betz companies, the missions as employers of labour became relatively unimportant.[149] Training in skilled manual work still continued under the Brothers; the mission received a grant of 23,500 francs for it in 1927, although the Belgians were not satisfied that enough was being done.[150] There were, however, only a very few jobs for such mission-trained men, and the most they could hope for in Kigali and Ruhengeri was a monthly salary of fifty to sixty francs.[151]

The mission stations were also centres of modest agricultural experimentation. The Fathers issued coffee plants to their catechists, who began cash cropping on their out-station grounds.[152] The success of the cigar factory at Rwaza inspired a number of Hutu to start buying tobacco at Nyundo themselves, make their own cigars and market them wrapped in banana leaves.[153] Some of the Bugoyi Christians took to buying fibre bracelets from the Hunde and selling them for cattle in central Rwanda.[154]

The missionaries were never enthusiastic about their role in trade and cash cropping, seeing it in moralistic terms as 'amour du lucre'.[155] Nor did they want the Hutu for ever sunk in a degrading poverty, eking out a meagre living from the soil. Far from it; they saw Tutsi domination as a reason for the damaging flight from Rwanda, and complained when the Belgians wanted to start hotels on Lake Kivu that Bugoyi would be turned into a human 'zoological park'.[156] They opposed the 'wrong type' of European coming into the territory and the cession of large tracts of land to Belgian companies.[157] But their training in apologetics had taught them only what to condemn; beyond the Bishop's call for private property they had few positive ideas on development save the belief that the Church ought to be both *Mater* and *Magister*.

By 1927 the political balance of power had swung decisively in favour of the *Inshongore* and away from Musinga; feeling that Rwanda was on the verge of social and economic transformation was common. There were cars on new roads, 'a race for the tin Klondike' in Gisaka,[158] imported hoes and cotton cloth in the markets, talk of a new Catholic vocational school at Astrida,[159] and CMS missionaries with qualified medical personnel. Musinga and the court traditions began to seem an irrelevance, an anachronism.

At this point the king, despairing of effective Catholic support, made the serious blunder of trying the Protestants. Not only had they little power but there had been brawls between Catholic and Adventist catechists around Kabgayi, and the Fathers resented the intrusion of the new sect.[160] The Adventists were quite successful among the Hutu, and had opened a training school for pastors at Gitwe.[161] A pastor was invited to teach the young Tutsi at court, and[162] a few months later the CMS were welcomed in Nyanza and allowed to give Bible lessons.[163] Whereas in 1926 the mwami wrote anxious letters if the Fathers failed to make their courtesy calls,[164] now there was silence. Musinga carefully noted the names of nobles confessing Catholicism; catechumens of five or six years' standing dared not receive baptism for fear of incurring the mwami's wrath.[165] 'The sultan Musinga,' wrote Classe to Algiers, 'has become, or rather revealed himself to be, absolutely anti-catholic.'[166] If the Bishop's 'fiat' counted for anything in the question of Musinga's deposition — and it seems probable that it did — then the mwami had alienated a useful ally and gained nothing in return.

After their appearance at court the Catholics took the Protestants seriously; the Vicar Apostolic ordered the throwing up of temporary structures throughout Protestant-threatened areas, and tried to pass these off to the Belgians as chapel schools.[167] Since Classe had faithfully echoed the administrators' social policy to the point where Tutsi rule was a resonating orthodoxy, he was somewhat affronted to find the Belgians limiting the proliferation of these poorly equipped mud-and-thatch chapel schools, the defiantly planted flags of the religious scramble.[168]

Protestant competition made Bishop Classe even more concerned that the missionaries should do nothing to offend the chiefs; he wanted the Tutsi's entry into the Church to be made as easy as possible. 'Special rules according to the taste of individual missionaries which are exaggeratedly severe' must go.[169] On no account must the Fathers threaten the chiefs with denunciation at the Residence for their misdemeanours: 'We need them and we will need them all the more when freedom of worship is better and more completely practised.'[170]

This is not to say, though, that the White Fathers suddenly lost all interest in the conduct of Tutsi rule; the behaviour of the chiefs during the particularly severe famine in 1928-29 appalled them. Over 35,000 died and 70,000 emigrated to Uganda, while chiefs hoarded grain and seed, and continued, as was their wont, to allow cattle to trample over the Hutu's crops.[171] Around Lake Mohasi and in Gisaka, where the rains failed completely, mortality was as high as 50-60 per cent; at the height of the famine 1,000 refugees a week were passing north through Gahini.[172] In thinly populated areas there were no reserves and no roads over which relief supplies could be brought. The Tutsi consistently opposed extension of arable land for fear it would eat into pasture land, and the Hutu saw the planting of food crops as yet another punishment or *kazi* labour.

It was shortly after informing the Governor of the gravity of the famine that Classe felt obliged to don the mantle of the reformer once more. He dwelt on two main injustices, suggesting that it was unfair to deprive dispossessed chiefs of their cattle and men when they lost political office, and deploring the failure of chiefs to recognise that the Hutu had more than usufruct right's over their land and cattle.[173] It was some measure of the Bishop's influence that the Governor circulated the following suggestions to the Rwanda Residents.

A second abuse ... is to recognise that natives of lower rank (*bahutu* or *batwa*) have even over goods produced by their labour . . . only incomplete rights (usufruct, use possession for life, etc) . . . By allowing property rights over wealth not created by them, and without their having truly contributed, a land concession or breeding cattle, to pass into the hands of the Batusi chiefs or other notables, the authorities would actually make themselves accomplices to an assumption of rights which neither custom nor tradition suffices to justify or authorise . . . If the native does not at the moment have any precise notion of these juridical ideas, it is incumbent on us to educate him on the matter, correcting his errors and forming his mentality with perseverance and patience.[174]

The Bishop saw the instructions as a '*point de départ* for the recommencement [*sic*] of certain property rights for the natives, rights without which the development of these regions will be impossible.'[175]

This liberal reform mooted in 1923 and now quite strongly pressed might seem out of keeping with Classe's reverence for the *status quo*. The Kigali Resident opposed agrarian revolution on the most Catholic of grounds. 'The muhutu farmer has been accustomed for generations to work the land . . . for himself,' he wrote. '. . . He is an individualist by nature. Now, the cult of the individual without any powerful cohesive bonds engenders anarchy. Will not the fact of proclaiming too baldly "rights over land" lead the primitive into an exaggerated idea of liberty and ordering of his life?'[176] Coffee and tobacco cash cropping did in fact produce a new form of land ownership. 'European' land with 'European' crops — for example, catechists' plots — tended increasingly to fall outside the chief's jurisdiction and to become Christians' private property.[177] But such change was essentially the result of continuing mission patronage and protection, and took place within a clientship context.[178]

Classe had not renounced his conservatism and become a social revolutionary, he was merely parroting the major theme of Leo XIII's encyclial *Rerum Novarum*. 'Private ownership . . . is the natural right of man; and to exercise that right, expecially as members of society, is not only lawful but absolutely necessary'[179] — a liberal doctrine belatedly espoused by the Church in order to defend herself against the onslaught of atheistic Marxism. The spectre of communism was never to leave the Catholics throughout the colonial period, and much that was doctrinaire and shortsighted may be attributed to the clerical 'Cold War' many a bush missionary imagined himself to be fighting. This obsession was shared by many Governors, Postiaux confided to Classe the disturbing news that 'communism and bolshevism, in other words the two parties which have inscribed on their programme the ruin of society, are about to turn their forces of destruction on the colonies.'[180]

The movement of the ruling class into the catechumenate continued unabated throughout 1928-29, especially in regions like Muramba and Rambura where there were newly arrived Banyanduga out to seek their fortune, and 'petits Tutsi' of long standing.[181] Important women, like Nyirashongore, a wife of Rwabugiri, and Mukamulera, one of Musinga's daughters, were swept up.[182] News that his favourite daughter, Musheshambugu, who was married to the Ega chief Rwagataraka, had begun to receive instruction, was too much for the king. He cursed her in a heart-rending letter which ended with a plea that she should show whether or not she was a true daughter of the mwami of Rwanda.[183]

Although the king was a very rich man, under Belgian rule he had become a powerless symbol, pathetic, irascible and fast aging. His sons manoeuvred for the succession and his daughters turned away from him. Under pressure from the Belgians, he threw caution to the winds and, for the first time, officially visited the provinces, possibly in the hope of drumming up support. Belatedly he crossed the Nyabarongo and was given a warm reception by the Hutu throughout the north.[184] If it was a last bid to save his throne it was somewhat half-hearted; attempts had already been made to contact the British with a view to his seeking asylum in Uganda with the royal herds and retainers.[185] Money poured into his treasury, Nyanza was strong, but the king was weak.[186] The crossing of the Nyabarongo in definance of the tradition of the 'Yuhi' kings was a final defeat for the *Abayoboke*. The king was trying another way but too late for both *Inshongore* and Belgians.

As the Great Depression brought commercial activity virtually to a halt young Tutsi flocked into the schools and catechism classes to secure the benefits of the Western bureaucracy and economy. Tutsi accounted for 1,934 of the 9,014 baptisms in 1930; at new stations like Nyamasheke, where Rwagataraka's influence was strong, figures were as high as 193 out of 393.[187] Tutsi now became the majority in the minor seminaries, and nineteen out of twenty-five *Bayozefiti* were from the ruling class.[188] The noviciates of the *Benebikira* had a similar lease of life; there were thirty postulants in all at Rwaza, Save and Kabgayi.[189]

At the capital only Musinga's two sons, Rudahigwa and Rwigemera, were not on the catechists' registers, and the king was openly mocked by catechemens.[190] The Fathers installed themselves at Nyanza with a permanent *pied-à-terre* for catechism lessons.[191] The mwami's ill-considered approach to the British had finally alienated the Belgians, while his hysterical outburst at his daughter's conversion had destroyed any lingering sympathy in the Vicar Apostolic; it was said that he raved openly and trampled a crucifix underfoot.[192]

While Classe had been willing to plead for Musinga in 1926, he now used his influence to prepare Belgian public opinion for the mwami's deposition. Shortly after the king's anti-Christian letter to his daughter Classe wrote the Governor a letter which described Musinga as 'haineusement anti-européen',[193] and sent off two articles to *L'Essor Colonial et Maritime*; one again pressed the case for guaranteed property rights, the other denigrated the mwami.[194] With the Colonial

Ministry behind him and public opinion in Belgium prepared, the new Belgian Governor could get rid of the king. Committed to social reforms that were being rendered ineffective by Tutsi intransigence, yet wedded to the Tutsi by the policy of Indirect Rule, the Belgians needed a scapegoat for their failure to provide the Hutu with real protection. 'He would quite deliberately wish stagnation on his people', wrote the Governor, Voisin, 'if an early dotage still allowed him any will for anything other than his perversity and hostility to the Christianisation of his country.'[195] The new Governor planned to raise and diversify Rwandan agricultural production, improve livestock, codify customary law on dues, provide new schools, and carry out a census. It was to be a clean sweep. He wanted a list of the king's sins for the Minister's use in case there were repercussions in Geneva.[196] Ten days after the Governor's first confidential letter to the Bishop the echo came back from Kabgayi. 'The peace, good order and good administration, on one side, and on the other the material, moral and social progress of Rwanda, will never be achieved in a lasting and profound manner as long as Musinga is mwami of Ruanda.'[197]

Musinga was to join Kabakas Mtesa and Mwanga in the Catholic chamber of horrors, but the problem of finding a successor remained. Voisin suggested Rudahigwa, but the Bishop was unenthusiastic; the man was 'craintif' and 'indécis', thought Classe, who feared the influence of his mother, the adroit politician Kankazi.[198] Rudahigwa had so far failed to make a good impression on Europeans; one observer had described him in 1929 as 'distinctly and artfully hostile to the missions . . . very intelligent but completely lacking in character, a knave and a deceiver'.[199] Much to Musinga's displeasure, since it put the prince close to the Kabgayi Fathers, Rudahigwa was appointed to Marangara province, where he inherited 10,040 cattle; Marangara was in chaos for the next year as Rudahigwa tried to wrest the cattle from the garagu of Tutsi lords and *ibikingi* holders.[200] Resistance was led by Kayondo's lineage, which was struggling to place Rwigemera in line for the succession.[201] Since few of the Marangara Tutsi would obey him, Rudahigwa began to court the Kabgayi Fathers[202] — a move that assured his future.

The Vicar Apostolic received two visits from Rudahigwa in June 1931, and spoke to the prince about the changes that had been taking place in Burundi, where the mwami lived in a luxurious house and drove around in a car. Classe had decided to make the best of a bad job, to wean the prince from the old style of kingship and to start him on French lessons.[203] The heir apparent next went to Bujumbura for a secret meeting with the Governor. 'Rudahigwa spontaneously asked me if you were *au fait* with my intentions,' wrote Voisin to Classe; '. . . on my assurance that you were in perfect agreement, he seemed very satisfied.'[204]

Under Voisin the amalgamation of provinces was given a fresh impetus, and new chiefs were appointed over newly enlarged jurisdictions. Mirenge province in Gisaka was unified under Simon Nyiringondo, a Christian from Zaza,[205] and other mission men gained several hills.[206] Kanuma complained of being 'slighted and rejected, though he had handed over his chieftancy to no one'.[207] Rudahigwa was given a car in which to return from Bujumbura; the mwami complained that everyone but the king rode around in cars.[208] As senior chiefs converted to Christianity, some fearing deposition,[209] the mwami was left alone with the Queen Mother; 'there would be no one left to conserve our customs and our cult to the ancestors,'[210] he lamented.

The Governor General of the Congo visited Bishop Classe in September to set a date for the deposition.[211] Rudahigwa was introduced to him, and a week later the notables were called to Kigali for discussion about the economic crisis.[212] Musinga was conveniently alone in Nyanza when he was informed that his son would succeed him. The king seemed to be expecting the news, cried a little and left almost immediately for a special residence at Kamembe. Rwanda appeared indifferent to his fate;[213] only *Le Drapeau Rouge*, the *Manchester Guardian*[214] and the Queen Mother protested — she was reported to be threatening suicide.[215] Musinga had ceased to rule long before; his whimpering departure simply removed the last major obstacle in the mission's path. The enthronement of his son was that of a Christian king.

Rudahigwa was proclaimed mwami by the Governor, and Monsignor Classe, replacing the *abiru*, supplied his reign name, Mutara IV. Only then were the six court *abiru* officially informed. Champagne toasts were drunk, a White Father acted as official photographer, and the royal drum Kalinga was shown to the crowd; Rwagataraka translated the speeches. Mutara made the first visit of his reign to Kabgayi, where the seminarians presented him with a Larousse and a childhood friend read a discourse on the divine dependence of kings.[216] The departed Musinga had been 'like the rock that stops the torrent'; 'once removed, the water surges on'.[217] More than ten thousand new catechumens enrolled at Kabgayi alone, and within the year nearly four thousand new Christians were baptised;[218] a rumour circulated that Rudahigwa wanted people to make the sign of the cross to greet him and desired them to register as catechumens;[219] even the new Queen Mother became a postulant.[220] Owing to the clientship structure of society in central Rwanda, the dense population and the absence of discrete villages, the movement, once started, soon involved massive numbers. The Fathers called it a *Tornade*, and indeed it did blow away the White Fathers' usual restraints and strict discipline for the catechumenate. Bishop Classe himself was carried away and, with the CMS beginning to take up the overflow, few could resist the eager

Tutsi who clamoured to join the catechumenate.[221] The end of Musinga's reign marked the end of the young Hutu Church. At first the 'petits Tutsi' and Banyanduga settlers north of the Nyabarongo, then the nobles, and finally women and old people, chiefs and their garagu joined the rush. The enthronement of the catechumen king came as a climax to the conversion of the ruling class that Classe had so ardently desired; it was a triumph for a mission that had held on to the hope of becoming the State religion against apparently insuperable odds.

The Belgians had not only recognised Rwanda's social stratification but had given it a new definition and rigidity by their political, educational and language policies;[222] the *Tornade* began simply as a response to the new qualifications now needed for chieftaincy and status, but as the *Inshongore* gained ground at court it took on a new meaning; the nobility were searching for a fresh religious legitimation for the mwamiship and their own offices. Traditional rituals had been stripped one by one from the king until the whole mystical support for his role disappeared. Obsessed by the doubtful legitimacy of his claims to the throne, Musinga could never share Kabare's cavalier attitude towards tradition, nor could he see, like the *Inshongore*, that a powerful intrusive religious system such as Christianity must be assimilated, as the Lyangombe cult had been in the past, if it were not to destroy the kingship.

The conversion of the Tutsi was a corporate recognition that the source of power within the State had shifted away from the mwami. For some it was a fatalistic acknowledgement of the bankruptcy of the old order and its religious system. 'My child,' Nyirashongore is said to have told her daughters, 'we have always believed in the spirits; we have offered them sacrifice and we have followed the customs of our ancestors in everything; what was the use of all that to us?'[223] For others there was the stark realisation that without Christianity a man might be excluded from wealth and prestige, that he might be left out of the new order. This fear, which drew strength from hell-fire sermons and perhaps even from the traditions of Nyiragongo Volcano, informed the dreams of at least one young Tutsi convert.

When we were sleeping together in a large hut — we were the king's *ntore* — I had a terrifying dream. I saw God in a beautiful court with lovely children who were enjoying themselves playing happily. As I tried to approached them, Imana [God] pushed me back towards a very deep chasm in which were hideous men weeping and groaning. 'There is your place,' He said to me. 'You are wicked and must suffer with the wicked.' Then I replied, 'Have pity on me, I will do all that you ask,' trembling all the while. He pushed me back again into this foul, smoking pit, when luckily I caught hold of some branches which were hanging by the abyss. I went on begging for pardon, and those who filled the pit, including my uncle who died some years ago, said to me, 'Come down. Do not waste your strength. It is no use saying that you didn't know. We said the same, and look, we are still here. The only thing is to do His will.' Even more angry, Imana came and pushed me back with his foot. I let go of the branches and made a grab for a tuft of grass, which gave way. Just as I was about to fall I awoke. That night I told the dream to my companions, and the next morning I took my leave of our chief. When I reached home I went straight to see the catechist, Augustin, who admitted me as a postulant. [224]

In a remarkable way Catholicism became 'traditional' the moment the Tutsi were baptised in large numbers. 'It was the "done thing" for almost all the chiefs to wear the medallion around their necks and to expect their people to accept the State religion without question,' a CMS missionary remarked. [225] The term 'State religion' was not merely a sour Protestant fancy. Residents warned the White Fathers when CMS missionaries appeared in their province, and Governor Tilkens encouraged Bishop Classe to multiply the number of Catholic stations to counteract the Protestant invasion of the 1930s. [226] The terms of the convention between the Holy See and the Congo government of 1906, to 'favour' and 'protect' the missions, were perhaps nowhere so broadly interpreted as in Rwanda; [227] Voisin contributed 50 per cent of the cost of new churches in Kigali and Astrida. [228] The Bishop's opinion was sought on weighty topics, from minimum wages to the mechanics of deposing kings. [229]

The key to the happy marriage between Church and administration was Monsignor Classe. He was what the Rwandans would call 'the man of the Belgians'. It was largely his definition of Rwandan politics and social structure which guided Belgian policy and initiatives in the early years. Or, to state the case less strongly, he gave the Church's *imprimatur* to policies that seemed to all right-thinking colonials self-evident. He was certainly as much a part of colonial administration as were the *abiru* of the traditional court. Indeed, the Vicar Apostolic could find no more fitting tribute for Monsignor Hirth in his eulogy of the veteran's fifty years of Christian ministry than 'doyen des coloniaux'. [230]

Intellectuals like Father Schumacher found Classe's 'seigneurial' style of episcopate insufferable, and downright dishonest or stupid his lumping of Musinga with the Uganda Kabakas, [231] but he pleased men like Tilkens, Declerck, Voisin and Postiaux: a few words between gentlemen, indiscreet Fathers to be kept in the dark, [232] nothing more was needed; that was the world in which he liked to move and the rock on which he hoped to build his Church. If the Catholic Church in Rwanda grew so quickly into a State Church it was largely because this was the part Classe was determined it should play, a part which few of his contemporaries would have found inappropriate. The Hutu Church had indirectly split the Tutsi and divided the missionaries; Classe had been toppled in its heyday and the king in its decline. If, after 1932, it became a Tutsi Church, in the sense that its life increasingly served the interests of the ruling class, it was because the nobility, having done away with Musinga, needed a new 'tradition' to legitimate their role as custodians of Rwandan culture and owners of its material wealth.

NOTES

1 Recommendation of the Apostolic Visitor to Nyasaland, 10 August 1928, Catholic Secretariat, Limbe, Malawi.

2 Musinga attended the consecration of Kabgayi cathedral; *Rapports annuels*, 1922-23, 500-1.

3 Van den Eede to Hirth, 18 January 1920, CO.

4 For example, a certain Makato appeared at Rukira claiming to be a son of the Gisaka pretender, Lukara; see Zaza diary, 13 March 1922.

5 Zaza diary, 7 February, 5 April, 16 April 1922.

6 The most provocative case was that of a peasant who refused to cook for Rwamuhama's son: Mr Allsop, the Resident, upheld the Hutu's complaint on the grounds that a married man should not have to perform humiliating work, see Zaza diary, 29 April 1922.

7 Allsop's appointee who was going effectively to take the place of the king, and destroy the 'sage et traditionelle politique', was Mulindahabi; see Zaza diary, 21 April 1922.

8 *Ibid.*

9 'During this first fortnight of May court cases have flooded into Lukira. Guided by a secret hope, encouraged above all by the new way of carrying out justice, litigants are coming in from everywhere. But in face of the number, and above all the oldness of the complaints, it has been made known to the litigants as a general rule that cases going back more than three or four years would not be dealt with,' Zaza diary, 15 May 1922.

10 Zaza diary, 18 May 1922.

11 Pagès, *Un Royaume*, 613.

12 Zaza diary, 25 April, 10 May 1922.

13 *Ibid.*, 25 April 1922, and see chapter eight.

14 *Ibid.*, 19 April 1922.

15 Although the missionaries were asked to sign a declaration pledging to refrain from political activity, the Rukira Resident sent tax defaulters to Zaza to work for the Fathers at one third the normal rate; Zaza diary, 7 May 1922.

16 Zaza diary, 18 April 1922.

17 *Ibid.*, 19 April 1922.

18 *Ibid.*

19 Zaza diary, 11 October 1922.

20 Classe made a speech on the subject of Gisaka at the Union Coloniale in Brussels, and returned to Rwanda in September 1922 the renowned defender of Musinga's kingdom.

21 Anet put a strong case before the mandates commission of the League of Nations; see Anet to Franck, 20 April 1921; *Le Chrétien Belge*, 16 September 1922, No. 18, 287; *Bulletin Missionaire*, No. 7, September 1923, 61, M.639, AA. Attached marginal notes in this file suggest that Anet made a considerable impact.

22 See chapter six.

23 See n. 33.

24 Pastor Monnier was joined by an American who slipped in from Uganda, only to be promptly expelled; he was followed by Pastor Delhove, a Swiss artisan, who survived; see Education Report for Ruanda-Urundi, 1921, M.634; Report on Missions in Ruanda-Urundi, 12 May 1921, M.639, AA; Zaza diary, 29 April 1922.

25 Ryckmans to Minister for the Colonies, 26 October 1920, M. 639, AA; *La Libre Belgique*, 20 January 1923; *Bulletin Missionaire*, No. 1, July 1922, 2.

26 *Bulletin Missionaire*, No. 3, December 1922, 22.

27 The missionaries were the Revs. Lewin, Stanley Smith and Leonard Sharp; see memorandum for Minister for the Colonies, 10 November 1920, M.639.

28 Anet to Franck, 5 September 1923, AE/II, No. 1918, AA. Nationalist sensibilities were less strained by this date.

29 Ryckmans to Minister for the Colonies, 26 October 1920, M.639, points out this danger and suggests that British missionaries might give rise to unfavourable comparisons.

30 Zaza diary, 19 April 1922; *Bulletin Missionaire*, No. 3, September 1922, 10; *Ruanda Notes*, No. 6, February 1923, 16. A collection of *Ruanda Notes* may be found at the CMS headquarters in London.

31 'With the change of administration, the position of a Protestant and English Mission had become, in the eyes of the natives, dubious; so I found that in nearly every place the work had gone back, and our teachers were no longer being supported by the chiefs. But our worst enemies were the R.C.'s.' See *Ruanda Notes*, No. 9, 28 March 1924.

32 *Ruanda Notes*, No. 9, 28 March 1924.

33 Mortehan to Classe, 10 September 1923, CO.

34 Bourgeois, R., *Banyarwanda et Barundi*, vol. I, 1957, 181-2; Paternostre de la Mairieu, B., *Le Rwanda: son effort de développement*, Brussels, 1972, 109, 112-14.

35 *Le Soir*, 29 March 1923, clipping in AE/II, No. 1847, AA.

36 Classe to Marchal, 23 September 1923, WFAR.

37 Van den Eede to Classe, 11 January 1920; Ryckmans to Hirth, 16 November 1921; Mortehan to Classe, 18 November 1922; Classe to Mortehan, 9 December 1922; Marzorati to Kigali Resident, 22 July 1927, CO. Marzorati to Classe, 14 February 1925, even requests 2,000 sheets of paper to complete that year's official *Bulletin*.

38 Lemarchand, R., *Political Awakening in the Belgian Congo*, Los Angeles, 1964, 134. This policy had been adumbrated by the Colonial Minister during his 1920 visit; see chapter six.

39 See Mallinson, V., *Power and Politics in Belgian Education*, London, 1963.

40 Mortehan to Kigali Resident, 16 April 1921, CO.

41 *Ruanda Notes*, No. 18, November 1926, describes Nyanza school and its equipment as 'Perhaps the finest in all Africa'.

42 Report on Senate session of 29 July 1921; memorandum by Kervyn to Minister for the Colonies, 9 April 1923, M.634, AA.

43 Classe to Van den Eede, 25 January 1920, CO.

44 Van den Eede to Classe, 9 June 1920; Classe to Van den Eede, 12 June 1920, CO; Marzorati to Minister for the Colonies, 4 July 1923, M.634, AA.
45 Memorandum from Kervyn to Minister for the Colonies, 11 March 1921, M.634.
46 Marzorati to Classe, 2 October 1924, 13 November 1924, 29 April 1925, CO.
47 Scanlon, D. G. (ed.), *Church, State and Education in Africa*, New York, 1966.
48 *Ruanda Notes*, No. 19, January 1927, 21.
49 Ryckmans to Franck, 2 December 1922, M.639.
50 Slade *English-speaking Missions*, 298 *et seq.*
51 Classe received his in 1922 for his defence of Gisaka.
52 Kabgayi diary, 6 November 1925.
53 Memorandum for Minister for the Colonies, 18 March 1921, M.634.
54 Kupens to Classe, 20 June 1925, trans. from French, CO.
55 See Weber, E., *Action Française*, Stanford, Col., 1962.
56 See chapter ten.
57 *Rapport sur l'administration belge du Ruanda-Urundi*, 1923, 6.
58 Bishibishi, Lwakadigi's son, became the leading figure in the district; see Nyundo diary, 22 September 1924, 4 January 1925; Rwaza diary, January 1925; *Rapports annuels*, 1924-25, 460.
59 The subjugation of Bukunzi was occasioned by the death of its *umuhinza*, Ndagano, in April 1923. On the pretext of averting ritual killings at the funeral Belgian troops occupied the kingdom. Bigirumwera, Ndagano's older brother, then ruled with the Queen Mother until the Belgians wanted him for tax defaulting, and he appealed to the Mibirisi Fathers for help in March 1924. He met Rwagataraka at the mission and agreed to pay a fine of twenty cows and submit peacefully to the Belgians. No cows were paid. Despite pleas from the Fathers and the efforts of the Tutsi, who feared the loss of an important rainmaker, the Belgians eventually tracked down the Bukunzi royal family in March 1925 and shot the Queen Mother dead. Five months later Rutasumbga, Queen Mother of Busozo, surrendered, and both kingdoms fell under Rwagataraka's jurisdiction. Few Tutsi wanted to live in either, and the Belgian conquests did not have Nyanza's support. See Mibirisi diary, 30 March 1923, 7-30 April 1924, 25 May 1927; *Rapports annuels*, 1923-24, 378; Pauwels, *Le Bushiru*, 215; Bourgeois, *Banyarwanda*, vol I, 182.
60 Des Forges, *Rwanda under Musiinga*, 252, 293, for examples from Nyanza and Mulera.
61 *Ibid.*, 252-323 *passim*, provides an exhaustive coverage of the inter-lineage politics at court in this period.
62 Lenaerts, M., 'Territoire de Nyanza. Rapport établi en réponse au questionnaire adressé en 1929 par M. le Gouverneur du Ruanda-Urundi à l'administrateur du territoire du Nyanza'. (Henceforth abbreviated to Nyanza report, 1929).
63 Classe to Marchal, 10 March 1923, WFAR.
64 Kabgayi diary, 17, 23 October 1923, 28 November 1924.
65 *Rapports annuels*, 1923-24, 370.
66 Kabgayi diary, 20 August 1924; Classe to Marchal, 18 March 1924.
67 Kabgayi diary, 15 February 1924.

68 *Rapports annuels*, 1923-24, 350, 360, 370, 375.
69 See also chapter five, p. 111.
70 *Rapports annuels*, 1923-24, 370.
71 *Ibid.*, 349; de Lacger, *Le Ruanda*, 520.
72 Des Forges, *Rwanda under Musiinga*, 259-60. This was Lwabutogo.
73 Statistics taken from *Rapports annuels*, and see Marzorati to Classe, 13 November 1924, CO.
74 Father Lecoindre had been Superior at Save and Kabgayi, positions liable to 'make or break' a missionary. He was made Monsignor Classe's *Econome Générale*, in charge of provisions and the vicariate's budget in 1922. He was, like Classe, a powerful patron, to whom even Musinga wrote begging letters; see Musinga to Lecoindre, 7 December, 12 December 1922, 29 January 1923, CO.
75 'umuntu iyabunze Abami 2 umwe aramanga amaze agakunda umwe'; Rwagataraka to Lecoindre, 25, 30 November 1962, CO.
76 Des Forges, *Rwanda under Musiinga*, 308-9.
77 Kabgayi diary, 15 March 1925; *Rapports annuels*, 1925-26, 8. Indeed, it was Classe who seems to have first warned the Belgians that there was something amiss at court. The Resident had jumped to the conclusion that Gashamura was planning an uprising; see Coubeau to Classe, 10 December 1924, CO.
78 Coubeau to Classe, 28 September 1924, CO.
79 *Umuganura* was stopped after Gashamura's deportation; see Father Martin's notes on Bumbogo, 23 November 1924, Derscheid papers.
80 This was on the occasion of Father Classe's silver anniversary as a priest. Rather pathetically, Musinga asked the Bishop to keep it a secret that he slept away; see Classe to Voillard, 22 April 1925; Kabgayi diary, 19 April 1925.
81 *Rapports annuels*, 1925-26, 8.
82 Kabgayi diary, 4 December 1925, 18 July 1926.
83 Serukenyinkware was the mwami's chief expert in court sacrifices, and his later defection to the pro-European faction was of great significance Mutara Rudahigwa seems to have been greatly influenced by him. After learning to read and write he was given Kanage and Bwishaza provinces. See Political Report for Rubengera, 1929, Derscheid papers; Rwagataraka to Lecoindre, 14, 23, 25 November 1926; Serukenyinkware to Lecoindre, 1 December 1926; Ntulo to Lecoindre, 12 December 1926, CO.
84 Kabgayi diary, 21 October 1926. Rwigemera was essentially the *Inshongore* candidate for the mwamiship as against Rudahigwa, who at this stage was still supporting the king.
85 *Rapports annuels*, 1925-26, 8.
86 Kabgayi diary, 21 October 1926.
87 It was here that the missionaries were most important, as the *Inshongore* successfully played on the Christianity *v.* traditional religion conflict. In Rwagataraka to Lecoindre, 1 December 1926, it is suggested that Bandora is a 'sorcerer' trying to poison the prince. The *Rapport sur l'administration belge du Ruanda-Urundi* speaks of the 'asservissement du mwami aux devins', 1926, 6. Bourgeois, *Banyarwanda*, vol. I, 183, paints the same picture.
88 Rwagataraka to Lecoindre, 1 December 1926.

89 De Lacger, *Le Ruanda*, 525.

90 *Rapports annuels*, 1930-31, 322.

91 Rwagataraka, saved from death on two occasions by treatment from the Fathers, was now something of a mission agent; he seems to have paid for the 102 hectares of the Nyamasheke site out of his own pocket; see Mibirisi diary, 18 February 1927.

92 Musinga to Classe, 6 January 1927: 'Kandi barashaka kugirngw' abantu bandje bazafatwe nkuko Gashamura yafashwe . . . Ninkuwakwangana n'Inkuba ntachyo yayitwara, ariko y'ibishatse yakimutwara.' CO.

93 *Rapports annuels*, 1925-26, 8; de Lacger, *Le Ruanda*, 525.

94 *Rapports annuels*, 1923-24, 1925-26, 1926-27, 23.

95 The mediums were said to have 'thousands' of adepts in Buganza. The Fathers concluded that the *mandwa* cult was for the Tutsi while 'the Nyabingi cult is no less widespread amongst the Hutu'; see Rwaza diary, 13 May 1928; *Rapports annuels*, 1924-25, 463-5.

96 *Ruanda Notes*, No. 16, April 1926, 11; *Rapports annuels*, 1924-25, 464, states: 'Sharangabo detests the Nyabingi and has on several occasions asked the Europeans to arrest one or another of them who live on a hill opposite the mission.'

97 *Rapports annuels*, 1927-28, 285-7; Zaza diary, 21 February 1928.

98 Classe to Mortehan, 21 September 1927, CO.

99 *Ibid.*; 'chefs nés, ceux-ci ont le sens du commandement'.

100 Zaza diary, 14 October, 19 November 1924.

101 He was consecrated on 1 June 1952 at Kabgayi; see chapter nine.

102 Nyanza report, 1929.

103 Political Report for Busiru 1925, Derscheid papers.

104 The same *umuhinza*, Nyamakwa, had been resisting since the days of the Ndungutse rising, leading the Gesera clan. In 1923, as a result of repeated clan feuds, the Tutsi chief, Nyangesi, was put over the region but commanded little allegiance while Nyamakwa was alive.

105 This was Nyamurasa; see Martin, 'Notes on Bumbogo', Derschied papers.

106 *Rapports annuels*, 1924-25, 454.

107 The Belgians began arresting Nyabingi mediums in 1927 in an attempt to subdue the north; see Rwaza diary, 31 May 1927, 13 May 1928. Still, four years later the Tutsi chief of Buberuka, Kahitakibwa, was murdered while trying to collect taxes; see Servranckx to Father Superior, Rwaza, 26 October 1931.

108 Servranckx, 'Rapport de sortie de charge', Shangugu, 1930.

109 For the effects of Hinsley's visit on education policy in another, British, colony see Linden, *Catholics, Peasants and Chewa Resistance*, 153-9.

110 A pastoral letter of 16 July 1927 in *Instructions pastorales de Monseigneur Classe, 1922-39*, Kabgayi, 1940, 31.

111 Quoted by de Lacger, *Le Ruanda*, 510.

112 De Lacger, *Le Ruanda*, 510.

113 *Ibid.*

114 For each French-speaking clerk who knew how to type the Fathers received 350-500 francs from the government; see Coubeau to Commissaire-Royal, 18 February 1924, CO; Deprimoz, White Fathers' school report for 1927-28.

Church and revolution in Rwanda

115 Deprimoz, school report.
116 *Ibid*. The system was modelled on that of the Congo; see Lemarchand, *Political Awakening*, 134.
117 De Lacger, *Ruanda*, 517.
118 Classe to confrères, 15 May 1928, CR.
119 Deprimoz, school report.
120 *Ibid*.
121 *Ibid*.
122 Quoted in de Lacger, *Le Ruanda*, 523.
123 Classe to confrères, 15 May 1928.
124 Discontent was shown by some chiefs at the quality of the bush schools; see Sandrart, Kigali report, 1929.
125 The monograph was first presented to the Institut Royal Colonial Belge in November 1930 and published in 1933.
126 Kisenyi report, 1929.
127 'Monophysite on their departure from Abyssinia, the Hamites, perhaps little by little in the course of their long exodus, forgot Christian beliefs and adopted superstitions and practices of the people in whose midst they lived.' See Pagès, *Un Royaume*, 8; *cf* Speke on Rumanyika: 'sprung from . . . the Abyssinians . . . They were Christians like ourselves, and had the Wahuma not lost their knowledge of God they would be so also'; see Speke, J., *Journal of the Discovery of the Source of the Nile*, London, 1863, 208.
128 Un Père Blanc, 'Traditions des Batutsi', *Missions d'Afrique*, 1907, 177-84.
129 One administrator had this to say about 'les rudes Bakiga': 'If the people of Kiga do belong to the black type they are far from having such low foreheads, such large, flat noses and thick, prominent lips as the Congolese type; in a word, this race has moved, as it were, towards what we consider a higher plane of beauty and has taken a step towards the European standard.' Stevens, 'Rapport de sortie de charge', Byumba, 1933, trans. from the French.
130 Stevens, *loc. cit*.
131 Dryvers, 'Rapport de sortie de charge', Mutara, 1932.
132 *Rapports annuels*, 1924-25, 454.
133 For the hostile reactions to *kazi* and compulsory crops see Rwaza diary, 28 July 1923; Nyundo diary, 20 March 1924; Zaza diary, 29 November 1925; *Rapports annuels*, 1923-24, 372; *Ruanda Notes*, No. 19, January 1927, 19.
134 Nyanza report, 1929; Paternostre de la Mairieu, *Le Rwanda*, 109-13.
135 An example is found in Nyundo diary, 3 May 1923.
136 The consensus of replies to the Governor's questionnaire in 1929 was that exactions were common but peasants too scared to complain.
137 Rwabukumba and Mudandagizi, *Les Formes historiques*, 24 n. 1.
138 Until 1924 the Belgians directed labour demands through the mwami, but he used them as a punishment. After 1927 they used supervised province chiefs, as the king's men were the worst offenders; see Zaza diary, 5 August 1926; Nyanza report, 1929; Leurquin, *Niveau de vie*, 22-3.
139 Wouters to Father Superior Rwaza, undated (*c*. 1930), Rwaza correspondence.
140 Mulera report, 1929.

141 Cotton acreage in Buganda had risen from 86,000 in 1922 to 185,000 in 1924; by the end of 1924 29 per cent, i.e. 1,394 of 4,834 labourers working for the Ganda were Banyarwanda. When the Ganda began to reduce their labour force in 1926 many of these men took jobs in the Public Works Department in Kampala. See *Rapports annuels*, 1924-25, 440, 473; Richards, A. I., *Economic Development and Tribal Change*, Cambridge, 1951, 28-9; Powesland, P. G., 'Economic policy and labour', in *East African Studies*, No. 10, 1957, 42-8.

142 Classe to Marchal, 18 March 1924; Nyanza report, 1929.

143 Zaza diary, 3 February 1927.

144 *Rapports annuels*, 1927-28, 274.

145 See Vidal, *Économie de la société féodale*, 52-75, for rich farmers in other areas.

146 Education Report for 1921, M.634, AA.

147 In 1924 Rwaza mission purchased 6,430 francs' worth of tobacco and paid out 3,132 francs in salaries to workers at their small cigar factory; profits from the sales amounted to 3,228 francs. The mission was buying over 6,000 kilos of local tobacco at five francs per kilo in 1931; the forty-seven workers produced 640,000 cigars worth 80,130 francs. The station took on the character of an industrial mission, with 130,000 francs paid out annually in employees' salaries; this included payment of construction workers, porters and teachers, as well as factory hands, millers, carpenters, sawyers and masons. Millers worked round the clock in five twelve-man shifts, producing flour at the mission sold for 2·5 francs a kilo. They bought in annually about 30,000 kilos of local wheat at 0·5-1·0 francs a kilo. The carpentry shop and sawyers made furniture, and provided construction materials for the growing town of Kigali.

148 The 1921 Education Report spoke glowingly of the missions' efforts in this regard: 'Everywhere native artisans are trained and guided in their work by the missionaries; bricklayers, tilers, sawyers, carpenters, heavy timber workers and many others have become useful auxiliaries in stations with private individuals.' M.634, AA.

149 For example, PROTONAG paid 1·50 francs per day for labour, and about 80 per cent of the men around Mibirisi mission were employed by the company; see Kamembe report, 1929, Derscheid papers.

150 Mortehan to Classe, 29 August 1928; Malfeyt to Classe, 8 December 1928, CO.

151 Coubeau to Classe, 15 December 1926, CO.

152 Zaza diary, 8 August 1926; Classe to confrères, 20 August 1928, CR; Leurquin, *Niveau de vie*, 59, 66. Plants were sometimes given in lieu of cash payment; see 'Compte rendu des séances de Conseil', Rwaza, 13 March 1928.

153 Personal communication, Father Manuel Daguerre, Rwaza mission.

154 *Rapports annuels*, 1928-29, 330.

155 *Ibid.*, 1926-27, 14.

156 *Ibid.*, 1927-28, 274.

157 *Ibid.*, 273. In Classe to Mortehan, 3 May 1928, there is a stiff remark about 'hundreds or even thousands of hectares free or to be sold free' to foreign buyers, and a reference to article 6 of the treaty of 18 April 1923 — the part concerning the safeguarding of African interests.

158 Classe to Marchal, 16 August 1927, WFAR.

159 The Brothers of Charity school was finally opened in the 1930s after many delays, and gave training in administration and veterinary science for Ruanda-Urundi.

160 Kabgayi diary, 4, 5 March 1926; Classe to Marchal, 7 May 1927, WFAR; *Rapports annuels*, 1926-27, 23.

161 *Ibid*., 1928-29, de Lacger, *Le Ruanda*, 501.

162 *Rapports annuels*, 1926-27, 23.

163 Church, J. E., 'Quest for the highest', 20, bound but unpublished typed MS prepared for the Makerere Religious Studies Project and covering the years 1927-71 of the CMS Ruanda mission. I am very grateful to Dr Church for allowing me to consult his copy.

164 *Rapports annuels*, 1925-26, 8.

165 Van Overschelde, A., *Un Audacieux pacifique*, Grands Lacs, 1948, 123.

166 Classe to Marchal, 7 May 1927. 'Sultan' was always a bad word.

167 The CMS, who were gaining their first Tutsi converts, had become more acceptable to the Belgians after Pastor Anet had done some skilful lobbying in Brussels; see Anet to Franck, 5 September 1923, 27 November 1923, AE/II, No. 1918, AA; *Ruanda Notes*, No. 18, November 1926; No. 19, January 1927.

168 Classe to confrères, 20 May, 15 June, 20 August 1928; Borgers to Vanneste, 2 July 1928; Coubeau to Classe, 7 June 1928; Marzorati to Classe, 5 August 1928, CR and CO.

169 Classe to confrères, 15 May 1928, CR. The period of postulancy was reduced to three to six months as a result of this prompting; see Smoor to Superior General, 22 March 1932, Dossier 221, WFAR.

170 Classe to confrères, 15 May 1928.

171 Zaza diary, 20 July 1928, 13 January 1929; *Rapports annuels*, 1928-29, 313-15.

172 Over 400 Christians died in Zaza parish, and the estimates of numbers moving north into Uganda ranged from 35,000 to 50,000; see Classe to Voillard, 10 August 1929, WFAR; Zaza Diary, 5 May 1929; Church, 'Quest for the highest'. 36; Richards, *Development and Tribal Change*, 36; Powesland, *Economic Policy*, 50.

173 Postiaux to Classe, 13 September 1929, CO.

174 Postiaux to Residents Territoriaux, 13 September 1929, CO.

175 Classe to Postiaux, 2 October 1929, CO.

176 Kigali report, 1929.

177 Mulera report, 1929.

178 The Catholic mission still reflected the impress of clientship; the authority of catechists, sent out in increasing numbers when limits were put on the number and quality of bush schools, was offset by that of the *bakuru b'inama*. On occasions the latter intimidated both chiefs and Christians, and meddled in cases. Even godparents were looked to as patrons. Once catechists settled on a hill they might expect their catechumens to hoe for them like for any chief. Much to the distress of the Resident, the Rwandan clergy at Murunda went to the point of taxing cattle crossing mission grounds. Nonetheless the existence of a strong hierarchy of Tutsi chiefs cushioned Rwanda

from the grosser Church abuses that occurred in the Congo during this period. See Nyundo diary, 4 February 1926, 24 Octover 1927, 5 November 1930; Zaza diary, 27 May 1927; Rwaza diary, 25 November 1930, 5 April 1931; Classe to confrères, 20 August, 21 September 1928, CR; Classe to Voillard, 24 April 1926, WFAR; Coubeau and Borgers to Classe, 3 February 1930, CO; *Rapports annuels*, 1933-34, 413; Arnoux, *Les Pères Blancs*, 140, 168.

179 The encyclical was published on 15 May 1891, a tardy response to Marxism, with its denial of class conflict, defence of family against the State, and upholding of private property. The same themes were taken up again in Pope Pius XI's *Quadragesimo Anno*, published in 1931.

180 Postiaux to Classe, 15 July 1929, CO.

181 *Rapports annuels*, 1929-30, 313-14. Both stations, significantly, had Rwandan clergy.

182 *Rapports annuels*, 1928-29, 317, 319.

183 Quoted in de Lacger, *Le Ruanda*, 529.

184 Rwaza diary, 8 December 1929; Nyundo diary, 14 December 1929; *Rapports annuels*, 1929-30, 301.

185 *Rapports annuels*, 1929-30, 300, 323; Des Forges, *Rwanda under Musiinga*, 346.

186 The value of tribute taken from Shangugu Province alone amounted to 72,000 francs in 1929, of which the most valuable item was 2,791 hoes valued at 34,492 francs. Total income included 5 per cent of the Belgian tax revenues; see Bourgeois, 'Rapport de sortie de charge', Shangugu, 1934; *Rapports annuels*, 1929-30, 301.

187 *Rapports annuels*, 1930-31, 277-8. Rwagataraka was the key to the Fathers' success in Shangugu since the 1920s.

188 Attempts had been made to start a postulancy for Brothers during the First World War, but only Brother Oswald persevered. Classe began again in an annex to the minor seminary at Kabgayi in August 1929; see Classe to confrères, 24 August 1929, CR.

189 *Rapports annuels*, 1930-31, 301; 1931-32, 271-3; de Lacger, *Le Ruanda*, 456-7.

190 Hymns were provocatively sung outside the royal enclosure; see Van Overschelde, *Un Audacieux pacifique*, 124. At the time all the Nyanza schoolchildren were catechumens; see Kabgayi diary, 9 May 1931.

191 Kabgayi diary, 1 January 1929.

192 *Rapports annuels*, 1930-31, 284

193 Quoted in Le Lacger, *Le Ruanda*, 524.

194 Classe, L., 'Pour moderniser le Ruanda', *L'Essor Colonial et Maritime*, Nos. 489-91, 4-11 December 1930; 'Un Triste Sire', Nos. 494, 495, 21 and 25 December 1930. The latter was subtitled by the editors 'Musinga must be got rid of'.

195 Voisin to Classe, 5 January 1931, CO.

196 Voisin to Classe, 15 July 1931, CO.

197 Classe to Voisin, 15 January 1931, CO.

198 *Ibid.*

199 Nyanza report, 1929, a comment made by the Belgian administrator, M. Lenaerts.

200 Kabgayi diary, 21 June 1931; Nyanza report, 1929.

201 Kabgayi diary, 15 August 1931.

202 Classe to Voisin, 23 July 1931, CO. He had probably been making moves in this direction in 1930, for Classe, when first approached, limited himself to the reflection: 'above all, have beside him "a well educated Administrator", balanced, prudent and capable of exercising over him a truly formative influence'; see Classe to Voisin, 15 January 1931. There was the implied reproof that this should have been done with Musinga; the Fathers certainly resented the power of the Nyanza Residents.

203 Classe to Voisin, 23 July 1931, CO.

204 Voisin to Classe, 15 July 1931.

205 See p. 153.

206 Zaza diary, 5 May 1931, September 1931; Mibirisi diary, 11 October 1931.

207 Zaza diary, 5 May 1931.

208 Kabgayi diary, 2 October 1931.

209 A good example of a political 'conversion' was that of Gakwavu at Rwaza; see Rwaza diary, 30 May 1930.

210 Classe to Marchal, 28 September 1930, WFAR. The king had, of course, approached Franck on just this point of ancestor veneration; see chapter six.

211 Classe to Marchal, 11 September 1931; *Rapports annuels*, 1931-32, 242.

212 Voisin to Coubeau, 21 September 1931; Coubeau to Administrateurs Territoriaux, 28 September 1931, CO — a deliberate ruse.

213 The king left with an escort provided by Ntulo on 14 October 1931; see Kabgayi diary, 16 November 1931; *Rapports annuels*, 1931-32, 243.

214 *Rapports annuels*, 1931-32, 247.

215 *Ibid.*, 243.

216 Van Overschelde, *Classe*, 74.

217 Kabgayi diary, 24 November 1931.

218 *Rapports annuels*, 1931-32; see also Zaza diary, 19 November 1931, for an immediate response to the deposition.

219 Kabgayi diary, 24 November 1931.

220 *Ibid.*

221 Classe wrote, 'To wish always to retard the baptism of the Batutsi is to discourage them and throw them into the arms of heresy.' See Van Overschelde, *Classe*, 62. Father Smoor complained,' the famous catechumenate of four years used by the White Fathers does not exist in Ruanda . . . Here two years are asked for — save for some exceptions — after the medal. To get it, three to six months only are required.' Smoor to Superior General, 22 March 1932, Dossier 221, WFAR.

222 The Kigali Resident wrote to Classe in 1928 informing him that 'The goal of the government being to get lucrative employment for the greatest number of our young Batutsi, a knowledge of French would be of the greatest use for these elements.' See Coubeau to Classe, 14 March 1928, CO. In response the Catholic schools gave French almost exclusively to the Tutsi. For educational and political policy see chapter six.

223 *Rapports annuels*, 1928-29, 319.

224 *Ibid.*, 1929-30, 328-9.

225 Church, 'Quest for the highest', 73; see also *Ruanda Notes*, No. 37, July 1931, 16.

226 Classe to Marchal, 11 September 1931.

227 The favour was not connected with 'ulterior' economic motives of imperialism; of the two most powerful prelates in the Belgian territories, Bishop de Hemptinne was from rich Katanga and Classe from destitute Rwanda.

228 Postiaux to Classe, 25 May 1930, CO.

229 Coubeau to Classe, 15 December 1926, 19 January 1927; Classe to Voisin, 15 January 1931, CO.

230 Classe to confrères, 12 May 1928, in *Instructions pastorales*, 37.

231 Schumacher to Governor, 15 August 1935, Dossier 221, WFAR. The Bishop had rightly spotted Schumacher as a dangerous customer, and had complained to Algiers about him long before; see Classe to Voillard, 10 October 1925, WFAR.

232 Classe to Voisin, 15 January 1931, *offers to keep the missionaries in* the dark about the coming deposition. See also Voisin to Classe, 26 October, 23 December 1931, CO, for a gentlemanly handling of the uppity Father Pauwels.

Dr A. C. Stanley-Smith with Mwami Musinga, his mother and his wives outside the royal hut, 1927

EIGHT

The Catholic chiefs

The Belgians had no intention before the Second World War of trying to govern Rwanda without the aid of the feudal system.[1] They did, however, wish to trim it to manageable proportions and reduce its gravest injustices to a minimum. When new economic opportunities became available to Rwandans in the 1930s the old feudal order began to be undermined; within it new types of social relationship grew up, and the nobility were transformed into a Belgian bureaucracy. The change from ascriptive to achievement criteria increased social mobility among the Tutsi but, after a few failed experiments, the Hutu were debarred from political office. The martial virtues were no longer appropriate as ruling class *mores*, but the Tutsi's position as a separate political class was assured as long as the Belgians artificially maintained the stratification of Rwandan society. What had once been a fluid ethnic boundary which aspiring Hutu could cross now became under Belgian rule an insurmountable caste barrier defining access to positions of political power. The ultimate means of coercion, military force, was firmly in Belgian hands, but the courts were successfully manipulated by the Tutsi. The latter were essentially weakened as a class; they depended on the Belgians, relied less on cattle wealth and clientship, and had lost their principal instrument of coercion, the State. Both in ideology and in practice the Church had an important contribution to make in training the administrative cadres, altering the ruling class behaviour of the Tutsi and in justifying segregation in terms of the Thomist organic society in which 'to each according to his function'.

In 1930 *ibikingi* were abolished, so removing the king's ancient weapon against the pretensions of landowners; chiefs controlling twenty-five men or less were brought into a system of sub-chieftancies containing at least one hundred Hutu. A year later the complex system of army, land and cattle chiefs was dismantled in favour of single regional commands, the Province chiefs.[2] From 1932 Hutu were allowed to pay crop dues in cash, two francs per adult working man to the sub-chief, one franc to the Province chief. Sub-chiefs were now legally entitled to only ten days' labour per man per year, chiefs to three days. Attendance at court was limited to one fortnight a year for chiefs, who were to be visited by their sub-chiefs for only ten to twelve days per annum.[3] The aim was to produce a tidy pyramid of chieftancies from king to peasant which was to be later transformed under the impact of the cash economy.

Such gross abuses as the high mortality among Hutu in their lord's retinue, forced even in the 1920s to stay without food and shelter for long periods at Nyanza, were stopped.[4] But in as much as the reforms set out ambitiously 'to alleviate the weight of the yoke placed on the Hutu by the host of Tutsi exactions since earliest times' they were bound to remain something of a paper exercise.[5] 'How were men tried?' wrote Marc Bloch. 'There is no better touchstone for a social system than this question.'[6] Despite the window-dressing of court clerks and a visiting Belgian Resident, the legal system remained in the hands of the Tutsi.[7]

Province chiefs with their chosen sub-chiefs acted as judge and assessors; the highest court of appeal was in the hands of the mwami and his councillors. The local *tribunaux indigènes* in Shangugu Province demanded thirteen francs for cattle disputes from the unsuccessful litigant, and eight francs for those involving land and livestock. Appeal to the provincial court in Shangugu itself cost forty francs for disputes involving more than five cattle, twenty francs for less; in 1933 208 cases came before the local courts and four went to appeal; in 1934 151 cases, and again only four appeals. During the famine years 1928 and 1929 366 and 322 cases repectively were brought, with a total of only three appeals in the two years.[8] Litigation seems to have been a counsel of despair for the Hutu; even the most outrageous extortion could be presented to the Resident by a skilful interpreter as customary practice.[9]

The quality of peasant life was little changed by the new *ubuletwa* regulations, they merely freed the Hutu for more onerous *kazi* labour for the Belgians. The weak and unproteced would end up with both.[10] The abolition of the army chiefs deprived the Hutu of an informal court of appeal; in the past peasants had been able to play these chiefs off against the *abanyabutaka* and had seen in them more of the ideal of feudal society, with its reciprocal bonds of loyalty and protection.[11] In the space of a few years the system of triple chieftancies was abruptly curtailed; in Kigali province 119 chiefs and 324 'sub-chiefs' in 1929 were pruned to eight chiefs and 278 'sub-chiefs' in 1930, and finally reduced to five chiefs and seventy-two 'sub-chiefs' in 1933.[12] The vast interlocking network of relationships in whose interstices Hutu found protection and rose to power was gone. When the Hutu of

Byumba province tried to reverse the process by commending themselves to more than one sub-chief the Resident intervened on behalf of the protesting Tutsi.[13] There were to be no liege lords in Rwanda.

A neat feudal pyramid, like the Norman monarchy of twelfth century England, could be directed from above more easily than the complex society of pre-colonial Rwanda. The Belgians wanted to rationalise the system, 'to strive to maintain and consolidate the traditional cadres of the Batutsi ruling class', as the Governor put it, for the usual 'Hamitic' reasons, 'their great qualities, their undeniable intellectual superiority and potential for command'.[14] The new mwami was intelligent enough to realise that his role was to acquiesce in reforms designed to create a showpiece for the mandates commission of the League of Nations, rather than preside over a revolution. He moved into a brick house, rejecting a vast body of court tradition.

But by 1934 the Belgians' drastic social surgery had weakened the nobility as scores of old chiefs lost their position or handed over to their sons. To every sorcerer his apprentice; the cash economy had its own momentum. Cotton production in Shangugu province rose from 38 tons in 1930 to 292 tons in 1934; widespread distribution of coffee plants after the Depression pushed up Rwanda's coffee production from 2.4 tons in 1930 to 39 tons in 1934.[15] British departure from the gold standard adversely affected the Ugandan rate of exchange, and more Hutu stayed on their hills to raise cash crops.[16] Exceptional growers might earn more than a thousand francs for a year's coffee crop, and some of the younger Tutsi began trying to buy their land outright from their chief.[17] Landowners and chiefs were generally opposed, as were the Residents. Despite talk about private property, it was decided that the land belonged to the mwami, the chiefs were his representatives.[18] This was not the conclusion drawn by the Germans, but the advent of an apparently compliant Rudahigwa, and the rapid superficial christianisation of the Tutsi, appear to have convinced the Europeans that land reform on the Uganda model would be misplaced and inopportune.[19]

Whatever their intentions, the Belgians had set in motion capitalist forces that were inexorably destroying the feudal system. They had inaugurated a major social transformation that was difficult to control and direct from above. The rush of the Tutsi into the Church was visible proof that the texture of Rwandan society was changing; new social relationships were growing up, old ideas were giving way, and the Church offered its clients free passage into the new world. By the mid-1930s the administrative cadres of chiefs and sub-chiefs were only 60 per cent literate, but they were 90 per cent Roman Catholic.[20]

The missionary Church was both stunned and delighted by its new role in Rwandan society. Anxiety there was, of course, particularly about the motives of the movement and the quality of the converts, but it seemed churlish to inspect too closely a prize that had so long been witheld. 'It is all very fine,' wrote one Father, 'but is it really the Faith that is working here and moving this crowd?'[21] An answer to this gnawing doubt about commitment tended to be relegated to a future realm of post-baptismal training. More common during the *Tornade* was the Zaza diarist's reflection: 'The motive is perhaps not the most disinterested, but with the help of God's Grace they will be turned into good Christians.'[22]

The White Fathers saw conversion primarily as an intellectual assent to the dogmas of the Catholic Church, and in this they bore the imprint of their Society's early Jesuit novice masters. Membership of the Church and access to its sacraments put the Christian into contact with the reforming and transforming action of Grace. Although great stress was placed on baptism as an important turning point,[23] conversion was thought of almost as a continuous process as well as a once-and-for-all commitment to the person of Christ;[24] man was neither radically sinful nor radically good — hence the need for regular confession and penance. In practice this meant that the Fathers were most concerned that the catechumens understood the Faith; they neither encouraged nor approved of the idea of conversion as an event taking place in an aura of crisis and emotion. The majority of Rwandans refused admission as postulants at Kabgayi in March 1932 were turned away on mundane grounds of illiteracy; seven hundred failed a simple examination, though six thousand, certainly not fully literate, were admitted.[25]

The role of the missionaries changed as a result of the *Tornade* from that of proselytism to one of leadership, formation, and government, within a hierarchical institution that overshadowed Rwanda. Although the Church numbered less than a quarter of the population it was politically the most important quarter. The Fathers no longer had to confront Rwandan society, to create conditions conducive to the building up of the Church from the unpromising material of the hill communities; they were now part of society and close to the centre of power. Lwabutogo, the outcast of Musinga's court because of his proselytising,[26] became Rudahigwa's closest associate.[27] The Catholic chief of Mirenge province, Simon Nyiringondo, paid the salaries of catechists working on the hills around Zaza mission.[28] As chiefs began to serve at Mass the custom of saying a Pater and an Ave for the mwami and chiefs was revived.[29] The mwami's personal catechist felt his position sufficiently important to ask for a brick house at Nyanza and *ibikingi* for his cattle and clients.[30] Bishop Classe enjoyed a position of unprecedented power as adviser to both court and administration. When writing to the Victor Apostolic, Governor Jungers could at times be positively obsequious: 'Car permettez-moi de vous le dire sans flagornerie, vous êtes pour moi un example de noblesse veritable et d'aimable distinction.'[31] Rudahigwa often went to Kabgayi to consult the Bishop, and took pains to talk and act publicly in ways pleasing to the White Fathers.[32]

Between 1932 and 1936 the *Tornade* almost tripled the membership of the Catholic Church from 81,000 to 233,000. The wave of converts swept from the forefront of Monsignor Classe's mind any thoughts of tampering with the foundations of Rwandan society.[33] Like the Belgians, he could see no need for upheavals; the body politic could be influenced in a rational and harmonious fashion from the head downwards by adjusting structures and instituting minor progressive reforms. The Catholic chiefs were to be to society as the missionaries and Rwandan clergy were to the Church. There was, it was felt, nothing intrinsically incompatible — to understate the case — between Christian government and the continuation of a rational feudal hierarchy.

Some of the Fathers were glad to use their parishoners' experience of feudal society to explain the Christian's relationship with God, 'relations that make us grow, engage us in total devotion and assure us of goods far superior to those which the Mututsi gives the Muhutu'.[34] The word *shebuja*, lord, did have the sense of 'father of a servant', and it was customary for the garagu to speak fulsomely of his devotion to his patron in public.

If the Vicar Apostolic ceased to be worried about Rwandan society it was because he assumed that the Tutsi class — which he now again called a 'caste'[35] — would be informed by Christian virtue whatever type of government prevailed. And by the remarkable sleight of hand that invariably occurs when the Catholic Church flagrantly represents ruling class interests, a political position of great power was felt, believed to be, and proclaimed by the Fathers as a mere spiritual authority, an apolitical stance. 'The revolution that we brought,' wrote Father Arnoux, 'was therefore limited to a purely religious aspect with nothing of politics [about it].'[36]

In consequence, the decade after the Tutsi movement found the Vicar Apostolic more inclined to restrain Belgian initiatives in the direction of social reform than to encourage them. When a systematic review of customary dues and *ubuletwa* was undertaken in 1933 Classe appeared as an advocate of the *status quo*;

Would it be better and more just to give the chiefs simply a suitable remuneration which would give them the wherewithall to live and maintain their position? In theory, yes. In practice, no! The error would be psychological; the people's mentality and the social conditions in the country make such a total change premature. At the present time it would amount to the virtual abolition of the country's social structure, an organisation that has always demonstrated its strength and remains the necessary and indispensable adjunct to the government's transformation and *mise en valeur* of the country.

The chiefs would no longer be the people's chiefs, attached to their way of life and their prosperity, those good elements without which there can be no social grouping. They would no longer be their 'head' who advises and leads them, arranges their affairs, their law suits, and plays the part of intermediary between them and government. In a word, the chiefs would lose their people's confidence because they would simply become 'government agents' who only executed the government's instructions and made people work. [37]

This plea for a truly Indirect Rule looks remarkably like opportunism. But it had its ideological side. The major intellectual stimulus to the flabby and slow-reacting body of Catholic sociology in the nineteenth century was a revived Thomism. At the time the majority of the White Fathers were trained seminary manuals were Thomist and, whatever else the missionaries took away from their studies, they came to Africa with a fundamentally organic view of society that presupposed the ideal centrality of the Church 'as the soul of the whole organism'.[38] For the more intellectual missionaries Rwandan society was like a living creature: it demonstrated a hierarchy and division of labour and service that was rational, necessary and harmonious.[39] The *Tornade* provided Rwanda with a group of potential Catholic patriarchs and allowed the priests to think in terms of 'the Christian society' and in the categories of Thomist sociology. There was a happy fit between the model of a feudal society in transition that historically informed Aquinas' thought and the Fathers' experience in Rwanda; even the Protestants with their emphasis on the individual, spoke of the 'social symbiosis' between Tutsi and Hutu.[40]

Belgian optimism that administrative decrees would curb excesses was paralleled in the mission by the faith and hope that membership of the Church would make Catholic chiefs charitable and just. The attitude is well illustrated in a letter written by Father Pagès to a Resident in 1933.

there are injustices committed, as some individuals are loaded with more *corvées* than should be their lot . . . but only little by little as the administration gets to know of abuses will they be able to remedy them. without overthrowing the present regime. The government will be able to direct the country with confidence, given the chief's intelligence and amenability . . . along the path of moral and material progress, the final goal of all colonisation.[41]

It was in a similar defensive vein that Pagès wrote his notes on land holding in Bugoyi, emphasising that no social system was perfect but that all were subject to 'the passions which are the common lot of all mortals'.[42]

The Vicar Apostolic and the more thoughtful missionaries saw themselves as nurturing the embryo of a future *corpus christianum*, a prized creation which now more than ever they wished to preserve from the over-hasty. Defects there were, but the Fathers were on hand to tutor the untutored and absolve the sinful. A repeated theme in Classe's pastorals was that this process of maturation must not be disturbed by the priests' authoritarianism, 'this mania or, if you prefer, this need to play at chief and, at whatever cost, to impose your authority'.[43] The missionaries were told to refrain from pointing out the chiefs' faults in front of their subjects, and never to insult them in public. The priest's function, as the soul of the social organism, must be formative, 'to lead them little by little into an awareness of the role they can and must fulfil in a Christian fashion and for their Catholic, and other, subjects'.[44]

Mission reports from Nyundo and Rwaza dutifully recorded that, although the Hutu had rejected former pagan Tutsi, they willingly accepted Catholic chiefs 'because they are more just and humane';[45] Lwabutogo was said to be one of the few impartial judges.[46] The northern missionaries tried to comply with instructions, moved catechists if they offended chiefs, and dwelt on the virtue of submission and loyalty,[47] but they suffered from the depredations of the Banyanduga.

The northern problem remained the same; the Banyanduga were government agents with no local support and with little wealth and prestige. In order to consolidate their position in regions where the Hutu shunned *ubuhake* they were obliged to oppress their subjects; the rich and densely populated land raised the stakes in the game. Having lent their support to the new Mulera province chief, Kamuzinzi, the Fathers discovered that he had been pillaging and even killing dissidents. When the Rwaza Father Superior testified against him at Ruhengeri three other Catholic chiefs promptly broke off relations with the mission. On the other hand, the Christian Hutu still looked on the missionaries as protectors, to such a point that the Ruhengeri Resident could find no one willing to fill the sub-chieftancies around Rwaza mission; Tutsi who were approached refused, saying that mission Hutu were ungovernable. What they meant, of course, was that mission Hutu defended their rights with more assurance than their neighbours.[48] To complicate matters dispossessed chiefs continued to influence the politics of the region by getting jobs as judges and forming cabals against the Belgian appointees.

The bush missionary's equivocal feelings about the Catholic chiefs were heightened by a small but ostentatious group of young Tutsi whose modernity they found reason to criticise. The group was known as *Basilimu*, Musinga's derisive term, the Europeans' followers. Their leader was Rwigemera; he had been left high and dry after his brother Rudahigwa's accession, so had grounds for rejecting mission patronage. The movement began around Rubengera, shifted to Nyanza and finally found its natural focus in the commercial centre of Kigali and among the young Banyanduga chiefs around Rulindo mission to the north. The members of the 'club' openly refused to genuflect in church or make the sign of the Cross, and did not go to confession in the customary fashion before receiving communion. Rwigemera took a second wife, and Father Schumacher hinted darkly that club members had communal women or, at least, practised 'libertinage'.[49]

It was a sign of the times that the adoption of European clothes , which the Belgians had heralded as a great breakthrough in the reign of Musinga, was now seen as provocative if not subversive. Rudahigwa dressed in traditional fashion and was felt to represent a happy marriage between old and new. A handful of nobles also had cars and smart brick houses, and many of the Fathers thought that the process of modernisation had gone far enough. Monsignor Classe had read attentively the report of the 1932 ecclesiastical conference in Leopold-ville at which Bishop de Hemptinne characterised the mood of the day as 'independence', with its necessary corollary, 'indiscipline'. The words struck a chord in Bishop Classe, who scribbled in the margin 'surtout chez déracinés et clercs, orgueilleux'; against the heading 'Dangers of communism' he noted that teachers and clerks ought to be given special attention.[50] Leopoldville was to Rwanda as London to rural Ireland, a terrible warning against the loss of simplicity and the death of moral virtue.[51] While few of the priests had a clear idea of developments in the Congo, they looked over their shoulders at it with some trepidation and saw Kimbangu, weak chiefs, towns, European dress and communism as different symptoms of a dangerous virus which must not be allowed to damage the growth of the *corpus christianum* in Rwanda.

Despite public compliance with the Belgians, there was much dissimulation and private resentment. Chiefs like Rwabusisi who had been dealing with Europeans for over a quarter of a century[52] knew exactly what they wanted to take from Western culture. He communicated with his sub-chiefs by letter, did a little trading, but maintained the traditional life style of a noble. 'It has often been written,' commented one sharp administrator, 'that Lwabusisi was entirely won over to our way of thinking, and that he was sincerely devoted to us. I am willing to admit my doubts on this. Lwabusisi works for his country and adopts every innovation he finds if it will be to Rwanda's profit.'[53] The old contempt for the running dogs of the Belgians was still there;[54] one Tutsi described his sub-chiefs disparagingly to the missionaries as 'government *karani*', and was warned that trouble was in store for him, since the *karani* were the whites' friends.[55]

The effect of the *Basilimu* and brash young chiefs was to draw the court and missionaries together in an unspoken opposition to some aspects of the new order. The passage of men like Ntulo and Kayondo into history enhanced their dignity and virtues in people's minds.[56] The White Fathers in victory found the aristocrats worthy opponents who should be respected in defeat.[57] The two sides were in some respects similar in outlook; Catholic Bishops decried minor variations in the liturgy with as much outrage as they forecast communist subversion.[58] The Tutsi conservatives clung to the rubrics of court ceremonies. Monsignor Classe froze into silence newly ordained priests who suggested tentatively that there might be a place for Rwandan hymns in church; it was only in 1939 that he brought himself to condone such startling innovations.[59] This respect for the old order had political implications; there was considerable conflict between the old-established Tutsi families who had settled around Rwaza in or before the German period, and the new Banyanduga. The Fathers gave 'old' families[60] their unwavering support. Ruhanga's son was constantly being denounced to the Belgians in the early 1930s by his ambitious sub-chiefs, but the mission lent their authority to him.[61] The policy paid off, and the Belgians at Ruhengeri began consolidating the power of the older 'Batutsi Balera' and sending back the worst of the new men to Nduga.[62]

The stations' difficulties were less complex outside the north, but the dominance of feudal over kinship bonds still caused problems. Attendance at school tended to depend on the presence of the Catholic chief, and the eagerness of the Hutu catechumens was often correlated with their hope of joining his retinue and receiving a cow.[63] The overall pastoral approach was 'to each according to his position in society'. The Hutu *inama* were revived and the powers of the *bakuru* circumscribed. Each *inama* consisted of about twenty-five men who elected their leader and met once a week on the hills for prayer and discussion of mutual help. *Bakuru* were now banned from becoming involved in court cases, and meetings were compulsory; political questions were strictly beyond the purview of both *bakuru* and *inama*. Once a month the group leaders reported to the Father Superior at their mission, so the priests were able to control their activities closely while maintaining an appearance of local initiative and autonomy.[64] From the beginning of 1933 each station held a monthly meeting for Catholic chiefs 'to explain their duties to them, especially from the point of view of justice and charity, but abstaining absolutely from all political questions'.[65] Ineluctable conflicts were spirited away in an organic concept of society.

This post-baptismal training came partly as a response to Pope Pius XI's call for Catholic Action to christianise society. The assumption was that harmony between the two Rwandan estates could be orchestrated by the Catholic clergy, while the Church as an institution remained impartial outside the politics which it criticised. So it was that Pius XI could issue within five days of each other the encyclicals *Mit brennender Sorge* against Nazism and *Divini Redemptoris* on the dangers of atheistic communism.[66] Such a stance was quite possible in

Rwanda before the Second World War, where changes planned and supervised by the government gave the impression of equilibrated progress; it became impossible to sustain without gross self-deception in later years, when an accelerated rate of unregulated change brought conflict to the surface.

The appearance in July 1933 of the Catholic vernacular language newspaper *Kinyamateka*, printed at Kabgayi, was another product of mission anxiety about the chiefs. At first an eight-page monthly produced by the teachers at the major seminary, it sold largely amongst the chiefs, clerks, teachers and seminarians whom the Fathers were keen to influence. Sales rose from 400 to 1,500 copies within a year, and by 1936 to 4,000 with an additional supplement for catechists selling 3,200 copies; eight pages, though of smaller size, were still being filled.[67] The readership was wider than the figures indicate, people reading *Kinyamateka* aloud spread its impact throughout Rwanda.

This favourable response was largely due to the absence of government gazettes or vernacular printed material for a growing, partially literate Christian population. The paper served the purpose of broadcasting directives from the mwami and Belgians as well as providing pious reading, traditional wisdom and folklore in the form of proverbs. Some censorship was exerted over letters to the editor, so the political and tendentious rarely got into print.[68] However, there were enough missionaries annoyed at the pettifogging behaviour of agricultural officers[69] for mild criticism of government measures to be permissible; for example, in *Kinyamateka* No. 15 of 1934 quite a violent reply was printed in the question-and-answer column to a query about *corvées*;[70] the exactions of sub-chiefs and the persecution of individuals with excess *kazi* labour was roundly denounced. But the pre-war *Kinyamateka* was far from being an organ of Hutu protest. After the initial enthusiasm for the printed word, and as the Belgians used the paper less and less as an administrative organ after 1937, readership fell.[71]

The pastoral emphasis on the elite made sense in terms of statistics; fifty-four out of sixty-nine chiefs and 756 out of 900 sub-chiefs were Catholic by 1936, though the percentage of converts in the entire population was only 18 per cent.[72] Father Schumacher chaired a group of eight chiefs, one ex-chief and five sub-chiefs from Astrida province who asked the missionaries for a course in *politesse européenne* and law. Rudahigwa gave the group his support, and wrote with a number of leading Tutsi to the Superior General of the White Fathers to inform him of their 'parlement', where such topics as the fusion of chieftancies were debated.[73] Likewise at each monthly mission meeting efforts were made to find the philosopher's stone that would turn the local Tutsi hierarchy into benign patriarchs.

The concern of Catholic Action to maintain a kind of social homeostasis in the Rwandan body politic was presented to the Governor as the goal of rational social policy. 'There is to be avoided,' Classe told him, 'a disequilibrium that brings the young trained and educated man into a different life style and standard of living and makes him despise his companions who have remained with a way of thinking and cultural level that is so different.'[74] The key word was 'equilibrium', and by the end of 1934 the Bishop was complaining to the Governor that primary school education was still inadequate and that only one eighth of the children who ought to be at school were ever taught.[75] Above all, the Bishop wanted the schools geared to the needs of the country, for otherwise 'mécontents' and 'déclassés' would result.[76] The Belgians were spending less than one franc per annum on each child's education.[77]

The mission was doing too many things at once with limited manpower and finance. Classe had to run the subsidised State school system and at the same time keep catechists and chapel schools functioning. He tried to follow Rome's instructions on the development of an indigenous clergy and religious Orders, whilst fostering Catholic Action in the context of the *inama* and chiefs' meetings.[78] From 1929 Classe pressed a Church tax, one franc per adult Christian but the results were disappointing;[79] sending out the *bakuru* caused too much trouble, and the Fathers themselves took to 'harvesting' the tax on their motor-bikes.[80] The seminaries at Kabgayi were a constant drain on resources, and baskets used to be placed outside the churches for offerings in kind or money for their upkeep.[81] Things improved somewhat after 1935, when the Belgians increased their subsidies considerably.[82] Classe's plea for an expansion of primary education was also motivated by the thought that Catholics would benefit most from money spent on the educational infrastructure.[83]

Since the cassiterite and gold mines did not employ Rwandans in professional positions before the 1940s,[84] all the available white-collar jobs were in the public sector as clerks, hospital workers and a few in veterinary medicine and agriculture. Entry to the Brothers of Charity school at Astrida (Butare) was pegged at fifty per annum; no more could be absorbed by Ruanda-Urundi. Pupils entered the school in 1933 aged thirteen to fifteen years for a basic three-year course in humanities followed by a specialised professional or vocational training.[85] The day began with mass and a lesson in Christian doctrine. Teaching was in French. The school was theoretically open to all, and non-denominational; it was in fact Catholic and almost entirely Tutsi; between 1946 and 1954 389 Tutsi and sixteen Hutu enrolled from the two kingdoms.[86] The Belgians lamely defended themselves at the League of Nations against complaints of religious discrimination by claiming that although 97 per cent of the pupils were Catholics the Protestants had been requested to open a chaplaincy.[87] Nyanza government school was finally closed in 1935, and when the first products of Astrida emerged in 1940 a new distinction arose in the Tutsi elite between a Nyanza 'old guard' and the new men, the 'Astridiens'.[88] These school loyalties were to play an important part in the politics of the 1950s.[89]

The closing of Nyanza marked the end of a major wave of amalgamations and fusions of chieftancies; there were no longer enough new sub-chieftancies to keep up Tutsi interest in the school. Both Classe and the Belgians were agreed that no useful purpose would be served by opening any new trade schools while existing bricklayers, carpenters and masons were unemployed.[90] The only school at Nyanza was now run by the White Fathers, who had built a mission on the site of Musinga's old residence.[91]

The essential characteristic of education between the wars was that it served only the Tutsi and was limited in its scope to filling the short-term needs of Belgian administration. Within this system the Church was the handmaid of the State. But within the Church the ideological commitment of the Vatican demanded not passive agents for European missionaries, but rather the development of a Rwandan Church in the image of, and in full communion with, the Church of Rome. Christian brotherhood found its most perfect expression in group solidarity among the clergy, a solidarity which was seen as an essential expression of the universality of the Church. 'There is but a single clergy', the Apostolic Delegate told the assembled Bishops at Leopoldville, 'without distinction of race or colour; the Catholic clergy.'[92] For this reason Rwandan seminarians had to have the same education as their European counterparts, and Monsignor Dellepiane saw his first duty as Vatican representative to be the overseeing of seminary education.[93]

Despite the cost, Monsignor Classe faithfully followed in Hirth's footsteps and championed the cause of an indigenous clergy. From five to ten per cent of the pupils finishing their course at the minor seminary went on to Kabgayi Major Seminary, which served the four vicariates of Rwanda, Urundi, Lac Albert and Kivu; they had respectively fifty-eight, twenty, nine and eight seminarians at Kabgayi in 1934.[94] The Rwandan contingent was always intellectually dominant, taking the first ten places in the examinations, and Classe repeatedly refused to cut down the Rwandan intake to make way for other vicariates, because it would mean excluding the more for the less able.[95]

Conditions at Kabgayi were harsh, but no harsher than life on the hills; the beds and reed mattresses with simple wool covers and plain food was prepared by the *Benebikira*.[96] Swahili and Kinyarwanda were forbidden, and the pupils were obliged to speak French or Latin to each other. They entered at the age of eighteen to twenty and followed a three-year course in philosophy, followed by five years of theology. Then came a trial period as sub-deacons when they spent a year or two in a parish before the diaconate and ordination. For literature Cicero and Victor Hugo were recommended, but Virgil, Ovid and Horace were thought too hard.[97] Only deacons were allowed to wear shoes, and all seminarians were cut off from their families for almost ten years under kind but stern professors. Each year four or five men emerged as Roman Catholic priests; from 1937 to 1940 the Rwandan clergy increased from thirty to forty-six, while the number of professed *Benebikira* rose from seventy-five to ninety.[98]

Classe's policy from the beginning was to form all-Rwandan parishes and convents, and by the late 1930s Rulindo, Janja, Muramba, Muyunzwe (near Kabgayi) and Save were all in Rwandan hands. He was anxious to maintain standards, demanding study in theology and curtailing too frequent visits home.[99] There was little friction with the White Fathers under his system in the early years, and when it did occur he was capable of taking the Rwandan side.[100] Seminarians were discouraged from joining European Orders. The mission clergy and that of the indigenous Church began and remained separate but unequal; whatever the theory, in practice most missionaries saw the Rwandan priests as on probation.

Since the first Normal school for lay women teachers only began at Save in 1939, and for men at Kabgayi in 1936, the majority of Rwandan religious capable of it were engaged in teaching.[101] By the mid-1940s half the clergy, *Bayozefiti* and *Benebikira*, were from Tutsi families; one or two of the old Hutu clergy like Abbé Gallicani were withdrawn from parish work to teach in the seminary,[102] but the Tutsi take-over of the Church was directly felt through the clerical role in education. To go to school was to find a Tutsi teacher, and the intellectual life of the Church was soon dominated by the new Tutsi abbés. Alexis Kagame came from a family of *abiru* and went to the school for chiefs' sons at Ruhengeri, whence he moved to Kabgayi minor seminary in 1929. He became editor of *Kinyamateka* while a seminarian in 1938, and was ordained in 1941. Stanislas Bushayija, another outstanding intellectual, had been one of Musinga's *ntore* and was baptised only in 1930; he was ordained in 1944 just as the writer Janvier Mulenzi was finishing his philosophy course.[103]

It was hard for the long-suffering seminary professors not to be impressed with men of this calibre whose social poise made them shine in comparison with the Hutu student. Rudahigwa was never far from their company, though his own Catholic career was fraught with difficulties. He married a descendant of the Gesera line of kings at Shyogwe in September 1933 — a prudent move in view of Gisaka's chequered history in the Rwandan kingdom — but the children of the marriage were stillborn. Classe cautiously refrained from baptising the mwami before a male heir was born; the marriage lingered on until

January 1942, when a little canonical legerdemain allowed it to be dissolved in favour of a baptised Christian, Rosalia Gicandwa. On 17 October 1943 the king was baptised in the presence of fifty Catholic chiefs, with the Governor General, Pierre Ryckmans, as godfather. [104]

Rudahigwa's cautious blending of politics, ancient and modern, had otherwise been to the Fathers' liking. The king was gracious in Mulera, telling them how pleased he was that the people accepted him as mwami of the north; in Buganza he allowed the Rwamagana Fathers to cut down trees on one of mwami Rwabugiri's residences.[105] In return Brother Adolphe was made available to him for private building and carpentry, and the Queen Mother was housed at Kabgayi in a building designed for her by Monsignor Classe, though espionage was more the motive than chivalry.[106] Nonetheless Kankazi retained much of her traditional power, and on her request insubordinate garagu in Marangara were whipped in front of the king.[107] The mwami succeeded in getting back the *ntore* in 1935, thanks largely to the cautionary example of the Europeanised *Basilimu*, but also because the Belgians needed to convince a sceptical world that 'Indirect' rule had not proved fatal to their trustee.[108] A year later the number of king's advisers was raised to six, although Rudahigwa's main supports remained Lwabutogo, his secretary, Godefroy Kamanzi, and Raphael Serukenyinkware, now a Catholic, who had successfully ridden the Belgian tiger during two decades at court[109]

As the Belgians increased the number of their administrative personnel, and the activities of the agricultural and veterinary departments affected more and more people's lives, the missionaries began to find their local authority seriously challenged for the first time since German days. Taking a lively interest in cattle and crops themselves, it annoyed them to watch the high-handed behaviour of inexperienced minor Belgian officials.[110] The convergence of feeling between old missionaries and old nobles was played on by the king; when the Fathers requested it he would summon a Tutsi who had taken another wife and publicly admonish him.[111] This may have been nothing more than annoyance that, being so much in the public eye, he was debarred from such an action himself, but it genuinely impressed the Fathers. Sometimes the play for a Catholic-Tutsi alliance against the Belgians was quite explicit, as in a speech reported in the Zaza diary in 1940:

He took the opportunity to tell the assembled chiefs in the strongest possible terms to put their house in order as regards behaviour on the hills and to lend their influence on behalf of the mission. He reminded them that they must not forget that Rwanda belongs firstly to the King and to the Banyarwanda, and they ought not to slip into the mentality of those who thought of them as salaried officials of the government. Their work as chiefs was not limited to executing material works as *serkali*, but they had a moral task to accomplish in the country in union with the missionaries.[112]

Such bold talk may have been produced by news of the German invasion of Belgium that May; nonetheless there is no indication that the missionaries felt anything but approval for the sentiments expressed.[113]

It would have been a bold man in 1940 who insisted that the Belgians held Rwanda *in perpetuo*. Owing to a growing sensitivity to the Protestant lobby in the 1930s, Brussels had placed restrictions on Catholics multiplying their stations and extending their land holding.[114] The Rwanda Resident foolishly toyed with the idea of bringing in divorce legislation, and Monsignor Classe began angrily brandishing the 1930 encyclical on Christian marriage, *Casti Connubii*.[115] The missionaries knew well enough that the ex-German colonies were counters in European diplomacy; Father Pauwels had burnt his fingers by saying that Rwanda, like Togo and the Cameroons, might one day be handed over to the Germans.[116] Relations were not so good that the missionaries refused to contemplate the thought that a Catholic king with Catholic chiefs might be able to guarantee the position of the Church in Rwanda with as much certainty as the Belgians.

Furthermore the Catholicism of the court was no mere facade. The ordination of cultured Tutsi priests brought about a deliberate attempt to baptise some of the traditions of the court. Alexis Kagame began to reconstruct ancient Tutsi society and culture in his writings.[117] The same mood prevailed among teachers and descendants of the families of dynastic poets, who produced a very rich and fascinating Catholic Tutsi poetry in the 1940s.[118] The *Isoko y'Amajyambere*, 'The story of progress', is a cycle of thirty songs telling of the court's glorious history, followed by a sequence relating the missionaries' works until Rudahigwa's baptism in 1943. In Kagame's words, 'from the historical *exposé* was deduced a moral conclusion which invited the present generation to reproduce the same *gestes* but on a higher plane, in keeping with the degree of our evolution'.[119] A catechist from Nyange mission, Frederiko Kaberuka, composed the praise poem *Igisinzo cya Papa Piyo XII* on the enthronement of Pope Pius XII in 1939; events like the building of a church, the presentation of a Papal medal to the king, were all occasions for the creation of new verses in the epic vein. Bruno Nkuriyingoma, a descendant of a court poet in the reign of Cyilima II Rujugira, composed his *Izuka cya Jesu* in the classical form of dynastic poems in praise of the abami.[120] Poetry was declaimed at court and sometimes brought forth thunderous applause from the assembled audience.[121]

De Lacger's *Ruanda* was essentially a Western prose version of epic poems like *Isoko y'Amajyambere*; his European model, though, is obvious when he writes about Rudahigwa's first visit to Bishop Classe at Kabgayi: 'It was on a more humble scale the repetition of the historic act of the catechumen Constantine greeting the Pope as his religious leader.'[122] Similar medieval echoes occurred in Rudahigwa's speech when he dedicated Rwanda to Christ the King: 'Lord Jesus, it is You who have made our country. You have given it a long line of kings to govern it in Your stead even at a time when they did not yet know You.'[123]

Rudahigwa had jettisoned the old rituals of kingship, and the idea of the mwami as the focus of Imana power, for the Catholic conception of the king as God's temporal representative. When Father Deprimoz was consecrated Bishop in 1943 the mwami handed over to him a herd of *nyambo*, royal cattle known as *Inkulirakwamuza*, or the Pope's herd, a nice gesture implying in one sense the subordination of the Bishop and in another the sharing of sovereignty. Conversely the condition for the reconstitution of two teams of *ntore* had been that they attend the Fathers' school at Nyanza.[124] As legitimation for kingship Christianity came a poor second to the old religion, but with the court considerably weakened the king was bound to tie its fortunes to the most powerful institution in the land. The Church was happy with the marriage, willingly advocated the mwami's claim to ownership of the land, and favoured more independence for the clergy and Catholic chiefs than the Belgians desired.[125] 'In correspondence with the government about concessions and other matters,' wrote the Byzantine Dellepiane, 'it is useful to avoid when speaking about the clergy or indigenous congregations, etc, etc . . . the words "autonomous", "independent" and the like.'[126] And there certainly was something that smacked of independence in the way the new Tutsi clergy set about shoring up the monarchy with a dynastic history, and in the manner in which the mwami himself sought autonomy sweetened by moral virtue rather than the bitter resistance of Musinga, with his warrior ethic.

Catholicism, with its hierarchical structures, elite of priests and religious, and emphasis on liturgy, was put on by the Tutsi ruling class in the late 1930s like a bespoke suit on a penniless gentleman. Saverio Naigisiki evokes the scene on Sunday morning at the capital:

La grande messe, à Nyanza peut-être plus qu'ailleurs, revêt de la part des fidèles un caractère singulièrement protocolaire. C'est la messe du beau monde. Car les pouilleux de Nyanza . . . ont honte de mêler leurs hardes de dimanche aux costumes de luxe.[127]

Even in popular culture the intrusive religious system effectively displaced traditional practices. Catholics clubbed together to make mass offerings, and masses were requested for success in childbirth and a happy marriage as well as for the more common purpose of assuring the spiritual well-being of deceased kin.[128] The entire *inzu* attended church on these occasions, went to confession and then communion in a type of celebration that, in the past, would have involved offerings to lineage spirits. The close connection between confession and communion[129] was easily understood as a purification, and gave an outlet for feelings of guilt that might have erupted in witchcraft accusation.

The impact of Christianity can also be detected in the way names containing 'Imana' became increasingly common in the 1930s. Only about 0·5 per cent of the names in Rwandan oral history are theophorous, like Habyarimana (It is God who begets), Hakuzimana (God makes things grow), Nsengimana (I adore God). Likewise only 0.6 per cent of the 518 baptismal names registered at Rwaza in 1914 contained Imana, but by 1946 7 per cent of the 755 baptisms inscribed were theophorous, and today school registers show a proportion as high as 19 per cent.[130] It seems that after Rudahigwa's accession Imana became less a neutral, otiose force and more a personal bringer of luck in people's daily lives; this popularisation of the Rwandan 'God' was balanced by a comparable decline in the Lyangombe cult and in lineage religion.[131]

It was fitting that, since Catholicism had been assimilated as the court religion, evangelical Protestantism should find itself inheriting the mantle of Nyabingi as the Hutu *culte de contestation*. Classe's demand that Catholic chiefs should be supported, come what may, meant both that dissidents tended to look for new patrons amongst the Protestants, and that Protestants tended to be looked on as dissidents by the chiefs. According to Monsieur Monnier — and this was amply corroborated by the CMS — Catholic chiefs accused their subjects of insubordination if they frequented the Adventists, made their Hutu build chapel schools for the Fathers, and were openly biased in favour of the Catholic missions.[132] 'We would be happy to see the chiefs solely in the service of the administration,' wrote Monnier much to the point, 'and not in the service of the Fathers.'[133]

The Adventists were now in the position of the Catholic 'northern faction' in German days.[134] Monnier courageously listed the Tutsi exactions: the way they forced their subjects to perform duties expected only of garagu in the south, obliged them to bring wood to make their fire during the hated night watch at the lord's *rugo*, and press ganged women and children into working for them to get round the *ubuletwa* restrictions.[135] The Resident's opinion was that 'the missions ought to adapt themselves — Catholics and Protestants have found their way to doing so — to the political organisation and local social structure of the natives that they find, and not transform these to suit themselves'; it was 'an understanding of this to which the Catholic missions owe a part of their success'.[136] True enough, but when another administrator said in a fit of exasperation that he preferred pagans to bickering Christians, and that the administration had no religion, a great number of postulants and catechumens stopped attending the Catholic classes at Rambura.[137] For many Catholicism had simply become the religion of the powerful, an opinion for which there was ample evidence in Rwanda.

Part of the tension between Protestants and Catholics had spilled over from the Congo; the Fathers there were given massive land grants, and Monsignor Dellepiane lived in a spacious villa set in nine-acre grounds next to the Governor General's. He flew from Leopoldville in a plane put at his disposal by the government.[138] The Protestant grievances were straightforward: 'Religious liberty in the Belgian Congo is neither fully established nor completely recognised . . . it is surely not necessary to be loyal to Rome to be loyal to Belgium.'[139] The pomp and luxury of an Apostolic Delegate disguised the poverty of the bush stations. Missionaries paid their employees poor wages, and many catechists were lost to the mines and plantations.[140] By 1938 Bishop Classe had over-committed the mission, and financial disaster threatened; for want of salaries the vicariate was able to put only three hundred catechists into the field. Financial pressure made the 'invasion' of ten Protestant stations difficult to counter and put the Fathers on their mettle.[141].

It was the CMS in the north-east, rather than the Adventists, who inherited the religious tradition of Nyabingi. The Ruanda Mission of the CMS represented the extreme evangelical wing of Anglicanism and coexisted uncomfortably with the Bishop and his archdeacons in Kampala who tried to supervise them.[142] An emphasis on sin, repentance and total conversion was soon heeded; at a mass meeting at Gahini in 1934 a number of people stood up to confess in public.[143] 'We have seen the spirit of God working in such a manifest form that one can only compare it with accounts of Wesley's time,' a missionary was reporting by 1936.[144] During a night meeting for prayer and hymn-singing people were 'smitten and fell down under a deep sense of sin'.[145] The Kigeme congregation also spent nights of intense devotion: 'One or two began to have trances in which they seemed to become possessed and spoke with another voice.'[146]

The centre of the movement was on the Rwanda-Uganda border, among the Kiga and in Ndorwa, in the very region that had for decades produced Nyabingi prophetesses. From the first response to the CMS conversion fell within the tradition of the shamans.

There is a little village far off the beaten track . . . and there lived there a woman fairly young in years who had already sold herself to the practice of the occult arts, and was frequented by the local inhabitants as a witch doctress of some power . . . She woke up at midnight, and said to her husband, 'Let us go and worship God' . . . In the morning she went off with her husband to the local chief, where she again said apparently almost in the language of the possessed that she was going to follow Jesus; and she exhorted all the people to do the same. They said to her, 'What do you know about Jesus?' And she replied. 'Was it not He that came to me at midnight?'   [147]

Such women gathered a following and directed people to Sunday worship by threats of dire punishment.[148] Although they were inevitably brought before the Resident, a promise that violence would be eschewed, and the Church orientation of their teaching, was enough to spare them imprisonment.[149]

The CMS missionaries recognised that the movement was 'fraught with great spiritual danger' but saw it in the context of the Christian revival they had been preaching for several years. As hundreds of Kiga flocked to church, some believing that the Second Coming was imminent, the revival became increasingly independent of mission control.[150] Known in Rwanda as the *Abaka*, 'Those who shine (with the power of the Holy Spirit)',[151] the converts began to criticise the missionaries' conduct. W. F. Church[152] described in 1937 how the *Abaka* at Gahini were 'beginning to subject our lives to a searching light, judging us by the standards we set them'.[153] The same element of contestation occurred in Kigezi, where the groups were called *Balokole*.

The real leaders of the movement seem to be Africans who feel they are specially inspired and resent correction from anyone. In some ways they seem to have the status of special prophets among their own followers, who honour them with the most extravagant expressions of regard, particularly by the girls and women, who, uttering loud cries of joy, embrace them even after a very short absence.[154]

The revival movement, which spread through eastern Rwanda to Burundi from 1937 to 1942, was a translation of the CMS teaching on the radical sinfulness of man, and of pagan society in particular, together with their emphasis on the Holy Spirit,[155] into the medium of witch-calling and Nyabingi shamanism. The aetiology of conversion involved a sense of Jesus's call and the in-dwelling of the Holy Spirit, occurring either in dream or in the emotional atmosphere of a mass meeting; the convert confessed his sins in public, and might sometimes accuse others around him, demanding that they too proclaim a 'conviction of sin'. Groups with a core of CMS members toured the hills, holding prayer meetings and seeking confessions.[156] Sometimes the accusations would be undisguised calls to admit to sorcery, and the CMS missionaries found people bringing in the leather crowns of cowrie shells that had traditionally represented spiritual power.[157] Thus the *Abaka* leaders became Christian witch-callers, *abahamagazi*, who felt chosen to root out the evil about which the missionaries preached incessantly,[158] and who legitimised their right to do so by reference to the Paraclete rather than to the Nyabingi Spirit.[159]

The feeling of being imbued with a malign force, the account of guilt given by the *Abaka* and sought from others, was partly anxiety caused by contemporary social and political upheavals and partly a product of the Catholic monopoly of chiefly office. Catholic chiefs used the whip freely on the peasantry and on recalcitrant sub-chiefs, and as the Belgian demand for forced labour mounted Protestant Hutu were discriminated against, loaded with *kazi* and beaten if they protested. A consciousness of being the oppressed outsiders of Catholic Rwanda was heightened by their acceptance of the CMS's view that Catholicism was a nominal and superficial form of Christianity; they alone clung to the 'true and pure faith'.[160] The jealousy and resentment engendered by discrimination became internalised as an intensified sense of personal wickedness; the *Abaka* were both 'pure' and 'dangerous'.[161] The movement appeared as a dialectical resolution of their experience of a basic conflict between righteousness and wickedness.

The *Abaka* also represented a renaissance of the old Shamanistic religion; they interpreted the universal claims of the Holy Spirit as directed to society as a whole, rather than to the more limited realm, into which the prophetesses had been forced, of offering personal cures for disease and infertility. This enlargement of spiritual scale to the whole of society was unacceptable to the CMS missionaries; they had only meant evil to be treated in its private, individual, familial context. After this movement Nyabingi possession tended to be relegated to the realm of the pathological, a private ailment requiring an exorcism of the evil spirit.[162]

The Protestant claim that Catholicism was a State religion was fully justified; the mass had become not simply the re-enactment of the foundation of the Christian community but the religious ratification of a stratified society divided just as surely by class as by altar rails. 'Our young notables take up the yoke of vanity when they receive a hill', wrote a Nyundo Father. 'From the first week their wives, who used to come to mass on foot, arrive majestically and proudly seated on a *tipoye* born on the shoulders of their new subjects.'[163] Even at its least visible and most spiritual it was a Catholicism experienced through the traditional categories of kingship. When Naigiziki's hero in *Escapade ruandaise* contemplates the altar it is Christ the king who is present, not the Suffering Servant, the Saviour of the poor. 'From there, today, the king who surpasses all kings, the king who commands all kings, sows, with the hand of divinity that excludes no one and embraces every horizon, a serene and perfect peace.'[164] Like the mwami whose paternity embraced all Rwandans, Christ the King held open the doors of heaven to all, even to those who dared not freqent High Mass for shame at their poverty.[165]

The Catholic Church had, as it were, captured the divinity of the mwamiship and made of Imana the God of kings and of hierarchy. Both geographically and structurally the CMS had moved into the zone of peripheral Hutu religion.[166] The most pious Protestant Christians built small huts in their *rugo* large enough for one man to say his prayers in peace; they were placed where the *ndaro* spirit houses had once been built for the veneration of lineage spirits.[167] Evangelical Anglicanism entered Rwanda and the Hutu household at a time when the Catholics were turning their back on a national Hutu Church; it became for a while, and in a limited area, a new Christian 'lineage religion' in contrast to the Catholic 'territorial cult'. Only Catholicism was allowed to speak to society as a whole in Rwanda, to offer the ruling class a religion of success on earth, and, to the poor, beatitudes and a place in Heaven. But on the other hand only evangelical Protestantism acknowledged the primacy of the problem of evil and provided an idiom in which fears of witchcraft might be articulated and resolved.

The mood of crisis, and the deterioration in the conditions of peasant life that were partly the cause of the *Abaka* movement were widespread phenomena by the beginning of the war. Labour was now being demanded for reclamation of swamps, clearing roads and building, in addition to the burden of compulsory food and cash crops. The Tutsi still tried to squeeze the maximum in *ubuletwa* from their subjects. *Arabica* coffee plants were distributed throughout the country in a wide range of soil types and climates, and when they did not grow the Hutus' incompetence was blamed.[168] Compulsory food crops like manioc were often not disease-resistant, but peasants refusing to go through the motions of planting them were subjected to severe penalties by the *ingénieurs agronomes*, fines of fifty to a hundred francs being imposed for failure to follow instructions to the letter.[169] Anti-erosion measures after 1937 increased occasions for punishment.[170] As the Banyarwanda manfully pushed up the production of coffee from 2,000 tons in 1937 to 4,800 tons in 1945 the farming of export crops became widely regarded as 'a European scheme for their own enrichment at the expense of the African'.[171]

Emigration to Uganda remained high after 1936, when Belgium followed Britain and abandoned the gold standard, thereby devaluing the franc.[172] Fear of being conscripted into the British army kept emigration down in 1939; in the first few months of 1940 about 14,000 passed across the Kakitumba bridge into Uganda; then Belgium devalued, and the numbers shot up to 57,000 in the second half of the year.[173] While the exodus was linked to high earnings and not simply to poor conditions in Rwanda, whole families were now moving and settling permanently. Belgian attempts to use the White Fathers to popularise a resettlement scheme in 1930 failed; the response was nil, and the missionaries did not appear enthusiastic.[174] After 1937 some 20,000 people were successfully moved to Gishari, north-west of Lake Kivu,[175] but with population increase in the 1930s at 2.52 per cent per annum this was a drop in the ocean. Despite signs of land shortage in some areas the Belgians carved out the enormous expanse of the Parc Albert, depriving the Nyundo Tutsi of pasture land and forcing them to move animals into Hutu plots. [176]

Wartime saw a growth in resentment against the Belgians' rule as their colonial territories were pressed to become economically viable. Musinga hailed the German invasion of Belgium as the end of colonial government; a number of nobles began to take a renewed interest in him, and he was hastily deported to the Congo.[177] *Kinyamateka* acted as an organ of war propaganda, treating its reader to lurid drawings of German air attacks on Belgian villages. The administration was sufficiently touchy to put two Italian priests under house arrest at Rambura mission.[178] The Tutsi had already suffered from repeated requisitions of cattle for meat and milk before the war, and with their herds decimated by sleeping sickness and cattle pest a number committed suicide.[179] The effect of pegging cattle prices at a level below their market value was, as the Protestant Mission Alliance explained, 'to defraud the native of a fair return for his produce and to keep him permanently on a low level of subsistence'.[180] Cattle requisitions during the war enriched Belgian middle men and impoverished cattle owners.

Drained and weakened by three years of wartime rule, Rwanda succumbed to an appalling famine that cost the lives of at least 300,000 people; the pea, sweet and ordinary potato harvests were blighted by mildew, but it was only at the end of 1943, after a year of hunger, that large quantities of food relief began arriving by road from the Congo.[181] Yet there was no let-up in the demands for forced labour, and by 1943 a Catholic diarist was speaking of 'the discontent which reigns in the population, particularly for the last three or four years'.[182] When the Protestant Alliance sent an appeal to the Governor General about conditions in 1944, they described' a steady deterioration in the morale of the country'.[183] Since the Catholic Church had become identified with the State, these changes had immediate effects on the Catholic missions.

From 1939 to 1943 the number of Catholics continued to rise slowly from 289,000 to 330,000; given the long catechumenate, this represented the response in the period 1935-39, the pre-war years. Numbers fell dramatically to 320,000 in 1944 and continued down to 312,000 in 1946.[184] Only 4,502 catechumens registered in all the thirty stations put together in 1944. Some of this drop was caused by emigration —

Father Pagès calculated that from 1941 to 1943 the adult male population on the eleven hills around Nyundo fell from 6,041 to 3,742[185] — but it was also what they called a 'baisse générale'; few of the baptised Christians continued to frequent the sacraments and a number of Tutsi took second wives.[186]

This massive slump can best be explained firstly as a reaction after the *Tornade*; many who had been swept up in the movement and received minimal instruction fell away; and secondly as disgust at the Europeans' administration and the search for more powerful patrons than the White Fathers. Temporary labour at the mines and on the pyrethrum plantations gave Catholic workers new bosses, and once independent of the mission they took the opportunity to emancipate themselves from the ethical restrictions imposed by Church membership; second wives and temporary liaisons with women became more common, and drunkenness was sufficiently rife for the adventists to be forced to turn a blind eye to beer-drinking.[187] Some Nyundo and Rwaza Christians profited from the situation by becoming wandering beer salesmen, *abachuruzi*, and at Kabgayi a Rwandan was the first priest to be defrocked for drunkenness and insubordination.[188]

Monsignor Classe was now aging rapidly after forty years on the missions, and thoughts of reform and protest were far from his mind. Despite ruthless Belgian tightening of the screw, he limited his complaints to a protest that forced labour was making it impossible for people to attend catechism classes.[189] With failing strength he worked diligently from 1937 to 1943 to gain privileges for Catholics, arranging exemptions from tax for Catholic pupils regularly at school, and from *kazi* and *ubuletwa* for catechists and *bakuru*.[190] His episcopate ended as it had begun in unremitting effort to obtain for the institutional Church the power, prestige and privilege it lacked in France. In January 1943 Father Laurent Deprimoz was consecrated Classe's co-adjutator and took over the administration of the vicariate.

The advent of Deprimoz allowed the missionaries to give vent to their feelings for the first time. Father Pagès wrote a letter of protest to the Kisenyi Resident about the brutal corporal punishment meted out to those who, in desperation, pulled up their potato crop before it was ready.[191] Two months later the Protestant Alliance sent their list of complaints to Leopoldville. Only then did the Catholics make a fully official protest; the Catholic chief of the Nyambo peoples in the north-east had pleaded with the Fathers to intercede on his behalf because his subjects were fleeing *en masse* into Karagwe to escape the whip and forced labour.[192]

But Catholic protest was too local and too late; the resounding silence of the early war years destroyed Rwandan confidence in the Fathers, and the close union between the missionaries and the Tutsi was never fully restored. From 1943 onwards a number of Tutsi from poorer families, followed by a few nobles, began to take an interest in the CMS, asking for their schools and some actually converting.[193] In Mulera, where Chief Kamuzinzi used to get information about his subjects from Catholic catechists, the Nyundo parishoners came openly to complain at the mission that the Fathers never denounced the chief's brutality;[194] several of his sub-chiefs became Protestants.[195] The Fathers increasingly found themselves recruiting from the very young or the very old.[196] Had not the Protestants seen education as a preparation for 'Satan's kingdom', and opened a secondary school before 1946, the movement might have been more extensive amongst the Tutsi.[197] As it was, the *Tornade* ended abruptly, and the Fathers could no longer take the allegiance of the Tutsi for granted. These early stirrings of anti-colonialism found 'the Whore of Babylon', if not in the Belgian bedchamber, at least badly compromised in Rwandan eyes.

During the war the Catholic chiefs became precisely what Classe had feared, nothing but government agents. Wealth and prestige were now the fragile preserve of the Belgians' elect; much of the brutality and oppression on the hills was the panic-stricken reaction of ambitious men who knew that they might lose all if their subjects did not fulfill the administration's increasingly onerous demands. Clashes between chiefs and mission-supported Christians over exemptions from labour became more common;[198] as a result a wedge was slowly driven between chiefs and missionaries. Thus at the very time the Tutsi take-over of the Church was under way the Rwandan laity was reacting against the White Fathers; the vicariate was run by an old man, a 'man of the Belgians'. The new Tutsi clergy therefore had every reason to look back wistfully to the days of true nobility and to wish for the disestablishment of the Rwandan Church and the disentanglement of the court from European overrule.

Although it was the hierarchical aspects of Catholic Christianity that found their fullest expression after the *Tornade*, the radical doctrine of the equality of man in the eyes of God continued to be heard at times, even though not seen, in church. The *bakuru* were elected by ballot, and the Hutu clergy were an example to everyone that the peasant class did not suffer from some genetic disability that precluded them from high office. The Catholic message that sacramental Grace in the Church could transform seemed to find a living proof in the first generation of Hutu priests. The Fathers, in Lemarchand's words, 'brought the Hutu into contact with a new set of values and metaphysical beliefs',[199] but they did so paradoxically in an institution which belied many of them.

The Hutu found in the seminaries the only path to secondary education open to them. Although the Fathers would have joined the CMS in deploring that 'their desire for Christ, in the first place, is simply to have a God of learning and civilisation',[200] they were not unduly disturbed. For the many, Catholicism, defracted through the prism of patronage, clientship, kingship and power, remained an instrument to ease Rwandans into a bitter-sweet dependence on the Belgians. But for some the radical promise of Christian brotherhood opened up new horizons and expectations. For them the realisation that a Christian ruling class could be as ruthless and tyrannical as the old Tutsi nobility brought an awareness of the inherent contradictions in Rwandan society denied to many of the blinkered missionaries.[201]

The early 1940s saw a *conscientisation* of the Hutu at Kabgayi Major Seminary as Tutsi seminarians began to dominate its life. Men like Joseph Gitera Habyarimana, Anastase Makuza, Aloys Munyangaju, Joseph Ndwaniye and Grégoire Kayibanda felt Tutsi disdain in a purely Christian setting. The experience of being treated as inferior, contemptible and stupid by pushing Tutsi seminarians brought about the realisation that something more than 'Grace' would be needed if the Tutsi were to change their attitudes, let alone relinquish their power. From inside Kabgayi it was plain that the Church had become an instrument in the hands of the ruling class.[202] Precisely because these Hutu seminarians believed in the Christian message, such experiences were formative; even among the clerical elite, where there was an unquestioned premise of equality, the Tutsi had become more equal than others.

Training for the Rwandan Josephites had the same impact on Hutu aspirants. Balthazar Bicamumpaka, the Singa clan head, became *économe* at the Josephite's house in Kansi, but he was treated by the Tutsi Brothers as a roughneck and an inferior. Though an individual Tutsi might invite him to share a meal, if several were present he was not welcome at table.[203] In October 1945 he left the Order to train fully as a teacher; his friend and contemporary, Jacques Hakizimana, fared little better at Astrida, where he bravely trained as a medical assistant. All those who later became Hutu leaders, like Lazare Mpakaniye, Froduald Minani and Calliope Mulindahabi,[204] received their education in Church-run institutions where Tutsi dominance was liable to lead to bitterness and resentment.

However conscious of injustice and humiliation the tiny group of Hutu white-collar workers were, they had as yet no definition of Rwandan society different from that of the Fathers. The Tutsi intellectuals were able to articulate the widespread anti-colonialism of the educated but largely ignored the internal stratification of Rwandan society in their critiques. After the cruelties of wartime Father Pagès still believed that the Tutsi-controlled legal system was 'despite everything relatively well adapted to the peoples for whom it was destined, and, far from being loathsome, was in general based on natural Law'.[205] In as much as this natural law was not informed by charity and love, and the ruling class in society were sinful men, the Rwandan system contained genuine and 'inherent miseries' that would disappear only in 'the light of and under the influence of the Gospel and with the joint aid of the European adminstration'.[206] It was the old story of patriarch and priest. To the crushing philosophy of each according to his station the Hutu could find no immediate answer.

The paring down of Rwanda's feudal society in readiness for a future capitalist economy had thrown up a new group of Catholic chiefs from whose membership the Hutu were totally debarred. The period 1932-45 saw the transition from a Hutu to a Tutsi Church and ended with a general turning away from the White Fathers as the anti-colonial feelings generated by Belgian rule, now a real and pervasive force, came to the surface. By the end of the Second World War there was far more than a Tutsi-dominated Church in Rwanda; there was a State Church. The rise of nationalist sentiment could not but have serious repercussions. On the other hand, resistance to the Belgo-Tutsi State found a natural outlet in the Protestant Ruanda mission in the *Abaka* movement. Only later was Hutu resistance to move from the purely religious plane among the Protestants to spring up within the Catholic Church in the social Catholicism of the Bahutu manifesto. The next few years were to see Monsignor Deprimoz contending with a national elite that shunned mission patronage and attempting to halt the virtual collapse of the Church on the hills.

NOTES

1 Lemarchand, *Rwanda and Burundi*, 79

2 Bourgeois, 'Rapport de sortie de charge', Shangugu, 1934, Derscheid papers.

3 Bourgeois, *Banyarwanda et Barundi*, 181-2.

4 The mortality of people from Bugoyi at court was about forty per annum; some were obliged to work there for two to three months before building for Lwakadigi, his mother and friends. Attempts by individual Residents to restrict the time spent at Nyanza were ignored; see Nyundo diary, 3, 27 May 1926.

5 Bourgeois, 'Rapport de sortie de charge', Shangugu, 1934.

6 Bloch, *Feudal Society*, 359.

7 Lemarchand, *Rwanda and Burundi*, 76.

8 Bourgeois, 'Rapport de sortie de charge', Shangugu, 1934.

9 Governor Jungers, 'Circulaire rélative à la nécessité de l'emploi de la langue indigène en lieu et place du Kiswahili', 25 November 1932, CO.

10 Nyanza report, 1929.

11 Delmas, L., 'Droits fonciers au Ruanda', undated MS (*c.* 1933), WFAR; Kagame, *Le Code des institutions politiques*, 7.

12 Schmidt, Report on the province of Bwana-Tshyambwe, 1934, Derscheid papers.

13 Stevens, 'Rapport de sortie de charge', Byumba, 1933.

14 *Rapport sur l'administration belge du Ruanda-Urundi*, 1938, 3.

15 Bourgeois, 'Notes sur l'administration des indigènes du territoire du Shangugu', 1934, Derscheid papers.

16 Powesland, *Economic Policy*, 57.

17 Verhulst, Report on East Ndorwa Province, 1933; Bourgeois, 'Rapport de sortie de charge', Shangugu, 1934.

18 '*Monsieur le Gouverneur* told us that he was very happy to have received the notes on native property. It now seems definite to him that the native receives his land from the king by the intermediary of the chiefs and that this is the basis of the latter's authority.' See Kabgayi diary, 11 October 1934.

19 Rubera report, 1929; for changes in land holding in Uganda see West, H., *Land Proprietary Structure in Buganda*, African Studies Series, Cambridge, 1971.

20 De Lacger, *Ruanda*, 557.

21 *Rapports annuels*, 1933-34, 407.

22 Zaza diary, 19 November 1931.

23 For example, catechumens were strictly forbidden to attend mass; see Classe to confrères, 5 June 1928, CR.

24 The Protestant formula of *semper reformanda* applied to the individual but not in the same way to the Church.

25 Kabgayi diary, 10, 18 March 1932.

26 See chapter seven, n. 72.

27 *Rapports annuels*, 1933-34, 417; de Lacger, *Ruanda*, 553.

28 *Rapports annuels*, 1933-34, 404.

29 Classe to confrères, 4 December 1931, CR; Zaza diary, 5 June 1932; *Rapports annuels*, 1933-34, 415.

30 Kabgayi diary, 6 December 1931.

31 Jungers to Classe, 20 December 1934, CO.

32 *Rapports annuels*, 1933-34, 415.

33 *Cf* Classe to Marchal, 23 September 1923, WFAR, chapter seven.

34 Arnoux, *Les Pères Blancs*, 142.

35 See Classe to confrères, 22 May 1934, in *Instructions pastorales*, 210.

36 Arnoux, *Les Pères Blancs*, 123.

37 Classe to Simon, 21 October 1933, CO.

38 Troeltsch, E., *The Social Teaching of the Christian Churches*, London, 1931, 289.

39 Pagès, 'Notes sur le régime des biens', 3-4.

40 Memorandum by the Alliance of Protestant Missions in Ruanda-Urundi to the Governor General, Leopoldville, 24 April 1944, Namirembe Archives, Kampala; notes kindly communicated to me by Catherine Robins, UCLA.

41 Pagès to Philippart, 6 November 1933, CO.

42 Pagès, 'Notes sur le régime des biens', 4.

43 Classe to confrères, 3 June 1937, in *Instructions pastorales*, 321.

44 Classe to confrères, 5 May 1938, *ibid.*, 342.

45 *Rapports annuels*, 1930-31, 259.

46 Nyanza report, 1929.

47 'Christians must be a model of respect, submission and obedience to the chief in everything that is not, of course, positively contrary to principles of

Divine and Natural Law.' See 'Compte rendu des séances de Conseil', Rwaza, 28 October 1932.

48 Rwaza diary, 19 February, 21 June 1933.

49 Schumacher to Governor Jungers, 15 August 1935, Dossier 221, WFAR.

50 De Hemptinne, J., 'L'Action Catholique dans nos missions', Bishops' conference, 1932, CR.

51 The Governor wrote to the Bishop about a joint scheme for training medical assistants: 'I objected that it would be regrettable to spread amongst our people who are peaceful, happy and relatively chaste, the AMI from the Belgian Congo.' See Jungers to Classe, 22 December 1934, CO.

52 See chapter five, nn. 124, 150, and chapter seven, n. 69.

53 Schmidt, Report on the province of Bwana-tshyambwe, 1934.

54 'Inshongore', 'the proud ones', was originally the name of one of Ntulo's packs of hunting dogs; see des Forges, *Rwanda under Musiinga*, 252.

55 This was Seruhanga; see Kabgayi diary, 26 February 1935.

56 Saverio Naigiziki, J., *Escapade ruandaise*, Brussels, 1949, 176-7; and see de Lacger's presentation of Kabare in *Ruanda*, 402-3.

57 See the account of the baptism of Ntulo in *Missions d'Afrique*, 1934, 97.

58 See the report on the eighth day of the Bishops' conference, 27 October 1932, Leopoldville, CR.

59 Personal communication from the Rev. Père Boutry. Bishop Classe's first letter on becoming Vicar Apostolic was to ban Rwandan hymns; see Classe to confrères, 28 April 1923, CR.

60 Rwaza diary, 14 February 1934.

61 *Ibid.*, 14 May 1935.

62 *Ibid.*, 19 June 1936.

63 Zaza diary, 5 February 1934.

64 Classe to confrères, 10 January 1933, in *Instructions pastorales*, 143-52.

65 *Ibid.*, 143.

66 On 14 and 19 March 1937.

67 *Rapports annuels*, 1933-34, 434; 1935-36, 347.

68 Nyundo diary, 1 February 1941.

69 Zaza diary, 13 September 1932, 17 February 1933, 11 May 1936; Nyundo diary, 2 September 1942; Grauls to Classe, 5 October 1943, CO. Even Classe had delivered a stiff rebuke to the agriculturalists in the past; see Classe to Namèche, 8 September 1927, CO.

70 An almost complete series of *Kinyamateka* is to be found at Archbishop's House Library, Kigali, Rwanda.

71 I am grateful to Monsieur Michel André of the University of Liège, who is making a study of the Catholic Press in Rwanda, for a very helpful discussion of the paper's role in the pre-war years. Anyone selling more than five copies was given a free issue.

72 Nothomb, *Church History*, 86, 93.

73 Rudahigwa *et al.* to Padré Voillard, 7 September 1935. The busy Schumacher soon abandoned the group for his pygmies; see Schumacher to Voillard, 6 December 1935, Dossier 221, WFAR.

74 Classe to Junger, 23 September 1935, Education file, CO.

75 Classe to Jungers, 25 December 1934, Education file CO.

76 *Cf* his comments on the 1932 Leopoldville Bishops' conference. The

1930s were the era of resentment at the 'jumped-up mission boy' in Rwanda, a good twenty years later than in most British colonies like Nyasaland and Nigeria, where the missions had arrived correspondingly early.

77 Rubbens to Jungers, 16 April 1935, Education file, CO. 1,942,605 francs were spent on education in Ruanda-Urundi in 1935; total tax collected was over 11 million francs. The Minister for the Colonies points out that in comparison with Tanganyika this is a favourable percentage of the tax income spent on education.

78 Deprimoz to Voisin, 18 December 1930, Education file, CO. When the Bishop thought he would be able to pass off a noviciate for *Benebikira* at Astrida as a subsidised girls' school he was eager for the project. When the Governor decided that he wanted it as a normal school for Tutsi girls the Bishop declined.

79 Classe to confrères, 14 June 1929, 14 January 1932, CR.

80 Kabgayi diary, 20 August 1934. A thousand parishioners at Murunda gave 1,101 francs; see *Rapports annuels*, 1933-34, 408.

81 De Lacger, *Ruanda*, 625-6. The vicariate was collecting an impressive amount of money by 1938, about 30,000 francs in the poor boxes and 85,000 francs as Church tax; the latter was graduated at about 100 francs for chiefs and two francs fifty centimes for peasants.

82 Minutes of the meeting of the Executive Committee of the Ruanda mission, 16 January 1936, 'Field Executive Minutes' file, CMS, London. The Catholics got 850,000 francs for 56,000 pupils; the Brothers of Charity at Astrida got an additional 480,000 francs for their school. Protestants got 574,000 francs for 12,000 pupils, fewer of whom were in sub-standard bush schools.

83 Appeals by Classe to bring schools up to the standard specified for grants-in-aid; see Classe to confrères, 13 April 1931, CR.

84 Jean-Baptiste Lukamba needed a special letter of recommendation from no less a person than Monsignor Deprimoz for such a position; see Zaza diary, October, 15 November 1943.

85 Difficulties in negotiations for the school between the White Fathers, the Brothers and the Belgian authorities delayed Astrida's opening from 1930 to 1933; see Simon to Classe, 22 September 1933, CO, and chapter seven, n. 119.

86 Lemarchand, *Rwanda and Burundi*, 138.

87 The CMS had lodged complaints with the Governor General at the end of 1935; see minutes of the meeting of the Executive Committee of the Ruanda mission, 12-13 November 1935; *Ruanda Notes*, No. 55, January 1936, 16; De Lacger, *Ruanda*, 573-4.

88 School affiliation remained often more important than class distinctions. In Africa, where elite schooling in the colonial period secured an individual his place in the ruling class, the 'old boy' network was quite as important as in the English public schools of the day, e.g. Michel Rwagasana's support for UNAR.

89 See chapter nine.

90 Classe to Jungers, 16 March 1936, quoting a letter from Postiaux to Classe, 28 October 1934, Education file, CO.

91 *Rapports annuels*, 1935-36, 366; Kabgayi diary, 6 June 1933, 8 August 1934.

92 Quoted in de Lacger, *Ruanda*, 587.

93 See Correspondence with Apostolic Delegate file, CR.

94 Classe to Dellepiane, 1 October 1934, Apostolic Delegate file, CR.

95 Classe to Dellepiane, 28 January 1935; Classe to Gorju, 8 May 1936, Apostolic Delegate file, CR.

96 De Lacger, *Ruanda*, 589.

97 *Ibid.*, 590.

98 *Rapports annuels*, 1937-41.

99 Classe to Voillard, 4 December 1925, WFAR; Classe to Rwandan clergy, 1 October 1929, CR.

100 Classe to confrères, 13 September 1930, CR; Jungers to Classe, 6 March 1933; Classe to Jungers, 13 March 1933, in which the Bishop supports Abbé Callixte in an important dispute involving Father Vanneste.

101 The question of starting Normal schools has been broached in 1934 but had been held in abeyance for lack of funds and manpower; see Jungers to Classe, 15 April 1934, CO.

102 Abbé Gallicani had been a fierce opponent of Pastor Lestrade while he was at Murunda. *Rapports annuels*, 1930-31, 289, speaks warmly of his 'Homeric battles'. However, since Lestrade was Belgian, Classe probably found it wiser to move the Abbé to quieter waters.

103 Details in a book celebrating the fiftieth anniversary of Catholic missions in Rwanda, in the possession of Father Dominic Nothomb; interviews with Father Boutry, teacher at Kabgayi seminary from 1936 to 1946; Kagame, *Répertoire bibliographique*.

104 De Lacger, *Ruanda*, 550, 663-4.

105 Rwaza diary, 17 February 1935; *Rapports annuels*, 1933-34, 417.

106 Kabgayi diary, 15 March 1935; De Lacger, *Ruanda*, 550.

107 Kabgayi diary, 21 January 1936.

108 Jungers to Rwanda Resident, 9 October 1935; Lemarchand, *Rwanda and Burundi*, 77, for Lord Lugard's views on Belgian 'Indirect' rule.

109 De Lacger, *Ruanda*, 553, and see chapter seven, n. 83.

110 The Zaza diary for April and May 1936 has a number of instances of disapproval shown of Belgian measures, unlike the early days when the Fathers were the main agriculturalists; see Mortehan to Classe, 18 November 1922; Classe to Mortehan, 9 March 1923. Classe was officially informed of attacks by *Camiostoma coffeela* on the coffee crop; see Hombert to Classe, 3 April 1935, CO.

111 Zaza diary, 21 July 1940, 13 September 1949.

112 Zaza diary, 21 July 1940.

113 The fact that it took place in Gisaka is not suprising; the court was never entirely sure of the Gesera chiefs' loyalty.

114 Classe to Father Superior, Rwaza, 23 March 1933, Rwaza correspondence; Dellepiane to Classe, 6 January 1938, Apostolic Delegate file, CR.

115 Classe to Paradis, 24 September 1941.

116 Voisin to Classe, 23 December 1931; Pauwels to Classe, 1 January 1932, CO.

117 Chanoine Louis de Lacger began his researches at the same time; he had known Monsignor Classe since his seminary days at St Sulpice in Paris. He finished the first part of *Ruanda* in 1938 just as Kagame's first articles were coming out.

118 For the richness of traditional oral literature see Coupez, A., and

Kamanzi, T., *Littérature de cour an Ruanda*, Oxford, 1970. Abbé Alexis Kagame has a collection of Christian poetry at the University of Butare.

119 *L'Ami*, Nos. 67-8, August 1950, 140.

120 *Ibid.*, 138-9.

121 *Ibid.*

122 De Lacger, *Ruanda*, 540.

123 Nothomb's appendix to *Ruanda*, 672.

124 *L'Ami*, No. 91, July 1952, 136; Jungers to Rwanda Resident, 9 October 1935, Education file, CO.

125 Kabgayi diary, 11 October 1934.

126 Dellepiane to Classe, 15 July 1933, Apostolic Delegate file, CR.

127 Naigiziki, *Escapade ruandaise*, 72: 'High mass at Nyanza perhaps more than elsewhere is surrouned on the side of the faithful with a singular aura of protocol. It is high-society mass. For the flea-bitten of Nyanza . . . are ashamed to mix their Sunday tatters with such sartorial elegance.'

128 *Rapports annuels*, 1935-36, 370.

129 There was little theological justification for this, but in the African context of a shortage of priests it was also a matter of convenience.

130 Rwaza parish registers and personal communication from the Rev. Father Heremans, Kigali Minor Seminary.

131 This decline, however, has not been very great in the north, where lineages are still important as a 'social calculus' and have not been broken by feudal bonds.

132 Monnier to Rwanda Resident, 18 September 1933, CO; *Ruanda Notes*, No. 37, July 1931, 16; No. 47, January 1934, 11-12.

133 Monnier to Rwanda Resident, 18 September 1933.

134 See chapters five and six.

135 Monnier to Philippart, 12 October 1933, CO.

136 Memorandum from Philippart to Rwanda Resident, 12 October 1933.

137 The speech, made by Jean Paradis, is reported in Witlox to Classe, 28 September 1933, CO.

138 Stonelake, A. R., *Congo Past and Present*, London, 1937, 133.

139 *Ibid.*, 135.

140 Classe to confrères, 11 February 1929, CR: an appeal to reduce domestic staff, since government is insisting on a minimum wage; Zaza diary, 7 November 1936, gives example of unpaid catechists working for the mission, *Rapports annuels*, 1935-36, 376, for loss of employees to mines.

141 The north-west was contested with the Adventists and the Belgian Protestants, the north-east with the CMS. Nyundo had some acrimonious disputes with the Adventists (see Nyundo diary, 26 November 1939), while the Rwandan clergy occasionally clashed with the Belgian Protestants; see Durand to Classe, 3 February 1927.

142 See Executive Committee meeting minutes of Ruanda mission, annual conference, 19 February 1935; missionary conference, 7 February 1942, CMS, London; interview with Dr J. E. Church, CMS missionary in Rwanda since 1927, Cambridge, February 1973; interview with the Rev. Albert Brown, head of Rwanda mission, CMS, January 1973.

143 *Ruanda Notes*, No. 48, April 1934, 18-20.

144 Arthur Pitt-Pitts was one of the several CMS missionaries in Rwanda

who had been in CICCU before the war: 'It was not an uncommon experience at a CICCU Prayer Meeting or Bible Reading to hear a loud thud, and the whispered explanation, "Pitt-Pitts has fainted again".' *Ruanda Notes*, No. 72, May 1940, 11; No. 57, July 1936, 3.

145 *Ruanda Notes*, No. 57, July 1936, 7.

146 *Ibid.*, No. 59, January 1937, 50.

147 *Ibid.*, No. 25, July 1928, 5.

148 See Linden, I., 'Chisumphi theology in the religion of central Malawi', Lusaka conference on Religion in Central Africa, July 1972, for a comparable instance of prophets directing people to a central cult. In the Christian context Alice Lenshina is also in this tradition.

149 At this time there were militant Nyabingi groups around Lake Bunyoni and northern Rwanda using the 'bullets to water' ideology; see Rwaza diary, 13 May 1928; *Ruanda Notes*, No. 25, July 1928, 7.

150 *Ruanda Notes*, No. 25, July 1928, 6; Church, 'Quest for the highest', 105, 120, 125-149.

151 *Ruanda Notes*, No. 67, February 1939, 38.

152 A younger brother of Dr Joe Church. The family is able to trace a line back to a female convert of Wesley.

153 *Ruanda Notes*, No. 61, July 1937, 23.

154 Memorandum by Dr L. L. Sharp in minutes of the meeting of the Executive Committee of Ruanda mission, 12-13 February 1942.

155 'The Snow Prayer' in Kiga and Kinyarwanda was distributed in some 3,000 copies in 1928: 'O God, our Father, wash me from all sin in the Saviour's Blood, and I shall be whiter than snow (*sic*). Fill me daily with the Holy Spirit, to serve thee for Jesus Christ's sake, our Lord, Amen.' *Ruanda Notes*, No. 25, July 1928, 4.

156 *Ruanda Notes*, No. 66, November 1938, 26-7; No. 68, May 1939, 20-1; Church, 'Quest for the highest', 117.

157 *Ruanda Notes*, No. 58, October 1936, 14; *Rapports annuels*, 1935-36, 375; *cf* the Lenshina movement in Zambia.

158 'As I walked down the hill from the hospital that morning my blood boiled within me because of the cruelty of it all; but the answer came to me. Sin was written across those withered bodies. Satan had dragged them down and given death and disease as his reward.' Comments on the famine, *Ruanda Notes*, No. 28, April 1929, 16.

159 For a good example see 'The story of a Gahini schoolboy', undated MS in Education file of Ruanda mission: 'I heard a voice telling me that I was a wicked sinner and that I should certainly perish. When I heard that voice I repented of my sin and knew that the judgement of Hell had passed from me. I heard the voice of the Lord Jesus once more, telling me that my sins were forgiven me.' *Cf* the large number of confessions registered by the Fathers at the height of the Abaka movement; see Kabgayi diary, 12 April 1941; and *cf* A. C. Stanley-Smith's remark: 'These people are spirit worshippers, their chief spirit being named Nyabingi, and their religious life is entirely one of fear' (*Ruanda Notes*, No. 1, 7 May 1921) and 'Day by day short addresses were given on the personality and the personal need of the Holy Spirit; on how to receive Him and how we may lose Him, on His fullness and His fruits' (*Ruanda Notes*, No. 24, April 1928, 7).

160 The *Abaka* 'tended towards the idea that only their party were real Christians'; *Ruanda Notes*, No. 67, February 1939, 39. This was identical to the Protestant view of the Catholics; see *Ruanda Notes*, No. 63, January 1938, 22.

161 Douglas, M., *Purity and Danger*, Harmondsworth, 1966, 122-36.

162 Lestrade, A., *Notes d'éthnographie du Rwanda*, Sciences Humaines, Annales Serie in 8 , Tervuren, Brussels, 1972, 331-2. A similar development of the Chisumphi cult is found; see n. 148.

163 Nyundo diary, 22 January 1948.

164 Naigiziki, *Escapade ruandaise*, 185.

165 See n. 127.

166 It is interesting that the first Rwandan to be ordained in the Anglican Church was Kosea Shalita, the Tutsi son of a prominent chief who backed Ndungutse in 1909 and had been forced to flee to Nkole. Born 1901 near Gahini, he was educated at Budo College in Uganda and was ordained on 25 January 1933; see *Ruanda Notes*, No. 43, January 1933, 15.

167 Church, 'Quest for the highest, 8, dates the first building of these huts to November 1933, before the Gahini revival; see also Church, J. E., *Forgive them*, London, 1968, 23.

168 Zaza diary, 11 May 1936.

169 Zaza diary, 25 January 1939; memorandum of Protestant Alliance, 24 April 1944.

170 Paternostre de la Mairieu, *Le Rwanda*, 131.

171 Memorandum of Protestant Alliance, 24 April 1944.

172 Richards, *Economic Development*, 50.

173 Powesland, *Economic Policy*, 67.

174 Postiaux to Classe, 13 February 1930; Classe to Coubeau, 29 May 1930, CO.

175 Simon to Classe, 4 October 1937, CO. Labour was also sent to Katanga from Rwanda.

176 Nyundo diary, 8 October 1943.

177 Paternostre de la Mairieu, *Le Rwanda*, 152.

178 Paradis to Classe, 11 December 1940, CO.

179 Nyundo diary, 24 September 1932, 30 April 1933, 3 August 1934, 8 October 1943; Zaza diary, 2 May 1943; *Ruanda Notes*, No. 50, October 1934, 23, 26. The Governor had made an attempt to stop Belgian abuses of the Tutsi cattle; see circular of 30 August 1932, CO.

180 Memorandum of Protestant Alliance, 24 April 1944.

181 Zaza diary, 3 January 1944; de Lacger, *Ruanda*, 658; Leurquin, *Niveau de vie*, 33.

182 Nyundo diary, 8 October 1943.

183 Memorandum of Protestant Alliance, 24 April 1944.

184 De Lacger, *Ruanda*, 658. The figure given for 1943 is actually 353,000, but this is certainly too high, owing to the Fathers counting in emigrants, so a correction of 7 per cent has been made in the text.

185 Nyundo diary, 8 October 1943.

186 Zaza diary, 19 October 1944; de Lacger, *Ruanda*, 658-9.

187 Nyundo diary, 8 October 1943.

188 Gesche to Administrateur territorial, 17 May 1946, Rwaza correspondence.
189 Classe to Simon, 16 December 1939, CO.
190 Rubbens to Classe, 31 July 1937; Classe to Rubbens, 2 August 1937; Simon to Classe, 19 January 1940; Classe to Paradis, 24 September 1942; Paradis to Classe, 29 June 1943, CO.
191 Nyundo diary, 14 February 1944.
192 Deprimoz to Grauls, 18 May 1944, CO.
193 The first signs are complaints from Shyira CMS mission; see Nyundo diary, 13 April 1942, 8 October 1943; *Ruanda Notes*, No. 88, January 1944, 13; No. 86, August 1944, 2-3; No. 92, May 1946, 3.
194 Nyundo diary, 8 October 1943.
195 Minutes of the meeting of the Executive Committee of Ruanda mission, 7-14 July 1943, CMS; Nyundo diary, 1 January 1943, 28 March 1945, 22 January 1948.
196 Nyundo diary, 8 October 1943.
197 When a school did open at Shyogwe in June 1946 it was quickly filled with Tutsi boy boarders; see 'The story of a Gahini schoolboy'; *Ruanda Notes*, No. 94, November 1946, 4, 11.
198 Vauthier to Deprimoz, 28 March 1947, CO; official notification by Governor of restriction of *bakurus*' powers, 12 December 1946, contained in *Trait d'Union*, No. 39, May 1947; *Rapports annuels*, 1947-48, 193.
199 Lemarchand, R., 'The *coup* in Rwanda', in *Protest and Power in Black Africa*, ed. Rotberg, R. I., and Mazrui, A. I., Oxford, 1970, 891.
200 *Ruanda Notes*, No. 61, July 1937, 21.
201 Interview with the (then) President, Grégoire Kayibanda, Kigali, June 1973.
202 Interview with Chanoine Ernotte, headmaster of Christ-Roi school, Nyanza, June 1973.
203 Interview with Balthazar Bicamumpaka, Rwaza, June 1973.
204 Mpakaniye was a teacher from Rwaza who became a sub-chief after schooling at Kabgayi Minor Seminary. From 1967 to 1971 he was national secretary of MDR-PARMEHUTU. Minani came from Gitarama, and spent three years studying philosophy before leaving the major seminary. He studied political science at Louvain and became a PARMEHUTU national *député* in 1965. Mulindahabi, also from Gitarama, went to Kabgayi Minor Seminary and became secretary for Catholic schools in 1956. He was Secretary General of PARMEHUTU in October 1959; he died on 7 September 1971.
205 Pagès, A., 'Au Ruanda. Droits et pouvoirs des chefs sous la suzeraineté du roi hamite: quelques abus du système', *Zaire*, April 1949, 359.
206 *Ibid*.

NINE

Elite and counter-elite

When Bishop Leon Classe died in hospital in Bujumbura on 31 January 1945 the Church he had fashioned was in dire straits. The threat was not external; Catholic missions dominated the north and south of the country, holding the Protestants at bay in the contested north-east and north-west corners. There were the perennial problems; the *bakuru* had risen during the war to became a law unto themselves, judging cases, avoiding labour dues and on occasions demanding labour, goods or money for representing the Christians before their sub-chiefs.[1] Even the most loyal of mission protégés, like Simon Nyiringondo, found cause to complain about the Catholics' insubordination to the administration.[2] Then there were the new ones; in 1946 only half the Christians inscribed on the Fathers' books were performing their Easter duties, the confession and communion without which a Catholic was normally considered to have 'lapsed'.[3] Nobles, lured by the new Protestant school at Shyogwe,[4] were spontaneously rejecting the White Fathers and seeking out the Anglicans.[5]

At a meeting of Superiors of mission stations held in September 1945 reforms of the catechumenate were mapped out. The period of postulancy was to last sixteen months, with two sessions of doctrine and reading per week. Those passing the final examination were eligible for a thirty-two-month catechumenate punctuated by eight-monthly examinations. From the beginning of postulancy to baptism the training was divided up into four-month sessions, *igice*, and no one could move from one unit to next without adequate attendances at class. Catechists had the *Gatikisimu isobanuye* (Cathechism commentary), which contained a set of relevant Bible references, and they were given a short manual on methodology.[6] The reforms seem to have been effective; statistics for Easter duties showed that the failure rate had dropped to 10 per cent by 1955.[7]

With the practice of the catechumenate restored to traditional White Father rigour, Monsignor Deprimoz turned to the problem of the *évolué*, a term for the Rwandan intelligensia that did not initially appear objectionable in its connotations,[8] and was used freely by Rwandans and Europeans alike. To counter secular newspapers like the new *La Voix du Congolais* coming out of Leopoldville[9] a small Catholic magazine, *L'Ami*, destined for French-speaking Africans in Rwanda, Burundi and eastern Congo, was published. It had a limited success, selling one thousand copies, though only four hundred were bought by Rwandans in the first few years.[10] The Brothers of Charity produced their own magazine, *Servir*, destined for the alumni of the Groupe Scolaire in Astrida. The seminarians contributed to their own *L'Écho du Séminaire*.[11] Each year a Sunday was set aside as 'Press Day' when the Fathers exhorted their congregations to read 'good' periodicals and to disseminate them.[12] The buying of Catholic newspapers was virtually an obligation for teachers and catechists, and the readership of *Kinyamateka* doubled to nine thousand by 1947.[13]

The growth of *cercles*, clubs for Catholic *évolués* where it was hoped they would make contact with the clergy in an informal atmosphere, and where books and sports facilities were provided, was also the fruit of the first years of Deprimoz's episcopate. Regular meetings at Astrida mission blossomed into the Cercle Secondien, named after the head of the Groupe Scolaire. At Kigali there was the Cercle Léon Classe and at Nyanza the Cercle Charles Lavigerie.[14] Similar groups had a modest success among the much larger educated Catholic population of Leopoldville. Deprimoz's commitment to the *évolué*, judged by that touchstone of episcopal concern, money, was sincere; an impressive hall and small library were built for the Astridiens.[15] His declared aim was 'garder toute notre influence sur cette génération montante qu'il faut éclairer dans le bon sens, diriger dans leurs revendications et orienter vers l'Action Catholique'.[16]

But despite the new Bishop's desire to keep Rwanda's two to three thousand *évolués* within the fold, his consecration at sixty-five had come, late for a missionary, at an age at which responses to new problems did not easily escape a narrow traditional framework. In the same mould as Bishop Classe — an outgoing Bishop could usually guarantee his favourite's appointment — he lacked any urgent sense that Africa, in a new stage of its history, needed new approaches.[17] It was with a certain regret that he acknowledged that the prestige of the bush catechist had declined in the face of the country's better educated youth.[18] He knew the *évolués* needed special treatment, like bright but difficult children, yet the fear remained that extensive education would create a group of *déclassés* who would leave the land and the assured piety of rural Catholicism.[19] He balanced the buildings in Astrida with the Institut Léon Classe in Kabgayi, a trades school giving training in carpentry and tailoring which opened its doors to forty-eight pupils in 1947.[20]

There was the same ambivalence in the attitude of the Belgian administration, which, while recognising that Rwanda's new position as a United Nations trusteeship territory implied a commitment to ultimate independence,[21] was slow to set the wheels turning. A Conseil du Gouvernement for Ruanda-Urundi was set up in 1947 and met annually, but it lacked Rwandan members; the two abami were admitted only in 1949, and then as a result of a visit the previous year by the first United Nations delegation.[22] Despite proddings from New York the Belgian administration stubbornly refused to think seriously about democratic reforms in Rwanda before the requisite level of economic and 'moral' progress was judged to have taken place.[23] The White Fathers were to sponsor the first Rwandans' travel to Europe before the Belgians sent Isodore Rwubisisi to the Université Libre de Bruxelles and the Hutu Fidèle Nkundabagenzi for trade union training at the École Sociale at Héverlée in the early 1950s.[24]

For both Church and administration the period after the war was one of wait-and-see and half-hearted measures. Significant changes, though, were taking place in the missionary personnel; Classe's death heralded the passing of a generation of missionaries who had grown up in the rigid conservatism of nineteenth century French Catholicism. The new missionaries who arrived in the late 1930s and 1940s were born into a fast secularising Europe. The percentage of unbaptised in industrial towns like Limoges rose from 2.5 per cent at the turn of the century to 34 per cent at the beginning of the first world war.[25] They grew up in a period of response to communism marked by movements like Cardinal Cardijn's Jeunesse Ouvrière Catholique in the late 1920s. Yet the proletariat-oriented apostolate of some movements in Catholic Action never broke through the middle class legacy of the nineteenth century, which continued to act as a brake on any widespread shift in the social policy of the Church.

The Second World War, by revealing the logical consequence of blind adherence to the *status quo* and obedience to 'lawfully constituted authority', was a turning point. After the collusion of the German hierarchy with the Nazis the institutional Church was called in question.[26] The visible structures of Catholicism were no longer seen as a consummation of the Faith but as its disposable instrument in the world; witness, not survival, was the message of the Third Reich, and many were ready to listen. Not only had Catholics fought alongside communists in resistance movements but Christian Democrat parties were obliged in post-war years to form coalitions with 'enemies of the Church', liberals and socialists. French worker priests quickly took up positions in trade union leadership, and the movement was only slowly and painfully crushed by the Vatican.

The new generation of missionary priests was drawn from a wider range of social backgrounds, and, although French and Belgians predominated, other nationals were more in evidence than in the past.[27] They were young, eager and zealous, bringing to Rwanda a sense of urgency that contrasted with their superiors, who, though not smug, had nonetheless grown, Vatican-fashion, to view the world in the 'perspective of eternity'. Men like Father Gilles, Dejemeppe, Adriaenssens, Pien, Perraudin and Ernotte were a different breed from the old royalist White Fathers.

Father Louis Pien grew up in a small town, one of a large Flemish family; his father was a self-made man who had risen to be *greffier en chef* in the local court.[28] Chanoine Eugène Ernotte worked after the war as director of the College St Barthélemy in Seurain, a working class industrial suburb of Liège; a close friend of the Belgian Superior Provincial of the White Fathers, Father Guy Mosmans, he came to Rwanda in 1956.[29] He was a tough but intellectual priest who would not have looked amiss on the shop floor. Father, later Archbishop, André Perraudin was the son of a schoolmaster in Le Chable-Bagnes in Switzerland. During the war he was professor of philosophy and rector of the minor seminary in Fribourg,[30] and thus in a unique position to contemplate the Church's role in Germany. He worked as a bush missionary in Burundi from 1947 to 1950 before taking up an appointment as professor of philosophy at Nyakibanda major seminary in Rwanda.[31] Father Gilles worked with the JOC for several years before coming to Africa.[32]

There were eighty-eight White Fathers in Rwanda in 1948; the indigenous Church was headed by eighty-one Rwandan abbés, fifty-eight Josephite Brothers and 155 *Benebikira*.[33] Only Abbé Aloys Bigirumwami was included on the all-white Conseil du Vicariat, after having served for fourteen years as Father Superior of Muramba parish. Another Tutsi priest, Abbé Decgratias Mbandiwimfura, was in Rome studying canon law.[34] With so few Abbés given positions of responsibility at the vicariate level, and with continuing pressure from Tutsi clergy in seminaries and parishes, friction grew up not only between European and Rwandan priests but between Tutsi and Hutu Abbés. Father Mosmans saw the Rwandan clergy as divided into two groups, 'priests with a touch of white and the all-blacks'. 'To the first the natives confide absolutely nothing,' he wrote, 'and the second relay to us nothing of what the natives have confided in them . . . in each camp may be distinguished a more nuanced and organised Tutsi group and a more simple, hard-working Hutu group.'[35]

As new stations opened after the war, the power of the indigenous Church on the hills increased. Both Tutsi and Hutu priests were able to translate their spiritual authority into a temporal sway over their parishoners. Members of an Abbé's family tended to settle around his mission or find employment there, and as Father Superior he was able to build up a network of clients, often becoming a confidant of the local chief;[36] several Astridiens passed through minor seminaries in the company of future Abbés, and school ties remained strong. False modesty or pretence that authority should be shorn of material expression was generally lacking; the priest was a local leader. When the Josephite Brothers elected their own Rwandan Superior the mwami presented him with fifty cows.[37] Before Monsignor Bigirumwami's consecration the Abbés at Nyundo caused the local Hutu much annoyance, and the White Fathers some consternation, by organising a 'voluntary' collection for the future Bishop's car.[38]

The first serious sign of conflict within the Church appeared in 1948, significantly the year of the United Nations delegation's visit. Abbé Deogratias' departure for Rome aroused a storm of protest from the Hutu clergy, who imagined, probably correctly, that he was being groomed for episcopal office.[39] Then there was the removal of Brother Secondien from Astrida. His return to Belgium seems to have been due to pressure on the White Fathers from Rudahigwa, who was jealous of the bright young men from the Groupe Scolaire.[40] The rise of the Tutsi Church increased the power of the mwami, a close friend of Abbé Alexis Kagame, who was able to intervene in Church matters from behind the scenes.[41] The king later forced the resignation of Abbé Eustache, Bishop Bigirumwami's vicar delegate, over a family quarrel; he was replaced by Abbé Alexandre Musoni, a close relative of Rudahigwa.[42] The Tutsi clergy, chafing at the restraints imposed on them by the missionaries, were increasingly anti-White Father and tended to form a common front with the chiefs.[43]

The White Fathers found few defenders. The Hutu Abbés accused them of indifference to social problems and failure to press for reform of *ubuhake*, while the Tutsi Abbés complained about the nationalism of the Belgian clergy and pointed to Protestant successes.[44] To escape from their influence Abbé Alexis Kagame requested permission to join the Jesuits.[45] He and the mwami were pressing for a Jesuit college at Nyanza, partly because of the Jesuits' educational reputation and partly because they were thought more pro-African and more in favour of African nationalism than other Orders.[46] Against a background of mounting tax evasion and general discontent at Belgian dilatoriness, the administration was soon talking of 'subversive elements';[47] the cultural nationalism of Kagame seemed threatening, especially since it had Nyiginya support. Father Mosmans wrote of Kagame with anxious admiration, '[he] is not only a learned and hard-working priest, a man of great talent; he is, what is more, a force of nature'.[48] The verdict of the disgruntled Deprimoz was 'this Abbé is closer to Nyanza than to Rome'.[49]

The Bishop's remark was some measure of the gulf between missionary and Rwandan clergy, for Kagame's nationalism was subtle and refined enough to find a place for Rome. His was a strikingly

Platonic position in which the role of the Tutsi elite was to salvage the Rwandan cultural heritage; for the warrior valour of the old order was to be substituted the moral virtue and intellectual excellence of Rwanda's guardians, the new *abiru*, the Tutsi Abbés.[50] They had consciously set out to, and would one day, control the Rwandan Church. His book, *Le Code des institutions politiques du Ruanda*, was an encomium of the old Tutsi system;[51] if there were defects in contemporary society they were products of arbitrary tampering with a balanced political system by the Belgians.[52] He was opposed to the new style of egalitarian preaching on the grounds that ordinary Rwandans were not ready for such 'esoteric' doctrines; commoners 'without proper intellectual formation' needed the constraints of Rwanda's stratified society.[53]

Abbé Kagame emerged as the most articulate and trenchant of the White Fathers' critics because he understood them so well. For the European cultural hegemony imposed in the seminaries the Tutsi elite wished to exchange their own, and could present it as the national culture of Rwanda. Kagame's devastating critique of the missionaries' *politicisme* is applicable, word for word, to the cultural nationalism of the Tutsi Abbés.

C'est un système de sa nature inavoué, latent qui, sous prétexte d'assurer les intérêts de la Religion, ou même a l'occasion des intérêts religieux réels, veut en réalité asseoir des bases solides à l'emprise dominatrice d'un corps culturel sur l'esprit des autochthones.[54]

And just as the Tutsi politicians were later to look to the United Nations in an attempt to force Independence, so the Tutsi clergy looked to Rome to deliver them from the White Fathers. Since the *Tornade* legitimation for the monarchy and for the divisions in society had come from Rome, but now it came to the court via the Tutsi Abbés; the White Fathers, seemingly dangerous democrats judged by their post-war missionaries, were by-passed. Kagame called for obediene to the dictates of the Holy See.[55] Permission for the *Benebikira* to wear shoes, and the introduction of private rooms instead of dormitory alcoves in the major seminary, granted in the early 1950s, were both attributed to the benign intervention of the Papal Delegate.[56] Rome was pro-Rwandan. Abbé Kagame was not anti-Rome, far from it; he was anti-White Father, and for good reason.

It was apparent to even the most other-worldly of Fathers by 1950 that their relations with the *évolués* had deteriorated to a disquieting degree. 'It would doubtless be hasty,' wrote Deprimoz, 'to consider this state of mind as an expression of an exaggerated and unhealthy nationalism. It must be considered rather as a new awareness which has not yet found its equilibrium, and which must at all events be treated with great delicacy.'[57] The old formulas for Catholic Action were not working any more; the *cercles* continued in the small Rwandan towns, but there was no life in them.[58] Membership of the Cercle Charles Lavigerie fell from seventy to thirty.[59] Anti-European feeling was running high; the mine bosses and plantation owners were despised for what they were, dishonest oppressors come to extract the maximum profits in the shortest time. The elite, despite diplomas and qualifications, found it hard to obtain employment with the pay and status to which they aspired, and resented being treated as ordinary parishoners by ignorant *bakuru b'inama*.[60] They were singularly isolated, suffering from both the opposition of the 'Nyanza old guard' and the contempt of the Europeans. Nor could they find solace in the Church. 'The *évolués* know perfectly well how much separates the native priests from the White Fathers,' wrote one missionary. 'The gulf is much greater than is generally realised, and many are still blind to it.'[61]

Although many Rwandans still practised a 'target' economy, not bothering to pick their coffee crop at the end of the harvest season if they had met their cash and clothing needs, the new elite began in the 1950s to take advantage of the opportunities afforded by commerce.[62] Older men with fixed ideas of the 'just price' taught them by the Fathers were easy prey for shrewd entrepreneurs who would buy up their coffee crop in exchange for salt, DDT or even quinine tablets.[63] Since they could hope only for minor positions in the administration, and the number of vacant sub-chieftancies was limited, many of the new elite turned to small-scale commerce; from only twenty-one African-owned shops in all Ruanda-Urundi in 1948 the number rose to 647 by 1951.[64] Coffee production reached a peak 28,800 tons in 1956.[65] Although there was a tendency for cash to be converted to cattle, a small group of literate entrepreneurs grew up who thought in modern terms of capital accumulation and market forces.[66]

The facile division between Tutsi cattle-owning wealth and Hutu subsistence farming poverty, always an oversimplification, became thoroughly misleading after the war. During the colonial period a large body of Tutsi became, or remained, impoverished and lacked cattle, while returning Hutu migrants and successful coffee-growers accumulated cows and were relatively prosperous. A survey of incomes undertaken in the mid-1950s, which excluded those in political office from the sample, gave the following figures:[67]

Caste	No. of families	Adult men	Average income/family (francs)
Tutsi	287	215	4,439
Hutu	914	727	4,249
Twa	2	1	1,446

Tutsi families on average had more cattle than Hutu families, but the difference was not great; for example, Nduga Tutsi had 2.4 animals against Hutu 1.2 animals per family. The greatest disparity was in Buyenzi province, with 1.9 animals against 0.3 animals respectively. Similarly, the Tutsi on average had only a slightly lower rate of child mortality.[68]

Even when considering the distribution of political office, the significant point is not so much a Tutsi monopoly of traditional and bureaucratic power as the closed oligarchy of a few noble lineages. A single Nyiginya lineage occupied almost a quarter of the country's forty-six chieftancies.[69] Nyiginya-clan Tutsi held a total of 276 offices in 1950, and the Ega 113 — over half the chieftancies and sub-chieftancies.[70] The Catholic chiefs and sub-chiefs formed a narrowly based political elite, wealthy in cattle, cash, coffee and clients. They were a mixture of Nyanza alumni and Astridiens with, at one elbow, the Belgian administrators and, at the other, dispossessed chiefs, their uncles and fathers who found positions as judges and cattle owners. Below them were the mass of poor Tutsi who identified with the nobles and clung to their precarious superiority by despising and exploiting those of Hutu birth.

The Hutu who rose through the Catholic schools and seminaries formed a counter-elite, totally excluded from traditional and administrative office; many found employment in teaching, a few in the veterinary or medical service, and some ran small shops or remunerative coffee plots. There were a few hundred carpenters, tailors, masons, craftsmen and lorry drivers, and seventy thousand salaried workers in the private sector, between them and the bulk of the peasantry.[71] Rwaza mission employed over a hundred men in its cigar factory,[72] several of whom branched out as independent cigar makers and tobacco buyers.[73]

The Tutsi elite, with its clerical core, and the Hutu counter-elite, with its clerical wing, appeared after the war as the leaders of a potential middle class that would not ultimately depend on a continuation of the feudal system. Though emotionally attached to the symbols and traditions of the past, they were also progressive in outlook, with nascent bourgeois aspirations. They were the hope of the Belgians and the modern-minded missionaries who could see a stable future for Rwanda only in the development of a Third Estate. That this new class was stillborn, and Rwandans increasingly identified themselves in the ethno-social categories of Hutu and Tutsi, or on the narrower basis of clan affiliation, was largely a product of its small size and of the continued existence of an important conservative faction among the Tutsi, whose intransigence and egregious sense of historical superiority attracted waverers and forced on the Hutu a militant ethnic consciousness. It did appear, even to D'Hertefelt, who was later to abandon the idea of 'caste,' that an ethnic-caste analysis of Rwandan society in the 1950s was sufficient and objective. 'Although the majority of the Tutsi were on the edge of the political sphere,' he wrote in 1961, 'all the members of the Tutsi caste participated in the social and economic advantages associated with the superior status of the conquering and owning group.'[74] 'Imagined they participated' would perhaps be more accurate; the poverty of the 'petits Tutsi' was hidden in the shadow of the mwami. The Belgians, by giving political office exclusively to the Tutsi, had created a sense of caste among even the poorest Tutsi, who felt themselves members of a privileged group from which the Hutu were for ever excluded.

Social tensions on the hills between 'petits Tutsi' and peasantry were aggravated after the severe famine of 1943-44 by a high rate of population growth, a 21 per cent increase in population from 1949 to 1958 while the number of salaried workers in the private sector was decreasing.[75] Population density crept up from eighty-nine per square kilometre in 1952 to ninety-five in 1959, but this average figure does not indicate the intensity of local pressures; Bugoyi, Bushiru, Mulera, Bugarura, Buhoma, Bukoma and Rwankeri, most of the north-west, had population densities of over 200 in 1952.[76] Emigration, at the rate of 2,258 per annum from Ruhengeri and 2,360 from Kisenyi, although high, was not enough to relieve the land shortage.[77] There were numerous disputes as Tutsi tried to take over clan lands for grazing; the Hutu around Rwaza were openly rebellious, refusing to work in road labour gangs on the usual pretext that they were catechumens.[78]

The new missionaries plunged into the milieu of the *évolués* and were impatient with the paternalistic approach of their older colleagues. Partly because they came to know the Rwandan intelligentsia well, and partly from their European experience, they saw the inadequacy of the museum categories 'Roi Hamite' and Tutsi patriarchate.[79] Their goal was initially no different from that of Bishop Classe, but their model was drawn from the twentieth century.

This position as an independent class seeking, because it is a class of intelligentsia, to play a part in the country's political life raises the following question: will it be for us or against us? . . . We have heard a hundred times how we lost the working class and why Catholic Action saw the light of day — I have lived through it all — and it is all indelibly imprinted on my mind. It is just the same issue here with this new class of *évolués*.[80]

Looking afresh at Rwanda, they saw, above all, a colonial Church suffering from the cleavage between European missionary and African *évolué*. They wanted urgently to put it right. Father Dejemeppe left for Belgium in 1950 to attend a conference celebrating the twenty-fifth anniversary of the JOC with Grégoire Kayibanda, a young teacher at the Institut Léon Classe. Kayibanda stayed with Dejemeppe's family for two months, and was able to make contacts among Christian Socialists and trade union leaders as well as having more formal meetings at the Belgian Colonial Ministry. 'The Fathers and whites, we do not understand the *évolués*,' wrote Dejemeppe on his return to Kigali. 'We do not put ourselves in their place when considering their problems. We subject them to an extraordinary degree of patronage. In talking with Grégoire Kayibanda I came to ask myself whether there had not already grown up among many of our *évolués* a sense of incompatibility between us and them.' 'This feeling can be dangerous,' he added, 'because it will logically be followed by that of opposition, then struggle and revolt.'[81]

Prophetic words. Within a few months the major seminary at Nyakibanda suffered a complete breakdown of its rigid discipline; the Protestants were to suffer in the same way only several years later.[82] The feeling had grown among the seminarians that the ascetic rigour of their life, designed to inculcate a spirit of sacrifice and little harsher than in Italian or Irish rural seminaries, was nothing more than deliberate colonial exploitation by the largely European staff. They refused to do manual work and bitterly resented the authoritarian response of the missionary teachers. Behind the petty grievances was a nascent nationalism. The Rwandan students would not join in activities with their Rundi and Congolese colleagues, and took every opportunity to shower them with abuse and contempt; they wanted Swahili removed as the *lingua franca* and Kinyarwanda imposed throughout. More upsetting for the White Fathers, they seemed to have had the support of Rwandan Abbés who taught there or visited frequently;[83] when four students were picked out as ringleaders and dismissed by the Rector, some Rwandan Abbés sent a joint letter to Bishop Deprimoz appealing for their reinstatement.[84]

The intense chauvinism of the seminary revolt was part of a wider movement by chiefs and *évolués* that had begun in the war years and amounted to a conscious repudiation of European authority. While such anti-colonialism was certainly nudged into nationalism by the cultural renaissance among the Tutsi Abbés and Tutsi old guard, its main impetus came from the disaffection of the 'independent class' that Dejemeppe had forecast. In this small sector Hutu-Tutsi divisions were in abeyance and Tutsi 'national' culture was a splendid riposte to the White Fathers. Indeed, the leading figure dismissed from Nyakibanda was Anastase Makuza, later a prominent Hutu politician.[85] Thus, while Tutsi and Hutu would separate on issues like Abbé Deogratias' training in Rome, they closed ranks as Banyarwanda against the mission.

By the end of 1951 there were eighty-nine Rwandan Abbés to eighty-seven White Fathers, and little love was lost between them. Abbé Joseph Sibomana was appointed alongside Abbé Bigirumwami to the Conseil Vicarial, and Abbé Stanislas Bushayija was made a *juge pré-synodal* for questions of canon law in the vicariate. Abbé Louis Gasore became deputy school inspector.[86] Sixteen of the country's thirty-three stations now had Rwandan Superiors and staff. Contemporary pressures, and the logic of Classe's policy, dictated the setting up of an all-Rwandan vicariate; tensions between European and indigenous clergy suggested the quicker the better.

In order to keep a watchful eye on Abbé Kagame, Bishop Deprimoz made him his personal secretary; Kagame naturally favoured the erection of a new vicariate and pressed the Bishop to centre it on Nyanza. Deprimoz was not to be caught. 'It goes without saying,' he noted, 'that if such suggestions were heeded the young Church in Ruanda would be set from its very first steps on the path of a dangerous caesaro-papism.'[87] The power of the Christian court made it imperative to head the Church away from the direction in which it had been proceeding for several years; Deprimoz chose instead the Hutu north-west, with a centre at Nyundo mission. On 1 June 1952 Abbé Aloys Bigirumwami was consecrated Bishop at Kabgayi.[88] The Rwandan clergy were given the alternative of staying under Deprimoz in the south or moving to the all-Hutu parishes of the new Nyundo vicariate.

Bishop Bigirumwami, an old-fashioned disciplinarian, had little personal appeal for the younger clergy; he was felt to be very much the 'seigneur' but at the same time under the White Fathers' thumb. Despite being a 'foreigner', as a descendant of the Gesera kings of Gisaka, his royal lineage gave him a certain distinction, an appeal that was not lost on the Tutsi Abbés.[89] No clear-cut split occurred among the clergy but it would be truer to say that Nyundo became the Tutsi, rather than the Rwandan, vicariate, with a powerful caucus of anti-colonial Abbés intent on championing ruling-class culture. The implications for a region that had jealously guarded its autonomy in the past were obvious.[90]

In January 1953 the Tutsi-dominated Josephites chose their own Rwandan Superior, Brother Laurent, together with four councillors, and over two hundred *Benebikira* elected their first Rwandan Mother Superior and four advisers.[91] Nyakibanda was finally given over entirely to Rwandan students, with Father André Perraudin as the new Rector;[92] the clerical 'federation' was broken, the Rwandan clergy and seminarians had driven the White Fathers to make a substantial move in the direction of autonomy for the Rwandan Church.

The Church's recognition that times had changed coincided with that of the Belgians. A decree of 14 July 1952 set out the procedures for forming representative and 'elective' councils at the levels of sub-chieftancy, chieftancy, territory or province, and State.[93] In late 1953 the Conseil Supérieur of Rwanda consisted of the mwami, presidents of the provincial councils, six elected chiefs and one notable from each of the provincial councils. In practice, sub-chieftancy councils were nominated by the sub-chief and the notables on the Conseil Supérieur were thoroughly unrepresentative; as an attempt at democracy the 'consultation populaire' was a mere charade. Nor did the councils thus formed have anything more than a consultative role. It was a process, as Maquet and D'Hertefelt wrote, 'of diffusion of power but principally among the group which already possessed it, that is to say the Tutsi caste'.[94]

The result of the Belgian exercise in civics was that the Tutsi oligarchy found its power base broadened rather than weakened by the inclusion of Hutu clients in the councils. On the other hand, since the 'elected' councils were the expression mainly of the Tutsi authorities' wishes, the Hutu counter-elite felt their exclusion from political office all the more keenly, and were increasingly embittered at the gulf between their expectations as educated Rwandans and the realities of the Tutsi monopoly of power. The Belgians were forced to toy with democratic reform because of United Nations pressure, but the commitment of even their ablest thinkers to the Tutsi order remained unchanged. This is Guy Malengrau's assessment of Tutsi rule in 1952:

> The Batutsi were capable of keeping a certain order, and their administration was certainly not without value. The internal cohesion of this administration, which has wrongly been called 'feudal', allowed it to resist victoriously the profound breakdown that European occupation very quickly inflicted on native Congolese institutions.[95]

The *évolués*' sense of being in the vanguard of change was fostered by the Catholic Church's emphasis on their uniqueness as a new class. The new missionaries' priorities found official approval, and the unwary were drawn into an unhealthy dependence on mission support. The spotlight on the *évolué* tended to accentuate the division between elite and counter-elite; well intentioned courses on social morality in the press and seminaries highlighted the Tutsi abuse of power for all who could apply Vaticanese to the society around them. *L'Ami* ran a series of 'Leçons de morale sociale' from 1950 to 1951; far from radical, they did point out nonetheless the dignity of human labour, the need for consent in a labour contract, and, most appositely, how consent could be invalidated by extortion and threats of violence.[96] The articles were a strange mixture. Bland preaching that 'rich and poor, high or low must show a fraternal spirit towards each other'[97] came next to the militancy of a JOC manifesto that called on workers to 'demand profound reforms in economic and social structures in order to make the injustices of capitalist exploitation and collectivist oppression disappear'.[98] There were news items concerning the referendum on the future of the monarchy in Belgium, and details of the debates in the Conseil Supérieur.[99] The seminarians were given a richer intellectual diet under Father Perraudin, including talks by radical priests like Abbé Sterckx on the improbable topic 'the rise of worker consciousness in nineteenth century Belgium'.[100] In short, the francophone elite had set before them a range of possibilities and wide horizons designed to stimulate all but Marxist thinking and to inform a Catholic social conscience.[101]

The first elite association to find the Church's approval was the Association des Amitiés Belgo-Rwandaises, formed in 1951 under the presidency of Jan Franz Goosens, Director General of the SOMUKI consortium, a Belgian married to a Tutsikazi. Father Dejemeppe was vice-president and Abbé Kagame secretary. The members were predominantly progressive Tutsi like Lazare Ndazaro and Chief Prosper Bwanakweri, but Grégoire Kayibanda and a brother of Bishop Bigirumwami joined, as well as court figures like Chief Kamuzinzi, a friend of the king.[102] The problem facing Rwanda had been defined by the Church in terms of race relations, and the Association was an attempt to improve them; throughout 1953 Kayibanda wrote ardently and faithfully on this theme.[103] Now a secretary of Father Dejemeppe at Kabgayi, he had become a spokesman for the White Fathers' latest thinking on crucial issues. He spoke of Rwanda's 'equilibrated evolution' and 'integration into the civilised world', putting reform before nationalism and co-operation before anti-colonialism.[104]

Bien comprise, la collaboration peut purifier nos problèmes sociaux d'un certain attachement parasseux ou égoiste à cette sorte de dupeuse ou nationaliste africanité propice à un maintien indefini du *status quo*.[105]

A deep hatred of the Tutsi order and a sincere love of the Church, far from being incompatible sentiments, combined to create a high level of political motivation that found a ready response in the young missionaries, with their social catholicism.[106]

Kayibanda was still firmly 'the good *évolué*' and dealt in the categories of elite politics. On his return from Belgium he formed the Association des Moniteurs to press the Church for higher salaries for teachers — they were far behind those of Tutsi in government employment.[107] The association later came to be used as an official pressure group against the secularisation of schools during the Buisseret administration.[108] At the same time the indefatigable Dejemeppe, soon to be made Deprimoz's pro-vicar, founded Rwanda's first *mutualité*, a friendly society whose members made monthly subscriptions of ten francs; the benefits were 400 francs on the birth of a child and 1,000 francs on the death of a spouse. The elite increasingly wanted to be buried in wooden coffins, rather than in the traditional mat. The society catered largely for the wealthy Hutu *bakonde* owners and teachers, and the new Tutsi chiefs and sub-chiefs around

Byumba.[109] The Church favoured friendly societies and co-operatives because they furthered development, brought together elite and counter-elite, and promoted a 'healthy and solid democracy' in a painless fashion.[110] Their role as midwife to the Rwandan bourgeoisie was applauded by the Belgians and seemed to prescind from the underlying Hutu-Tutsi conflict; Kayibanda's editorials in *L'Ami* stressed the need for unity against the 'ferment de désagrégation' which he saw in the country.[111]

But the failure of the *cercles* and the fall in readership of *L'Ami* spoke as much of indifference to this moderate Catholic position as of anti-white sentiment. The consciousness of injustice was too deeply rooted in the counter-elite for it to be overlaid by hopes of a prosperous 'Third Estate'. A contributor to *L'Ami* asserted that the *cercles'* decline was due to 'the injustices and general poverty, the bad treatment we are given and the misunderstandings [we suffer] from our patrons and other leaders, our aspirations brutally stifled, our proverbial shyness which holds us back and makes any initiatives so difficult'.[112] The sermonising of *L'Ami* was in the traditional Catholic style of generalities that allowed the complacent reader to avoid applying the lessons to himself; it was not adequate in view of such bitter litanies. Another writer went so far as to describe *L'Ami's* contribution as *peureuse*.[113] The 1953 'elections' had raised, then dashed hopes; yet within a year of even these tentative changes there was a backlash from the court: Prosper Bwanakweri, son of the Nyiginya chief Ntulo and hero of the progressive Astridiens, narrowly missed banishment to the Congo. He had incurred the mwami's wrath by instituting major land reforms and running his chieftancy along mildly democratic lines. After remonstrations from the Belgians the mwami accepted his relegation to the distant province of Kibuye,[114] but the incident made plain how much of a mirage a progressive multi-racial bourgeoisie had been. If reformist Tutsi like Bwanakweri could not survive in 1954 the hopes for a bourgeois 'buffer' between nobility and peasantry in the 1960s were illusory.

By the end of 1953 the ideas and language of the two leading Hutu spokesmen, Grégoire Kayibanda and another ex-seminarian, Aloys Munyangaju,[115] had slowly begun to change. *L'Ami* editorials were pressing for concrete reforms, the codification of customary law, and legal recognition of rights of private property. More important, Kayibanda was beginning to define the counter-elite less in terms of the mythical 'Third Estate' and more in the new category of 'rural *évolué*'. He now wanted a Catholic elite who would not reject the men of the hills but whose task it would be to help 'their cadre and the people to struggle against their moral, intellectual and economic distress'.[116] The rural *évolué* was modelled on the missionary: 'he spends time with them, chats to them often, knows their aspirations better, their distress, their complaints, and sees better the injustices of which they are the victims'.[117] It was a philosophy for the Hutu school-teacher, cut off from the flashy smartness of the Tutsi in the small towns, and still a peasant in the eyes of the Catholic chiefs. Thwarted ambition and a burning sense of injustice were driving Kayibanda from the institutional role of 'good *évolué*' to dangerous new ground of prophecy. 'These islands of Europeanised intellectuals,' he wrote, 'could, sooner or later, find themselves uprooted by the inexorable mounting wave of peasant discontent.'[118] Few of the Catholic missionaries could have shared this startling premonition.

The change of emphasis and the appearance of key words like *masses populaires* in the Hutu propagandists' articles were symptoms of a new awareness and urgency as the Belgians increased their pressure on the court. *L'Ami* carried a new series of articles on 'Formation politique' which offered its readership a simple course in political science; the slant was conservative-Catholic, warning that the Church did not consider the right to rule necessarily linked to any political form. The Fathers were following Pius XI's encyclical *Dilectissima nobis* in 1933: 'the Catholic Church is never bound to one form of government more than another, provided the divine rights of God and Christian conscience are safe. She does not find any difficulty in adapting herself to various civil institutions, be they monarchic or republican, aristocratic or democratic'.[119]

On 13 February 1954 the mwami made a major speech in which he spoke of the need to jettison outmoded institutions and to move towards a modern State. *Ubuhake* was abolished by decree in April in a three-stage process: the first year required the consent of both parties, in the second unilateral dissolution of the 'contract' was permitted, and all other 'contracts' had to be terminated by the end of the third year.[120] The king had been willing to abolish *ubuhake* for some time but the Belgians had been frightened of the effects of widespread dissolution of clientship ties.[121] Rudahigwa's willingness to sweep away what seemed to be the mainstay of the feudal system was a good indication that it was nothing of the sort. The donation of cattle had always been an expression of Tutsi control over land rights, the basis of the feudal economy, and this remained unchanged after 1956. Hutu who accumulated cattle from the severance of *ubuhake* ties still had to find pasture for them. To get *igisati* they again had to seek the patronage of land-owning Tutsi. In several regions the dissolution of *ubuhake* remained a dead letter; Tutsi ideology thoroughly dominated the Hutu of central Rwanda and had been internalised, with the resulting psychological dependence and sense of inferiority that limited the potential for creative political action, even among the Hutu counter-elite.

Although commodity exchange was increasing fast, Hutu selling *ubuhake* cattle[122] and Tutsi running dairies or cash cropping,[123] a feudal economy survived in central Rwanda. If anything it was a harsher feudalism then before as the new Catholic chiefs mercilessly dunned their peasantry to gain the land and wealth promised by their education and political office.[124] In as much as the king's decree did result in the breakdown of clientship ties and the pastoral idiom was removed from the relationship between chiefs and peasants, the Hutu were more able to see the nature of their exploitation. Population increase and the resultant land hunger highlighted the chiefs' coercive role as landlords and contained the seeds of future peasant revolt.

Throughout 1954, when Kayibanda was made lay director of *Kinyamateka*, the Hutu spokesmen struggled towards an independent analysis of Rwandan society. On the one hand Kayibanda saw the danger of a leadership which could neither understand the masses nor gain their allegiance; on the other, he realised the difficulty of weaning an illiterate and conservative peasantry from the monarchy. His articles lacked a sense of perspective; the few hundred masons, carpenters, tailors and craftsmen with primary education he referred to alongside the illiterate plantation workers and miners as 'the working class'. 'The term "proletariat" is hardly known,' he wrote; 'its reality is becoming their daily experience.'[125] But the JOC vocabulary was incongruous in the Rwandan context; it was difficult to get an objective view of society from under the ample skirts of Mother Church, tied as she was to a continuation of Belgian rule and an obsessive fear of communism.

Kinyamateka's readership rose to 22,000 in 1954 and to the remarkable figure of 24,900 in 1955, so Kayibanda's ideas of Christian democracy reached a wide audience.[126] As an organ disseminating a rival ideology to that of the Tutsi elite *Kinyamateka* was vitally important in the political evolution of Rwanda during the 1950s. For a vernacular-language paper of twelve pages with a pronounced Catholic content this was an extraordinary achievement. As the paper was read and re-read aloud, Catholic social teaching was broadcast throughout Rwanda;[127] in Father Dejemeppe's words, 'Il [Kayibanda] en fit rapidement un journal vraiment démocrate où la doctrine sociale de l'Eglise était distilée habilement sans des habits "royalistes".'[128] But the Church was also able to employ the paper to rally its forces against the policies of the Buisseret administration, which again threatened to wrest control of the schools from the clergy.[129] The mwami favoured the Belgian policy, since it would loosen White Father control of education. The idea of 'ecumenical' (lay) schools was accepted in the February 1954 session of the Conseil Supérieur, but when it seemed likely that the Liberal Minister for the colonies would push through secular schools a pastoral was issued defending the Church's right and mandate to educate.[130] Much to the mwami's annoyance, the Tutsi Abbés on the *Conseil* stood firm on this issue. The mwami accused Abbé Bushayija of leading a cabal against him, and appealed to Deprimoz for his removal. The Bishop categorically refused. Later he also had the courage to remove and laicise Abbé Thaddée Ngirumpatse, who had become little more than an agent for the king.[131] Rudahigwa found himself isolated. The Astridiens and learned Abbés privately thought of him as a man 'who had not done his studies', and the European clergy did not like the control he tried to exert over the indigenous Church.[132]

However much Kayibanda tried to fit the complexities of Rwandan society into a European model, the primary social relationships remained those of patron and client in the south, clan and lineage in the north. 1955 saw a resurgence of clan-based politics around Rwaza; the heads of the leading Hutu clans held meetings on the hills. The best organised group, the Singa under the leadership of Balthazar Bicamumpaka, collected a twenty-franc contribution from adult members to the clan treasury which amounted in 1957 to 2,820 francs.[133] These clan *mutualités* were more politically motivated than their Church prototypes, and concentrated on questions of land rights. Bicamumpaka became sufficiently powerful to be elected as a notable on the Ruhengeri Conseil de Territoire. Although the Tutsi laughed at the pretensions and wranglings of the clan meetings, the Province chief, Jean-Baptiste Rwabukamba, was impressed enough by Bicamumpaka's rising fortunes to offer him his daughter in marriage.[134]

After a minor famine in Ruhengeri, aggravated by sub-chiefs' hoarding of food, there were a number of violent incidents in 1956 involving the Rwaza Hutu.[135] In an atmosphere of rising hopes created by forthcoming elections in November, a sub-chief's hut was burnt down and the Hutu refused to accept the Belgian appointee as chief of Gashashi.[136] When D'Arianoff, the Ruhengeri Resident and a man of known Tutsi sympathies, insisted, more than 250 angry men descended on the *bureau du territoire*.[137] The group was predominantly Singa and seems to have been acting on Bicamumpaka's orders. It amounted to a Rwaza Christian revolt; Bicamumpaka was doyen of the mission and a close friend of its flamboyant Spanish Superior; the mob was headed by catechists. Belgian security officers sent to arrest Bicamumpaka were foiled when he hid in a back room of the mission.[138] D'Arianoff had infuriated the priests, who saw him as a sinister Russian, and the Hutu, who resented his handling of land cases and his willingness to accede to Tutsi demands for *bakonde* plots.[139]

In the 1956 elections all adult men were eligible to vote to choose candidates for the sub-chieftancy councils. In theory the councils expressed the will of the people; in practice many sub-chiefs managed to push their own candidates forward. The elections suffered from two principal defects; firstly the administration left less than two weeks for campaigning, with the result that the better organised Tutsi could use existing administrative machinery to their advantage; secondly the largely unprepared Hutu masses sought the advice of authority figures, scribes, missionaries or sub-chiefs. Kabgayi diocese issued the usual pastoral encouraging citizens to fulfil their civic duty according to an 'informed conscience', but the caucus of traditionalist Tutsi Abbés at Nyundo used teachers and catechists to press parishoners to vote for 'the mission's men'.[140] As a result many stayed at home.[141] The missions were centres for the diffusion of government information about the election, and naturally tended to put pressure on voters to select their co-religionists.

The 1956 elections clearly demonstrated how little consciousness the Hutu peasantry had of themselves as an ethnic group. With the exception of Kibungu in rebellious Gisaka, where a Hutu campaigned on a ticket of reduced Tutsi power, neither did class conflict enter the election. As in all peasant societies, there was a certain distrust of the local man who pushed himself forward, and even had the Belgians not banned propaganda it would have been difficult for poor Hutu to build up a following. So it was that Ruhengeri and Kisenyi, where there was Hutu leadership of long standing, registered the greatest Tutsi losses; after 1953 Tutsi representation, compared with other provinces, had been disproportionately great in relation to the total Tutsi population, and land hunger was marked.[142] In Bushiru, for example, Tutsi representation at the level of the sub-chieftancy fell from 38:141 in 1953 to 19:324 in 1956; the Ndorwa Tutsi suffered similar 70 per cent losses, as did Tutsi in the Hutu kingdom of Bukunzi that had only recently been colonised.[143] Yet country-wide, at the level of the *territoire*, the Tutsi suffered only a 5 per cent loss; on the Conseil Supérieur Hutu representation was actually reduced. To quote Maquet and D'Hertefelt, 'Le filtrage de la volonté populaire . . . à travers sept scrutins pour arriver au Conseil Supérieur a eu pour effet, en 1956, de renverser l'orientation que le vote populaire manifestait.'[144]

Bishop Deprimoz broke his leg in April 1955, and decided to resign. his replacement a year later by Father André Perraudin, a man who had considerable sympathy for the social bias of the younger missionaries, significantly altered the attitude of the Church in Kabgayi vicariate. Deprimoz had never outgrown the Classe mould; his last pastoral spoke of respect for established authorities, 'the sole depositary of divine authority'.[145] His sole concession to the *Zeitgeist* was an insistence that the human personality should be cultivated and grievances should be aired — 'legitimate grievances', that is.[146] Bishop Perraudin was no less authoritarian in his conduct of the episcopacy, but he shared the European experience of the new missionaries. His first speech to his old seminarians at Nyakibanda set the tone for his episcopate; he wanted 'the priests to insist, from the pulpit and in the confessional, on the very grave obligations of social justice'.[147]

It would be easy to point to Perraudin's consecration as inaugurating a *volte-face* in the Church's handling of the Hutu-Tutsi conflict,[148] and it is undeniable that the Tutsi were at loggerheads with the official Church after 1956, but who jettisoned whom? One opinion was that 'the moment the ruling class realised it could no longer make use of the Church's influence to defend its privileges, the conflict was born'.[149] As in all broken marriages, both partners had changed since the happy early days, and the apportionment of blame is not very illuminating. Nonetheless Bishop Perraudin cannot be justly accused of being anti-Tutsi; he annoyed Dejemeppe, who had been running the vicariate while Deprimoz was in hospital, by replacing Kayibanda on the editorship board of *Kinyamateka* with a Tutsi Abbé, Justin Kalibwami.[150] Another Tutsi, Abbé Gasabwoya, was appointed the new vicar delegate.[151] Perraudin was no more radical, no more pro-Hutu, than Pope Pius XII in his 1954 Christmas message, which called for priests and laity to speak out against social injustice. *Kinyamateka* faithfully printed moderate Catholic social teaching from 1956 to 1958; in particular the Papal social encyclicals, a simplified version of the course given to seminarians by Father Adriaenssens and, earlier, by Perraudin himself. In the context of Rwanda, though, any statement that the Church had a right and duty to speak out about social issues could be interpreted as a betrayal of the ruling class and the court.[152]

The real pressure came from the Hutu Abbés, the young White Fathers and the Hutu counter-elite. Anyone who listened would have seen the force of their arguments; but very few did listen. At a *Journée d'Études Sociales* held by the Bishops in July 1956 the Hutu Abbés tried to bring up the Hutu-Tutsi problem but were squashed by the Burundi Bishops and by Monsignor Bigirumwami's Tutsi representative.[153] No one wanted to hear about 'tribalism' and 'racialism', though Monsignor Martin from Burundi roundly declared that Tutsi were always selected for secondary schools because they were more intelligent than the Hutu.[154]

Bishop Perraudin did modernise the vicariate. One priest was put solely in charge of Catholic Action, while another was released from all other duties to supervise the Catholic Press. Another man was withdrawn from mission work to head the education office at Kabgayi. Five new missions were founded, each with two priests and two Josephite Brothers, and more Rwandan clergy were sent abroad for further training.[155] Father Pien dedicated himself to social projects after a period of chaplaincy with the Josephites.[156]

Father Louis Pien spent 1950-54 in Europe and took an immediate interest in developing co-operatives on his return, when he found that Kayibanda had already started a small coffee co-operative in Gitarama, with a shop in Kabgayi. The Bishop made a hectare of land available in 1956 and TRAFIPRO (Travail, Fidélité, Progrès) headquarters were built, with a sorghum mill and a small shop selling salt, soap, beans, sugar and coffee. Each member contributed an initial fifty francs' capital, and profits were distributed annually. Coffee sales were such a success that by 1958 TRAFIPRO had a capital of over half a million francs and a membership of more than a thousand. Its first members and directors were mainly Hutu, teachers from the Normal school at Zaza forming the nucleus; but by 1958 the membership and the board of ten directors were largely Tutsi.[157] The ruling class had waited, watched and then engulfed yet another Hutu initiative.[158]

Not only had the small numbers coming out of the training colleges each year mounted to produce a strong lobby of teachers, who sought to supplement their income and status in organisations like TRAFIPRO and the Association des Moniteurs, but education itself had become a commodity as highly valued as cows. 'Knowledge is riches' was taken literally, and the Fathers spoke anxiously of 'the almost emotional desire of our youth for education'.[159] When a Jesuit college scheduled for a site a few miles from Nyanza was moved to Bujumbura there was anger and consternation. A new Catholic college intended for Nyundo was obliged to move south. The mwami insisted on having an institute of higher learning at the capital. Christ-Roi College was therefore started in a predominantly Tutsi milieu but, much to the court's displeasure, the doughty Chanoine Ernotte had a 50 per cent Hutu entry by 1959.[160] The geography of education was firstly a question of finance, and thus under Belgian control; but within these limitations a tug-of-war went on between the court and the White Fathers over Hutu higher education and the threat of Jesuits.[161]

The moving of the Jesuit college did not improve European-Tutsi relations and disqualified Rudahigwa from leadership of the educated elite. Despite the superficial modernisation of court life, the familiar jostling for position among the principal lineages continued with the mwami trying to consolidate the hold of the Nyiginya;[162] the Ega and Gahindiro had been driven to form clan-based mutual help societies.[163] Although Bwanakweri had been toppled, he remained an uncomfortable presence in the country, a hero martyr of the Astridiens.[164] The mwami found himself increasingly relying on the support of the less progressive and more traditionalist members of his entourage.

A frightening new development for Rudahigwa was the first official broaching of the 'Hutu problem' at the Vice-Governor General's council in May 1956. M. A. Maus, president of the Union Euroafricaine and a moderate by any standards, declared that 'the day when universal suffrage is really introduced into Ruanda-Urundi among a people conscious of their rights there will not indeed be a single Mututsi elected to the native councils, not one Mututsi tolerated as a chief or sub-chief, nor a single big cattle owner allowed on the hills'.[165] His solution was the familiar 'Third Estate', and like Kayibanda he saw the 'elected' councils as associations of nineteenth century patrons trying to stifle a working class trade union movement.[166] If the mwami feared that elections would sharpen the debate, he needed no further proof.

But the danger to the court still did not seem immediate in 1956. The Belgians, following their sociologists, saw the evolution of Rwanda in terms of a controlled and equilibrated movement to democracy.[167] Though the nightmare of the French Revolution did come to disturb their reveries, the sociologists assured them that the transfer of power to the Hutu would find a balance in the continuing social and economic dominance of the Tutsi.[168] Rocked into complacency by the unquestioned equilibrium model of society — a model that suited the organicism of the missionaries as much as the torpor of the administrators — the Belgians continued with their piecemeal reforms.

The period after the Second World War had seen the White Fathers moving their attention from the Catholic chiefs to the broader category of better educated Rwandans, the *évolués*. This was the group which, in its modernity and anti-colonialism, seemed to pose the greatest threat to the Church. But no sooner had the missionaries identified their priorities than the rapid pace of change, elections and reforms, made them out of date. Against the rising tide of elite Hutu protest, supported by the new missionaries with their social catholicism, the *évolués* began to break down into factions along ethnic lines. Within a short while these groups were to harden into political parties with different goals, and carry the ethnic conflict into the ranks of the clergy.

NOTES

1 *Trait d'Union*, No. 17, October-November 1944; No. 39, March 1947.

2 Zaza diary, 19 June 1945.

3 Annual confession and communion were a minimal requirement for membership of the Church; *Rapports annuels*, 1946-47, 363.

4 The Collège Central des Missions Protestants opened with seventy-five Tutsi boarders on 28 June 1946. In 1948 an Ecole d'Apprentissage Pédagogique was also opened at Shyogwe, with a two-year teachers' training course. After separate lodgings with a chaplain were provided at Astrida, five or six Protestants began to enter the Groupe Scolaire annually; see 'The story of a Gahini schoolboy'; *Ruanda Notes*, No. 94, November 1946, 4, 11.

5 *Ruanda Notes*, 1947-50, for increase in number of Tutsi conversions.

6 Deprimoz to Vauthier, 9 April 1947, CO; de Lacger, *Ruanda*, 669-71. Catechumens were divided into two groups, *banyamategeko*, who were given

two weekly lessons on the commandments, and *banyamasakramentu*, who moved on to three weekly lessons on the sacraments.

7 The process was slow, and even in 1948 only 70 per cent of Catholic families were bothering to send their children to first communion classes; see de Lacger, *Ruanda*, 704.

8 For an interesting discussion of *Évolué* attitudes see Anstey, R., 'Belgian rule in the Congo and the aspirations of the *évolué* class', in *Colonialism in Africa, 1870-1960*, vol. 2, Cambridge, 1970, 194-226.

9 The monthly was founded in 1945 as a forum for the Congolese *évolués* by the Belgian Information Service in Leopoldville, but had a Congolese editor, A. R. Bolamba, and some freedom of expression despite censorship at times; see Anstey, 'Belgian rule', 200.

10 Boutry, *Rapports annuels*, 1945-46, 216.

11 Many of these early periodicals may be found in the library of Archbishop's house, Kigali.

12 The Catholic Press was designed to fortify Christians against 'publications with advanced opinions and subversive doctrines that show scant regard for morality'; see Deprimoz to confrères, 8 November 1946, in *Trait d'Union*, No. 35, November 1946.

13 After 1943 *Kinyamateka* had six pages and cost ten francs. Its topics were evenly spread over the following during the war years: religious instruction, explanation of the news, monthly calendar of events, scientific and agricultural information, war propaganda and sport. In 1946 the front page significantly switched over from religious instruction to social and agricultural questions, with religion on page 2, and two instead of one page of news.

14 *Rapports annuels*, 1945-46, 216-7.

15 Astrida, later Butare, was originally to have been the educational centre of Ruanda-Urundi to vie with the commercial and administrative capital, Kigali. By the 1950s, though, Bujumbura was becoming more important than either.

16 *Rapports annuels*, 1945-46, 216.

17 Boutry.

18 *Rapports annuels*, 1946-47, 368. This was not suprising when the Belgians requested that *évolués* should even be given special places in church; see *Trait d'Union*, No. 54, June 1948.

19 *Rapports annuels*, 1946-47, 370.

20 Nothomb, *Church History*, 113.

21 Ruanda-Urundi was given tutelary status on 13 December 1946. Article 766 of the United Nations charter defined the goals of the tutelary power as follows: 'favoriser ... leur évolution progressive vers la capacité de s'administrer eux-mêmes ou l'indépendance compte tenu des conditions particulières à chaque territoire et à ses populations, des aspirations librement exprimées des populations intéressés et des dispositions qui pourront être prévues dans chaque accord du tutelle'.

22 Paternostre de la Mairieu, *Le Rwanda*, 164.

23 Lemarchand, *Rwanda and Burundi*, 79.

24 Kanza, T., *Conflict in the Congo*, Harmondsworth, 1972, 11-12.

25 Dansette, A., *Religious History of Modern France*, vol. II, London, 1963, 417.

26 See Zahn, G. G., *German Catholics and Hitler's Wars*, New York, 1962; Lewy, G., *The Catholic Church and Nazi Germany*, London, 1964.

27 Dansette, *Religious History*, 432, gives the change in the percentage of French missionaries in the world missionary population as from 4,500-6,100 in 1875 to 3,000-8,398 in 1930.

28 Interview with the Rev. Father Pien at the Bureau Episcopale du Développement (BED), Kigali, June 1973.

29 Interview with the Rev. Chanoine Ernotte, College Christ-Roi, Nyanza, June 1973.

30 Durrieu to Fumasoni-Biondi, Cardinal Prefect of the Propaganda, 17 May 1955, Dossier 542, WFAR.

31 The position of Rector in the major seminary was a common stepping stone to the episcopacy. Deprimoz had held the position for a while.

32 Gilles to Superior General, 8 December 1948, Dossier 543, WFAR.

33 *Rapports annuels*, 1948-49, 276-7.

34 *Trait d'Union*, No. 51, March 1948.

35 Mosmans, G., 'Climat du Ruanda indigène en 1952', MS, typewritten, undated (1952), Dossier 543, WFAR.

36 Unattributable interviews.

37 *L'Ami*, No. 103, June 1953, 140.

38 'Brève réponse à quelques grossières calomnies que l'on a lancées contre l'Église au Rwanda', undated duplicated booklet produced by a group of White Fathers in Rwanda *c.* 1964, 8.

39 De Meire to Superior General, 2 May 1948, Dossier 543.

40 Dejemeppe to Superior General, 5 January 1951, Dossier 543.

41 De Meire to Superior General, 15 June 1948, Dossier 543.

42 Mosmans 'Climat du Ruanda', 1952.

43 De Meire to Superior General, 2 May 1948, Dossier 543.

44 *Ibid.*

45 Kagame to Superior General, 17 August 1948, Dossier 543.

46 This was probably due to the high reputation of the Centre Universitaire Lovanium, which was directed by Jesuits, but may have stemmed from the pro-nationalist stance of the Jesuit Bishop Guffens of Kwango-Kwilu province. Whatever, the Jesuits offered a chance to break the White Fathers' monopoly in Rwanda with educationalists of a high standard and sympathetic outlook. The Jesuits were almost the only Order to encourage the recruitment of Africans and to attempt to found African provinces of their Society.

47 Drijvers to administrateurs territoriaux, 26 January 1948; Proud'homme to Deprimoz, 23 May 1949, CO.

48 Mosmans, 'Climat du Ruanda', 1952.

49 Deprimoz, L., 'Note au sujet de l'érection d'un vicariat indigène au Ruanda', MS, undated (*c.* 1951), Dossier 543.

50 Dodds, E. R., *The Greeks and the Irrational*, Boston, Mass., 1957, 207-24.

51 Published in 1952, so presumably researched in 1947-50.

52 Review by Kagame, A., of Maquet, J. J., *Le Système des relations sociales dans le Rwanda ancien*, Tervuren, 1954, in *Zaire*, March 1955, 310.

53 Kagame, A., 'Le Rwanda et son roi', *Aequatoria*, vol. 8, No. 2, 1945, 56.

54 'It is a system, by nature unavowed and latent, which, under the pretext

of assuring religious interests, or even with real religious motives, wants in reality to build a solid foundation for the dominating ascendancy of a body of culture over the native mind'. Kagame, A., *Le Colonialisme face à la doctrine missionaire à l'heure du Vatican II*, Butare, 1964, 144. The book was conceived in 1953 and written in 1955.

55 *Ibid.*, 145-6.

56 Interview with Monsignor Matthieu, ex-Rector of Nyundo Seminary, Rwaza, May 1974.

57 *Rapports annuels*, 1950-51, 281.

58 *L'Ami*, No. 66, June 1950, 102.

59 Derson to Superior General, 23 March 1951, Dossier 543.

60 Gilles to Superior General, 19 August 1950, Dossier 543.

61 See n. 59.

62 Christians had, of course, been doing so in small numbers since the early days.

63 Leurquin, *Niveau de vie*, 250.

64 Report by visiting UN Trusteeship Council delegation, 2 March 1954, 11.

65 Centre de Recherches de l'Information Socio-politique, *CRISP*, No. 51, 5 February 1960, 3.

66 Leurquin, *Niveau de vie*, 250.

67 *Ibid.*, 203.

68 Neesen, V., 'Quelques données démographiques sur la population du Ruanda-Urundi', *Zaire*, December 1953, 1019. Regions with a population of 25 per cent Tutsi had a child mortality of 22.4 per cent; 15-25 per cent Tutsi had 28.9 per cent and less than 15 per cent had 27.6 per cent.

69 *Rapport du Groupe du Travail concernant le problème politique du Ruanda-Urundi*, Brussels, 2 September 1959, 35.

70 Bourgeois, *Banyarwanda et Barundi*, vol. I, 62.

71 There were only 296 men being given trade and craft training in all Ruanda-Urundi in 1952 — some measure of the small size of the group of skilled craftsmen; see Maquet, J. J., 'Le problème de la domination Tutsi', *Zaire*, December 1952, 1056.

72 Statistics for cigar factory and mission budget in loose papers, Rwaza mission.

73 Joseph Ruburankoma, an uncle of Bicamumpaka, started work in Rwaza cigar factory, then moved on to commercial brick-making. He was sufficiently successful to provide his nephew with a car in the 1950s.

74 D'Hertefelt, M., *La Revue Nouvelle*, 15 May 1960, 454-5.

75 *CRISP*, No. 51, 4.

76 Bourgeois, *Banyarwanda et Barundi*, vol. I, 11.

77 This was the number of those who had left for more than thirty days but less than a year, so the loss was only temporary in part; see Neesen, *Quelques données*, 1023. Certain areas, though like Gisaka, did show a natural regulation of density by emigration. Mirenge Province, for example, had a density 108 people per two square kilometre, in 1929 and 100 people per two square kilometre in 1952; see Rubura report, 1929; Bourgeois, *Banyarwnada et Barundi*, 10-11.

78 Gaupin to de Rennesse, 6 December 1951, Rwaza mission correspondence.

79 Pages, 'Au Ruanda. Droits et pouvoirs', 359; 'Au Ruanda. A la cour du Mwami', *Zaire*, May 1950, 472-85.

80 Gilles to Superior General, 19 August 1950, Dossier 543.

81 Dejemeppe to Superior General, 5 January 1951, Dossier 543.

82 *Ruanda Notes*, No 135, February-April 1957, 12-13.

83 Report on Nyakibanda Seminary, 26 March-3 April 1952, MS sent to Superior General, author not given, Dossier 543.

84 Rwandan clergy to Deprimoz, 10 May 1951, Dossier 543.

85 Makuza was twenty-four when he left the seminary and went for four years to train in the administrative school in Kisantu. In 1955 he began work for the Belgian administration, and was a signatory of the Bahutu manifesto.

86 Nothomb, *Church History*, 119-22.

87 Deprimoz, 'Note au sujet de l'érection d'un vicariat'.

88 In his speech there was another allusion to the divine dependence of the aristocracy: 'All of you, the notables who make up the elite of the country, it is God who has made you who you are and it is from him that you hold all that you own.' See *L'Ami*, No. 91, July 1952, 131.

89 Bishop Bigirumwami was born on 22 December 1904 and baptised the next day at Zaza mission. He was the son of Joseph Lukamba and Magdalena Nyirabushundobo, see chapter seven. Ordained on 26 May 1929, he served at Kigali and Muramba missions until 1951, when he was made Superior of Nyundo. His name meant 'All things belong to the mwami', a prudent choice by the Gisaka royal line.

90 See chapter ten and epilogue.

91 Nothomb, *Church History*, 132.

92 Father Perraudin took over Nyakibanda in November 1952; the ex-Rector, Father Seumois, became secretary to the Superior General in Rome. The same policy of intervicarial seminaries was also pursued at Kachebere, on the border between Zambia and Malawi; this finally broke down for nationalistic reasons in 1973.

93 Maquet, J., and D'Hertefelt, M., *Élections en société féodale*, ARSOM, vol. 21, 1959, 19.

94 *Ibid.*, 26.

95 Malengreau, G., *Zaire*, November 1952, 965.

96 The series seems to have been inspired by Dautais, E., *Leçons élémentaires de morale sociale*, Paris, 1946; see *L'Ami*, Nos. 62-85, 1950-52; No. 64, April 1950, 63-4.

97 *L'Ami*, No. 73, December 1950, 6.

98 *Ibid.*, No. 74, January 1951, 23.

99 *Ibid.*, No. 64, April 1950, 76; No. 102, June 1953, 110; No. 116, August 1954, 302.

100 *Ibid.*, No. 102, June 1953, 103.

101 In 1953 monthly sales were at only 812 copies, 355 sold in Rwanda, 246 in the Congo and 103 in Burundi.

102 *L'Ami*, No. 78, June 1951, 105; see also chapters eight and ten for these personalities.

103 *L'Ami*, No. 102, June 1953, 122-4; No. 104, August 1953, 155-6; No. 105, September 1953, 170.

104 *L'Ami*, No. 105, September 1953, 170.

105 *Ibid.*

106 I was impressed during an interview with Grégoire Kayibanda, then President of Rwanda, in June 1973, by the intensity of his feelings against the Tutsi. Interviews with missionaries who had known him intimately during the years 1950-61 convinced me that social Catholicism, rather than any other philosophy, informed his actions and planning.

107 Interview with Balthazar Bicamumpaka at Rwaza, June 1973.

108 Kayibanda was secretary of the Association, and Cassien Murengeratwali president; see *L'Ami*, No. 85, January 1952, 16. Their publication was *Barerera Imana* — 'Those who educate for God'.

109 The *mutualité* was founded in June 1951 at Buhambe, Byumba, with Phocas Kabageme as president, Aloys Rukeribuga as vice-president and Étienne Zamu as secretary. The Belgians brought in legislation in 1949 exempting co-operatives from tax for the first three years and allowing a 50 per cent rate thereafter. Agricultural development was the main ingredient of the ten-year plan developed between 1949 and 1951.

110 *L'Ami*, No. 107, November 1953, 234.

111 *Ibid.*

112 *L'Ami*, No. 80, August 1951, 145.

113 According to an editorial by Kayibanda; see *L'Ami*, No. 108, December 1953. Kayibanda took over the editorship of *L'Ami* from Abbé Alexis Kagame in November 1953, when Kagame went to Rome for four years to do his doctorate in philosophy (on the Bantu philosophy of being) at the Gregorian University.

114 Lemarchand, *Rwanda and Burundi*, 154, puts the incident in 1956, but Nkundabagenzi, F. and Verhaegen, B., *Rwanda politique*, CRISP, Brussels, 1962, 16-18, 407, date the quarrel with the mwami to 1954.

115 Aloys Munjangaju was born at Save in 1924 and spent three years in the major seminary studying philosophy. He worked from 1947 to 1957 for a Belgian company in Bukavu before launching out into journalism.

116 *L'Ami*, No. 110, February 1954, 57; No. 118, October 1954, 352.

117 *L'Ami*, No. 110, February 1954, 59.

118 *Ibid.*

119 The encyclical was published on 3 June 1933 and addressed to the Spanish hierarchy.

120 *CRISP*, No. 51, 6.

121 Lemarchand, *Rwanda and Burundi*, 128.

122 UN *Report on the Trust Territories of Ruanda-Urundi*, 8 December 1954, 29.

123 Maquet, *Domination Tutsi*, 1955; see n. 71.

124 For the way Tutsi power maintained feudal relations even into the 1960s see Gravel, *Remera*, 163, 166.

125 *L'Ami*, No. 120, December 1954, 424.

126 *Rapports annuels*, 1953-54, 280.

127 *Ibid.*, 1956-57, 177. From 1953 *Kinyamateka* had a twelve-page format and conducted campaigns on behalf of Sunday observance and against alcoholism and secular schools, as well as airing social issues with political overtones. Even in apparently bland historical descriptions of the French Revolution Kayibanda was able to get his message through the censor, Father

Aelvort. One example from *L'Ami*, No. 112, April 1954, just after the mwami's concessions: 'Generous sentiments were to be found in the nobility. They were interested in the people's lot, helped the poor and relieved the suffering. But they kept political power, material goods, culture of the mind, the refinement of the arts, to themselves, leaving only for the masses' share the roughest work and the most elementary education. This aristocratic society is dead. Democratic society took its place.'

128 Dejemeppe to Linden, 19 July 1973. I am very grateful to Father Dejemeppe, now heading Caritas in Khartoum, for replying in great detail and with great promptness to my questions.

129 The Belgian elections of 11 April 1954 brought a coalition government to power with eighty-six Socialist and twenty-five Liberal *députés* in the Chamber. The sixty-six-year-old Auguste Buisseret, who had been Minister of Education from 1949 to 1950, was the Liberal leader; he was given the Colonial Ministry under Prime Minister Gaston Eyskens. His anti-clerical bias and desire to break the Church's monopoly of education made the 'question scolaire' a burning issue at a time when the colonies were given an unusual amount of public attention in Belgium; see Lemarchand, *Political Awakening*, 145-50; Anstey, R., *King Leopold's Legacy*, Oxford, 1966, 220.

130 On 25 October 1954; see *Rapports annuels*, 1954-55, 629.

131 Adriaenssens, J., 'La situation politique et sociale du Ruanda', memorandum sent to Superior General in May 1960, Dossier 543; 'Brève réponse'.

132 Gilles to Superior General, 23 March 1951, Dossier 543.

133 Bicamumpaka; Lemarchand, *Rwanda and Burundi*, 149 n.

134 Bicamumpaka.

135 D'Arianoff, A., 'An investigation into Gashashi chieftancy', undated MS (*c.* 1957), Rwaza mission correspondence; Marien to Administrateur Territorial, 2 March 1956.

136 *Ibid.*

137 It was, presumably, difficult for men like D'Arianoff with experience in central Rwanda and Gisaka to get used to the entirely different balance of power at Rwaza.

138 Interview with Father Manuel Daguerre, Rwaza mission, June 1973.

139 Father Daguerre pointed out by way of explanation for D'Arianoff that he was 'part Russian'.

140 Maquet and D'Hertefelt, *Élections*, 43.

141 *Ibid.*, 43. There was only a 22 per cent vote at Nyundo, 271 out of 1,212, a nice retort to the Abbés.

142 See n. 77.

143 Maquet and D'Hertefelt, *Élections*, 101, 196, 156.

144 *Ibid.*, 221.

145 'Mandement de Carême', 1 February 1955, CR.

146 *Ibid.*

147 Quoted in Nothomb, D., 'Note concernant la "Motion des étudiants Rwandais Hutu en Belgique" sur le problème socio-ethnique au Rwanda', duplicated MS, 10 April 1973, 4 n.

148 Other writers in the Belgian Liberal anti-clerical tradition, or Marxists, tend to take the Tutsi account of the Church between 1956 and 1961

somewhat uncritically. For example, De Heusch, L., 'Nationalisme et lutte des classes au Ruanda', in *Afrika im Wandel seiner Geselleschaftsformen*, ed. Frohlich, W., Leiden, 1964, 103, overstates his case: ' Perraudin dont l'ascendant sur M. Kayibanda est considérable appuiera sans réserve le Parmehutu.' Similarly Lemarchand, *Rwanda and Burundi*, 107: 'Whether because of his national origins, or because of his personal predispositions, Perraudin's democratic convictions found expression in what can only be described as a flagrant *parti pris* for the Hutu.' My own account does not pretend total objectivity, since it is largely an interpretation of predominantly Catholic sources, but it does try to escape from simplistic, monolithic accounts of the Church's action.

149 Adriaenssens, 'La situation politique'. This was also the opinion of Father Pien and Grégoire Kayibanda. The latter described Rwandan Church history as divided into three phases: (1) the Hutu are converted while the Tutsi size up the Church's potential; (2) the take-over of the 1930s; (3) the rejection of the 1950s. The ideas of viewing from the outside, take-over and manipulation were expressed by Kayibanda, for the Church, and by Pien, for TRAFIPRO, and were thus something of a stereotype of Tutsi behaviour.

150 Abbé Justin Kalibwami's outlook may be glimpsed from his portrayal of pre-revolution France, which 'presented the spectacle of some of the most refined and brilliant people. She still kept some of her moral prestige of former years in the eyes of Europe. How was it that this collapsed suddenly in the midst of scenes of indescribable cruelty and ignominy?' The answer was the Freemasonry of Voltaire and lack of religion. 'From that time a frivolous people whose religious convictions were more than diminished fell easy prey to frenzied and conscienceless agitators.' See *L'Ami*, No. 107, November 1953, 279.

151 Likewise Monsignor Gahamanyi, now Bishop of Butare, would have had Perraudin's blessing and recommendation to Rome. Gahamanyi is the brother of Michel Kayihura, the UNAR leader, who led a violent campaign against Perraudin at the Vatican in 1964. Tutsi Abbés like Kalibwami, Gasabwoya and Gahamanyi were first and foremost Churchmen, and this left them open to attack from all sides. Dejemeppe saw Kalibwami as a 'gift' to the Tutsi, while UNAR spoke of him as a pro-Hutu 'extremist'; see 'Brève réponse', 11.

152 *Cf* the White Fathers' withdrawal from Mozambique in 1972 and the fate of outspoken priests under the Caetano regime.

153 Adriaenssens, 'La situation politique'.

154 This was not simply a question of there being more Hutu educated in Burundi in comparison with Rwanda. Bishop Martin saw the Hutu as the wards of Tutsi rulers, their 'natural protectors'; see *CRISP*, No. 51, 14, quoting Maus to Vice-Governor General, 25 April 1956. A more tragically erroneous view could scarcely be imagined.

155 Nothomb, *Church History*, 146-8.

156 Pien, L., 'Fondation et premières années de la co-opérative TRAFIPRO', undated typed MS kindly lent to me by Father Pien.

157 *Ibid*.

158 Pien.

159 *Rapports annuels*, 1954-55, 629.

160 Ernotte. Nonetheless the Hutu were blocked from progressing much further, as the scholarships for study abroad, instituted by the Buisseret administration in 1954, went largely to the Tutsi with connections at court. Abbé Innocent Gasabwoya was suspected of bias in this matter, according to Kayibanda.

161 Boutry.

162 Pien; Boutry; Paternostre de la Mairieu, *Le Rwanda*, 206.

163 *Temps nouveaux d'Afrique*, 7 June 1959.

164 Interviews with an 'Abbé Ruandais', *Presse Africaine*, 21 July, 3 August 1956, quoted in Nkundabagenzi and Verhaegen, *Rwanda politique*, 16-18.

165 Nkundabagenzi and Verhaegen, *Rwanda politique*, 13-15.

166 The speech was reported in *La Libre Belgique*, 25 May 1956. He spoke of 'an intermediary class between nobility and the people . . . the third estate that I have tried in vain to introduce into the council', made up of assimilated Hutu.

167 Speech by Jean-Paul Harroy before Vice-Governor's Council, 1 December 1958, quoted in the 'Report of the Commission of Enquiry', 26 February 1960, MS signed by F. Peigneux, G. Malengrau and S. Fredericq.

168 Maquet and D'Hertefelt, *Élections*, 217: 'In the *ancien régime* the caste system was stabilised. This equilibrium was apparently largely accepted at least in the region of central Rwanda . . . Should it not be feared that, as the Hutu caste become more politically aware, a system of universal suffrage whose results will not be buffered by successive ballots like today will allow them to dominate the country's political life in such a way that the Tutsi will be deprived of all power and be sacrificed? Such a fear places too much weight on political power . . . It may be predicted that universal suffrage will only lead to a situation of greater equilibrium between the two castes.' See also Maquet, *The Premise of Inequality*, 138, 143, 158. Lloyd, P. C., has briefly pointed out the way equilibrium models led Maquet to underestimate the Hutu movement; see *History and Social Anthropology*, ed. Lewis, I. M., ASA Monographs, 1968, 26.

TEN

Freedom for oppression

Nationalism or social justice

The formation of political parties and independence were in the air by the end of 1956. In Leopoldville a group of Catholic intellectuals led by Abbé Joseph Malula, Joseph Ngalula and Joseph Ileo had issued a manifesto in which the eventual independence of the Congo was discussed.[1] A largely Catholic Democrat party, representing the interests of the 'menu peuple', had been formed in Buganda.[2] The Catholic Church was being dragged into the political arena by its elite, and Rwanda could not avoid taking notice.

Rudahigwa met Kabaka Mutesa II of Buganda on two occasions in the latter half of 1956,[3] and shortly afterwards the Conseil Supérieur, always something of a Tutsi mouthpiece, suggested the creation of four Ministries entirely within Rwandan hands, Finance, Education, Public Works, and the Interior — virtual self-government. In February 1957 the Conseil called for a speedy transfer of power and the promotion of a trained elite to staff new Ministries.[4] For the counter-elite this surge of nationalist feeling seemed nothing but an expression of the Tutsi will to continue their oppressive rule. Their language was now strident: 'To those who want to abandon this country we say: No! Three million times no!' wrote an anonymous Abbé in *Presse Africaine*. 'In the name of three million Bahutu delivered up to fear.'[5]

On 24 March 1957 Kayibanda, head of TRAFIPRO, Calliope Mulindahabi, Bishop Perraudin's secretary, and Aloys Munyangaju, a clerk in a Belgian company, in consultation with other Hutu leaders and under the guidance of Ernotte and Dejemeppe, published the Bahutu manifesto from Kabgayi. At the same time the Bishops of Burundi and Rwanda published a joint pastoral pointing out once more the Church's right to speak on matters of social justice and to call attention to abuses.[6]

The manifesto contained little that was new, and the Hutu had to wait a year for its impact to be felt fully. It suggested that the malaise in the country was attributable to the evils of Indirect Rule, the prevalence of *ubuhake*, and the Belgian destruction of equilibrating institutions without their replacement by modern ones;[7] it called for the establishment of a strong middle class and for *syndicalisme*. The writers wanted forced labour and the remaining *ibikingi* abolished, recognition of private property and the development of credit unions. To counter a letter to the *Courrier d'Afrique* by some Rwandan chiefs it asserted that ennoblement of Hutu had been a rare privilege in the past. Finally there were vague calls for economic union with Belgium and for freedom of expression: a very Catholic package, with the bogey of communism in the background.

The one striking new element in the manifesto, sharpening its menace, was the accusation that to the political and social disadvantages of the Hutu 'is added the element of race which is becoming more and more accentuated and acrimonious'.[8] Going right to the heart of the Tutsi Church, the writers went on to say, 'The monopolist interests' brandishing of the sword of national custom [*umuco w'igihugu*] is not of a nature to favour the establishment of the necessary confidence, nor justice and peace, in the face of the people's present aspirations.'[9] More important, the 'racist monopoly' was labelled 'Hamite'. The Hutu counter-elite were moving towards a dichotomous analysis of Rwandan society on the basis of their experience of an ethnic 'ceiling' on advancement, and after ready acceptance by the ruling class of the 'Hamitic hypothesis' introduced by the Europeans. Their anti-colonialism had been guided by the social democrat missionaries on to the internal coloniser, the Tutsi class, now seen as a closed ethnic group. They rejected the powerful movement of cultural nationalism as 'Hamitisation', a deliberate attempt to exclude them from administrative posts. Finally they insisted on the retention of ethnic designations in official documents, claiming that their proposed removal was Tutsi obfuscation.[10] The cultural nationalists were hoist with their own petard.

In contrast to the position in the early 1950s, when the *évolués* formed a common front against Europeans, the growing disillusionment of the counter-elite had driven them back amongst the Hutu masses and semi-skilled labour. The degree to which they became an *élite manqué* seems to have been the degree to which they experienced what Kayibanda called 'une prise de conscience fondamentale'.[11] They looked to the new missionaries for advice and support, and these in turn saw them as willing agents of Catholic social policy. The solidarity of the indigenous bourgeoisie was a hopeless chimera; Rwanda's ethnic boundaries had become too rigid where they mattered most, in competition for the key roles and status in the colonial administration. Under the pressure of the Tutsi cultural renaissance the counter-elite slipped easily into a racial analysis of its woes.

Was this a subtle plot by the colonialist Church to divide and break a potentially powerful nationalist movement led by a Tutsi vanguard?[12] Or was it an upwelling of Hutu political consciousness that for the first time saw through the mystification of Tutsi rule? These were to be the final battle cries, but the reality was far from clear-cut. The young missionaries at the elbow of the counter-elite were both in favour of drastic social reform and sympathetic towards independence movements, but conservative Tutsi 'nationalism' disqualified itself by its elitist contempt for the mass of the population. Few educated Tutsi contemplated sharing power with the Hutu and radical policies. As in the emirates of northern Nigeria, the 'nationalism' of the traditional rulers was not a movement for change but an entrenchment of ruling class privilege.[13] The masses were called to worship at the shrine of the 'natural leader', and some of the old Fathers were happy to bless the liturgy.

Likewise in Nkole protest movements developed in the wake of enforced modernisation; a type of ethnic consciousness seems to have grown up among the Iru peasantry, and the ruling Hima came to be seen as 'Hamitic invaders'. The difference was that the Iru were divided between Catholic and Protestant Churches, and were quickly assimilated into government after 1955.[14] In Rwanda the Hutu counter-elite became Catholic protégés, and Hutu protest was ignored by Belgians and Tutsi alike. On the twenty-fifth anniversary of his accession Rudahigwa said not a word about the Bahutu manifesto, which had been given excellent coverage in *Kinyamateka*, and his silence astonished both priests and Hutu leaders.[15] And it was precisely the failure of the 1956 elections to give the Hutu adequate representation in government that gave their movement momentum.

In September 1957 the White Fathers sent Aloys Munyangaju and Gregoiré Kayibanda to Belgium for training as journalists. They left behind them the Mouvement Social Muhutu (MSM) born at the publication of the manifesto. During his year on the staff of *La Croix* Kayibanda was able to renew contacts with members of the Parti Social Chrétien (PSC) and its supporting trade unions, the Confédération des Syndicats Chrétiens (CSC). It seems likely that both the CSC and the Flemish Catholic Boerbond pledged financial support for the MSM at this time.[16] Munyangaju wrote for another pro-Catholic paper, *La Cité*, and both Hutu leaders were able to popularise their cause during their stay. Their absence from Rwanda, on the other hand, weakened the MSM, which at the beginning was little more than a loosely knit group from Gitarama and Ruhengeri, with only Hutu origins and grievances in common.[17]

In November 1957 the flamboyant Joseph Gitera, an ex-seminarian of the 1930s,[18] who saw politics more as a Christian crusade than an organised *syndicat*, formed his own movement with its base at Save mission, the Association pour la Promotion Sociale de la Masse

(APROSOMA). He was a more passionate and perhaps compassionate man than many of the other ex-seminarians, with an unshakeable commitment to Christian radicalism. But the intensity of his feelings militated against calculated, consistent political action; he was often erratic and sometimes fanatical. When Gitera trumpeted he expected the walls of Jericho to fall; his first letter to the United Nations was sent in September 1957, and at each succeeding petition he appeared to be shocked to find the Tutsi class still firmly in control.[19]

Gitera stepped up his campaign for Hutu emancipation in March 1958 by arranging an audience with the mwami and an article in *Kinyamateka*.[20] The meeting was stormy; Gitera threatened to hold a demonstration in Nyanza, and the mwami at one point grabbed him by the throat.[21] As a compromise Rudahigwa finally agreed to receive a Hutu delegation at court. Fifteen representatives, led by Gitera, arrived at Nyanza on 31 March, only to be studiously ignored by the mwami and the Conseil Supérieur. They were denied lodgings and told that the Conseil was not ready to sit.[22] Chanoine Ernotte took the party in and they waited at Christ-Roi College for over a week before the mwami deigned to greet them. The petitioners were met with contempt, upbraided for being separatists and accused of being rebels, *inyangarwanda*, haters of Rwanda.[23] It was alleged that Rwanda's troubles were caused by European interference; if the delegation wished to have Hutu judges and chiefs in the future they should all work harder.[24] When they arrived the party had been monarchist to a man, referring to the mwami as 'our father', and congratulating themselves on being 'called to Nyanza'.[25] To discover that Rudahigwa was an arrogant Tutsi came as a shock, so strongly had the myth of kingship been believed in, even by educated men.

After the public chastisement a number of minor concessions were made in private. Rudahigwa tried to buy off the ringleaders; Bica-mumpaka was offered a sub-chieftancy, but initially refused.[26] Gitera was co-opted on to an enlarged meeting of the Conseil Supérieur, as were Makuza and Hakizimana[27] later in the year; a ten-man commission with equal Tutsi-Hutu representation was formed to study and report back on Hutu grievances. But the Catholic voice at court remained largely Tutsi and clerical, with Abbés Kagiraneza and Mbandiwimfura from the Nyundo caucus[28] and Abbé Musoni from Rwamagana on the Conseil Supérieur. When, with the king's approval, large cuts were proposed in the primary education budget — the Hutu gained from these schools most — it was noticeable that the only forceful rebuttal came from Gitera and Bishop Perraudin.[29]

At this treatment of the Hutu delegation the scales fell from a number of moderates' eyes, and a note of militancy appeared in both *Kinyamateka* and *Temps Nouveaux d'Afrique*, a more radical successor to *L'Ami* run by the White Fathers from Bujumbura. Despite his

Tutsi origins Abbé Innocent Gasabwoya, the director of *Kinyamateka* during the critical period 1957-59, maintained the paper's social bias, running a series of articles in debate form on 'Rwanda and her native government' (*Rwanda n' abategetsi kavukire*).[30] Of a horatory nature, they suggested reforms, calling for *amajyambere*, progress, and *demokrasi*.[31] Yet two divergent strands could be detected: admonitions to work and progress together towards Independence, *umujyanama*, and calls for concrete changes in law, education and political structure.[32] Still present were letters from the *évolués* complaining of persecution by unlettered chiefs. The chiefs' replies bemoaned the impoliteness of the younger generation, who refused to take off their hats in greeting, ignored the mwami, and spoke badly of the whites, revealing the intricacy of the sub-themes that embroidered the fundamental conflict between elite and counter-elite.[33] The Belgians had profoundly modified the nature of chieftancy; according to one White Father source many children at school did not know who the mwami was.[34] When the chiefs branded youth as *abagome*, rebels, it was easy to see from where a conservative faction at court would draw its strength.[35]

Kinyamateka, otherwise scrupulously fair under Abbé Justin Kalibwami, with an open 'Tribune libre' column, became a powerful weapon in the armoury of the MSM and APROSOMA writers after April 1958. They made no bones about writing to drum up support for the Hutu cause among the people, *ni ugutega amatwi*, to open their ears, as they called it.[36] *Temps Nouveaux d'Afrique* carried headlines like 'A council representative of what?' and letters baldly attributing the plight of the Hutu to Tutsi racialism.[37] Abbé Kalibwami would probably not have passed such letters, but he allowed a full airing of Hutu grievances in moderate language; the 1 May *Kinyamateka* gave a blow-by-blow account of the Hutu delegation's experiences at Nyanza. It contained the first frontal assault on the king, refuting the idea that he was above race and politics; this was continued a fortnight later in language every villager could understand. The writer asked the readers why, if the mwami was the parent, *umubyeyi*, of Gatutsi, Gahutu and Gatwa, and had the power, *ubushobozi*, to sign documents and direct the country, the whites should take the blame when he favoured one of his children.[38]

After such a savage prodding the court traditionalists, dinosaurs of Tutsi evolution, lumbered dangerously into action. On 15 May a letter signed *bagaragu b'ibwami bakuru*, elder servants of the mwami's court, was sent to the commission studying the Hutu problem. It contained an old tradition of the Nyiginya conquest of Rwanda; Kigwa was said to have found the indigenous Hutu Zigaba clan under the leadership of Kabeja. Kigwa, his brother Mututsi and his sister Nyampundu then taught Kabeja the use of iron, and in return were accepted as his lord, *shebuja*; thus the only bond between Tutsi and Hutu was feudal; no blood tie existed. It was demonstrably false, they asserted, that everyone was a son of Kanyarwanda; Ruganzu killed the Hutu *abahinza*, so how could they have been his brothers? In a second letter sent a day later to the Conseil Supérieur history as ideology gave way to day-to-day politics; a group of fourteen 'Banyarwanda' appealed to the mwami to apprehend the Hutu revolutionaries who were disturbing the established order and asked for permission to retain their *ibikingi*; adequate uncleared land remained for the Hutu to settle and cultivate, they claimed.[39]

The traditionalist wing of the Tutsi, representing the thinking of many poor Tutsi, whom Gitera naively hoped to recruit for APROSOMA, was an Achilles heel to Rudahigwa. Childless and treated with contempt by the Astridiens, estranged to a great degree from the Catholic Church, yet in the past tied to it for legitimation of his rule, the mwami must have been tempted again by the feudal mythologies. But against the background of the new Hutu propaganda they were political poison. As early as 1956 Rudahigwa had told the Vice-Governor's council: 'it is very difficult to define the terms Tutsi and Hutu today, in view of the fact that it would be difficult to find any criterion to differentiate them'.[40] Nothing was more likely to arouse the peasantry quickly than tying ethnic labels to the growing problems of land shortage. Both Tutsi and whites could be easily identified in a revolt; but which was to be the butt of the peasants' fury?

The importance of the MSM and the Bahutu manifesto was not that they aroused the peasantry — they remained as quiescent as ever in the south and centre of the country — but that the counter-elite forced on Rudahigwa and the Tutsi elite a radical change in the mythology of power, a reformulation of ruling class ideology and history; dynastic history and Catholic theology were replaced by nationalism. Every step taken by the Hutu towards a racial analysis of Rwandan society drew from the mwami and his entourage a further emphasis on national unity. Every article in the Catholic Press on caste and social justice brought forth a surge of Tutsi anti-colonialism. D'Hertfelt sums up succinctly the change that took place:

L'intelligentsia traditionaliste a créé un *Wunschbild* mythique du passé, qui, dans la conjuncture politique présente, remplit une fonction analogue a celle qu'avaient les mythes traditionnels dans l'ancien régime stabilisé. Lorsque à la suite d'influences étrangères, celui-ci fût mis en cause par des politiciens égalitaires Hutu, les 'mythes d'inégalité' durent structurellement céder la place aux 'mythes d'unité et d'harmonie' qui s'opposaient tant à la volonté des rebelles pour l'émousser, qu'aux colonisateurs pour affirmer l'unité du peuple rwandais dans la lutte anti-colonialiste.[41]

Observers noticed the rabidly anti-Belgian tone of a speech made by the mwami after he returned from the Brussels exhibition,[42] and from this time onwards his contacts with the CMS became more frequent.[43]

It is difficult to assess how far Rudahigwa was master in his own house. He had tended to bend before powerful men throughout his reign, coming successively under the influence of his mother, Monsignor Classe, Father Witlox, his chaplain, Abbé Kagame, Chief Kamuzinzi, Goosens, D'Arianoff and, from 1949 to 1952, the Nyanza Resident, Drijvers. After 1952, when he had offered to resign, he was increasingly influenced by the conservatives at court and the nationalist promptings of a coffee buyer, allegedly of communist sympathies, Monsieur Poelart.[44] 'He is superior when on the defensive,' wrote Mosmans, 'shrewd to the point of duplicity; and patient to the point of humility.' 'But,' he added, 'he is quickly lost when on the offensive; the femininity of his personality shows itself and the weakness of his general formation. He steps down before obstacles, hesitates between different solutions, instinctively seeking the support of a strong will.'[45] Evidence is too scanty and contradictory to determine whether his intermittent bouts of vacillation and intransigence from 1956 to 1959 may be attributed to his own personality or to the different pressure groups at court. Nevertheless his failure to respond in a moderate and consistent fashion to Hutu demands was an important element in turning the Europeans and counter-elite against him. Not believing in his own myth, he destroyed the faith of others in it.

The Tutsi elite had a powerful case and presented it subtly. They decried conflict between *imiryango*, lineages, as destructive of unity — a fact the northern Hutu were coming to acknowledge — but by *imiryango* they referred to 'abatutsi, abahindiro, abega, abahutu' with complete confusion of level, class and clan; the mwami was father of them all.[46] To escape from the trap the Hutu tended to use the word *ubgoko*, clan or tribe, and spoke of Gatutsi, Gahutu and Gatwa to underline historic differences of race and caste by reference to the eponymous ancestors.[47]

The Conseil Supérieur met from 9 to 12 June 1958 to consider the cursory findings of the commission on the Hutu-Tutsi 'problem'. It declared that no such problem existed and that henceforth ethnic designations should disappear from official documents.[48] 'The enemies of the country shall not succeed. Moreover the entire country has come together to seek out the bad tree that has produced the bad fruits of division,' warned the king. 'When it is found, it will be cut down, uprooted and burnt; it will be made to disappear and nothing will remain of it.'[49]

The position of the institutional Church in the face of mounting racialism and nationalism was awkward. It was plain that Independence would leave the Church internally weakened by conflict between

Hutu and Tutsi clergy, and externally attacked by a triumphant court which wanted to dismiss the missionaries as colonialists. While sympathising with the aspirations of APROSOMA and MSM, and relatively happy in a discourse which dealt in social categories, most Church leaders were loath to get on to the dangerous ground of race. Gitera, who was capable of invoking the Trinity and threatening to castrate all Tutsi in the course of a single letter,[50] frightened them. Monsignor Bigirumwami spoke out boldly in March and July 1958 about the demands of justice. His pastorals decried those in authority who had 'a baleful tendency to make use of it improperly to their own advantage'. 'How much more does someone who allows an innocent man to be condemned deserve the anger of God,' he wrote in reference to the widespread Tutsi abuse of the courts.[51] But by September developments led him to write an article for *Témoignage Chrétien* placing his authority behind the national unity line of the Conseil.[52] His argument was more tellingly couched in social terms and contained a measure of truth; in the past considerable inter-marriage had taken place between Hutu and Tutsi, he declared, so the difference could not be important. Secondary education was not the privilege of one racial group but of the new independent class, so why were the Hutu complaining? Was he not himself the member of a Hutu clan, the Gesera, but of royal blood? The facts were accurate but the social mobility he spoke of had ended with European rule when Hutu and Tutsi became closed castes.[53]

The tempo of events in Belgian territories accelerated towards the end of 1958. Prince Louis Rwagasore, determined on immediate independence for Burundi, pushed UPRONA[54] into a more nationalist stance.[55] In the Congo Lumumba founded the Mouvement National Congolais, which broke away from the narrow Bakongo politics of ABAKO, moving towards a more radical nationalism.[56] With a new PSC-Liberal coalition in Belgium, and Maurice van Hemelrijck as Colonial Minister, a man able to sympathise with the urgency and intensity of African nationalist sentiment, the question of de-colonisation was no longer in doubt, only the timing.

Thanks to the Buisseret administration's reduction of subsidies to Church schools,[57] the close relationship between Church leaders and Belgian officials came to an end in the Congo.[58] But in Rwanda the language division between Flemish- and French-speaking Belgians had the unexpected result of cementing ties between local administrators and missionaries. Despite Rwanda's early experiments in elections[59] the territory was looked on as something of a rural backwater where the less able could serve out their time in tranquillity. Jean-Paul Harroy, who was responsible to the Governor General for Ruanda-Urundi, thought along lines that ran from his headquarters in Bujumbura through Katanga to Leopoldville. A French-speaking

Freemason, he tended to relegate Flemish and Catholic administrators to Rwanda, keeping the 'bright young men' for service in Bujumbura.[60] So the Rwandan administration had much in common with the young missionaries, and took to their protégés, the Hutu leaders, more readily than to the Tutsi. The superciliousness of the Tutsi, even their height, easily evoked a class reaction in men who had experienced discrimination in their own country and who had a respect for the peasant virtues.[61]

Pressure from the local Ruanda-Urundi administration, which seems to have heeded the Catholic chorus in *Kinyamateka*, convinced the Colonial Ministry by November 1958 'of the necessity for bold and profound reforms'.[62] Mosmans wrote from Brussels, 'They are now therefore distinctly partisans of a real and quite definite democratisation which they want brought about fast.'[63] This was a defeat for Rudahigwa, who spent his time at the Brussels exhibition trying to convince the Colonial Ministry that no Hutu-Tutsi problem existed. He had seen the Jesuit Bishop, Monsignor Guffens, who was in charge of the Congolese pavilion, and complained bitterly of the way some clergy were compromising the Catholic Church in Rwanda.[64] The days of the mwami's alliance with an anti-clerical Liberal Minister for the Colonies against a common enemy, the White Fathers, were over; he now faced the peril of Catholic administrators, reformist missionaries and educated Hutu.

Although the Belgians decided that Rudahigwa should 'reign and not rule', the decision was difficult to implement.[65] Apart from the peasantry, he had the support of 40 per cent of the leading chiefs, mainly those who had passed through Nyanza in the early days. The Astridiens, tired of paying an annual tribute of cows to keep their pasture lands, wanted his power reduced, but rising Hutu militancy had driven several back into the ranks of the conservatives.[66] The number of Africans in the lower administrative ranks rose sharply from 782 in 1955 to 1,221 in 1959;[67] they were mostly Astridiens, and many were opposed to the Nyanza old guard, with its traditionalist rhetoric.[68] The Tutsi progressive moderates were in Belgian employment; the easy way out of the perils of court intrigue was to find European patronage.

The leaders of the Tutsi conservatives were predictably the insecure chiefs of the north-west, Rwangombwa and Kayihura, who had the most to lose from Hutu emancipation, and Mungalurire. They formed an Association des Eleveurs Ruandais (ASSERU) as a counter to MSM and called on the Tutsi Abbés at Nyundo to support them.[69] By concentrating on an anti-colonialist platform they and the mwami were tapping a rich vein of support in the countryside. The interference of Belgian agricultural officers was irksome and humiliating to the peasants, and memories of the unreformed Belgians of 1943-45 were still keen. Thousands of coffee plants were pulled up around Ruhengeri in November 1958 as a protest against fines imposed by the agricultural department for infringements of regulations.[70] Two months later schoolteachers at Zaza came out on strike because their wages were paid late by the mission.[71]

The Hutu propagandists worked hard in *Kinyamateka* and *Temps Nouveaux d'Afrique* to draw the fire towards the Tutsi landowners. The MSM statutes were published in November, and Hutu efforts were rewarded by the first official recognition of their movement on 1 December. 'My first affirmation will be that a problem exists,' declared Harroy. 'Assuredly, as the mwami Mutara pointed out in his speech, it is simplistic and dangerous to entitle it, baldly, the Tutsi-Hutu conflict. But in this country of inequality of conditions a problem undeniably exists.'[72] Good sense and enlightened self-interest had prevailed in the Colonial Ministry; but the recognition was long overdue. By the end of 1958 Harroy's statement that the division in Rwandan society was between 'rich and poor, capitalists and labourers, governed and governors'[73] appeared simply trite. The counter-elite could name those who got the scholarships and those who sat in judgement on their poor relatives; they saw the cleavage as between Hamite and Bantu, and they were beginning to force the political pace, imposing their definition of the problems.

With the return of Kayibanda and Munyangaju to Rwanda in October 1958 the Hutu movement was given a tighter organisation and more calculating leadership. Communication in the mountainous terrain remained a difficulty; only Bicamumpaka owned a car,[74] though many of the Tutsi chiefs had vehicles in varying states of dilapidation. Only Church organisations were available to the counter-elite, and they made use of the Press and lay associations in an unofficial manner for propaganda and recruitment. Kayibanda was able to extend his contacts through TRAFIPRO and the Association des Moniteurs; as head of the Legion of Mary, which had praesidia throughout Rwanda,[75] he could discuss the MSM programme with Hutu members after the prayers and official business.[76] Major Catholic events brought the counter-elite together, and the first memories of serious discussion amongst the Gitarama, Save and northern Hutu were from the celebrations for the fiftieth anniversary of the founding of Save mission.[77] Members of Kayibanda's class at seminary, Abbé Apollinaire and Deogratias Rugerenyange, with Anastase Makuza, formed a natural group of friends. The attractive, warm personality of Bicamumpaka and the age of Gitera assured them a place, and Kayibanda was a frequent visitor to Rwaza.[78]

The Leopoldville riots of January 1959 and the subsequent government declaration that the Congo would be led 'without precipitous haste' to independence alerted the Church in Rwanda to the impending crisis. Monsignor Bigirumwami, who returned from Brussels that month, had the difficult task of putting a brake on the Nyundo Tutsi caucus and arresting the growing polarisation of his clergy into two hostile camps. But the middle ground had disappeared. The Bugoyi Tutsi took Bigirumwami's 1957 statements about exactions and injustice to be pro-Hutu, and called on the CMS to send them a Protestant Bishop from Uganda.[79] The mwami become a close friend of Dr Joe Church at Gahini;[80] the threat of widespread Tutsi defection was real and worrying to those reared, like Bigirumwami, on the dictum 'outside the Church there is no salvation'. Learned Tutsi Abbés, like Janvier Mulenzi, began broadcasting a moderate version of the conservatives' case, and the Bishop of Nyundo no longer knew which way to turn.[81]

Monsignor Perraudin was more decided and had the conviction to press his viewpoint home. A joint pastoral letter issued on 11 February 1959 bore the mark of conflicting and divergent opinions resolved by compromise in favour of Perraudin. There was an ardent appeal for reform: 'Christian morality demands that the authorities should be at the service of all the community and not only one section, and that they should be attached with a particular devotion and by all possible means to the emancipation and cultural, social and economic development of the mass of the population.'[82] The idea of class warfare was rejected, but the legitimate interests of the different classes in society were accepted as worthy of promotion; at the same time a warning was given that 'the diversity of social groups and above all of races risks degenerating into baleful divisions'.[83] The admission that a racial element existed was offset by a moving call to forget ethnic differences in the higher unity of the Catholic Church.

However, from the Christian point of view, racial differences must dissolve into the higher unity of the Communion of Saints. Christians, to whatever race they belong, share more than brotherhood; they participate in the same life of Jesus Christ and have the same Father in Heaven. Whoever excludes from his affection a man of another race than his own when he says 'Our Father' is truly not calling on the Father that is in Heaven, and he will not be heard. There is no Church by race; there is only the Catholic Church.[84]

The pastoral was easily seen as pro-Hutu in its call for reform and dangerously anti-Tutsi in its calculated undermining of the conservatives' rhetoric. 'In our Ruanda,' Perraudin wrote, 'social differences and inequalities are for the large part linked to racial differences, in the sense that, on the one hand riches, and, on the other, political and even judicial power, are in reality to a considerable degree in the hands of people of the same race.'[85] The White Fathers had come out officially in favour of the MSM analysis, though in moderate and unexceptionable language.

Unfortunately the political evolution of Rwanda had reached a point where the language of theology and common sense was heard as the language of the coloniser, and the Church *qua* institution was unable to direct or moderate the course of events. The Bishop wrote to his clergy, appealing to them to refrain from partisan politics and emphasising that the social and economic organisation of society was the sole prerogative of the State. Headmasters of secondary schools were requested to give pupils in the top forms copies of the pastoral and to run sessions on Catholic social teaching before they went home on holiday.[86] It was too late; social justice had become a Hutu rallying cry, whilst the conservatives successfully posed as fiery radical nationalists against the background of Lumumba in the Congo. Tracts produced by the nationalists, signed 'Abatabazi' — the saviours of Rwanda who died on her soil — began to circulate denouncing APROSOMA.[87] The Hutu in Ruhengeri were taking the law into their own hands and expropriating large tracts of Tutsi-controlled pasture land.[88] Twa guards appeared at the side of Tutsi at Save on Christmas Day 1958 when rumours spread that the Hutu were about to attack.[89] It was impossible for the Rwandan clergy not to take sides and most improbable that the White Fathers' neutrality would be more than superficial.

The essential defect of the Church's official position was woolly thinking about its institutional relationship to politics. The orthodox position was to assert that the Church as moral teacher had a right to comment on the social content of politics. And when it came to racism it could be argued that this right became a duty. Yet Pope Pius XI and the early articles in *L'Ami* insisted that the Church could coexist with any political structure.[90] Older clergy solved the problem by agreeing that the Church had the right to comment on specific violations of the moral law within a political system, yet no right to criticise the system as a whole. Younger men who had watched the Nazis hypnotise the German Church were disturbed by this limitation. Father Adriaenssens had this to say about the Rwandan crisis: 'It is not a matter of simply advocating some tampering with [society], or partial reforms that do not go to the root of the evil. The Church must aim at a veritable transformation of the social system.'[91]

However much Adriaenssens might argue to himself that this was the logic of Catholic social teaching, it was nonetheless a radical departure from the traditional position of the Church. 'Revolution' had once meant a total personal transformation in Christ. The benign patriarchs who formed the *terminus ad quem* of Pagès', Kagame's and indeed the CMS's social morality were men who had undergone this metanoia, this Christian revolution.[92] There was a difference between the view which saw structure and system as morally neutral, with the individual as the custodian of social ethics, and the new 'social Catholicism' of the Jocistes and recently arrived European priests. The mwami was right when he complained to Guffens that the Church, as he had been taught to see it, was being compromised.

Behind this social-individual distinction in thinking and the attempts to gloss over its import was the more profound equivocation which at one instant identified the Church with clergy and laity in communion with their Bishop and, the next, equated the Church with its hierarchy alone. When the laity formed political parties 'in the light of their Catholic Faith', and through these furthered the interests of the institutional Church, it could be denied that 'the Church' was involved in politics. But when such parties or movements set Catholic against Catholic it was not thought incongruous to appeal that dissensions 'in the Church' come to an end. It was not only an inadequate theology of incarnation[93] but sheer naivety to expect the clergy to refrain from committing themselves to a particular interpretation of events, and like all men seeking the political kingdom, even without formal membership of a political party.

Neither Bishop Bigirumwami nor Perraudin could ultimately escape political issues to find sanctuary in the *civitas dei*. The days when Monsignor Classe could put the Church's authority squarely behind the ruling class and enjoy the esteem of one 'above politics' were past. In times of political and social crisis, and especially in the holistic cultural environment of African societies, the Church, dogged by a mystifying Western philosophy, reaped the rewards of its inauthenticity. The Bishops were obliged to respond rather than lead and to suffer the taunts of the politically motivated who interpreted moderation as pusillanimity and positive social teaching as factionalism.

If it is true to say that the CMS came to support the conservative 'nationalists', then it was true to the same degree that the Catholic Church was pro-Hutu.[94] The CMS, with its public school, Cambridge and army background leant naturally towards the Tutsi aristocracy, personality and culture.[95] As Father Adriaenssens admitted to the Superior General, 'almost everyone is susceptible to the Tutsi physique and manners for a certain time'.[96] The personal preferences of missionaries, based on class and social attitudes developed in Europe, determined reactions to Rwanda's social problems as much as pastorals and directives. As late as 1959 the CMS could conceive of no other future for Rwanda than a Tutsi-dominated one: 'They have an innate capacity to rule born of centuries of experience. Will it be selfish, domineering, cruel and corrupt as in the past, or will it be in the highest interests of all, enlightened and pure?' *Ruanda Notes* wanted to know.[97] Most of the Catholics had left this position behind in the late 1940s; the difference was that they were socially, and therefore politically, more heterogeneous than the CMS.[98]

In the months before Rudahigwa's death Monsignor Perraudin

struggled to hold his vicariate together. The Belgian administration, stalled by foot-dragging in Leopoldville, found it difficult to put the Colonial Minister's plans into practice.[99] Gitera petitioned both Van Hemelrijck and King Baudouin,[100] and there was a general hardening in the position of the conservatives and the counter-elite. Munyangaju and Gitera, in a vernacular tract, *Idjwi rya rubanda rugufi* ('The voice of the small people'), were now aiming at the heart of Tutsi supremacy, the potent symbol of Kalinga, the dynastic drum of the Nyiginya. The drum was believed to be festooned with the dried genitalia of defeated *abahinza* and to contain in mystical fashion the power of kingship; scarcely a more evocative target for Hutu resentment could be imagined. Moreover by concentrating on historical symbols the Hutu were able to push the newspaper debate back into traditional categories more vulnerable than the populist language of Tutsi nationalism. Rudahigwa took the attack quite literally, and secretly sent the drum off to a hiding place from where it was finally smuggled out of the country some months later.[101]

The mwami was drinking heavily by 1959 and seemed to be expecting deposition.[102] Apart from his chaplain, he had little contact with the White Fathers, nor seemed to want it. With Lumumba calling for the disappearance of ethnic differences and denouncing 'saboteurs' of national independence in the Congo,[103] the White Fathers' mission in Rwanda appeared not only anti-Independence but anti-unity. When the Belgian Groupe de Travail, a parliamentary delegation investigating the political situation, toured the country from April to May 1959 a strong lobby of Tutsi complained to them that the Catholic mission Press was deliberately sowing discord.[104] Whereas in the Congo the Church was simply one facet of a many-sided problem, in Rwanda, which lacked a settler voice of significance and the complexities of multi-tribal politics, the Church was omnipresent: on the hills, in the schools and training colleges, leading co-operatives and *mutualités*, influencing the *évolués* and the *bakuru b'inama*, nudging the administrators and chiefs and ready with advice in Bujumbura, Leopoldville and Brussels. The Church had no legions, its members fought on different sides, but the Tutsi did not underestimate its importance in 1959 as a factor in the political equation.

The official Church stolidly maintained its apolitical stance, but its members had long since toppled over into partisanship. *Temps Nouveaux d'Afrique* replied archly to Tutsi accusations: the Catholic Press 'will always struggle for the truth and will never drag the poor in the mud to merit the graces of the rich'.[105] Battle had been joined. When the mwami died of a cerebral haemorrhage in Bujumbura on 25 July 1959 it was rumoured that the White Fathers had plotted his murder with the connivance of the Belgians. Shortly after, a truck driven by a Brother carrying *Kinyamateka* from Kabgayi to Nyanza was stopped on the road and stoned; on the hills around the capital, medals were snatched from catechumens and Christians had their rosaries torn from them by monarchists.[106]

The funeral of Mwami Rudahigwa at Mwima, near Nyanza. Seated, left to right, are Rosalie Gicanda, his widow, the Queen Mother and a sister of the deceased mwami. Among those standing are Bishops Bigirumwami and Perraudin.

The new mwami, twenty-four-year-old Jean-Baptiste Ndahindurwa, a son of Musinga who had studied at Astrida, was proclaimed in a tense scene at Rudahigwa's grave without any reference to the Belgian authorities. Eye witnesses reported that the Belgians' Congolese troops were each shadowed by Twa court agents, and any attempt to stop the proclamation would probably have resulted in bloodshed. This minor Tutsi *coup* heralded Rwanda's descent into civil war. On 15 August 1959 the northern Tutsi chiefs joined with conservative nationalists at court and Muslim merchants in the few towns to form the Union Nationale Rwandaise (UNAR). A half-Congolese Hutu educated by the Josephites who had spent much time with Musinga during his exile, was selected as president; François Rukeba was something of a soldier of fortune,[107] but it was a canny appointment to give the lie to Hutu propaganda.

At its first public meeting in September UNAR demonstrated the degree to which the nationalists had become estranged from the Church.

Swahili traders toured Kigali in their cars and vans, calling on people to fight those dividing Rwanda, while trucks picked up people coming out of mass to take them to Nyamirambo market. Rukeba is reported to have said sarcastically amid much applause, 'You have all come without being called by the Bapadri.' Chief Kayihura attacked the missionary monopoly of education. 'It will no longer be admissible,' he is alleged to have said, 'for Banyarwanda children to know the history of Napoleon and know nothing of the conquests of Rwabugiri.'[108] This was the full-blooded language of nationalism, of Lumumba and Fanon. There were cries of 'À bas les blancs.' À bas les missionaires!' and *Benebikira* were mocked in the street.[109] A week later UNAR members heckled the preacher at mass in Gitarama, and there were some scuffles.[110] About three thousand people were present at the UNAR meeting,[111] and it was apparent that the party, with its financial superiority, access to typewriters, cars and lorries, and its monopoly of nationalist rhetoric, would be able rapidly to broaden its base to form a mass organisation. However, its strength lay in the towns among those who, like the Swahili petty merchant capitalists, had become politically aware under the economic restraints of Belgian rule, and its rump of old conservatives representing the vestiges of the feudal economy was a liability.

The mwami's death heightened tension within the Church. Seminarians, politically active since the publication of the Bahutu manifesto, had been leaving to join the struggle, some to Kayibanda's ranks, others to the Jesuits.[112] In a desperate attempt to paper over the cracks Monsignor Perraudin called a synod at Nyakibanda seminary. After stormy scenes he was able to persuade Bishop Bigirumwami, now pushed into the UNAR camp by his clergy, to sign a joint letter to Catholics in Rwanda;[113] like communiqués after the breakdown of diplomatic talks, it was aimed at minimising conflict and avoided substantive issues. The two Bishops asserted their authority and appealed for unity in the Church; Christ had formed *umuryango umwe* (one lineage) and mankind came from *inda imwe* (one womb); men were true brothers.[114] In as much as the UNAR presented itself as *Abashyirahamwe b'Urwanda* — those putting Rwanda together — the letter might be interpreted as a minor victory for the Tutsi Abbés. Similarly, the Catholic view of the dynastic drum, Kalinga, presented in the pastoral was something of a rebuff to APROSOMA and Gitera's campaign; considered as a flag, the drum itself was declared to be unobjectionable, though the human remains were offensive. The idea that Kalinga contained the power of kingship was criticised, but this was beside the point once it was acknowledged by the Church to be a symbol of the nation.[115] The clergy were informed of the decision about Kalinga in a letter to which Perraudin appended his episcopal SOS call: 'Communism is not a myth but a sad reality. Very serious enquiries have shown that it has already infiltrated into our regions.'[116] The reference was doubtless to Monsieur Poelart, who could be found clapping enthusiastically at UNAR meetings.[117]

On 19 August a joint pastoral of the Bishops of the Congo and Ruanda-Urundi, which had been in preparation for some time, was issued. Another attempt to rise above local disputes, it approved in general terms of Independence, quoting Pius XII's *Fidei Donum* on the necessity of political liberty. The Belgians, of course, had already decided to grant independence. Positive leadership, rather than ratification of government policy, came in a small section which bore Monsignor Perraudin's imprint. 'The fate of the little ones, the poor, the still numerous disinherited masses, must be the first priority of the authorities . . . Social, political or economic evolution which favours a minority, or neglects the well-being of a large part of the people, would create an unjust and unacceptable situation.'[118] Politics, it was declared again, did not escape from the realm of morality, and a final appeal was made for the development of a strong middle class. It was a shot across UNAR's bows, and the influence of 'social Catholicism' was apparent.

One day after the first UNAR meeting, and with what Lemarchand called 'almost indecent haste',[119] the Rassemblement Démocratique Ruandais (RADER) was formed. It was headed by Chief Bwanakweri[120] and Lazare Ndazaro, a protégé of the Belgians who had spent some time in Brussels.[121] Another familiar figure was Rwigemera, the modernist of the late 1930s.[122] The party represented the progressive Astridiens and Belgian employees, a last bid by Father Dejemeppe and the Belgians to create an inter-racial party which would consolidate the 'middle class', the dependants of colonial administration and missions. RADER was several years too late and had no natural constituency beyond the elite.

The UNAR attack on Catholic schools, contained in its manifesto and presented at its meetings, was a serious error of judgement. While there was resentment at the Eurocentric and authoritarian teaching in mission schools, there was no revolt among pupils. It was educated Rwandans looking back on their barefoot days who put another interpretation on phrases like 'little monkeys' which once had seemed innocuous. Though some wished for the psychological liberation of rejecting all that was European-given, others did not need to deny the Church's clumsy efforts towards their emancipation. The Church in Rwanda had ridden out the Buisseret administration, and the UNAR attack was one that tended to unite Tutsi, Hutu and White Father clerics against an affront to their authority in the State. The crowd might roar 'Down with the Fathers' in the heat of the moment, but, if they reflected, it was clear that the Church had been mediator of all

Graces, especially the grace of salaried white-collar jobs.

UNAR's anti-clericalism gave Monsignor Perraudin sufficient leverage to get the Bishop of Nyundo's signature to an emotional joint letter condemning the party as anti-Catholic and under 'influences communisantes et islamisantes.'[123] More revealing of the Bishop's thinking were the following sentences:

The UNAR party seems to wish to monopolise patriotism on its behalf and to say that those who are not with them are against the country. This tendency strongly resembles the national socialism that other countries have known and which has done them so much harm.[124]

It may be that Perraudin — like Bishop de Hemptinne, who once spoke of black Zionism[125] — was looking round for any club to beat an Independence movement; it seems more likely in the light of his experiences that he was drawing on a European model in a serious fashion. To Father Boutry and other French priests the Rwandan monarchists seemed comparable to Action Française, the French Catholic fascist movement of the 1920s ultimately condemned by the Pope.[126]

Despite the warning against UNAR, six of the Tutsi Josephites at Kabgayi joined the party, so strongly did they feel the White Fathers to be a colonial agency.[127] Gitera, however, leapt on the statements as a sign of the Church's blessing on APROSOMA. Addressing large crowds at Save, he called on the people to applaud the courageous gesture of the Vicars Apostolic in condemning Kalinga as idolatrous superstition.[128] They had said nothing of the sort. With the realisation that the Church was now in the political arena, the two Bishops took the opportunity to reassert their neutrality by issuing a warning against the racism of APROSOMA and a protest against the way they had been used as an umbrella for Gitera's fanaticism. Only a letter of apology from Gitera after the meeting restrained Perraudin from placing APROSOMA under a full-scale ban.[129]

In October 1959 Kayibanda moved on from MSM to form the Parti du Mouvement de l'Émancipation Hutu (MDR-PARMEHUTU) with the blessing of Chanoine Ernotte and Father Endriatis and the support of most of the Hutu Abbés. The dialectical conflict between elite and counter-elite had now reached the point where Kayibanda was talking of Independence, though under a constitutional monarchy;[130] UNAR was including some land reforms and a call for higher education in its programme. Since Bishop Perraudin made Abbé Kalibwami editor of *Kinyamateka*, there were limits to what Kayibanda could get printed.[131] But PARMEHUTU was showing the effects of Kayibanda's organisational talents; the party worked on a cell basis reminiscent of the Legion of Mary, with a propagandist on most hills. The Association des Moniteurs provided him with a second network among the Hutu teachers. Nonetheless, able neither to activate clientship ties, except in the north, nor use the emotive language of kingship and unity, the party had only patchy grassroots support, with its main centres around Gitarama and Ruhengeri, where land shortage or lineage allegiance aided the Hutu.[132]

The Belgians decided to remove the northern Tutsi chiefs, Kayihura, Rwangombwa and Mungalurire, on 17 October 1959, on the ground that they had abused their positions by inciting people to violence at UNAR meetings.[133] The fact that the Tutsi politicians held traditional office enabled the Belgians to stifle them by claiming that as government agents they had no right to engage in political action. A group of two hundred men descended on the Kigali Residence to protest about the depositions, and were finally dispersed with tear gas, leaving one dead.[134] Tension was high, with rumours circulating and new tracts appearing daily; Perraudin and the RADER leaders, Bwanakweri and Ndazaro, were singled out on one UNAR hand bill as enemies of the people 'to be made to disappear by all possible means'.[135] Anything Belgian or White Father was suspect; hosts were said to poison people and DDT to kill crops.[136] An anti-tuberculosis team was rumoured to make people sterile; schoolchildren fled from Zaza school to escape them.[137] Around the missions it was bruited that an all-Tutsi vicariate was to be formed by dividing Nyundo.[138] The rejection of the European presence and the assertion of Tutsi Independence was soon translated from the symbolic world of rumour to the real world of violence in which the Hutu were the only acceptable victims. In the first few days of November Abbé Joseph Sibomana and Dominique Mbonyamutwa, both old MSM leaders, were attacked. Kayibanda went into hiding; it was generally thought that UNAR was going to crush PARMEHUTU by selective assassination of its leaders. It looked as if Rwanda was entering a period of nationalist struggle, with the PARMEHUTU and RADER parties acting as European quislings.

The peasant revolt against the Tutsi that began on 3 November 1959 broke with the spontaneity and intensity of a tropical thunderstorm. Beginning in Ndiza and Bumbogo, the centres of the worst Tutsi repression during the aftermath of the Ndungutse rising,[139] it spread to Kisenyi and Ruhengeri, tracing in reverse the path of the old Nyabingi prophets into regions of ancient clan autonomy and recent land shortage. Anarchic in its conduct, the revolt was predominantly monarchist in its ideology. Groups of ten men led by a 'president'[140] with a whistle, blazed a trail of destruction across the hills until, either exhausted or drunk, they handed on, relay fashion, to another group, who continued the burning of Tutsi huts. In Ruhengeri not a single Tutsi habitation was spared. The Hutu raiders were recruited 'on orders from the mwami', and so firmly convinced were some of official sanction that they stopped at the Residence to ask for petrol.[141] The idea that the king had called for the destruction of the Tutsi, or was held prisoner by them, was widespread among the incendiarists. If PARMEHUTU propagandists did organise groups, this must have been a very minor part of a movement that spread rapidly across the country, leaving several hundred dead, and thousands of Tutsi as refugees. In some areas Tutsi with their garagu and subjects put up resistance and fought off the attackers, but this was not widespread.[142]

The raids which had been sparked off by the attacks on Hutu leaders took the Tutsi by suprise. At Nyanza spearmen formed a human wall around the mwami's house, and the Twa are said to have been dispatched to seek out and kill prominent members of the counter-elite.[143] As the Belgians were slowly restoring the country to a semblance of order on 7 and 8 November wall posters entitled 'Declaration of the authentic Rwandans' appeared.[144] Just as the court ritualists had directed State policies in the past, so it was imagined the power of PARMEHUTU could be traced back to its *éminence grise*, Monsignor Perraudin. The posters now declared the enemies of Rwanda to be Kayibanda and 'his chief Monseigneur Perraude[sic]'.[145]

Banyarwanda! These are the men who are betraying Rwanda today; these are the men who wish to keep us in the slavery introduced to the country by the Belgians; these are the men who under the presidency of Perraude have held councils at Kabgayi with a plan to kill His Majesty our Kigeli V Ndahindurwa in order to displace the monarchy in Rwanda and keep us in slavery.[146]

The prime menace was again the White Fathers; the Tutsi, on the edge of the Church again, as in the 1920s, could see the Hutu as nothing but the priests' passive clients.

The mission stations, both Catholic and Protestant, were turned into sanctuaries for escaping Tutsi, and a number of Fathers had to bring out their hunting rifles to frighten off Hutu mobs. Perraudin and Bigirumwami immediately issued a joint pastoral on 6 November appealing for calm and charity and denouncing all violence.[147] Perraudin was shocked by the ferocity of the Jacquerie[148] and by the campaign implicating him in it. He immediately went to see Ndahindurwa to seek his assurance that the king was not responsible for the posters; the mwami told him that the Swahili had written them.[149] This was possible: the Muslim traders had suffered more than most from the Catholic monopoly of education, and the Catholic Press had even run a successful campaign against Sunday commerce.[150] The co-operative movement, sponsored by the Church, threatened their position as capitalist entrepreneurs, and their future in a Catholic Rwanda was uninviting.

On 8 November Bishop Perraudin wrote a letter to Rome which

demonstrates how little he fulfilled the revolutionary role assigned him in Tutsi diatribes.

We are all of us deeply broken-hearted by this civil war — one must call it by its rightful name — which has broken out . . . The atmosphere is heavy with hatred, panic and vengeance . . . I am very saddened by these attacks, above all because they paralyse my freedom of action. I don't set much store by my personal safety, and I offer this up for our poor Rwanda, but the Christians are certainly suffering from it all.[151]

This was hardly the letter of a man pushing ruthlessly for a Catholic Hutu republic. Two days later news that the Vatican had formally instituted the Catholic hierarchy in the Congo and Ruanda-Urundi came through. The Rwandan vicariates were no longer ruled by Vicars Apostolic but by Archbishop Perraudin and Bishop Bigirumwami as head of two dioceses of a local Church. The indigenous Church had come of age, and the missionary task was essentially finished . . . but in bloodshed and anarchy and with the Church racked by divisions.

APROSOMA, RADER and PARMEHUTU reacted to the UNAR attack on Perraudin by sending a letter to Pope John XXIII branding the 'nationalist' party as totalitarian and denouncing its 'fascist intentions'.[152] The letter coincided with a directive from Perraudin which identified the Church's enemies as 'communists': 'Communism is active. Satan is alive.'[153] The note of hysteria is explained by continuing personal attacks on the Archbishop from UNAR activists outside Rwanda. Protestants spoke of him as 'l'impie évêque', while others calumnied the Catholic Press as divisive, aimed at the removal of the mwami in favour of a minority goverment. In a petition to the United Nations in May 1960 Perraudin replied to the accusations; he was preceded by Abbé Jean-Baptiste Gahamanyi, a Tutsi, who wrote to refute the charges in a remarkable gesture of solidarity.[154]

The Jacquerie of November 1959 nonetheless drove another wedge between Hutu and Tutsi clergy; more than twenty-one Tutsi chiefs and 332 sub-chiefs had left their positions by the time the trouble died down.[155] 'If, at the beginning, there could be found a fairly wide range of opinion amongst the Tutsi clergy,' wrote Adriaenssens, 'as the Hutu movement gained ground a regrouping took place which will doubtless end by their being gathered, almost all of them, in a single group.'[156] Abbés Thomas and Alexandre Ruterandongozi fled from Rwanda to Tanzania to organise support for UNAR outside the country.[157] Monsignor Bigirumwami, seeing in the revolt the outcome of the White Fathers' social catholicism, swung over to the conservative nationalists, and the Governor had to reprimand him for his opposition to Belgian policy.[158] When the UN trusteeship delegation visited Nyundo in March 1960 the roads were lined with PARMEHUTU supporters all the way to the mission grounds, where 'a large crowd of several thousand, including a number of schoolchildren accompanied by European and African nuns, were voicing pro-UNAR sentiments demanding Independence, at the same time as other demonstrators were shouting anti-Tutsi slogans'.[159] Because of its large preponderance of Tutsi clergy and religious, Nyundo had become a UNAR island in a PARMEHUTU sea; the European Sisters were faithfully following their Bishop, but even in the missionary ranks there were genuine UNAR supporters.[160]

Monsignor Perraudin struggled to restore the Church's neutrality and moral authority, narrowly missing death during one tour of his stations when his car broke down at Gahini and a Tutsi crowd recognised him.[161] Tutsi Abbés were withdrawn from the Conseil Supérieur and a more hard-line Tutsi, Abbé Ntezimana, put in charge of *Kinyamateka*. Deeply wounded by events, Perraudin was inclined to retreat from further commitment to the Hutu cause. But even had he been willing to press Catholic social policy more actively, matters were now out of his hands. The Jacquerie had imposed its own dynamic on the pace of political change.

Political developments following the revolt were dominated by three major factors: a resolute bias on behalf of the Hutu by the Special Resident of Rwanda, a Catholic Social democrat, Colonel Bem Logiest, the increasing sophistication of the PARMEHUTU propaganda, and the success of Kayibanda's men on the hills at a time when hundreds of new sub-chieftancies were becoming available. In December 1959 the Flemish Residents in Ruhengeri simply took teachers from the Catholic schools and made them sub-chiefs.[162] Logiest was convinced that the Tutsi regime was oppressive, and the presence of his paratroopers held counter-revolution in check.[163] At last the phantom communists materialised; Michel Rwagasana, the UNAR delegate to the United Nations, was detained in Kampala by the British and found to be carrying communist literature.[164] Even if UNAR had not yet turned to Lumumba's MNC on the other side of Lake Kivu, it seemed only a matter of time before they would try.[165] The Belgians' worst fears were confirmed when it was discovered that the mwami had been trying to enlist Russian support.[166]

PARMEHUTU propaganda on the hills focused on the issues of *ibikingi* and *igisati*, genuine peasant grievances against Tutsi landowners. At the national level the Hutu took over the language of nationalism and anti-colonialism and turned it successfully against UNAR. The mwami became 'the Tutsi sultan' again, just as in the old mission documents when Musinga was behaving badly; the ruling class were 'colonialists of the Ethiopian race' who were invited to return to 'their fathers in Abyssinia'.[167] What was once legitimation now was condemnation; the structural transformation was complete.

The fact of independence for the Hutu people *vis-à-vis* Tutsi colonialism will be definitely and solemnly consecrated by the total abolition of the triple myth of the Tutsi feudal colonialists, 'Kalinga-Abiru-mwami'. [168]

The Hutu had become a Bantu people in the face of an Hamitic invader. Gitera spoke wildly of 'hitlerisme' and 'hamitisme', spoiling his rhetoric by claiming to be the mwami of the Hutu and Kayibanda their Imana.[169]

Despite the fact that PARMEHUTU was still only a loose congeries of local parties over which Kayibanda exerted little direct control, in an atmosphere of intimidation and violence MDR-PARMEHUTU scored a landslide victory in the July 1960 elections.[170] The slow process of building up a national party was circumvented when, on 28 January 1961 the PARMEHUTU leadership seized power with the connivance of Logiest.[171] Dominique Mbonyamutwa, a forty-year-old ex-teacher and Belgian company agent from Gitarama, a sub-chief since 1952 and a close friend of Kayibanda, with whom he shared the leadership of PARMEHUTU, was elected President of the new republic, with Grégoire Kayibanda as Prime Minister. Formal independence was granted by Belgium on 1 July 1961. The king, Kigeri, went into exile, PARMEHUTU having abandoned thoughts of a constitutional monarchy after their election successes. The Hutu had discovered themselves as an ethnic group in the 1950s; now they were a nation.

Whatever its intentions, the Church had presided over a dramatic transfer of power from the Tutsi noble lineages to the counter-elite of teachers and ex-seminarians. The struggle divided both indigenous and missionary Churches. At the level of doctrine it had pitted two Catholic defences against communism, the individualist piety and institutional triumphalism of the nineteenth century, and the social Catholicism of the mid-twentieth. The change in Catholic social policy during the colonial period was essentially a change from one to the other — a change that threw Churchmen into a spectrum of views ranging from the patriarchate of Pagès, Classe and Kagame to the 'total social transformation' of Adriaenssens. It was as if the insights of Europe were delayed twenty years before making their impact on the missions. While the traditional model of atheistic communism remained the stock-in-trade of missionary fears about political movements, monarchist and fascist developments provided new reference points against which African and settler nationalism could be judged.

But perhaps the most persistent resonances were those between the late Middle Ages and colonial Rwanda, the glorious epoch of the Church, the ubiquity and inevitability of patronage, lulling the Churchmen into complacency. The churches were for ever full, with the Hutu before the 1930s, with the added Tutsi after the *Tornade*, and again with Hutu after the Jacquerie had swept out the landowners. The Bishops were galvanised into action only by grave crises, the collapse of the Rwandan Church after the Second World War and the nationalism of the late 1950s.

The static organic society proved the most dangerous of myths for the Church in the post-war period; enforced modernisation had greatly modified the feudal economy of old Rwanda and given rise to a small, vociferous, anti-clerical class. After this new class had split along ethnic lines as a result of Belgian limitations on access to political office, the Hutu counter-elite alone seemed ready to move out finally from the feudal world with the aid of the social democrat clergy. Pro-Tutsi clergy were essentially trying to keep alive an anachronism. That the colonial process had not been completed, with a capitalist elite firmly in the neo-colonial net, is perhaps one reason why Belgium continued to support PARMEHUTU.

It would be easy to portray the divisions of the post-war years as a temporary aberration caused by an unfortunate conjunction of political circumstances. But the cracks had appeared with the first squabbles between northern and central missions in 1905. Rwanda's stratified society, the regional differences between kinship-based and feudal economies, and finally the country's partial insertion into the colonial capitalist world, exposed the inherent contradictions in the Church's structure and ideology which agnostic, secular Europe had been able to ignore. Social class, hardened into ethnicity, was the anvil on which the Rwandan Church was hammered. The apparently abrupt change of policies, Hutu Church to Tutsi Church, *évolué* to counter-elite, was not the opportunism of the Roman monolith but the result of divisions within Church and society, of conflicts an omnipresent *corpus christianum* could not avoid.

Rome and the Bishops made policies, but there was ultimately no decision that did not require the consent of the bush missionary for it to work, no directive that a wilful Father Superior in an isolated station could not ignore. In the 1958-61 crisis it was group loyalties, idiosyncratic preferences based on culture and history, rather than any ideal catholicity that were the operational terms of the Church's actions. 'There are some who have taken to speaking badly of the mwami and who deprive him of the respect to which he is due,' wrote Bishop Bigirumwami in his 1960 Easter pastoral. 'These people hate Rwanda. Those who do not respect their chiefs and refuse to obey them hate Rwanda and the Church.' And as he wrote Hutu laymen and Abbés were comparing the 'Tutsi sultan' to Farouk: 'Tell the Tutsi lords that the liberation of the Bantu people of Rwanda will soon be achieved and that Rwanda does not need the pharasaical interventions of the feudal imperialists for her Independence.'

Precisely because the Catholic Church was so successful in Rwanda, because it became Rwanda's Church, it bore the impress of its society and its imperfections. The Word was made class-conscious, vacillating, ambitious flesh, unwilling and unable to opt out of history, however high the price. That the social catholicism of the post-war missionaries and Hutu laymen triumphed, that the egalitarian themes of basic Christianity overcame the powerful symbols of kingship and hierarchy, was ultimately thanks to Belgian paratroopers. So it was that a Rwandan republic born from the principles of social catholicism limped to Independence, taking with it the anachronism of a Tutsi-dominated and highly conservative indigenous Church.

NOTES

1 Young, C., *Politics in the Congo*, Princeton, N. J., 1965, 276.
2 Apter, D. E., *The Political Kingdom in Uganda*, Princeton, N. J., 1961, 340-4.
3 *La Libre Belgique*, 24 January 1957.
4 Nkundabagenzi and Verhaegen, *Rwanda politique*, 19.
5 *Ibid.*, 16-18; as chapter nine, n. 164.
6 Pastoral letter of Bishops of Ruanda-Urundi, April 1957, Dossier 543, WFAR.
7 This was very much a consensus opinion shared by Maquet and Kagame as well.
8 The choice of words here, 'race' rather than 'tribalism', would not have been alien to the Hutu leaders. The evidence at my disposal suggests that the Hutu did not see themselves as a tribe in conflict with another tribe but, on the model of European-African relations, an oppressed race ruled by a minority. They were 'the Hutu counter-elite' only in relation to the Tutsi elite, just as the *évolué* was essentially a term relating to colonial European culture. For a short comparative treatment, see Kuper, L., 'Race structure in the social consciousness', in *Race and Social Difference*, ed. Baxter, P., and Cansom, B., Harmondsworth, 1972, 77-97.
9 Nkundabagenzi and Verhaegen, *Rwanda politique*, 26-7.
10 *Ibid.*, 29
11 Kayibanda.
12 Fanon, F., *The Wretched of the Earth*, New York, 1968, 160-1: 'Colonialism pulls every string shamelessly, and is only too content to set at loggerheads those Africans who yesterday were leagued against the settlers . . . etc.'
13 For the way this correlated with differences in religious ideology see Paden, J. N., *Religion and Political Culture in Kano*, Berkeley, Cal., 1973.
14 Doornbos, M. R., 'Kumanyana and Rwenzururu: two responses to ethnic inequality', in *Protest and Power*, 1089, 1094.
15 Boutry and Bicamumpaka.
16 Lemarchand, *Rwanda and Burundi*, 107-8.
17 *Ibid.*, 151.
18 See chapter nine.

19 *CRISP*, No. 51, 12-13.
20 *Kinyamateka*, 1 March 1958.
21 Ernotte.
22 *Temps Nouveaux d'Afrique*, 13, 20 April 1958.
23 *Ibid.*, 27 April 1958.
24 *Ibid.*, 15 May 1958.
25 Ernotte.
26 Bicamumpaka.
27 Loose papers contained in a dossier entitled 'Rwanda avant 1962' in Kigali White Fathers' archives.
28 See chapter nine.
29 'Procès verbal de la réunion du cadre élargi', 5 May 1958, 11-13, in 'Rwanda avant 1962', dossier Kigali.
30 *Kinyamateka*, 15 November, 1 December 1957, 1 January, 1 February, 1 March 1958.
31 See article by Rukiramacumu, C. A., in *Kinyamateka*, 15 November 1957. 'Progress' was also rendered by *kuzana ibishya*, literally 'the sending of new things', and Rwanda was already spoken of as *mu nzira yo kwigenga*, 'on the road to Independence'. Ghana's independence acted as a model and catalyst; see *Kinyamateka*, 15 March 1958.
32 'Koko Rwanda ruzakizwa na bene rwo' ('How Rwanda will be saved by her people'), in *Kinyamateka*, 1 January 1958, is a good example of the Tutsi emphasis. *Kinyamateka*, 15 February 1958, 1 June 1958, has good examples of specific Hutu complaints.
33 *Kinyamateka*, 15 March 1958.
34 Mosmans, G., 'L'avenir politique du Ruanda-Urundi', August-September 1958, typed MS, Dossier 543. It is difficult to dismiss Mosmans' observations as the bias of a pro-colonialist. His *L'Église à l'heure de l'Afrique*, Tournai, 1961, was an impartial dissociation of the Church from colonial government, and he was writing in the same vein in *La Revue Nouvelle*, April 1956; see Lemarchand, *Political Awakening*, 148.
35 The term was still in use, as was *inyanga Rwanda*, 'haters of Rwanda'; see Félicien Kambanda in *Kinyamateka*, 1 February 1958.
36 *Kinyamateka*, 1 April 1958.
37 *Temps Nouveux d'Afrique*, 15 May 1958.
38 'Abahutu bati: Ntiwumwa ubuntu umwami yaba umutware wa parti politique kandi ali umubyeyi rusange w'abanyarwanda bose.' 'The Hutu said: how can the mwami's prestige be behind one political party when he is the father of all the Rwandan people?' *Kinyamateka*, 15 May 1958; *Temps Nouveaux d'Afrique*, 6 July 1958.
39 Nkundabagenzi and Verhaegen, *Rwanda politique*, 35-7.
40 *CRISP*, No. 51, 13.
41 'The traditionalist intelligentsia created a mythical *Wunschbild* (Legitimation-fantasy picture) of the past, which, in the present political circumstances, fulfils an analogous function to that of the traditionalist myths in the stable *ancien régime*. When, following foreign influences, the egalitarian Hutu politicians called the latter in question, the "myths of inequality" had structurally to give way to "myths of unity and harmony" which were as much opposed to the rebels' aims that they were designed to thwart, as to those of

the colonisers against which they sought to affirm the unity of the Rwandan people in the anti-colonialist struggle.' Unedited text of a paper read by Professor M, D'Hertefelt before an IAD seminar on ethno-history, 1961, quoted in 'Évolution des structures sociales rwandaises', an article by Abbé Janvier Mulenzi *Culture traditionelle et christianisme*, proceedings of a seminar held at Nyundo, July-August 1969, kindly lent to me by Abbé Alexis Kagame.

42 Bicamumpaka remembered the surprise caused by the tone of the speech made at a hotel in Ruhengeri in November 1958.

43 Relations were cordial before he left; see *Ruanda Notes*, Review Number, 1957 58, 21. It was plain from the interview with Dr Joe Church that Rudahigwa was a close friend in the last two years of his life, and a photograph of the mwami has a prominent position in the Church's hallway.

44 Adriaenssens, 'La situation politique'; Mosmans, 'Climat du Rwanda indigène'.

45 Mosmans, 'Climat du Ruanda indigène'.

46 'Umwami Gihuza-miryango'; see *Kinyamateka*, 1 January, 1 May 1958.

47 *Kinyamateka*, 1, 15 May 1958.

48 Reported in *Temps Nouveaux d'Afrique*, 6 July 1958.

49 *Ibid*.

50 Unattributable interview.

51 Quoted in Mosmans 'L'avenir politique', 6.

52 *Témoignage Chrétien*, 5 September 1958. A major propaganda war was going on in the Belgian periodicals at this time, with G. Cyimana putting the Hutu case in *La Revue Nouvelle*, March and November 1958.

53 The fact that Bishop Bigirumwami swung round in the course of 1958 to the court position was a measure of the way both Tutsi and Hutu communities with their priests were becoming polarised. He was essentially a Churchman but, like Perraudin, who swung in the opposite direction in this period, subject to intense pressures from his clergy and friends.

54 'Parti de l'Unité et du Progrès National'.

55 Lemarchand, *Rwanda and Burundi*, 328-9.

56 ABAKO, 'Association pour la Sauvegarde de la Culture et des Intérêts des Bakongo'; see Kanza, *Conflict in the Congo*, 33-8, 49-51.

57 The Buisseret-Moermans-Thompson agreement of March 1956 provided that 45 per cent of the education budget would go to the construction of new lay schools, 45 per cent on Catholic missions and 10 per cent on Protestant missions; see Lemarchand, *Political Awakening*, 148.

58 *Ibid*., 147-50.

59 Lumumba, for example, pointed to the 1956 Ruanda-Urundi election in comparison with the political stagnation of the Congo; see Lemarchand, *Political Awakening*, 160.

60 Interview with Baudoin Paternostre de la Mairieu, Kigali, June 1973.

61 Interview with David Weston, ex-Director of the Études Practique de Langues Modernes, May 1973, Butare. David Weston was in Rwanda in the late 1950s and pointed out to me the obvious embarrassment of Flemish administrators who barely reached to Rudahigwa's shoulder.

62 'À mon retour de voyage (fin septembre) j'ai remis au Ministère le rapport sur les perspectives d'évolution politique du Ruanda-Urundi. Ce

rapport a fortement impressioné les Conseillers de la politique indigène du départment qui, apres divers échanges de vues, se sont ralliés aux principes généraux énoncés . . . Au début des ces réunions d'étude (certaines avaient eu lieu pendant le séjour en Belgique de M. Harroy) il a fallu convaincre ces personalités de la nécessité d'une réforme hardie et profonde.' Mosmans to Superior General, 17 January 1959, Dossier 543. Mosmans' account perhaps exaggerates his own role in rousing the Ministry from their natural torpor, but it gives the lie to Lemarchand's portrayal of the Church favouring African independence because of a rupture with Belgian administration; see Lemarchand, *Political Awakening*, 148.

63 Mosmans to Superior General, 17 January 1959.

64 Mosmans, 'L'avenir politique', 5.

65 Mosmans to Superior General, 17 January 1959.

66 Adriaenssens, 'La situation politique'.

67 *Rapport de l'administration belge du Ruanda-Urundi*, 1959 (published 1960), 42.

68 Adriaenssens, 'La situation politique'. Both Mosmans and Adriaenssens are highly intelligent and experienced men making reports for the Superior General of the White Fathers. Their bias seems to be a commitment to social justice and perhaps an overemphasis on the discreteness of the Tutsi factions, though, of course, Adriaenssens points out that the events pushed all the Tutsi factions together by 1960. They are probably more reliable as sources for political change than anything in Belgian archives, since neither Mosmans nor Adriaenssens is essentially pressing the Maison-Mère in Rome to do anything; they are reporting back with information rather than attempting directly to influence policy.

69 Mosmans, 'L'avenir politique', 5.

70 *Temps Nouveaux d'Afrique*, 16 November 1958.

71 Zaza diary, 25 January 1959.

72 *Temps Nouveaux d'Afrique*, 7 December 1958.

73 *Ibid.*

74 This was just another indicator of the differences between the land-owning northern clan leaders and the Gitarama Hutu. Personality differences were equally striking: Bicamumpaka moderate, self-confident and radiating bonhomie, Kayibanda retiring, intense and seemingly embittered (he was, of course, within one week of deposition when we met and doubtless knew the end was near).

75 The Legion of Mary began in Rwanda in May 1950. Though not obligatory, it was strongly recommended for leading Catholics. Sixteen of the Rwandan missions had praesidia by 1954 and all of them had groups by the late 1950s. There were thirty-five Curia divided into praesidia with 6,000 members in 1959. A major meeting of the Legion took place at Kabgayi in April 1959, with Calliope Mulindahabi as secretary and Kayibanda as president.

76 Grégore Kayibanda denied categorically that he ever used Church organisations for political propaganda, and this was literally true. However, in an unattributable source, 10 November 1959, there is a complaint about Mulindahabi and Kayibanda: 'they take advantage of their visits to the praesidia and Curiae in the country to make propaganda for their political

party after completing the Legion's business'.

77 To questions as to when the MSM programme originated and when the first organisation took place, replies invariably hit on a major event in the Church calendar; the 1950 Save celebration was the commonest, though all questioned appear to project social consciousness further in the 1940s than the documentary evidence would warrant.

78 According to Bicamumpaka, Kayibanda immediately left for Rwaza on hearing of the mwami's death.

79 Mosmans, 'L'avenir politique', 5. Bishop P. J. Brazier, who had authority over the Ruanda CMS, unfortunately did not reply to detailed questions about the period beyond the comment that 'It was ironic that we were left with the criticism that we favoured the Tutsi regime while the RC's switched their support to the rebelling Hutu!' Brazier to Linden, 11 April 1973.

80 See n. 43.

81 Unattributable interviews.

82 'Urukundo mbere ya byose' ('Charity before all things'), 11 February 1959.

83 *Ibid.*

84 *Ibid.*

85 *Ibid.*

86 Circulars of 11 February 1959 and 15 April 1959, Nos. 20, 21. Older pupils were to have special lessons on '(1) The dignity and fundamental equality of all men. (2) Accidental, inevitable and providential inequalities needed for the common good. (3) Racism and race in Catholic doctrine. (4) Nationalism and patriotism. (5) The role of the governed: obedience to the law, taxes, class interests and the common good. (7) The Church and the temporal sphere (social or political). (8) Catholic Action, one of the organs best suited to carry the Christian spirit into the lives of people and into institutions. Every Christian is committed because he is a member of a living body, etc. I recommend the social encyclicals, speeches by Pius XII . . .'

87 APROSOMA was putting out 'Idjwi iya rubanda rugufi', and these were the Tutsi reply; see *CRISP*, No. 51, 12-13.

88 'Report of the Commission of Enquiry', 21.

89 *Temps Nouveaux d'Afrique*, 11 January 1959.

90 *L'Ami*, No. 113, May 1954, 178-80; chapter nine, n. 119.

91 Adriaenssens, 'La situation politique'. He saw the Church's mission as 'not to please everyone but to preach truth and justice'. 'The Church has the right to judge according to unchanging principles even the foundations of a social system . . . The Church has the right and duty to intervene in this issue [racism] in as much as it touches moral law . . . To abstain from speaking would be complicity.'

92 'Then at last they understood. The kingdom was not self-government and a Welfare State but forgiveness of personal sins, a changed attitude to life and a call to preach a Gospel which would change mens' hearts.' See *Ruanda Notes*, No. 147, March-May 1960, 16, a statement that any older White Father would concur in wholeheartedly.

93 It seems to me that this is also the root of Bishop Lamont's dilemma in dealing with the Smith regime after the Land Apportionment Act. In the course of the 1971 Rhodesian Church-State crisis Lamont had both to

maintain that he had a right to speak on social and racial issues and that he was not 'meddling in politics'. But what politics are not about social or racial issues?

94 *Ruanda Notes*, No. 147, March-May 1960, 13; Church, J. E., *Forgive them*, London, 1968; St John, P., *Breath of Life*, CMS, London, 1971, 208, all show the preference unashamedly.

95 They were also tightly knit lineages. Dr Joe Church's family goes back to Samuel Church, bo's'un on Charles II's yacht, whose daughter-in-law was converted by Wesley. Stanley Smith and Leonard Sharp were double brothers-in-law who studied medicine after going to Harrow and Winchester, and both served in the East African Rifles. Captain Holmes, an international ice hockey player, was a regular officer who had been seconded to Canada. The *ntore* were, of course, fine athletes and accomplished high-jumpers.

96 Adriaenssens, 'La situation politique'.

97 *Ruanda Notes*, No. 142, 1958-59, 6.

98 There were a number of recruits from lower middle class families in the CMS, but these tended in English fashion to be politically unwaveringly Conservative.

99 Mosmans to Perraudin, 3 June 1959, No. 02946, Dossier 543: 'A brake is being put on the execution of all the decisions that have been taken by all possible means.'

100 *Temps Nouveaux d'Afrique*, 29 March 1959; *CRISP*, No. 51, 12.

101 Unattributable interview.

102 Church.

103 Lemarchand, *Political Awakening*, 201.

104 *Rapport du Groupe du Travail*, 37.

105 *Temps Nouveaux d'Afrique*, 31 May 1959.

106 Nkundabagenzi and Verhaegen, *Rwanda politique*, 89.

107 UN Visiting Mission to Trust Territories' *Report on Ruanda-Urundi*, 1954, 34, describes a meeting with Rukeba in which he complained about the administration's refusal to give him a concession for mining talc and about the tyranny of chiefs and judges. He deplored the lack of access to higher education. The topics broached provide an interesting indication of the way the political focus altered dramatically from 1954 to 1959; see also Lemarchand, *Rwanda and Burundi*, 158.

108 *Temps Nouveaux d'Afrique*, 27 September 1959.

109 'Because they realise they are in danger of losing their lives and thus becoming lost to their people, these men, hot-headed and with anger in their hearts, relentlessly determine to renew contacts once more with the oldest and most pre-colonial springs of life of their people.' Fanon, *The Wretched of the Earth*, 209-10.

110 *Temps Nouveaux d'Afrique*, 27 September 1959.

111 'Report of the Commission of Enquiry', 32-4.

112 Father Boutry recalled that fourteen seminarians had left in 1957.

113 Unattributable interview; *Temps Nouveaux d'Afrique*, 20 September 1959.

114 'Urwandiko Abepiskopi b'u Rwanda bohereje abakristu babo' (Joint letter of the Bishops of Rwanda to their Christians), 27 August 1959, White Fathers' archives, Kigali.

115 'Déclaration des Vicaires Apostoliques du Ruanda sur le Kalinga,' read before the two synods held at Nyakibanda, 24-9 August 1959: 'Comme pour tout emblème national, l'Église admet que des marques de respect ou même des cérémonies nationales aient lieu autour du Kalinga. Il faudrait expliquer à ceux qui en auraient besoin, que ses marques de respect s'adressent, à travers le Kalinga, à la nation ou au détenteur de l'Autorité.'

116 'Consignes et directives des Vicaires Apostoliques du Ruanda-Urundi à leur clergé et aux congrégations religieuses', 24-9 August 1959.

117 *Temps Nouveaux d'Afrique*, 27 September 1959.

118 *Ibid.*, 30 August 1959.

119 Lemarchand, *Rwanda and Burundi*, 160.

120 See chapter nine.

121 Lazare Ndazaro had been present at the Brussels talks in the Colonial Ministry at the end of 1958 and had been prominent in the Belgo-Rwandan friendship society of 1950. RADER was clearly an attempt at creating a moderate party against the racial extremism of UNAR and PARMEHUTU.

122 See chapter eight.

123 'Mise en garde contre l'UNAR', 24 September 1959.

124 *Ibid.*

125 For negritude see Lemarchand, *Political Awakening*, 238.

126 It is interesting that the model that came to Bishop Galen in his isolated rejection of Nazism was also the Action Française movement; see Lewy, *The Catholic Church and Nazi Germany*, 125. Similarly, Bishop Lamont was motivated by his experiences in Nazi Germany during the war in his condemnation of the Smith regime's racial policies: interview with the Rev. Father Traber at Archbishop's House, Blantyre, Malawi, 1971. Father Traber had just been deported from Rhodesia, and Bishop Lamont had compared the Smith regime with the Nazis in a speech for Traber's send-off. Père Boutry has a vivid memory of his father's sudden rejection of the Action Française movement in the 1920s.

127 Unattributable source.

128 He was now in some danger, having been threatened by Twa while leaving a bar; see *Temps Nouveaux d'Afrique*, 4 October 1959.

129 Ernotte; 'Mise en garde contre l'APROSOMA', 11 October 1959, joint directive of Bishops Bigirumwami and Perraudin, which speaks of a 'non-Christian spirit of racial hatred'.

130 *CRISP*, No. 51, 11.

131 The exact workings of the editorial board are a little confusing owing to Kayibanda's reticence on the topic. It seems that from 1957, Abbé Kalibwami was put over Kayibanda, who became an important lay adviser. From late 1958, however, Kayibanda was removed from the editorial board because of his involvement in politics. The important point is that, from 1957 to 1959, Abbé Kalibwami had a right of veto over articles and acted as a censor. Kayibanda was adamant in an interview that he was forced to rewrite many articles in this period to get them through.

132 *Ruanda Notes*, Review Number, 1957-58, 21, speaks of a scramble for land, with evangelists wishing to return to their homes to stake their claims. *Temps Nouveaux d'Afrique*, 19 October 1958, describes an appeal made by the Kiga concerning the way Tutsi were forcing them to emigrate.

133 *CRISP*, No. 51, 18.

134 *Ibid.*

135 *Temps Nouveaux d'Afrique*, 1 November 1959. RADER, of course, looked most dangerous to UNAR, since it threatened to split off moderate Tutsi support, especially the Astridiens.

136 Some Tutsi began to refuse communion at the hands of White Fathers; see Pauwels, *Le Bushiru*, 306; Zaza diary, 29 October 1959.

137 Zaza diary, 29 October 1959.

138 Rwaza diary, 26 September 1959.

139 See chapter five.

140 It would be interesting to know whether the name originated in the many Catholic associations on the hills and at the stations.

141 Rwaza diary, 4, 11 November 1959; 'Report of the Commission of Enquiry', 52-63.

142 *Ibid.*

143 Chanoine Ernotte and Father Endriatis, who took communion to Kayibanda in hiding, believed that his life was in grave danger.

144 'Itangazo ry' Abanyarwanda b'ukuli.'

145 'Umutware wabo ni Monseigneur Perraude w'i Kabgayi.'

146 'Banyarwanda! aba bantu nibo bagambanir' Urwanda, aba nibo byitso bishaka kuduheza mu buja bw' ababiligi, aba ni bo baremy' inama i Kabgayi, umuyobozi w'iyo nama yari Perraude, iyo nama yal' iyo kwica S.M. wacu Kigeli V Ndahindurwa ngo bace ubwami mu Rwanda tube abaja.' Note the opposition between councils at Nyanza and councils at Kabgayi.

147 Pastoral letter of 6 November 1959 signed by Perraudin and Bigirum-wami: 'Au nom de Notre Seigneur Jesus Christ dont nous sommes les représentants sur terre, nous vous disons qui tout cela n'est pas chrétien, nous le déplorons et nous le condamnons absolument.'

148 I am using the analogy given by Lemarchand, *Rwanda and Burundi*, 159; it seems appropriate to this peasent rebellion.

149 Unattributable source.

150 *Rapports annuels*, 1953-54, 280.

151 Perraudin to Cauwe, 8 November 1959, Dossier 543.

152 *Temps Nouveaux d'Afrique*, 6 December 1959.

153 'Présentation de la Sainte Vierge', circular No. 23, 21 November 1959.

154 Petitions from UNAR representatives of 11 November 1959; Rwaga-sana, 21 November 1959; M. M. Ntauhurunga and B. K. Kavutse (From CMS High School, Kampala), 24 November 1959; 'Banyarwanda' (Kampala), 14 December 1959; Archbishop Perraudin, 18 May 1960; Abbé Jean-Baptiste Gahamanyi, 22 April 1960, to the fourteenth session of the General Assembly of the United Nations.

155 Lemarchand, *Rwanda and Burundi*, 173.

156 Adriaenssens, 'La situation politique'.

157 Unattributable source.

158 Unattributable source.

159 UN *Report on the Trust Territories of Ruanda-Urundi*, 3 June 1960, 15.

160 Father Jules Guyssens, the king's chaplain, for example, left the

country, and Fathers De Schrevel, Van Overschelde (Gérard) and Bazot were thought to be pro-Tutsi.

161 Church. A Protestant pathologist at Gahini hospital, Yohane Kanyambo, helped the Archbishop to escape from the mob.

162 Landmeters to Speltinck, 9 December 1959, copy in Rwaza mission correspondence.

163 Paternostre de la Mairieu; Lemarchand, *Rwanda and Burundi*, 109-11.

164 Adriaenssens, 'La situation politique'; unattributable source.

165 Lemarchand, *Rwanda and Burundi*, 176.

166 'Breve response', 18: unattributable source.

167 Nkundabagenzi and Verhaegen, *Rwanda politique*, 247-8.

168 *Ibid*., 244.

169 *Ibid*., 258.

170 Lemarchand, *Rwanda and Burundi*, 180-2.

171 No one interviewed seemed in any doubt but that Logiest had deliberately held back from the PARMEHUTU meeting at Gitarama and, indeed, applauded the *coup* openly.

Epilogue

The situation after Independence was obviously unstable: tension between Nyundo vicariate, with its caucus of Tutsi priests led by Bishop Bigirumwami, and Kabgayi vicariate, led by Archbishop Perraudin, mounted against a background of guerilla attacks from UNAR groups in exile. Raids by *Inyenzi* guerillas, the 'Cockroaches', resulted in savage popular repression at the end of 1963, in which an estimated 5,000 to 8,000 Tutsi died. The Jacquerie broke out intermittently throughout the early 1960s. Letters from the Rwandan episcopate condemning violence were sent out on 24 August 1961 and an appeal against 'odious crimes' at Easter 1962. The killing of innocents after guerilla raids was again condemned at Christmas 1963; it could 'only draw down on our country the curse of God'. Another letter was circulated on 1 January 1964 deploring the UNAR terrorist attacks but adding that it 'cannot be silent either on the repression'. Four Tutsi Abbés suspected by the government of having contacts outside Rwanda, Abbés Gerard Mwerekande, Tharcisse Rwasubutare, Ferdinand Marara and Vianney Kivivo, were temporarily imprisoned at this time.

The Tutsi case against the government of Grégoire Kayibanda was presented to the Vatican by Michel Kayihura, Bishop Gahamanyi's brother, and by Jean-Baptiste Kayonga. Kayonga had been *Econome-Générale* of the Josephite Brothers before leaving to become a Trappist at Mokoto, Leopoldville. After taking his vows he left in 1957 to do refugee work but never returned to the monastery.

On 4 February 1964 *Le Monde* published an article by a Swiss technical assistant from Neuchâtel, M. Vuillemin, who had resigned as a UNESCO lecturer at the Groupe Scolaire in Butare on the grounds that he was unwilling to be an accomplice to genocide. Accused of being a Marxist by the missionaries, he claimed that the Church was condoning Tutsi genocide and intervening only discreetly, in order to safeguard its position in Rwanda. On 10 February 1964

Vatican Radio broadcast an impassioned message to Monsignor Perraudin as head of the Rwandan hierarchy in the most inflated language: 'Since the genocide of the Jews by Hitler, the most terrible systematic genocide is taking place in the heart of Africa.' The Rwandan episcopate sent a telegram to the Vatican the same day, requesting that Red Cross estimates be broadcast and adding that 'the comparison with Hitler is monstrous and gravely offensive to a Catholic head of State'. A letter sent by Monsignor Perraudin correcting the grossly inflated estimates of dead in *Le Monde* was never printed.

The implication of the European Press (e.g. *France-Soir*, 4 February, and *Le Figaro*, 11 February 1964) was that Rwanda was a clerical State in which Catholic Churchmen feared to 'rock the boat'. 'Le mince vernis du christianisme a craqué,' gloated *Le Figaro*. But independent Rwanda was far less clerical than ever before; the issue of secular schools had arisen again, and Kayibanda was doing his best to allay fears that he was a puppet of Belgian syndicalists and the White Fathers. The hierarchy's pastoral of 2 February 1963, 'The mission of the Church in relation to temporal Society', was a balanced renunciation of theocracy and an enlightened account of the Church's contribution to a developing nation. There was nothing mealy-mouthed about the Bishops' condemnation of Hutu violence in January 1964:

Knowing of certain violent reactions by the population in some regions of the country — murder of innocents, arson, personal vengeance killing, robberies and other disorders — we condemn them absolutely, not only as unworthy of Christians but also quite simply as shameful and degrading . . . We wish to draw the attention of those responsible in the public forum to the duty which is incumbent on them always to respect the human person even and above all in the exercise of justice.

Far too many *bourgemaistres* and priests had clashed over the treatment of Christians for the Church to suffer disorder silently at any level.

Racial tension within the Church naturally remained high. It was difficult to find Hutu Abbés who were 'episcopabile', and the most brilliant of them, Abbé Bernard Manyurane, ordained Bishop of Ruhengeri on 28 January 1961, fell ill on 11 February and died in Rome on 8 May; it is possible that he was poisoned. As the republic was purged of the Tutsi class, Tutsi Abbés closed ranks. Thanks to their academic pre-eminence they took up key positions in seminaries and, since so much of Rwanda's education was *de facto*, though after 1964 not *de jure*, in clerical hands, it seemed as if the Tutsi controlled secondary education as a whole. The culturally conditioned disdain for 'le petit Hutu' meant that Hutu pupils in minor and major seminaries still experienced the humiliating contempt of their superiors, which acted as a brake on their attainment. They were *expected* to be inferior to Tutsi pupils and, as recent educational experiments on black children in the United States have shown, such predictions tend to be self-fulfilling, even in conditions of unconscious discrimination. Whether Hutu pupils had 'a chip on their shoulder', or whether their Tutsi teachers deliberately tried to humiliate them into failure, is of secondary importance to the fact that in the post-colonial period the Hutu *experienced* no psychologically satisfying academic success, and attributed this continued failure to the prominence of Tutsi in positions of power within the educational system.

What is not in dispute is that a disproportionately high percentage of Tutsi seminarians passed through seminary education in the decade after Independence in all dioceses save that of Monsignor Perraudin, who tried, according to government policy, to peg his intake to the 10-15 per cent level of the population as a whole. This might seem shocking were it not for the fact that the Tutsi were trying to gain through the Church what they had lost during the revolution in the State. However little active support Monsignor Bigirumwami gave to conservative, reactionary Tutsi Abbés in Nyundo diocese, they were tolerated, and their manner was resented by the northern Hutu, who had never fully accepted the feudal system of central Rwanda. Attempts to form councils of priests had to be abandoned, since they polarised Tutsi-Hutu opinion in the diocese; the resulting lack of communication between priests and their Bishop facilitated a process in which the Tutsi Abbés became increasingly antipathetic to the Hutu and were seen as aliens.

By the beginning of 1973, for a number of reasons, including the economic one that many Hutu left the seminaries for government employment, where they were desperately needed, Rwanda's seminaries stood out as havens of Tutsi ascendancy, and the education system as a threatening stronghold of undiminished Tutsi power. Hutu pupils, frightened that they were about to be cheated of the revolution's fruits, and having tasted few of them, reacted violently to an imagined Tutsi menace and expelled their Tutsi colleagues and teachers from educational centres, convents, noviciates and seminaries. Initially a movement at the University of Butare in reaction to diminishing job opportunities, orchestrated by northern dissidents unhappy at the Gitarama bias of Kayibanda's government, the purge grew into a minor internal revolution within the Catholic Church, which had come to epitomise for young Rwandans the wily retention of power by their former overlords, now disguised in soutanes. The Jacquerie of 1959-61 that had lapped at the Church's door now burst through into the sacristy; the Rwandan Church had been spared the consequences of its Tutsi hegemony for long enough.

The Bishops of Rwanda met in extraordinary session on 22 and 23 February 1973 to discuss the problem of racial violence that had resulted in Tutsi being expelled from almost all secondary schools. They spoke unequivocally of racism:

These disorders aimed at eliminating pupils of one ethnic group. Some went as far as wounding and pillage. In the last few days these threats and the taking of the law into individuals' hands have grown to include employees and workers in private enterprise. Rumours are spread against priests and even prelates . . . The Law of God, as well as the Declaration of the Rights of Man, to which Rwanda subscribes, and the Rwandan constitution, are fundamentally opposed to these procedures of eliminating people and this persecution, with its racial basis . . . If there are social problems to be resolved, and there is no lack of them, let those who are in charge, and not individuals and anonymous groups, do so by means of dialogue.

By 25 February the pupils at the St Pius X Seminary at Nyundo were divided into ethnic groups, and the Tutsi were fleeing back to their hills by the evening. Two days later, pupils at the École d'Art, opposite the seminary, were circulating a list of people who had to leave. During the night of 27-8 February the Tutsi teachers at the seminary fled into Zaire via Goma, together with twelve Tutsi major seminarists. In the prefectures of Kisenyi and Kibuye several hundred Tutsi were attacked. Nyamasheke mission was attacked by school pupils on 12 April and Abbés Robert Matajyabo, Modeste Kajyibwami and Mathias Kambali were wounded. On the 27th Abbé J. Kashyengo of Kisenyi Mission fled to Zaire, the twelfth Tutsi Abbé to escape since the beginning of the troubles.

Tension remained high around Nyundo throughout March, with anonymous notices put on the church door calling for the departure of Monsignor Bigirumwami with all his Tutsi clergy. On 26 March the head of the seminary, Monsignor Matthieu, was dismissed and his place taken by Major Alexis Kanyarengwe, and four days later the same compulsory secularisation took place at the Mater Ecclesiae *Juvenat* at Muramba; it was made into a girls' college under the direction of Sister Twagiramariya Euphrasia. After broadcasting an appeal for calm on 22 March, the President, Dr Grégoire Kayibanda, presided on 4 April over a meeting of the Conseil du Gouvernement which condemned the violence in terms reminiscent of the Bishops.

The fact that the Church condemned the racial violence one month before the government did not escape the notice of Rwandan students studying in Belgium, who were incensed at such meddling in affairs of State. They condemned the Church for controlling education, ignoring social problems and engaging in politics. Monsignor Perraudin was described as 'the brake on all attempts at development and growth by the Rwandan people'. The wheel had turned full circle. The Archbishop could, had he wished, listen to Radio Bujumbura condemning him as the pro-Hutu agent of Belgian syndicalism, or read about his reactionary pro-Tutsi attitudes in a Hutu student manifesto.

Many observers felt that the hierarchy had gone too far in the February pastoral by calling the disorders 'racial' and failing to elaborate on the social dimension. On the other hand, it was difficult to find any other word for a situation in which 'pure' Hutu students checked the noses and fingers of their colleagues to ascertain their ethnic origin. Even the government spoke of attacks on people 'en raison de leur appartenance raciale'. The type of explicit reference to physical characteristics that occurred was necessary in the mixed environment of the classroom, unlike in the hill communities, where lineages were known; like the South African pencil test, fingers and noses provided a quick method.

The school disorders were something of a dress rehearsal for the army's seizure of power in July. Northern students were involved in many of the violent incidents, and the army demonstrated its discipline and power in the country by bringing the situation rapidly under control. Few of the priests found anything to complain about in the way Major Kanyarengwe ran the seminary at Nyundo. When Major General Juvenal Habyarimana set his armoured cars rumbling through the streets of Kigali on 7 July 1973 resistance was minimal. The men of Rambura, Janja and Rwaza missions had seized power; the internal revolution in the Church had been a prelude to a northern *coup*. The internal dynamics of the 1959-61 movement had taken the political evolution of Rwanda one step forward. The rebellious north that had killed missionaries and Tutsi, spawned prophets and tried several revolts, had finally succeeded. Its task was now to transcend the regionalism and ethnic conflict that had scarred Rwandan history.

Glossary

ababyakurutsa   Wandering mediums possessed by the spirit Biheko who claimed curative powers

abahamagazi   Witch-finders or witch-callers

abahennyi   Court functionaries who cursed the king's foes

abaja   Female servants or concubines (*umuja*, sing)

Abaka   The name for Rwandan revivalists who were believed to 'shine' with the power of the Holy Spirit

abanetsi   Manual labourers

abanyabutaka   Tutsi chiefs with rights in land who collected crop dues from peasants

abanyamukenke   Tutsi chiefs with rights in pasture land who collected dues for grazing cattle

abasangwabutaka   Those found on the land, the Gesera, Singa and Zigaba clans

abase   A relationship involving intercessory duties in which abasangwabutaka clans are said to be fathers to the Tutsi

abasemyi   The interlocuters, interpreters

abashobya   Ritual experts at court in charge of sacrifices

abasizi   Poets who composed dynastic poems at court

abatware   pl. of *umutware*

abayeyi   pl. of *umuyeyi*

Abayoboke   'Those who know but a single way', the name given by the progressives at court to the traditionalist faction

abazimu   Lineage spirits

Abbé   The Rwandan secular clergy, i.e. not attached to any religious Order

abiru   Court ritualists in charge of the esoteric code and therefore with influence over succession

akidas   Political agents in Tanganyika, the highest position held by educated Africans in local administration

APROSOMA   Association pour la Promotion Sociale de la masse

Badatchi   Germans

bakuru w'inama   Catholic lay leaders in charge of groups on the hills

banyamuliro   Keepers of the royal fire at Nyanza

banyanduga   Tutsi from Nduga, a name used by the northern Rwandans to describe new arrivals in the colonial period from the south *barozi*   Sorcerers of a malign type, wizards

Basilimu   A group of ultra-progressive young Tutsi in the 1930s

Bayozefiti   Rwandan Josephite Brothers

Benebikira   Rwandan Sisters

Bezirk   The German administrative unit of a circle

Boma   Colonial government district headquarters

Bulamatari   'Breaker of rocks', the Belgians

burozi   Sorcery, a malign charm

CICCU   Cambridge Inter-collegiate Christian Union

corvée   Forced labour

culte de contestation   Religious movements and cults that contest the established order and express the anguish of oppression

Econome   Bursar in charge of material provisioning of stations

fundi   Skilled artisans

gufaha   The payment of crop dues between Hutu on leased land

guhakwa   To pay court, with a view to becoming the client of a noble

ibikingi   Plots of land given by the king or nobles to favoured clients

ibirongozi   A group of Hutu leaders descended from disbanded German porters who controlled the region around Rwaza

ibisonga   Intermediaries between the Tutsi and the northern Hutu in charge of collecting crop dues

igihugu   The country, the geographical extent of any region

ikigabiro   A royal burial site marked by a sacred grove

ikoro   The royal annual tribute in crops and commodities

Imana   The creative force of the land and nation; original meaning unknown

imisigati   Summer pastures

ingénieurs agronomes   Belgian agricultural officers

inka   Cow

Inshongore   Chief Ntulo's hunting dogs, the name given to those who complained to the Belgians, the 'progressive' faction at court

intore   The 'chosen ones' (from *gutora*, to choose), catechumens selected by strong-arm methods

inyangarwanda   'Haters of Rwanda', traditional pejorative term for those rebellious to the Nyanza court

inzoga   Sorghum beer

inzu   Minor patrilineage

ischanga   Sub-clan

itondo   The virtue of self-control, the Tutsi 'stiff upper lip'.

itorero   Military training schools largely for Tutsi; see *ntore*

journalier, journeyman   Impoverished day labourer

Kalinga   The sacred drum of the Nyiginya dynasty

kapitao   Foreman, headman, lay leader

karani   A secretary

kazi   Forced labour for the Belgians on public works

kubitsa   The loan of a cow for usufruct

kukiza   To save (spiritually or literally)

kwatisha   Temporary usufruct rights over land in Bugoyi

mandwa   A class of powerful protective spirits

mazimano   Provisions of food collected for travellers, etc

Mpara   The court mandwa mediums
mshenzi   A pagan
MSM   Movement Social Muhutu
Mungu   The Christian High God
mwami w'imandwa   The head of the court mandwa mediums
mwami w'imvura   The name given to respected rain-callers
ngabo   The Rwandan regiments
ntebe   The provincial seat of a Tutsi lord
ntore   Elite warriors renowned for the martial arts
nyambo   The royal herds (elite cattle)
nyampara   The head of a work party or caravan, a mission agent
Nyiginya   Rwanda's ruling Tutsi clan
Nyina   Mother, as in Nyina'rupfu, Mother Death, and NyinaYuhi, the Queen
   Mother, Kanjogera
rugo   The enclosure, Rwandan home
serkali   A government agent
Serwakira   A mandwa spirit
shebuja (*shobuja*)   A lord or noble, patron
succursales   Catholic mission out-stations
'Terebura'   Father Alphonse Brard
'Tikitiki'   The German officer Von Grawert
La Tornade   'The tornado', the rush of Tutsi conversions, 1929-34
TRAFIPRO   Travail, Fidélité, Progrès: the main co-operative in Rwanda
Tutsikazi   A Tutsi woman or girl
tribunaux indigenes   Native courts
ubgoko   Clan, tribe, race
ubugabo   Manliness
ubuhake   The clientship relationship in which a *shebuja* gives usufruct rights
   to an *umugaragu* over a cow or cows for service
ubukonde   Hutu-owned lands in the north leased out for usufruct
ubuletwa   Labour demanded of peasants by their chiefs
umugaragu ('garagu' in the text)   The client in an *ubuhake* relation to a Tutsi
   lord
umuganuza   A functionary bringing the first fruits to court for the first fruits
   ceremonies
umugome   A rebel, someone who is in opposition to the Nyanza court
umuhinza   A Hutu land priest who shows characteristics of divine kingship
umukonde   A rich Hutu landowner who leases his land for usufruct
umwami   'Mwami' in text when referring to the Rwandan king, *umwami* when
   referring to the umuhinza-like Hutu religious leader/land priest
umupfumu   A diviner
umuryango   Major patrilineage
umutabazi   A saviour king in Nyiginya tradition

Bibliography

Unpublished sources

1. White Fathers' records have been progressively centralised during the past decade in the White Fathers' Archives, Rome, where they are being catalogued and are available to researchers. There are still important archives, however, at Archbishop's House, Kigali, with documents from 1905 to the present day. Individual missions retain occasional letters, a useful set being still at Rwaza. The process of centralisation has been subject to the vagaries of individual Fathers Superior and Regionals, and has been somewhat haphazard, some documents reaching Rome a long time ago when a parish was handed over to indigenous clergy; some papers are still at the bottom of the mission cupboard.

The Rome material consists essentially of diaries and correspondence between the Superior General and the Rwanda mission, though sometimes mission administration letters came back in a pile from a particular station. Bishops Hirth and Classe's letters form a valuable numbered series. The only diary I came across in Rwanda was a copy of the first years of Save mission at the University of Butare; an almost complete set may be found in Rome, largely originals, with valuable material for the period 1900-35, after which the content and quality of observation drop off.

The bulk of documents at Kigali are letters between Vicar Apostolic and missionaries or civil authorities, with some copies of intra-administration correspondence and circulars. These are contained in unnumbered dossiers marked with vague titles like 'Correspondence officielle', etc. Two such dossiers contain useful material from the German period. I was also able to consult a valuable Church history by Father Dominic Nothomb which provided a number of valuable details; this work was held back from publication and was made available to me in MS form, though its substance is appended to copies of de Lacger's *Le Ruanda*. I am most grateful to Father Nothomb for permission to consult this work and for conversations with him about it.

CMS records, a few dossiers of the minutes of the Executive Field Committee for the Ruanda mission, 1935-43, were made available to me at the CMS headquarters. Dr Joe Church was kind enough to allow me to read his unpublished history of the Ruanda Mission, 'Quest for the Highest', which provides many useful insights in the working of the CMS in the period 1925-71.

2. German records are to be found at three major archives, Potsdam, Dar es Salaam and, now, Brussels. The archive consulted by Professor W. M. Roger Louis consisted of documents removed in the early 1920s from Dar es Salaam by the Commissaire Royal at Bujumbura, Pierre Ryckmans. These disappeared from Bujumbura *c.* 1961 and only reappeared again in Brussels in 1971. Researchers are not permitted to consult catalogues in Brussels, but, as far as may be gathered, this material, in microfilm and in dossiers, contains the bulk of German material for Ruanda-Urundi. Since Ryckmans, with the exception of one or two files, cleared the Dar archives of material relevant to Ruanda-Urundi, and Potsdam contains only a small number of mission papers, the Brussels collection is of great importance, and conditions for historians in the Archives Africaines all the more deplorable. For example, documents quoted by Louis from Bujumbura have appeared in the mission collection at Kigali but I found no trace of them in Brussels, nor was it possible to check their existence. I have been unable personally to consult vol. G9/19 of the National Archives of Tanzania, which deals with White Father-mission disputes, 1902-06.

3. Belgian records are open to researchers within the limits of a strict fifty-year rule. Notebooks must be presented to the archivist for checking each evening and all citations listed for approval. I have consulted the period 1916-19 of military rule and 1919-23 of civilian rule. No catalogue is available to researchers. The Derscheid papers are fortunately richest for the period 1925-35, so compensate for the dearth of primary sources for this period.

4. The most useful thesis on Rwandan colonial history, as yet unpublished, is Alison Des Forges' 'Rwanda under Musiinga, 1896-1931', from Yale University, 1972. Catherine Newbury is also publishing a local study of Kinyaga from a doctoral dissertation, *The Cohesion of Oppression: Clientship in Kinyaga*, but I have been unable to consult this MS. Alison Redmayne's B.Litt. thesis 'The concept of feudalism', Oxford, 1961, has been of great help in clarifying problems of feudal terminology. A useful survey of the literature on Rwandan sociology is contained in J. L. Van Meeren's M.Phil. thesis for the University of London at the School of Oriental and African Studies, 'The social system of the Banyarwanda', 1969. My own thesis at SOAS, 'The White Fathers' Mission in Rwanda, 1900-32', 1974, provides the substance of the first seven chapters of this book.

5. The exciting work by Claudine Vidal and others has alerted me to the potentiality of oral sources in Rwanda. I have used these sparingly, as the political climate in Rwanda was particularly charged during early 1973 when I carried out interviews, and emotions were running high on the subject of Church and society.

Articles, periodicals and newspapers

L'Ami, 1950-54, Catholic periodical published at Kabgayi

Anstey, R., 'Belgian rule in the Congo and the aspirations of the *évolué* class', in Gann and Duignan (eds.) *Colonialism in Africa; 1870-1960*, Vol. 2, Cambridge, 1970, 194-226

Arnoux, A., 'Le culte de la société secrète des Imandwa au Rwanda', *Anthropos*, vol. VII, 1912, 287-90, 541-3

Church and revolution in Rwanda

Beattie J. H. M., 'Bunyoro: an African feudality?' *Journal of African History*, vol. VI, No. 1, 1964, 25-36

Bessel M. J., 'Nyabingi', *Uganda Journal*, vol. VI, 1938-39, 74

Bulletin Missionaire, Protestant Belgian Reformed Mission in Rwanda, mission magazine

Bulletin des Missions d'Afrique, White Fathers' Mission magazine for the Belgian province of the Society

Cahiers d'Études Africaines, vol. XIV, No. 53, 1974; issue on Rwanda

Centre de Recherches de l'Information Socio-politique, CRISP

Chanock, M. 'The political economy of independent agriculture in colonial Malawi: the Great War to the Great Depression', *Malawi Journal of Social Science*, vol. I, 1972, 113-29

Chrétien, J. P., 'La révolte de Ndungutse (1912): forces traditionelles et pression coloniale au Rwanda allemand', *Revue française d'histoire d'outre-mer*, LIX, 1972, 645-80.

Chroniques Trimestrielles des missionaires de Notre-Dame d'Afrique, 1896-1907

Classe, L., 'Pour moderniser le Ruanda', *L'Essor Colonial et Maritime*, Nos. 489-91, 4-11 December 1930, 'Un triste Sire', *L'Essor Colonial et Maritime*, Nos. 494, 495, 21 and 25 December 1930

Culture traditionelle et christianisme, Proceedings of Nyundo seminar, July-August 1969

Delmas, P. L., 'La vache au Ruanda', *Anthropos*, vol. XXV, 1930, 950-2

Deutsches Kolonialblatt

Doornbos, M. R., 'Kumanyana and Rwenzururu: two responses to ethnic inequality', in Rotberg and Mazrui (eds.), *Protest and Power in Black Africa*, Oxford, 1970, 1089-94

Goody, J., 'Feudalism in Africa?' *Journal of African History*, vol. IV, No. 1, 1963, 16

Grands Lacs, illustrated White Fathers magazine for the French province

Gravel, P. B., 'Life on the manor in Gisaka (Rwanda)', *Journal of African History*, vol. VI, No. 3, 1965, 328

Gwassa, C.GK, 'Kinjikitile and the ideology of Maji-Maji', in T. Ranger and I. Kimambo (eds.), *The Historical Study of African Religion*, London, 1972, 202-19

de Heusch, L., 'Nationalisme et lutte des classes au Rwanda', in *Afrika im Wandel seiner Geselleschaftsformen*, Leiden, 1964, 103

Hiernaux, J., 'Notes sur une ancienne population du Ruarda-Urundi: Les Renge', *Zaire*, April 1956, 351-60

Holy, L., 'Social stratification in Rwanda', in *Social Stratification in Tribal Africa*, Czechoslovak Academy of Sciences, Prague, 1968

Hopkins, E., 'The Nyabingi cult of south-western Uganda', in R. Rotberg and A. Mazrui (eds.) *Protest and Power in Black Africa*, Oxford, 1970, 258-337

Johanssen, E., 'Mysterein eines Bantu Volkes. Der Mandwa-Kult der Nyaruanda verglichen mit dem antiken Mithras-Kult', Leipzig, 1925

Kagame, A., 'Le Rwanda et son Roi', *Aequatoria*, vol. 8, No. 2, 1945, 41-58

Kinyamateka, 1934-61

Lemarchand, R., 'The *coup* in Rwanda', in R. Rotberg and A. Mazrui (eds.), *Protest and Power in Black Africa*, Oxford, 1970, 891

Mair, L., 'Clientship in East Africa', *Cahiers d'Études Africaines*, vol. VI, 1961, 315-25

Bibliography

Neesen, V., 'Quelques données démographiques sur la population du Ruanda-Urundi', *Zaire*, December 1953, 1019

Nord Deutsche Allgemeine Zeitung

Pagès, A., 'Notes sur le régime des biens dans la Province du Bugoyi', *Congo*, 1938, 8-9

—'Au Rwanda. Droits et pouvoirs des chefs sous la suzeraineté du roi hamite', *Zaire*, April 1949, 372

—'Au Ruanda. A la cour du mwami', *Zaire*, 1950, 472-85

Pauwels, M., 'Le Bushiru et son Muhinza ou roitelet Hutu', *Annali Lateranensi*, vol. 31, 1967, 205-322

Philipps, J. E. T., 'The Nabingi: an anti-European secret society in Africa', in 'British Ruanda, Ndorwa and the Congo (Kivu)', *Congo*, vol. I, 1928, 313-4

Rapports sur l'administration belge du Ruanda-Urundi, 1916-61

Rapport du groupe de travail concernant le problème politique du Ruanda-Urundi, Brussels, 1959

Rapports annuels des missionaires de Notre-Dame d'Afrique, 1906-59

Rennie, J. K., 'The pre-colonial history of Rwanda: a reinterpretation', *Transafrican Journal of History*, vol. 2, No. 2, 1972, 11-55

Répertoire bibliographique de Monsieur l'Abbé Alexis Kagame, 1938-66, University of Butare

Robins, C., 'Rwanda: a case study in religious assimilation', Dar es Salaam UCLA conference on the History of African Religion, June 1970

Ruanda Notes, CMS mission magazine, 1923-61

Schumacher, P., 'Das Sachenrecht in Ruanda', *Koloniale Rundschau*, 1932, 292

Temps Nouveux d'Afrique

Témoignage Chrétien

Trait d'Union, Catholic magazine for the Rwanda vicariates, 1945-61

Un Père Blanc, 'Les idées principales du Cardinal Lavigerie sur l'évangélisation de l'Afrique', *Revue d'Histoire des Missions*, vol. II, No. 3, 1925, 351-96

UN Reports on Trust Territories of Ruanda-Urundi, 1948-61

Verdonck, P., 'Décès du Mwami Rushombo: intronisation du Mwami Bahole', *Congo*, vol. I, 1928, 294-308

Vidal, C., 'Anthropologie et histoire: le cas du Rwanda', *Cahiers Internationaux de Sociologie*, vol. 43, 1967, 143-57

—'Le Rwanda des anthropologues ou le fetichisme de la vache', *Cahiers d'Études Africaines*, No. 35, 1969, 384-401

—'Enquête sur le Rwanda traditionnel: conscience historique et traditions orales', *Cahiers d'Etudes Africaines*, No. 44, 1971, 532

Books (local)

d'Arianoff, A., *Histoire des Bagesera*, IRCB, 1951

Arnoux, A., *Les Péres Blancs aux sources du Nil*, Namur, 1953

Austen, R. A., *Northwest Tanzania under German and British Rule*, New Haven, Conn., 1968

Baumann, O., *Durch Massailand zur Nilquelle*, Berlin, 1894

Bourgeois, R., *Banyarwanda et Barundi*, vols. I and II, Brussels, 1957, 1959

Bushayija, S., *Le Mariage coutumier au Rwanda*, Brussels, 1966

Church, J. E., *Forgive them*, London, 1968

Codere, H., *The Biography of an African Society Rwanda, 1900-1960*, Brussels, 1973

Coupez, A. and Kamanzi, T., *Littérature de cour au Rwanda*, Oxford, 1970

Delmas, L., *Généalogies de la noblesse du Ruanda*, Kabgayi, 1950

Denoon, D., *A History of Kigezi in South-west Uganda*, Kampala, 1972

Dufays, Rev. F., *Pages d'épopée africaine. Jours troublés*, Ixelles, 1928

Dufays, F., and de Moor, V., *Au Kinyaga. Les enchaînés*, Paris, 1938

Edel, M. M., *The Chiga of Western Uganda*, Oxford, 1957

Ekitabu kyo kufutula bigambo bye dini, Einsiedeln, 1902

Gorju, Monseigneur, *En Zigzags à travers l'Urundi*, Namur, 1926

Gravel, P. E., *Remera: a community in Eastern Rwanda*, The Hague, 1968

Hellberg, C. J., *Missions on a Colonial Frontier west of Lake Victoria*, Studia Missionalia Upsaliensia, 1965

d'Hertefelt, M., *Les Clans du Rwanda ancien: éléments d'ethnosociologie et d'ethnohistoire*, MRAC, vol. 70, 1971

d'Hertefelt, M., Trouwborst, A. A., and Scherer, J. H., *Les Anciens Royaumes de la zone interlacustre méridionale*, London, 1962

de Heusch, L., *Essais sur le symbolisme de l'inceste royal en Afrique*, Brussels, 1958

Le Rwanda et la civilisation interlacustre, Brussels, 1966

Iliffe, J., *Tanganyika under German Rule, 1905-12*, Cambridge, 1969

Instructions pastorales de Monseigneur Léon Classe, 1922-39, Kabgayi, 1940

Johanssen, E., *Ruanda. Kleine Anfänge, grosse Aufgaben der evangelischen Mission in Zwischenseengebiet Deutsche-Ostafrikas*, Bethel bei Bielefeld, 1915

Kagame, A., *Le Code des institutions politiques du Rwanda précolonial*, IRCB, vol. 26, 1952

—*L'Histoire des armées-bovines dans l'ancien Rwanda*, ARSOM, vol. 25, 1961

—*Les Milices du Rwanda précolonial*, ARSOM, vol. 28, 1963

—*Le Colonialisme face à la doctrine missionaire a l'heure du Vatican II*, Butare, 1964

Kandt, R., *Caput Nili*, Berlin, 1921

de Lacger, L., *Le Ruanda*, Kabgayi, 1939

Lemarchand, R., *Political Awakening in the Congo*, Los Angeles, 1964

Rwanda and Burundi, London, 1970

Lestrade, A., *Notes d'ethnographie du Ruanda*, Brussels, 1972

Leurquin, P., *Le Niveau de vie des populations rurales du Ruanda-Urundi*, Louvain, 1961

Louis Roger, W. M., *Ruanda-Urundi, 1884-1919*, Oxford, 1963

Maquet, J. J., *Le Système des relations sociales dans le Rwanda ancien*, MRAC, vol. 1, 1954

—*The Premise of Inequality in Ruanda*, Oxford, 1961

Maquet, J. J., and D'Hertefelt, M., *Élections en société féodale*, ARSOM, vol. 21, 1959

Mecklenburg Herzog zu A., *Ins innerste Afrika*, Leipzig, 1911

Mirbt, C., *Mission und Kolonialpolitik in den deutschen Schutzgebieten*, Tübingen, 1910

Saverio Naigisiki, J., *Escapade ruandaise*, Brussels, 1949

Bibliography

Nkundabagenzi,' F., and Verhaegen, B., *Rwanda politique*, CRISP, Brussels, 1962

Nothomb, D., *Un Humanisme africain*, Brussels, 1969

Van Overschelde, A., *Un Audacieux Pacifique*, Grands Lacs, 1948
Monseigneur Léon Paul Classe, Kabgayi, 1945

Paas, J., *Unter der Aequatorsonne. Padri Donatus Leberaho*, Trier, 1927

Pagès, A., *Un Royaume hamite au contre de l'Afrique*, IRCB, 1933

Paternostre de la Mairieu, B., *Le Rwanda et son effort de développement*, Brussels, 1972

Pauwels, M., *Imana et le culte des Mânes au Ruanda*, ARSOM, vol. 17, 1958

Ryckmans, P., *Une Page d'histoire coloniale*, IRCB, vol. 24, 1953

Schäppi, F. S., *Die Katholische Missionsschule im ehemaligen Deutsch-Ostafrika*, Vienna and Zurich, 1937

Schweitzer, G., *Emin Pasha: his Life and Work*, London, 1898

Slade, R., *English-speaking Missions in the Congo Independent State*, ARSC, vol. 16, 1959

St John, P., *Breath of Life*, CMS, London, 1968

Stanley, H. M., *Through the Dark Continent*, New York, 1878

Stonelake, A. R., *Congo Past and Present*, World Dominion Press, 1937

Vansina, J., *L'Evolution du royaume rwanda des origines à 1900*, ARSOM, vol. 26, 1962

Books (general)

Adam, K., *The Spirit of Catholicism*, London, 1929

Ajayi, A. J. F., *Christian Missions in Nigeria, 1841-91*, London, 1965

Anstey, R., *King Leopold's Legacy*, Oxford, 1966

Apter, D. E., *The Political Kingdom in Uganda*, Princeton, N.J., 1961

Barth, F., *Ethnic Groups and Boundaries*, London, Bergen and Oslo, 1970

Beattie, J., *The Nyoro State*, Oxford, 1971

Bloch, M., *Feudal Society*, vols. I and II, London, 1971

Bonilla, V. D., *Servants of God or Masters of Men*, London, 1972

Burridge, W., *Destiny Africa*, London, 1966

Daneel, J. M., *The God of the Matopo Hills*, The Hague, 1970

Dansette, A., *A Religious History of Modern France*, vols. I and II, London, 1963

Dautais, E., *Leçons élémentaires de morale sociale*, Paris, 1946

Descartes, R., *Discours de la méthode*, vol. I, Paris, 1898

Duchêne, Rev. P., *Les Pères Blancs, 1868-92*, Algiers, 1902

Fanon, F., *The Wretched of the Earth*, New York, 1968

Ganshof, F., *Feudalism*, London, 1952

Goody, J., *Technology, Tradition and the State in Africa*, Oxford, 1971

Gorres, I., *The Hidden Face*, New York, 1959

Hindness, B. and Hirst, P. Q., *Pre-capitalist Modes of Production*, London, 1975

Kanza, T., *Conflict in the Congo*, Harmondsworth, 1972

Karugire, S. B., *A History of the Kingdom of Nkore in western Uganda until 1896*, Oxford, 1971

Lewis, I. M. (ed.), *History and Social Anthropology*, ASA, 1968

Church and revolution in Rwanda

Lewy, G., *The Catholic Church and Nazi Germany*, London, 1964

Linden, I., *Catholics, Peasants and Chewa Resistance in Nyasaland*, London, 1974

Marx, K., and Engels, F., *Die Deutsche Ideologie*, Berlin, 1953

Mallinson, V., *Power and Politics in Belgian Education*, London, 1963

Morel, E. D., *History of the Congo Reform Movement*, ed. Louis, R., and Stengers, J., Oxford, 1968

Mosmans, G., *L'Église a l'heure de l'Afrique*, Tournai, 1961

Mulders, A., *Missiologisch Besteck*, Hilversum and Anvers, 1962

Paden, J. N., *Religion and Political Culture in Kano*, Berkeley, Cal., 1973

Powesland, P. G., *Economic Policy and Labour*, East African Studies, No. 10, 1957

Rahner, K., *Mission and Grace*, vol. II, London, 1964

Ranger, T. O., *Revolt in Southern Rhodesia, 1896-97*, London, 1967

Richards, A. I., *Economic Development and Tribal Change*, Cambridge, 1951
East African Chiefs, London, 1960

Scanlon, D. G., *Church, State and Education in Africa*, New York, 1966

Speke, J., *Journal of the Discovery of the Source of the Nile*, London, 1863

Troeltsch, E., *The Social Teaching of the Christian Churches*, London, 1931

Ullman, W., *A History of Political Thought: the Middle Ages*, Harmondsworth, 1965

Vansina, J., *Oral Tradition*, London, 1965

Weber, E., *Action Française*, Stanford, Cal., 1962

West, H., *Land Proprietary Structure in Buganda*, African Studies Series, Cambridge, 1971

Addendum

Feltz, G., 'Evolution des structures foncières et histoire politique du Rwanda (XIXe et XXe siecles)', *Études d'Histoire Africaine* (University of Lumbambashi), VII, 1975, 143-54

Index

Abaka, 204-5, 211
Abanyamukenke, 16, 60
Abiru, 5, 13, 15, 22, 33, 43, 106, 159, 160, 174, 198, 225, 271
Absolute monarchy, ix, 20-1
Action Française, 156, 266, 279 n. 126
Adriaenssens, Father, 223, 260, 261, 269, 271, 276 n. 68
Agriculture: agricultural officers, 195, 198, 206, 208, 257, 208; Belgian reforms of, 165, 166, 168, 171, 180 n. 133, 205, 208; cattle and, 16, 18; missions and, 39, 60, 77, 90 n. 43; pre-colonial, 10-12, 37, 104; rewooding, 129; wartime, 127-8
Alsace, 31, 33, 90 n. 32
Ancestral spirits, 11, 15, 44, 102, 173; Christian adaptations to, 202, 206; Nyiginya, 52, 119 n. 101, 137
Anglo-Belgian delimitation commission, 63, 82, 85, 87, 92 n. 83, 104
Anthropology, 1, 4, 10-12, 24 n. 1, 137, 165
Apostolic Delegate, 197, 201, 203, 225
APROSOMA, 251-2, 253, 254, 256, 260, 264, 266, 269
d'Arianoff, 236, 255
Askari, 3, 40, 50, 62, 84, 85, 107, 108, 113, 114 n. 3, 132
Association des Amitiés Belgo-Rwandaises, 232
Astrida, Astridiens, 167, 174, 195, 196, 197, 210, 221, 224, 227, 233, 236, 239, 240, 254, 257, 263, 265, 280 n. 135
Bakuru, 134, 182 n. 178, 194, 196, 209, 220, 226
Bahutu manifesto, 7, 249-50, 251, 254, 264
Balokole, 204
Bananas, x, 16, 26 n. 42, 154, 166
Banyanduga, 63, 68 n. 29, 87, 123, 137; and expansion in north, 108, 124, 126, 130, 156, 164, 169, 173, 192, 194, 202; resistance to, 75, 88, 95 n. 134, 96, 106, 107, 128, 134, 192
Baptisms: literacy required for, 189; numbers, 40, 64, 170, 207; of first nobles, 130, 170; seen as sorcery, 42; *see* Conversion, *Tornade*
Barthélemy, Father, 38, 59, 68 n. 15
Basebya, 85, 105, 108
Basilimu, 192-3, 199
Bayozefiti, 135, 170, 198, 210, 223, 224, 230, 238, 263, 266
Belgians: admit Rwandans to administration, 257; and education, 155, 163, 196, 235, 239; and ethnicity, xi, 165, 258, and German Rule, 50, 54, 85, 92 n. 83; and Independence, 222, 230-1, 240, 248 n. 168, 258, 267, 269, 271, 272; policy and government, 125-8, 132-3, 136-7, 154, 162, 168-9, 170, 171, 172-3, 186, 199, 231, 257; political attitudes of, 137-8, 140, 155, 159, 169, 235, 257; political reforms of, 186-8, 197; resistance to, 199, 207, 210, 211, 257-8; support Hutu, 251; wartime, 123-5; and White Fathers, 83, 129, 132, 135, 155-6, 168, 174
Benebikira, 135, 170, 197, 198, 214 n. 78, 223, 230, 264, 270
Bethel bei Bielefeld, *see* Lutherans
Bicamumpaka, 210, 236, 252, 258, 275, 276 n. 74
Bichubirenga, 123, 125
Bigirumwami, Bishop, 223, 224, 229, 230, 232, 238, 244 n. 89, 256, 259, 261, 264, 266, 268, 269, 272, 282, 284-6
Biheko, *see* Nyabingi
Bloch, Marc, 23, 187
Brard, Father, 32, *et seq.*, 40, 44, 54, 57, 65-6, 71 n. 92, 73, 79
British, 123, 125, 128, 146 n. 90, 155, 157, 170, 270; army, 206; in Gisaka, 138, 152, 153, 154, 161
Brothers of Charity, 196, 221, 224; *see also* Astrida
Buganda, 23, 110, 135, 181 n. 141, 249
Buganza, 12, 74, 134, 152, 179 n. 95, 199
Bugesera, 15, 128
Bugoyi, 10, 15, 28 n. 73, 35, 82, 127, 128, 134, 167, 191, 211 n. 4, 228, 259
Buhoma, 15, 107, 108, 228
Buisseret Administration, 232, 235, 246 n. 129, 256, 265
Bujumbura, 21, 31, 33, 46 n. 23, 50, 65, 79, 101, 118 n. 73, 160, 171, 172, 220, 239, 241 n. 15, 252, 256, 257
Bukoba, 19, 35, 85, 87, 93 n. 110, 103, 109, 111, 124, 130, 135
Bukumbi, 31, 56
Bukunzi, 12, 20, 74, 82, 156, 237
Bumbogo, 107, 108, 119 n. 112, 162, 267
Burundi, viii, 14, 16, 20, 30-1, 32, 33, 44, 50, 80, 103, 110, 119 n. 102, 139, 141, 171, 204, 238, 256

297

Index

Court, 18, 78, 87; attitude to religion, 45, 52, 87; Catholics' first arrival at, 32-4; Fathers teach permanently at, 170; language of, 34; liturgy of, 43, 68 n. 17, 80, 91 n. 65, 107, 137, 159, 160, 162, 188; mission built at, 197; mpara, 15; nomadic, 9; poetry, 17, 200; religious debate at, 101; residence and life at, 81, 100, 101, 116 n. 45, 136, 187, 211 n. 4; resistance to, 35, 36, 37-8, 47 n. 52, 81, 144 n. 57; source of rumour, 53; White Fathers banned from, 85
Culte du Salut, 15, 40, 64, 106
Culture contact, 1, 2, 4-5, 22, 29, 31, 33-5, 38, 40, 42-3, 44, 46 n. 20, 49 n. 114, 57, 60, 62, 74-5, 78 98, 114 n. 1, 117 n. 60, 173, 201
Cultural renaissance, 200, 250, 272, 278 n. 109
Cwezi cults, 12, 44
Cyitatire, 33, 34, 81, 101, 102, 115 n. 45, 130, 131, 136
Czekanowski, Dr, 89 n. 21, 92 n. 73, 82
Dar es Salaam, 50, 120, 164
Declerck, Major, 128, 129, 130, 132
Dejemeppe, Father, 223, 228, 229, 232, 235, 238, 249, 265
Deogratias, Abbé, 223, 224, 229, 252
Deprimoz, Bishop, 201, 208, 211, 220, 221, 224, 225, 229, 230, 232, 236, 237
Dhanis column, 31
Disease, 102, 117 n. 54, 128, 134, 144 n. 65, 149 n. 167; *see* Medicine
Divination, diviners, 11, 14, 15, 22, 34, 52, 101-12, 106, 153, 161, 178 n. 87
Drunkenness, 208, 262, 267
Duke of Mecklenburg, visit, 69 n. 38, 81, 82, 88 n. 29, 91 n. 71, 72, 92 n. 84, 85
Economy: gold standard, 188, 206; Great Depression, 170, 188; *see* Agriculture, Cattle, Industry, Markets, Trade
Education: at court, 64, 100; controlled by Tutsi, 198, 248 n. 160, 256, 258; Contrat Scolaire, 163; creates needs, 104; desire for, 158, 160, 161, 239; elementary, 137, 180 n. 124, 196, 252; German policy, 75, 76, 110; key to political office, 3, 7, 109, 152, 158, 161, 164, 173, 196; limited to Hutu, 79, 109; missions' monopoly of, 264; missionaries' view of, 76, 113, 152; Phelps-Stokes commission, 155; post-Independence, 284-6; Protestant, 111-13, 209, 214 n. 82, 220; secular, 135, 140, 155; serves Tutsi, 197; statistics, 162-4, 214 n. 77, 82; in Tanganyika, 120 n. 139, 164
Elections, 230, 233, 236-7, 239, 251, 271, 275 n. 59
Elite, xi, 4, 7, 211; Church and, 162, 193, 226, 231; culture, 225, 232, 255; and economy, 226; and education, 76, 109, 113, 161, 162; fear of *déclassés*, 193, 196, 221; form political parties, 249; *see* Nyanza Government School, Astridiens
Emigration, 4, 109, 166, 168, 207, 208, 243 n. 77; priests opposed to, 79, 103; resettlement schemes, 207; statistics, 182 n. 172, 206, 228; and Ugandan economy, 166, 188, 206
Encyclicals, 90 n. 39, 169, 194, 200, 234, 265
Ernotte, Chanoine, 223, 239, 249, 252, 266
Ethnicity, x, xi, 1, 4, 6-8, 18, 23, 165, 180 n. 129, 186, 188, 227; and choice of priests, 76, 197, 209; in Church membership, 164, 168, 210; Church's attitude to, 256, 259, 276 n. 86, 91, 285; conflict between Hutu-Tutsi, 240, 249, 250, 253, 254-6, 258-9, 262, 272; and education, 163-4, 196, 239
Évolués, 7, 221, 225, 228, 229, 231, 232, 240, 250, 272; rural, 233
Evangelicals, 29, 203, 206
Famine, 21, 36, 43, 62, 127-8, 133-4, 182 n. 172; compulsory food crops, 165, 166, 168, 180 n. 133 206-8, 228, 236; food economy, 166; Tutsi behaviour during, 168
Fascism, 156, 222, 223, 260, 266, 269, 271, 283
Feudalism: based on land, 234; Belgian reform of, 129, 186-8, 211; Classe's view of, 126, 137; cohesion of, 231, 234; complexity of, 97-8; 120 n. 122, 143 n. 44, 46, 187; definition of, vii-viii, 23; feudal idiom, 190, 235, 254; German view of, 97; gives way to rural capitalism, 103-4, 169, 186, 188; growth of, 18-19, 23, 62; mission view of, 33-4, 38, 57, 60, 61, 119 n. 110, 126, 191; as mode of production, ix-xii, 235; nobility v. monarchy, ix, xi, 15, 16, 20, 23, 65, 81, 82, 97, 101, 113, 127, 156-7, 160, 173, 186, 271, 272; romantic view of, 5; survival of, 3, 169, 234-5
First World War, 3, 113, 123-7, 129-32, 141 n. 1
Franck, Louis, 136-7, 140
Gahamanyi Abbé, 247 n. 151, 269
Gahindiro, Yuhi, 15, 16
Gahini mission, 154, 168, 203-4, 259, 270
Ganda: British agents, 104, 153; catechists, 30-40; employ Banyarwanda, 181 n. 141; return of, 79, 103; slaughter of, 50-4; withdrawn from mission, 41, 52
Gashamura, 126, 158, 159, 160, 161, 178 n. 77
Germans: civil administration, 67, 74, 75, 104; conflict with mission, 52, 56, 60, 68 n. 9, 96-97, 114 n. 8, 10, 125; conquest, 22-3, 31; and education, 79, 112-13; policy and rule, 50, 56, 65, 67 n. 1, 71 n. 88, 81, 97, 188; possible return of, 200, 207; punitive raids, 36, 54, 60, 65, 82, 84, 96, 107-9, 114 n. 3; in wartime, 113, 123-5, 141 n. 1
Gesera, 11, 25 n. 21, 130, 179 n. 104, 198, 215 n. 113, 230, 256
Gilles, Father, 223
Gisaka, 12, 15, 16, 19, 22, 37, 63, 75, 79, 84, 85, 101, 111, 125, 230, 237; cession of, 138-9, 152, 182 n. 167; monarchy, 35-6, 152, 153, 167, 168, 172, 175 n. 4; return of, 154, 157, 161
Gitarama, 239, 251, 258, 267, 271, 276 n. 74

299

Index

Kigali, 84, 85, 103, 107, 108, 110, 113, 117 n. 65, 125, 128, 129, 130, 155, 160, 162, 164, 166, 169, 174, 187, 192, 221, 264, 267

Kigezi, 104, 153, 204

Kingship, 7, 23-24; Catholic teaching on 172-3; centralisation of, 15-16, 136; Christian king, 57, 110, 152, 161, 172-3, 201, 206; Christ the King, 205-6; Hutu, 11-12; legitimacy of, 126; longevity of, 6, 7; manipulation of symbols of, 19, 24, 106, 107, 260, 271; as mystification, 228, 235, 252, 253, 255; saviour king, 106, 160; source of unity, 23-4, 78; support from Germans for, 50; traditional religious authority of, 15, 19, 44, 118 n. 95, 131, 135, 159, 173, 200-2; Tutsi, 13

Kinyamateka, 195, 198, 207, 221, 235, 238, 241 n. 13, 245, 251, 252, 253, 258, 262, 266, 270

Kisenyi, 75, 83, 110, 125, 126, 128, 130, 165, 208, 228, 237, 267, 285

Kivu, 20, 31, 33, 50, 83, 87, 127, 160, 167, 207, 270

Labour: control of, ix-xi, 60, 98, 103, 104; forced, 124-5, 165, 166, 168, 187, 191, 195, 205-7, 228, 250; impact of trade on, 111, 166; journeymen, 17-18; and kinship, 10-11; for mission, 33-4, 36, 59, 61, 65, 117 n. 69, 124, 203; movement of, 103; and new companies, 166, 208, 227; plantation, 4, 208, 226; service at court, 100; wages, 166, 181 n. 149, 203

de Lacger, Chanoine, 5-6, 200-1

Land: appropriated by Hutu, 260; buying of, 188; ceded to companies, 167; clearing, 10, 12; forest ownership, 12, 87, 99; grabbed by mission, 41, 56, 59, 62, 81, 93 n. 92, 130, 203; mission and clientship, 98; ownership in pre-colonial period, 12, 25 n. 21, 59-60, 116 n. 47, 169; pasture, 16, 18, 168, 207, 228, 234, 235, 270; poverty of, vii, ix, royal control of, 15-16, 19, 69 n. 45, 188, 212 n. 18; shortage, ix, 167, 207, 228, 234-5, 254, 267; size of mission, 59-60, 69 n. 46, 179 n. 91

Language: ability of Belgians, 165, of Germans, 56, of White Fathers, 32, 34, 42; in Belgian schools, 158; Belgian policy, 173; French, 132, 134, 158, 163, 184 n. 222, 196; German policy, 75, 79, 90 n. 32, 112; and king, 56, 64, 80; Kinyarwanda, 34, 39, 49 n. 109, 132, 138; Latin and seminary, 78, 90 n. 51, 112, 197-8, 229; of ruling class, 18, 87; Swahili, 32, 44, 56, 79, 80, 117 n. 57, 158, 164, 165, 197, 229; origins of Tutsi, 12, 25 n. 17

Lavigerie, Cardinal, 3, 29, 30, 38, 66, 88, 97, 161

Leberaho, Abbé, 77, 135, 138

Lecoindre, Father, 124, 125, 147 n. 122, 156, 158, 159, 178 n. 74

Legal system: Belgian, 129, 130; feudal obligations in, 98, 100; German, 113; mission's, 133-4; mission adaptation to local, 137; mission interference with colonial, 52, 75, 81, 133, 159, 194; in pre-colonial times, 11, 13; reform of, 165, 192; training for colonial, 158; Tutsi control of, 88, 96-7, 100, 104, 154, 165, 175 n. 9, 186-7, 256, 258

Legion of Mary, 258, 266

Lemarchand, René, 2, 209, 247 n. 148, 265

Leopoldville, 193, 197, 208, 249, 256, 262; riots, 258

Lineages: Hutu, 10-13, 17, 23, 43, 267; and political office, 227; ritual roles, 25 n. 21; Tutsi and kingship, 15, 20, 116 n. 45, 171; and unity, 255

Livinhac, Leon, 31, 75, 139, 141

Loupias, Father, 87, 95 n. 133, 135, 96, 108

Lukamba, Joseph, 153, 161, 214 n. 84

Lukara (Gisaka), 35-6

Lukara Iwa Bishingwe, 82, 87, 92 n. 82, 95 n. 130, 133, 135, 96, 105, 107, 128

Lumumba, 256, 260, 262, 264, 270, 275 n. 59

Lutherans, 65, 73-4, 82 *et seq.*, 101, 111, 112, 115 n. 27, 124, 125, 154, 156

Lwabutogo, 178 n. 72, 189, 192, 199

Lwakadigi, 89 n. 27, 128, 134, 136, 145 n. 84, 211 n. 4

Lyangombe cult: decline of, 202; development of, 14-15, 25 n. 26; mission attitudes to, 49 n. 115; opposition to kingship, 27 n. 59; opposition to missions, 44-5, 102-3; opposition to Nyabingi, 19, 105, 123, 179 n. 95, 96; as preparation for Christianity, 40, 41, 64

Maji-Maji war, 65, 85

Makuza, Anastase, 229, 252, 258

Mandwa spirits, 14, 19, 27 n. 59, 45, 102; girls consecrated to, 44; mediums, 15; merge with household spirits, 44; Nyabingi as a, 19

Maquet, J. J., viii, 6, 231, 237

Marangara, 56, 68 n. 24, 101, 124, 125, 134, 157, 171, 199

Markets, 21, 70 n. 61, 103, 111, 117 n. 65, 118 n. 73, 167

Marriage: alliances, 64, 70 n. 71, 81, 82, 236; ban on polygamy, 199, 208; bride price changes, 103; divorce, 200; of king, 198; mission's attitude to, 137; social mobility and, x, 6, 18, 121 n. 145, 256

Mashira, 13, 14

Mass, 43, 113, 189, 201, 205-6, 264

Matabaro, Father, 34, 39, 40, 77, 135, 138

Mbonyamutwa, Dominique, 267, 271

Medicine, 79, 102; vaccination, 128, 145 n. 66, 267

Mfumbiro (Bufumbiro), 21, 82, 87, 92 n. 83, 93 n. 111, 104, 123

Mibirisi mission, 36, 59, 60, 82, 110, 124, 130, 147 n. 57, 162, 177 n. 59

Military service. vii, viii, 3, 13-14, 17, 19-20, 108

Mines, 166, 167, 196, 203, 208, 226, 232

Index

DATE DUE

DATE DUE